Study Guide

Introduction to Physical Anthropology

2009–2010 EDITION

Robert Jurmain
Professor Emeritus, San Jose State University

Lynn Kilgore
University of Colorado, Boulder

Wenda Trevathan
New Mexico State University

Russell L. Ciochon
University of Lowa

Prepared by

Joanne Bennett Devlin
The University of Tennessee

WADSWORTH
CENGAGE Learning

Australia • Brazil • Japan • Korea • Mexico • Singapore • Spain • United Kingdom • United States

ISBN-13: 978-0-495-60335-1
ISBN-10: 0-495-60335-X

Wadsworth
10 Davis Drive
Belmont, CA 94002-3098
USA

Cengage Learning is a leading provider of customized learning solutions with office locations around the globe, including Singapore, the United Kingdom, Australia, Mexico, Brazil, and Japan. Locate your local office at: **www.cengage.com/global**

Cengage Learning products are represented in Canada by Nelson Education, Ltd.

To learn more about Brooks/Cole, visit **www.cengage.com/wadsworth**

Purchase any of our products at your local college store or at our preferred online store **www.ichapters.com**

Printed in the United States of America
1 2 3 4 5 6 7 13 12 11 10 09

TABLE OF CONTENTS

PREFACE

This Study Guide is a supplement to the textbook *Introduction to Physical Anthropology,* 2009–2010 Edition, by Jurmain, Kilgore, Trevathan, and Ciochon. As such, it is intended to guide your learning and understanding of the foundations of physical anthropology and to assist you in preparing for exams in your introductory course. In addition, it is hoped that this Study Guide will stimulate you to explore this fascinating subject beyond the limits of your text and class; to engage in anthropological thought and practice via the internet and other media resources.

Success in any class is dependent upon establishing a personal program and maintaining a consistent approach to synthesizing course materials. The layout and design of this Study Guide was intended to provide you with the tools and suggestions to achieve success in your class. Each of the seventeen chapters that comprise this guide corresponds to the same numbered chapter in your textbook. Following is an overview of the basic components of each chapter and recommendations for how to best incorporate this guide into developing your own positive study program.

- Familiarize yourself with the theme of the chapter by first reading the **LEARNING OBJECTIVES** in the Study Guide. This will give you a general overview of those ideas that comprise that portion of the text.
- Next, review the **CHAPTER OUTLINE** as these emphasize the major concepts and many of the minor points discussed in your text. The outlines comprise the majority of this guide and are written in order to prepare you to understand the concepts and themes as well as possible. Think of the outline as your road map to manage the chapter.
- Then consider the list of **KEY TERMS** to further expose you to the ideas, processes, and perspectives that comprise the chapter.
- **READ THE TEXT CHAPTER**.
- Return to the Study Guide to examine how well you have assimilated the knowledge, by completing the "test questions" (these can be found in the latter portion of each Study Guide chapter). A variety of formats including **TRUE-FALSE, MULTIPLE-CHOICE** and **SHORT ANSWER** are offered. Even if your instructor is partial to one format practice all as a means to challenge yourself in processing the ideas and concepts.
- Following completion of the tests correct them with the answers and textbook page references found at the end of each Study Guide chapter. Note your strengths and weaknesses and use this to guide your continuing study of the chapter.
- Finally, attempt the sample **ESSAY QUESTIONS** (reference pages in the text are provided with those as well) to assess your synthesis of the materials.
- Expand your thinking by exploring the practical resources contained in the sections identified below.

The challenge and the excitement of learning comes from developing an understanding of the subject matter and then reaching beyond the class text to experience the ideas and concepts. As such, each chapter in the Study Guide has sections entitled **CONCEPT APPLICATIONS** and **MEDIA RESOURCE EXERCISES.** These are designed to challenge you to examine major issues, or to apply concepts or processes introduced in that text chapter. You will find internet addresses of many useful and content-rich websites relevant to physical anthropology. Further, you may be asked to engage in guided exploration within these sites to gain a greater understanding of, and perhaps attain new perspectives about, the information you have learned in class. If you have subscribed to *InfoTrac College Edition,* you are directed to access the internet site that is produced and maintained by the publisher of your text and Study Guide as it provides an online repository of over 11 million articles that is updated daily. Your Study Guide will point you to these *InfoTrac College Edition* resources to broaden your understanding of the field. The aim of these sections and this guide overall is to provoke you to think more critically about physical anthropology.

ACKNOWLEDGMENTS

I would like to thank Erin Abney, assistant editor for Wadsworth / Cengage Learning for her assistance in working on this guide. Especially my thanks are owed to Jeff and Liam, for their encouragement and also to Ms. Sandy Cridlin for her assistance in the completion of this task. Thanks to the authors for writing a solid and informative course text.

Joanne Bennett Devlin
Department of Anthropology
The University of Tennessee

CHAPTER 1
INTRODUCTION TO PHYSICAL ANTHROPOLOGY

CHAPTER OUTLINE

Anthropology is the scientific discipline that focuses upon the human species as its subject matter. Anthropologists study all aspects of humanity including our biology, which is examined from an evolutionary perspective.

I   INTRODUCTION
   A. Humans *Homo sapiens* belong to the evolutionary group known as hominins.
      1. A critical feature of hominins is that we are bipedal, which means that we walk on two legs.
         a. Important evidence for early upright walking (i.e. footprints) was found at a site in Africa called Laetoli.
         b. We will consider explanations for the evolution of bipedalism in Chapter 10.
         c. Anatomical and archaeological evidence for upright walking is presented in greater detail in Chapter 11.
      2. While we are unique in the Animal Kingdom, we are subject to the same evolutionary forces as all other species.
      3. Humans are members of the Order Primates, the group of mammals that also includes apes, monkeys, and prosimians; and their ancestors.
         a. Members of the order share certain anatomical and behavioral characteristics.
   B. The study of human evolution, variation and adaptation is the focus of Physical anthropology, also known as biological anthropology.
      1. Physical anthropologists study human biology from an evolutionary perspective.
         a. Human biologists approach the study of humans from a clinical perspective.
      2. Humans are the dynamic products of evolutionary forces.
      3. Evolution is any change in the genetic makeup of a population over time.
      4. Evolution can be defined and studied at two different levels.
         a. At the population level (microevolution), there are genetic changes within the population from generation to generation.

1

b. At the species level (macroevolution), the result is the appearance of a new species.
C. Humans are similarly a product of their culture and our examination must consider the influence of culture on the development of our species.
1. Culture is the strategy by which humans adapt to their natural environment.
   a. It includes technologies ranging from simple stone tools to computers and also includes subsistence patterns ranging from hunting and gathering to agribusiness.
2. Other aspects of culture include religion, social values, social organization, language, kinship, marriage rules and gender roles, among others.
3. An important property of culture is that it is learned and shared by group members.
   a. Culture is not biologically inherited.
   b. Likely humans inherit a predisposition to acquire culture
D. Biocultural Evolution
1. Throughout time, the role of culture has increasingly assumed greater importance as a factor in human evolution.
2. We say that humans are the result of biocultural evolution; i.e. the mutual long-term interaction between biology and culture.
3. This distinguishes humans from others in the Animal Kingdom

II **WHAT IS ANTHROPOLOGY?**
A. Anthropology is the scientific study of human evolution, adaptation, and culture.
B. In the United States anthropology consists of four subfields:
1. Cultural, Archaeology, Linguistic, and Physical (or Biological) anthropology.
2. Within each of these subfields, there are areas of specialization.
C. Many of the subfields of anthropology have a practical application; this type of anthropology is called applied anthropology.

III **CULTURAL ANTHROPOLOGY**
A. Cultural (or social) anthropology is the study of aspects of human belief and behavior.
B. The descriptions of traditional lifestyles are called ethnographies.
C. Ethnographic accounts form the basis for comparative cross-cultural studies (ethnologies) which broaden the context within which cultural anthropologists study human behavior.
1. This enables cultural anthropologists to formulate theories about fundamental aspects of human behavior.
D. The focus of cultural anthropology has shifted over the twentieth century. Some of the new subfields of cultural anthropology include:
1. Urban anthropology which deals with issues of inner cities.
2. Medical anthropology explores the relationship between various cultural attributes and health and disease.

IV **LINGUISTIC ANTHROPOLOGY**
A. Linguistic anthropology studies the origin of language, as well as specific languages.
B. The spontaneous acquisition and use of language is a unique human characteristic.
1. Research in this area may have implications for the evolution of language skills in humans, making this area of research of interest for physical anthropologists.

2

V   ARCHAEOLOGY
   A. Archaeology studies and interprets material remains recovered from earlier cultures.
   B. Archaeologists are concerned with culture and human behavior, but obtain their information from artifacts and other material culture (for example the. remains of buildings), rather than from living people.
   C. Archaeologists excavate sites to answer specific questions about past behavior not simply for the artifacts present at a site.
      1. By identifying human behavior patterns on a larger scale, archaeologists attempt to recognize behaviors shared by all human groups, or commonalities such as the development of agriculture or the rise of urban centers.
      2. Archaeological techniques are used to recover materials that are of interest to physical anthropologists.

VI   PHYSICAL ANTHROPOLOGY
   A. Physical anthropology is the study of human biology within the framework of evolution.
      1. Physical anthropologists emphasize the interaction between biology and culture.
      2. Physical anthropology is sometimes called biological anthropology to reflect the inclusion of genetics, evolutionary biology, nutrition and other subfields.
      3. The origins of physical anthropology are traced to the 19th century.
         a. Natural historians became interested in how species came into existence.
         b. The publication of Darwin's *Origin of Species* in 1859 marked the beginnings of modern evolutionary science and heightened interest concerning human origins.
   B. Physical anthropology is divided into a number of subfields.
      1. Paleoanthropology, which is the study of human evolution, focuses particularly on the fossil record.
         a. The goals of paleoanthropology are to identify early hominin species, establish their chronology and ultimately reconstruct their evolutionary relationships.
         b. Primate paleontology is the study of the primate fossil record extending back 65 million years.
      2. Human variation is a field which considers the observable physical traits in humans and the genetic factors that influence them.
         a. Today anthropologists study human variation to obtain clues about how humans adapted to the environment over time.
         b. Humans vary in the ability to cope with stress induced by the environment.
         c. The technique used to measure human physical variation is called anthropometry.
         d. Data are collected from populations living in different environments (high altitude, cold, and hot) to measure biological adaptation.
      3. Genetics is the field which studies gene structure and action as well as the patterns of inheritance.
         a. Molecular anthropologists use genetic data and technologies to study evolutionary relationships within our species and between humans and non-human primates.
         b. Advancements in DNA extraction have generated information regarding human evolution.
      4. Osteology, the study of skeletal biology, is a critical focus of physical anthropology.
         a. The subdiscipline of osteology that studies disease and trauma in archaeologically derived populations is paleopathology.

3

b. Forensic anthropology is a field directly related to osteology and paleopathology that applies these techniques to the intersections between anthropology and law.

c. Forensic anthropologists have played a very important part in the identifications of victims from the 9/11 terrorist attacks.

5. Many physical anthropologists are expert anatomists.

a. Anatomists study the soft tissue as well as the skeleton.

b. Anatomy is essential for anthropologists studying paleoanthropology.

6. Primatology is the discipline that studies nonhuman primates.

a. Because primates are humanity's closest living relatives, anthropologists feel that the study of these animals can shed light on our own behavior and other aspects of our biology.

b. The declining number of primates species in their natural environments has placed a greater urgency on the study of these animals.

VII   **INTERDISCIPLINARY APPROACHES**

A. Biocultural anthropology

1. Cultural anthropology and biological anthropology share interests in particular subject matter.

a. Nutrition has biological and cultural implications

b. Health too is product of both biology and culture

B. Applied anthropology

1. Uses methods and theories of anthropology outside of the academic setting.

a. Forensic anthropology is performed for medicolegal field.

VIII   **PHYSICAL ANTHROPOLOGY AND THE SCIENTIFIC METHOD**

A. Science is a process of explaining natural phenomena through observation, developing hypotheses, and testing hypotheses.

1. Scientists rely on the empirical approach which is based upon experimentation and/or observation.

2. As scientists, physical anthropologists must adhere to the scientific method, whereby a research problem is identified and information is subsequently gathered in order to generate a solution.

B. After the research problem has been identified the following steps are taken.

1. Exploration of the scientific literature to find out what is already known.

2. Develop and refine a hypothesis.

a. An hypothesis is a provisional explanation of phenomena.

3. Develop a research design or methodology that will test the hypothesis.

4. Collect and analyze data.

a. An approach should be used in which the investigator can precisely describe their techniques and results in a manner that facilitates comparison with the work of others.

5. In physical anthropology, data are usually expressed numerically, or quantitatively.

6. The testing of hypotheses with the possibility of demonstrating them to be false is the very basis of the scientific method.

4

C. If a hypothesis stands up to repeated testing it might become a theory.
    1. A theory is a statement of relationships as demonstrated through testing and through the accumulation of evidence.
    2. Scientific theories are not "guesses" nor "hunches" but tested explanations of facts.
D. Scientific hypotheses and theories always allow the possibility of being falsified.
    1. A hypothesis that cannot be tested rationally through experiment or experience is not scientific.
E. Bias
    1. The scientific method permits various types of biases to be addressed and controlled.
    2. Bias occurs in all studies due to many different factors such as the training of the scientist and the skills that she or he possesses.
    3. Science is an approach used to control bias.

IX THE ANTHROPOLOGICAL PERSPECTIVE

A. All branches of anthropology seek to broaden our viewpoint through the anthropological perspective.
    1. This perspective views humanity over time and space.
B. From this viewpoint we can grasp the contemporary diversity of the human experience and more fully understand our potentialities and constraints.
    1. The anthropological perspective can teach us to avoid ethnocentrism.
    2. Ethnocentrism is the bias of viewing human behavior based uniquely on one's own culture.

X A CLOSER LOOK: EVALUATION IN SCIENCE: LESSONS IN CRITICAL THINKING

A. Scientific evaluation is a critical component of critical thinking
    1. The acquisition of such skills is a benefit of education
        a. Critical thinking consists of comparing, analyzing, critiquing and synthesizing information.

KEY TERMS

adaptation: functional response of an organism or a population to the environment.
anthropology: the scientific discipline that studies all aspects of the human species.
anthropometry: the measurement of the human body.
archaeology: the discipline of anthropology that interprets past cultures through material remains recovered through excavation.
artifacts: objects that have been modified or, in some other way, used by ancient humans.
biocultural evolution: the interaction between biology and culture in human evolution.
bipedal: walking habitually on two legs as in humans and ground birds.
cultural anthropology: the area within anthropology that focuses on the study of human behavior.
culture: the behavioral aspects of humans, including our technology and institutions, which we learn and transmit between generations.
data: scientific facts
DNA: deoxyribonucleic acid is the double-stranded molecule that contains the genetic code.

empirical: relying on experiment or observation.

ethnocentrism: viewing other cultures from the inherently biased perspective of one's own culture.

ethnography: descriptive study of a human society.

evolution: changes in the genetic structure of a population

forensic anthropology: the field that applies the techniques of anthropology to the law. This usually refers to the techniques used by osteologists and sometimes archaeologists.

genetics: the study of gene structure and action and the patterns of inheritance of traits.

Homininae: the taxonomic family that includes humans and great apes.

hominin: evolutionary group that includes humans and our ancestors; members of the taxonomic subfamily Homininae.

hypothesis: a provisional explanation.

linguistic anthropology: the area within anthropology that studies the origins and cultural perceptions and uses of language.

material culture: the physical remains of human cultural activity.

osteology: the study of skeletal biology. Human osteology focuses on the interpretation of the skeletal remains of past populations.

paleoanthropology: the subdiscipline within physical anthropology that studies human evolution.

paleopathology: the branch of osteology that studies the evidence of disease and injury in human skeletal remains.

primate: a member of the mammalian Order Primates. Primates include lemurs, lorises, tarsiers, monkeys, apes and humans.

primatology: the study of the mammalian Order Primates. Humans are members of this order.

quantitative: a measurement and testing approach in which data are evaluated numerically.

science: knowledge obtained through observation and experimentation.

scientific method: a problem is identified, a tentative explanation is proposed and data are collected to test the explanation.

scientific testing: how hypotheses are verified, modified or discarded.

species: a group of interbreeding organisms that produce fertile offspring and are reproductively isolated from other such groups.

theory: an explanation of scientific observations that has withstood repeated empirical tests.

world view: common perspective shared by members of a society.

MEDIA EXERCISES

1) Are you interested in becoming a physical anthropologist someday? If so, then check-out the official site of the "American Association of Physical Anthropologists" (http://physanth.org/). What kind of graduate programs and career opportunities are there for undergrads aspiring to a career in physical anthropology?

2) Want to learn more about the activities of archaeologists, cultural anthropologists and other anthropologists? Log on to the website for the American Anthropological Association (http://www.aaanet.org/) or the Society of American Archaeology (http://www.saa.org/).

3) Why is evolution such a controversial topic in America today? Browse the "Talk Origins Archive" (http://www.talkorigins.org/) for answers to frequently asked questions ("FAQs") such as:
   1. Isn't evolution just a theory?
   2. Don't you have to be an atheist to accept evolution?
   3. If evolution is true, then why are there so many gaps in the fossil record? Shouldn't there be more transitional fossils?
   4. Where can I find more material on the Creation/Evolution debate?

4) Find some specific examples of current research conducted by physical anthropologists in the various subdisciplines. Use an Internet search engine such as Google (http://www.google.com/) to locate researchers' web sites. Be specific in your search criteria, e.g. "primatology chimpanzees communication".

INFOTRAC

1) In *InfoTrac*, do a Keyword search on "ethnocentrism" and read some articles demonstrating how the lack of an anthropological perspective can have important social and political ramifications for our public policy and policy makers.

2) In *InfoTrac*, do a Subject search on "paleoanthropology" and see how many different topics this rather small subset of physical anthropologists can actively engage in research.

CONCEPT APPLICATIONS

1) Fill in the "Anthropology Flow Chart" below with the appropriate labels provided in the accompanying list. One correct answer for each level has been provided for your assistance.

Choices:

1. Primatology
2. human identification
3. biology & culture
4. Archaeology
5. human evolution
6. Linguistic Anthropology
7. cross cultural studies
8. Human variation
9. Physical Anthropology
10. Paleopathology
11. language & culture
12. Forensic Anthropology
13. Paleoanthropology
14. Ape behavior

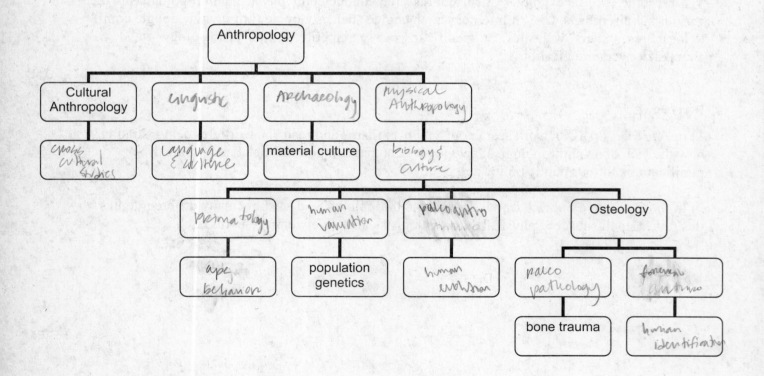

2) Fill in the "Scientific Method Concept Map" on the page below using the following choices:

1. Analyze data
2. New data inconsistent with hypothesis
3. Reject hypothesis
4. Develop theory
5. Collect data
6. Identify problem

7. Collect and analyze more data
8. Form hypothesis
9. Verify hypothesis
10. New data consistent with hypothesis
11. Reject hypothesis

Scientific Method

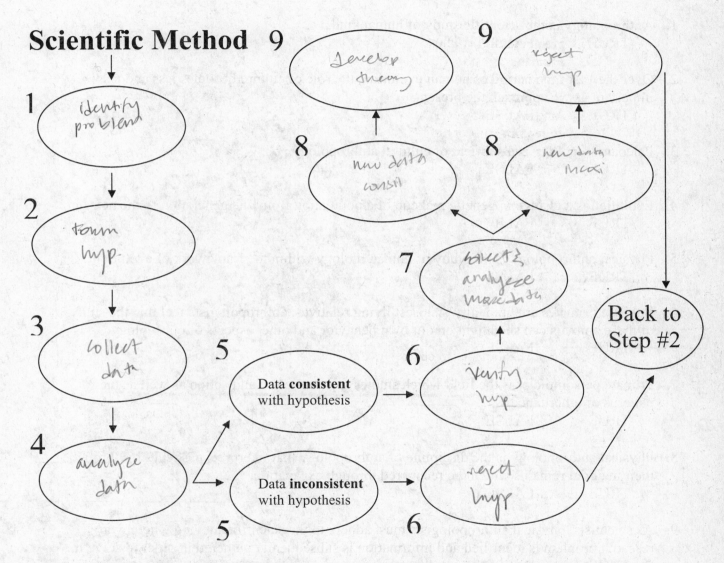

After completion of the cells in the chart, consider how this format dictates the process of a scientific examination. Think about what you would actually do if you were engaging in a scientific examination of several artifacts that you had unearthed. What specific actions could you place in each of the cells?

9

Now answer the True/False, Multiple Choice and Short Answer sample test questions. Following completion of the tests, correct them with the answers and textbook page references at the end of this Study Guide chapter. Note the areas in which you are strong and weak to guide you in your studying. Finally, answer the sample Essay Questions.

TRUE/FALSE QUESTIONS

If false, consider what modification would make the statement true.

1. Anthropology is the scientific study of humankind.
   (TRUE)   FALSE

2. Over the vast time period of human evolution, the role of culture becomes less and less important as we approach the present.
   TRUE   (FALSE)

3. Paleoanthropology is a subfield of cultural anthropology.
   TRUE   (FALSE)

4. Evolution is a change in genetic makeup of a population from one generation to the next.
   (TRUE)   FALSE

5. Physical anthropology is the study of human biology within the framework of evolution.
   (TRUE)   FALSE

6. Because primates are humanity's closest living relatives, anthropologists feel that the study of these animals can shed light on our own behavior and other aspects of our biology.
   (TRUE)   FALSE

7. Primate paleontology is the field which studies gene structure and action as well as the patterns of inheritance.
   TRUE   (FALSE)

8. Physical anthropology is the discipline of anthropology that interprets past cultures through their material remains which are recovered through excavation.
   TRUE   (FALSE)

9. As scientists, physical anthropologists must adhere to the scientific method whereby a research problem is identified and information is subsequently gathered in order to solve it.
   (TRUE)   FALSE

10. The anthropological perspective can teach us to embrace ethnocentrism, a valid viewpoint in which other cultures are seen as inferior to one's own.
    TRUE   (FALSE)

10

MULTIPLE CHOICE QUESTIONS

1. Walking on two legs, as humans and chickens do, is referred to as
   A. bipedalism.
   B. quadrupedalism.
   C. cursorial.
   D. brachiation.

2. The mammalian group to which humans belong is the Order
   A. Carnivora.
   B. Rodentia.
   C. Primates.
   D. Chiroptera.

3. Culture is
   A. inherited by a simple genetic transmission.
   B. a biological trait of our species.
   C. learned.
   D. the strategy by which most mammals adapt to their environments.

4. The biological characteristics of humans enabled culture to develop and culture, in turn, influenced human biological development. This is called
   A. biocultural evolution.
   B. microevolution.
   C. quantum evolution.
   D. convergent evolution.

5. Anthropology differs from other disciplines which study humans in that anthropology
   A. studies humans exclusively.
   B. allows no biases from other disciplines to interfere in anthropological studies.
   C. never uses an evolutionary perspective.
   D. is integrative and interdisciplinary.

6. An anthropologist who is studying the child-rearing practices of the Maasai people of Tanzania is likely to be a(n)
   A. archaeologist.
   B. cultural anthropologist.
   C. forensic anthropologist.
   D. paleoanthropologist.

11

7. Anthropologists who conduct excavations in order to recover artifacts and other aspects of material culture are
    A. archaeologists.
    B. cultural anthropologists.
    C. linguistic anthropologists.
    D. medical anthropologists.

8. Why do archaeologists dig for artifacts?
    A. To sell to collectors.
    B. To fill museums.
    C. To gain information about human behavior.
    D. To gain notoriety.

9. Physical anthropology has its origins in
    A. physics.
    B. natural history.
    C. anatomical observation of human physical variation.
    D. both B and C are correct.

— 10. Physical anthropologists became interested in human change over time (i.e. evolution) with the publication of
    A. Blumenbach's *On the Natural Varieties of Humankind.*
    B. Malthus' *An Essay on the Principle of Population.*
    C. Darwin's *Origin of Species.*
    D. Wood Jones' *Man's Place Among the Mammals.*

11. Anthropologists who specialize in the fossil remains and the physical evidence of early human behavior are called
    A. cultural anthropologists.
    B. linguists.
    C. paleoanthropologists.
    D. geneticists.

—12. Contemporary physical anthropologists, whose main interest is in modern human variation, consider their subject matter from the perspective of
    A. racial typologies.
    B. adaptive significance.
    C. behavioral genetics.
    D. constitutional typology.

13. Researchers that use state-of-the-art genetic technologies to study evolutionary relationships both within our species and between humans and non-human primates are
    A. contract archaeologists.
    B. cultural anthropologists.
    C. ethnographers.
    D. molecular anthropologists.

14. A researcher is studying the nutritional ecology of howler monkeys in Panama. Her area of expertise is
    A. primatology.
    B. paleoanthropology.
    C. osteology.
    D. genetics.

15. A family reports to the police that their dog has brought home a leg bone that appears to be human. The police also believe this bone is human. To find out whether or not this bone is indeed human the police will consult a(n)
    A. forensic anthropologist.
    B. primatologist.
    C. paleoanthropologist.
    D. evolutionary geneticist.

16. A physical anthropologist who studies bones exclusively is called a(n)
    A. primatologist.
    B. anthropometrist
    C. mammalogist.
    D. osteologist.

17. The study of the origins of human languages would be the focus of which subfield of anthropology?
    A. ecology.
    B. anatomy.
    C. linguistic.
    D. cultural

18. A scientific hypothesis
    A. must always be a correct statement.
    B. is not a necessary part of the scientific method.
    C. is the same thing as a law.
    D. must be testable.

19. If a researcher measures some biological variable and then uses the obtained numerical data to arrive at conclusions we would say that this study is
    A. quantitative.
    B. qualitative.
    C. descriptive .
    D. natural history.

20. Viewing other cultures from the inherently biased perspective of one's own culture is known as
    A. linguistics.
    B. ethnocentrism.
    C. ethnography.
    D. paleopathology.

21. A healthy skepticism about claims that are made about science, politics, or medicine is often called
    A. critical thinking.
    B. ethnocentrism.
    C. ethnography.
    D. biocultural adaptation.

22. What is it called when one species transforms in another?
    A. microevolution.
    B. macroevolution.
    C. natural selection.
    D. iocultural evolution.

23. What is anthropometry?
    A. The smallest unit of measure of the yard.
    B. Measurement of the human body.
    C. Measurement of any primate.
    D. A type of computer program used for statistics.

24. What chemical has been recently extracted from fossilized hominin bones?
    A. Lycine.
    B. RNA.
    C. DNA.
    D. Uracil.

25. The areas of Forensic Anthropology, CRM and Medical anthropology are all examples of:
   A. primatology.
   B. applied anthropology.
   C. Cultural anthropology.
   D. Human biology.

SHORT ANSWER QUESTIONS (& PAGE REFERENCES)

1. What is biocultural evolution? (p. 6)

2. Why is archaeology relevant to human evolutionary reconstructions? (p. 8)

3. Why is primatology important to human evolutionary studies? (p. 13)

4. What do forensic anthropologists do? (p. 12)

5. What is the difference between a theory and a hypothesis? (p. 16)

ESSAY QUESTIONS (& PAGE REFERENCES)

1. Explain what cultural anthropology can tell us about the human condition? (pp. 6-7)

2. Why is it important to physical anthropologists to study human variation? (pp. 8-9)

3. What is the scientific method and how do physical anthropologists put it into practice? (pp. 16)

ANSWERS, *CORRECTED STATEMENT* IF FALSE & REFERENCES TO TRUE/FALSE QUESTIONS

1. TRUE, p. 6

2. FALSE, p.5, Over the vast time period of human evolution, the role of culture becomes *more* important as we approach the present.

3. FALSE, p.8, Paleoanthropology is a subfield of *physical* anthropology.

4. TRUE, p. 4

5. TRUE, p. 8

6. TRUE, p. 13

7. FALSE, p. 10, *Genetics* is the field which studies gene structure and action as well as the patterns of inheritance.

8. FALSE, p. 7, *Archaeology* is the discipline of anthropology that interprets past cultures through their material remains which are recovered through excavation.

9. TRUE, p. 16

10. FALSE, p. 21, The anthropological perspective can teach us to *avoid* ethnocentrism, a *biased* viewpoint in which other cultures are seen as inferior to one's own.

ANSWERS & REFERENCES TO MULTIPLE CHOICE QUESTIONS

1. **A**, p. 3	11. **C**, p. 8	21. **A**, p. 18
2. **C**, p. 3	12. **B**, p. 10	22. **B**, p. 4
3. **C**, p. 4	13. **D**, p. 10	23. **B**, p. 10
4. **A**, p. 5-6	14. **A**, p. 13	24. **C**, p. 10
5. **D**, pp. 6	15. **A**, p. 12	25. **B**, p. 16
6. **B**, pp. 6-7	16. **D**, p. 11	
7. **A**, p. 7-8	17. **C**, p. 7	
8. **C**, p. 7-8	18. **D**, p. 16	
9. **D**, p. 8	19. **A**, p. 20	
10.**C**, p8	20. **B**, p. 21	

CONCEPT APPLICATIONS SOLUTIONS

"Anthropology flow chart"

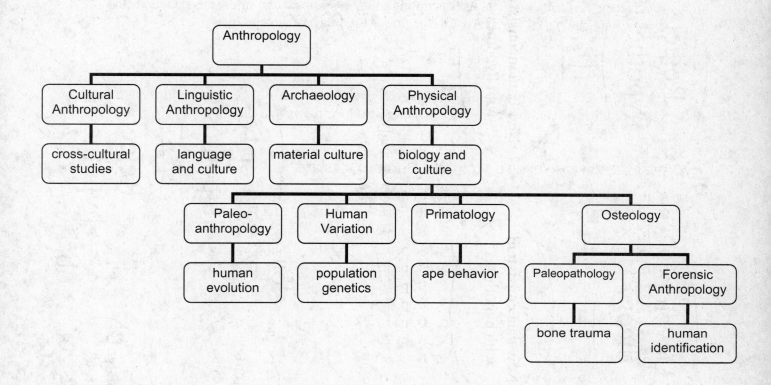

Scientific Method

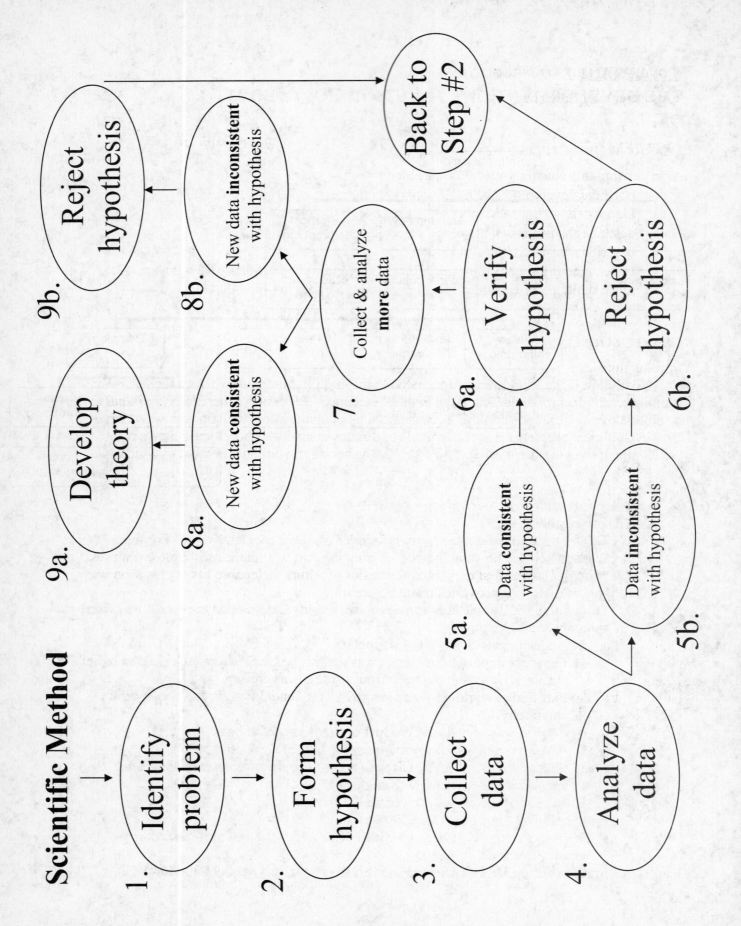

1. Identify problem

2. Form hypothesis

3. Collect data

4. Analyze data

5a. Data **consistent** with hypothesis

5b. Data **inconsistent** with hypothesis

6a. Verify hypothesis

6b. Reject hypothesis

7. Collect & analyze **more** data

8a. New data **consistent** with hypothesis

8b. New data **inconsistent** with hypothesis

9a. Develop theory

9b. Reject hypothesis

Back to Step #2

CHAPTER 2
THE DEVELOPMENT OF EVOLUTIONARY THEORY

LEARNING OBJECTIVES

After reading this chapter you should be able to
- trace the development of evolutionary thought (pp. 25-37)
- identify the major influences on Charles Darwin (pp. 33-37)
- describe the processes of natural selection (pp. 28-33)
- describe a case of natural selection (pp. 38-42)
- understand the shortcomings of Nineteenth-Century evolutionary thought (pp. 42)
- understand historical and current opposition to evolution (pp. 43-45)

CHAPTER OUTLINE

Introduction

Evolution is the single-most fundamental unifying force in biology. As a theory, it has been increasingly supported by a large body of evidence. Evolution is particularly crucial to the discipline of physical anthropology because its subject matter deals with human evolution and the physiological adaptations we have made to our environment. This chapter presents the development of evolutionary thought as well as the social and political context in which it developed.

I   A BRIEF HISTORY OF EVOLUTIONARY THOUGHT
  A. The pre-scientific view:
    1. The foundations of evolutionary principles can be traced to Western Europe.
    2. Western science however borrowed from the Arabs, Indian, and Chinese cultures.
    3. Though Darwin first explained the basics of natural selection, his explanation was possible due to discoveries made before him.
    4. Throughout the middle ages the European worldview was that the world was fixed and unchanging.
      a. This idea is known as "fixity of species."
        i) The most important influence was that of the Christian church and the belief that all life was unchanged from when it was created.
        ii) Part of this worldview was shaped by the feudal system that was a rigid hierarchy.
      b. The world was seen as the product of the "Grand Designer".
        i) All observable aspects of nature were part of a deliberate plan.
        ii) Anatomical structures existed to meet the purpose for which they were required - an "argument from design".
      c. It was considered heresy to contradict these views.
    5. Earth believed to be less than 6000 years old.
      a. This was a major obstacle to the idea of evolution, which requires immense amounts of time.
      b. Arch bishop James Usher claimed earth created on October 23, 4004 BC.

19

B. The scientific revolution:
1. The discovery of the New World challenged the traditional ideas of Europeans.
   a. The world could no longer be perceived as flat.
   b. Discoveries of new plants and animals increased awareness of the biological diversity on our planet.
2. Copernicus challenged the old idea that the earth was the center of the universe.
   a. This was already known in India.
3. Catholic Church doctrine was more favorable to Aristotle's view that the Earth and therefore humans were the center of the universe.
4. Galileo's work further pushed the notion that the universe was a place of motion rather than of fixity.
   a. Galileo was punished for his views.
5. By the 16th and 17th centuries scholars began searching for natural laws rather than supernatural explanations.

C. Precursors to the Theory of Evolution
1. John Ray (1627-1705) distinguished groups of plants and animals from other such groups.
   a. Organisms capable of reproducing and producing offspring classified as species.
      i) Members of a species are reproductively isolated from other species.
   b. Similar species grouped together into a genus.
2. Carolus Linnaeus (1707-1778) developed a system of classification and laid the basis for taxonomy.
   a. Linnaeus standardized the use of genus and species to identify every organism
      i) A procedure called binomial nomenclature.
      ii) Recall you are *Homo sapiens*
   b. Linnaeus' most controversial act was to include humans among the animals in his taxonomy.
   c. Linnaeus believed in the fixity of species but in later years began to question it.
   d. Wrote *Systema Naturae,* first published in 1735.
3. Comte de Buffon (1707-1788)
   a. Buffon stressed the important of change in nature.
   b. Buffon recognized that the environment was an important agent of change.
   c. Wrote *Natural History*, first published in 1749.
4. Erasmus Darwin (1731-1802)
   a. Grandfather of Charles Darwin, he expressed ideas similar to those that his grandson would publish over half a century later.
      i) Erasmus wrote that life originated in the seas and that all species descended from a common ancestor.
   b. Charles did read his grandfather's writings but the extent of the elder's influence on his grandson is unknown.
5. Jean-Baptiste Lamarck (1744-1829)
   a. Lamarck was the first scientist to produce a systematic explanation for the evolutionary process.
   b. Lamarck postulated that the environment played a crucial role in the physical change an organism could experience.
      i) As the environment changed, the organism would adjust to the environment by changing also.

20

     c.   Lamarck believed that as an organism used certain body parts, or did not use those regions, the structures would change in response to the environment.

        i)   Future offspring would inherit the modified condition.

        ii)   His idea known as Inheritance of acquired characteristics, or use-disuse theory.

        iii)   Common example relies upon the giraffe (see Figure 2-5).

            a) A need arose in the environment to grow a long neck and this change in the adult body form was transmitted to the offspring.

            b) We know today that this is not genetically possible.

6. Georges Cuvier (1769-1832)

     a.   Despite founding vertebrate paleontology (as well as comparative anatomy and zoology), Cuvier believed strongly in the fixity of species.

     b.   Cuvier is strongly associated with the idea that animal and plant species disappeared because of local disasters.

        i)   This theory was called catastrophism.

        ii)   Following a set of extinctions, new life forms migrated in from unaffected neighboring areas.

7. Thomas Malthus (1766-1834) was a political economist.

     a.   Malthus concerned with the relationship between food supply and population size.

     b.   He stated that population size increases geometrically while food supplies remained relatively stable.

     c.   Malthus' ideas contributed to the thinking of both Darwin and Wallace, particularly concerning competition for food and other resources.

     d. Wrote *An Essay on the Principle of Population*, published in 1798.

8. Charles Lyell (1797-1875) is considered the founder of modern geology.

     a.   Lyell emphasized that the earth had been molded by the same geological forces observable today. This theory, originally proposed by Hutton is called uniformitarianism.

     b.   These forces continue to operate today.

     c.   In order for uniformitarianism to be explanatory, the earth would have to be immensely old.

        i)   Implied earth millions of years old.

9. Mary Anning (1799-1847) was an intrepid fossil collector.

     a.   To support her family after her father died, Anning collected and sold fossils to some of the most famous scientists in England.

     b.   She discovered the first complete fossil of *Icthyosaurus*, an extinct marine reptile from the Age of Dinosaurs.

     c.   Although not given her due during her lifetime, her portrait now hangs in a position of honor in the British Museum (of Natural History) in London.

II   THE DISCOVERY OF NATURAL SELECTION

   A. Charles Darwin (1809-1882) grew up in a large family of privilege in rural England.

   B. As a boy, Charles developed a love of nature by fishing and collecting shells, birds' eggs and rocks.

     1. Sent to college in Edinburgh to study medicine by his father where he became acquainted with the theories of Lamarck.

        a.   After 2 years in Edinburgh, he enrolled at Cambridge to ostensibly study theology.

21

  b. Spent most of his time, however, in the field with geology and botany professors.

  c. After graduating, he was recommended by one of his professors to join a scientific expedition that was to circumnavigate the globe.

C. Served as the naturalist aboard the *H. M. S. Beagle* from 1832-1836.

D. Many of Darwin's ideas were formed from his observations during the voyage.

  a. At the Galapagos Islands, off of the coast of Ecuador, Darwin collected many finches that shared similarities with mainland species but were not identical.

  b. Later, these variations would lead Darwin to think that these birds descended from a common ancestor who lived on the mainland.

E. In the late 1830's a number of ideas coalesced for Darwin.

  1. Darwin saw that biological variation within a species was critically important.

  2. Darwin also recognized the importance of sexual reproduction in increasing variation.

  3. Malthus' essay was a watershed event for Darwin. From Malthus, Darwin realized:

   a. animal population size is continuously checked by the limits of food supply,

   b. and there is a constant "struggle for existence."

F. The basic idea of selection derives from the concept that breeders choose the best mating pairs to produce desirable offspring.

G. By the year 1844 Darwin essentially had completed the work that he would publish fifteen years later.

  1. Darwin knew that his ideas were a threat to current thinking about the world.

H. In Darwin's Shadow: Alfred Russell Wallace (1823-1913)

  1. Wallace grew up in a family of modest means with little formal education.

  2. Wallace was a naturalist who worked in South America and Southeast Asia.

  3. Wallace's observations led him to conclusions similar to Darwin's, namely that

   a. species are descended from other species

   b. the emergence of new species is influenced by the environment.

  4. The coincidental development of evolution by natural selection by both Darwin and Wallace was resolved by the joint presentation of their papers to the Linnaean Society of London in 1858.

  5. Darwin published his most important book, *On the Origin of Species*, the following year.

III NATURAL SELECTION

A. Natural selection, the key to evolution, is based upon the following processes:

  1. All species can produce offspring at a faster rate than food supplies increase.

  2. There is biological variation within all species.

  3. Over-reproduction leads to competition for limited resources.

  4. Those individuals within a species that possess favorable traits are more likely to survive than other individuals and to produce more offspring.

  5. The environmental context determines whether a trait is favorable or not.

  6. Traits are inherited.

   a. Individuals with traits favored by the environment contribute more offspring to the next generation.

   b. Over time such traits will become more common in the population.

  7. Over long periods of geological time, successful variations accumulate in a population so that later generations may become distinct from their ancestors; thus, in time, a new species may appear.

8. Geographical isolation may also lead to the formation of new species.
   a. When populations of a species inhabit different ecological zones they begin to adapt to the different environments.
   b. Over time each population responds to the different selective pressures and the end result, given sufficient time, may be two distinct species.
B. Natural selection operates on individuals, but it is the population that evolves.
   a. The unit of natural selection is the individual.
      i) Individuals cannot change genetically over time
   b. The unit of evolution is the population.
      i) Populations can change genetically over time

IV NATURAL SELECTION IN ACTION

A. The most frequently cited example of natural selection is the change in moth populations associated with the industrial revolution.
   1. Two forms of peppered moth exist: a light gray mottled form and a dark form.
      a. Prior to the industrial revolution the light form predominated.
         i) When resting on lichen covered tree trunks the mottled moth was camouflaged from birds.
         ii) In contrast, the dark forms stood out on light, lichen covered trees.
         iii) Birds served as selective agents which resulted in few dark moths surviving to produce offspring.
      b. By the end of the nineteenth century the dark form was the more common.
         i) As the industrial revolution progressed coal dust settled on trees.
         ii) The light moths stood out on the dark tree trunks and were preyed upon by birds; this resulted in dark forms leaving more offspring in the next generation and subsequently becoming the more common variety.
   2. Though this example has been criticized throughout the years, the premise still valid.
B. The medium ground finch of the Galapagos
   1. Drought in 1977 killed off plants that produced soft seeds.
      a. These were favored by medium ground finch
      b. Medium ground finches varied slightly in the size and robustness of beaks in the population.
   2. Available food resource consisted of larger, harder seeds.
      a. Those with smaller beaks less able to process these seeds
   3. This selected for finches with thicker beaks to open harder seeds.
      a. Those with thicker beaks passed on their genes.
   4. Through time, though population size decreased, average beak thickness for the population increased.
   5. With ecological shift to wet environment, through time, the average beak thickness across the population decreased.
C. Another example of natural selection with relevance to humans is antibiotic resistant bacteria.
   1. With the introduction of antibiotics in the 1940s, it was commonly thought that infectious disease would soon be a thing of the past.
      a. However, genetic variation in bacteria was not taken into account.
      b. A bacterium may have genetic ability to survive an antibiotic
         i) These antibiotic resistant bacteria with pass on their ability to survive.

23

2. As a result, many types of infection are untreatable with current medicines.
   a. Some infectious agents, thought to be nearly eradicated, are making a comeback.
   b. An example of this would be the bacterium that causes tuberculosis.
D. The above examples emphasize several of the mechanisms of evolutionary change through natural selection.
   1. A trait must be inherited for natural selection to act on it.
   2. Natural selection cannot occur without population variation for that particular trait.
   3. Fitness is a relative measure that changes as the environment changes.
   4. Natural selection can only act on traits that affect reproduction.
E. Differential net reproductive success refers to the number of offspring produced by an individual that survive to reproductive age.
F. See At A Glance on page 41.

V CONSTRAINTS ON NINETEENTH-CENTURY EVOLUTIONARY THEORY

A. Variation
   1. The source of variation was a major gap in 19th century evolutionary theory.
B. Transmission
   1. Darwin did not understand the mechanisms by which parents transmitted traits to offspring.
   2. The most popular contemporary idea was blending inheritance; the idea that offspring expressed traits intermediate between the traits of their parents.
   3. Modern genetics provides the critical information earlier evolutionists lacked.

VI OPPOSITION TO EVOLUTION

A. Darwin's publication of *On the Origin of Species* was controversial because it denied humanity was unique and many assumed it contradicted the existence of God.
B. A century and a half after the publication of *On the Origin of Species*, debates still revolve around evolution.
   1. For the vast majority of biological scientists evolution is an accepted scientific theory.
   2. Nevertheless, almost half of all Americans believe that evolution has not occurred.
C. Why evolution is not readily accepted
   1. Evolutionary mechanisms are complex and cannot be explained simply.
   2. Most people want definitive answers to complex questions, rather than the tentative and uncertain answers that scientists provide.
   3. While religions and belief systems deal with some natural phenomena, none propose biological change over time.
D. The relationship between science and religion has never been simple or clear.
   1. Scientific explanations are based on analysis and interpretation; they are testable and capable of being falsified.
   2. Religious beliefs are not falsifiable and are based on faith.
E. Catholics and mainstream Protestants generally do not see a conflict between evolution and religion.
   1. Pope John Paul II issued a statement in 1996 re-affirming the Catholic Church's acceptance of evolution as a sound scientific theory.
   2. In contrast, Fundamentalist Protestant groups do not accept evolution in any form.

F. History of Religious-based opposition to evolution in the US.
1. After WWI conservative Christians sought a revival of traditional values.
2. Prevented mention of Darwinism in public schools.
3. Scopes Monkey Trial in 1925 tested the validity of the law banning the teaching of evolution.
    a. Scopes was convicted and fined $100.
4. It wasn't until 1968 that the US Supreme court struck down the ban on teaching evolution in schools.
5. Christian fundamentalists renewed efforts to ban evolutionary teaching and promoted creation science.
    a. The premise of creation science is that the biblical account of the earth's origins and the Noah flood can be supported by scientific evidence.
6. Creation science is now called "intelligent design" or ID.
7. Creation science or ID are not scientific, as there are no hypotheses amenable to falsification.
    a. These practitioners believe that their views are absolute and infallible.
    b. This breaks the primary rule of scientific thinking.
8. Since the 1970s creationists have been active in local school boards.
    a. In Louisiana, Arkansas, and Pennsylvania, US judges ruled in favor of science and clearly stated that creationism and ID are not sciences.
        i) These subjects have no place in a science curriculum.
9. The first amendment of the US Constitution ensures that religion and state stay separate. Public education cannot promote religion. This is called the establishment clause.

KEY TERMS

binomial nomenclature: identifying each organism by two names, the genus and the species.

biology: the study of life.

catastrophism: a view that the earth's geology is the result of a series of cataclysmic events.

"creation science": a view that explains the existence of the universe as a result of a sudden creation. "Creation science" asserts its views to be absolute and infallible and therefore is religious and not scientific.

differential net reproductive success: the number of offspring that are produced, survive, and reproduce themselves.

deoxyribonucleic acid (DNA): double-stranded molecule that codes for genetic information.

evolution: changes in the genetic structure of a population from generation to generation.

fitness: a measure of the relative reproductive success of individuals and, hence their genetic contribution to the next generation.

fixity of species: the idea that species do not change, i.e., they do not evolve.

genome: the genetic makeup of an individual.

genus: the taxon (category) in biological classification that consists of closely related species.

Intelligent design: twentieth century creationist perspective that the world was created by an intelligent designer.

natural selection: the mechanism of evolutionary change in which certain traits from among existing variation are favored resulting in an increase in those traits in the next generation.

reproductive success: the number of offspring that an individual produces and the genetic contribution to the next generation that this implies.

selective pressures: forces in the environment that influence reproductive success in individuals.

species: a group of organisms capable of interbreeding under natural conditions and producing fertile and viable offspring.

stasis: in biology, this was the view that nature and all of its organisms were unchanging.

taxonomy: the biological discipline that names and classifies organisms.

uniformitarianism: the theory that the earth's geology is the result of long-term processes, still at work today, that requires immense geological time.

world view: general cultural orientation or perspective shared by members of a society.

MEDIA EXERCISES

1) Take a virtual tour through the University of California's Museum of Paleontology. In the "Evolution Wing" (http://www.ucmp.berkeley.edu/history/evolution.html) click on the "What is the history of evolutionary theory" link. Choose one of the "1800" time period link and click on one of the links. Read the biography of one of the figures that was not discussed in the text and discover something new that you had not learned from your book.

2) Next, take a tour of Berkeley's Evolution 101 course. http://evolution.berkeley.edu/evolibrary/article/evo_01. This brief internet site will give you some supplementary information about understanding evolutionary processes.

3) 2009 marked the 150 year anniversary of the publication of *On the Origin of Species* and the 200 year anniversary of his Darwin's birth. Many publications were dedicated to him and his works that year. Find a web site, or an article dedicated to Charles Darwin and the development of his theory. The American museum of natural history (www.amnh.org), the public broadcasting service (www.pbs.org), and National Geographic are good places to start.

4) The current anti-evolutionary approach of "intelligent design" can be traced back, at least in part, to the publication of Lehigh University biochemist Michael Behe's 1996 publication of *Darwin's Black Box: The Biochemical Challenge to Evolution*. In this book Behe presents his idea of "irreducible complexity" which he characterizes as absolutely incompatible with Darwinian natural selection. Read about Behe and his ideas online in TalkOrigins.org (http://www.talkorigins.org/faqs/behe.html). What is irreducible complexity and does it stand up to mainstream scientific scrutiny?

INFOTRAC

1) In *InfoTrac*, do a Keyword search on "uniformitarianism" and read the article by Richard Monastersy that shows how this two-century-old concept still resonates in today's geology. Does this article support Cuvier's "catastrophism"?

2) Follow-up with a keyword search on "catastrophism" to see how this concept is interpreted today.

CONCEPT APPLICATION

Using your text, match the historical figures and events to the time-lines on the next page.

A. Carolus Linnaeus publishes the first edition of *Systema Naturae*

B. Charles Darwin publishes *On the Origin of Species*

C. Archbishop Ussher determines Earth was created in 4004 B.C.

D. Comte de Buffon and Linnaeus are born

E. Georges Cuvier is born

F. Aristotle proposed the sun revolved around the earth

G. Charles Darwin reads Malthus' essay

H. Charles Darwin is born

I. Erasmus Darwin dies

J. Charles Darwin dies

K. Copernicus proposes heliocentric solar system

L. Lamarck is born

M. John Ray's ideas about species are accepted by scientists of his time.

N. First volume of Lyell's *Principles of Geology* published

O. Alfred Russell Wallace dies

P. Malthus writes his "Essay on the Principle of Population"

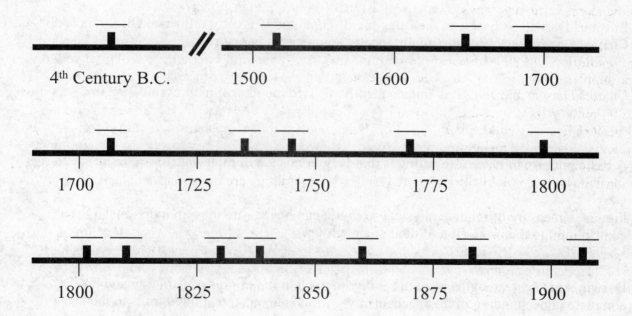

Now answer the True/False, Multiple Choice and Short Answer sample test questions. Following completion of the tests, correct them with the answers and textbook page references at the end of this Study Guide chapter. Note the areas in which you are strong and weak to guide you in your studying. Finally, answer the sample Essay Questions.

TRUE/FALSE QUESTIONS

If false, consider what modification would make the statement true.

1. The belief that life forms could not change came to be known in European intellectual circles as the fixity of species.
   (TRUE)   FALSE

2. The Comte de Buffon developed the system of classification that became the basis for taxonomy we still use today.   *→ adaptation*
   Linnaeus   TRUE   (FALSE)

3. The inheritance of acquired characteristics was an early mechanism of evolution proposed by Georges Cuvier.   *Lamarck*
   TRUE   (FALSE)

4. Charles Lyell's geological research supported the theory of uniformitarianism, an idea that states that processes observed in the present are the same as those that occurred in the past.
   (TRUE)   FALSE

5. Erasmus Darwin's "Essay on the Principle of Population" greatly influenced his grandson Charles Darwin's view of the importance of competition in nature.   *Malthus →*
   TRUE   (FALSE)

6. Charles Darwin and John Ray independently devised the idea of natural selection in the mid-17th century.   *→ Wallace*
   TRUE   (FALSE)

7. A basic premise of natural selection is that variation is the normal state of affairs in species.
   (TRUE)   FALSE

8. Fitness, a measure of relative physical strength, can be measured by an individual's contribution to the protection of their social group.
   TRUE   (FALSE)

9. Darwin's greatest strengths were his ability to explain the origins of variation and his complete understanding of the mechanism by which parents transmitted traits to their offspring.
   TRUE   (FALSE)

10. Creationism is not testable and cannot be considered science.
    (TRUE)   FALSE

28

MULTIPLE CHOICE QUESTIONS

1. The idea that organisms never change is called
   A. catastrophism.
   B. fixity of species.
   C. transmutation of species.
   D. evolution.

2. Which of the following is a **correct** statement?
   A. Scientific knowledge is usually gained through a series of small steps rather than giant leaps.
   B. Wallace developed the idea of natural selection a decade before Darwin.
   C. The predominant world view of the Middle Ages was that there was constant change in life forms with the exception of humans.
   D. The Great Chain of Being is an evolutionary scheme in which the organisms are arranged beginning with those whose ancestors first appeared in the fossil record and ending with those forms whose ancestors are the most recent.

3. The naturalist who first developed the concepts of the genus and species was
   A. Charles Darwin.
   B. John Ray.
   C. Carolus Linnaeus.
   D. Jean-Baptiste Lamarck.

4. The discipline within biology that is concerned with the rules of classifying organisms on the basis of evolutionary relationships is
   A. anatomy.
   B. genetics.
   C. taxonomy.
   D. ethology.

5. Which of the following is an example of binomial nomenclature?
   A. vole
   B. chimpanzee
   C. human
   D. *Homo sapiens*

6. The formal science of classifying animals and plants is called _____ and was invented by _____.
   A. natural selection; Wallace
   B. taxonomy; Linnaeus
   C. genetics; Mendel
   D. bioeconomics; Malthus

7. The first person to class humans with another animal group, the primates, was
   A. Linnaeus.
   B. Aristotle.
   C. John Ray.
   D. Archbishop James Ussher.

29

8. The naturalist who believed that species could change by adapting to new environmental conditions, yet rejected the notion of one species evolving out of another, was
    A. Linnaeus.
    B. Buffon.
    C. Lamarck.
    D. Cuvier.

9. Lamarck believed that
    A. organisms do not change.
    B. only genetically determined traits are passed from parent to offspring.
    C. the environment leads to the modification of body structures that are passed to offspring.
    D. only populations evolve.

10. The first natural historian to codify evolutionary ideas in a comprehensive system that attempted to explain the evolutionary process was
    A. Linnaeus.
    B. Buffon.
    C. Lamarck.
    D. Erasmus Darwin.

11. The opposite of Fixity of Species is
    A. evolution.
    B. typology.
    C. stasis.
    D. immutability of species.

12. A body builder works hard to build large muscles. He marries a beauty queen/life guard. The body builder expects his male offspring to be born muscle bound. His beliefs resemble those of
    A. catastrophism.
    B. uniformitarianism.
    C. the inheritance of acquired characteristics.
    D. evolution by natural selection.

13. The idea that species were fixed, but became extinct due to sudden, violent events and were replaced by neighboring new species is called
    A. evolution.
    B. phyletic gradualism.
    C. catastrophism.
    D. uniformitarianism.

14. Which scientist was most associated with the concept of catastrophism?
    A. Lamarck.
    B. Cuvier.
    C. Buffon.
    D. Lyell.

15. The idea supported by Lyell that the geological forces active today are no different from those acting in the past is known as
    A. Catastrophism.
    B. Uniformitarianism.
    C. Creationism.
    D. Conservatism.

16. Uniformitarianism implies which of the following
    A. new species are created by natural disasters.
    B. the earth is millions of years old.
    C. the earth has a living history, short as it may be.
    D. biological species evolve.

17. Which of the following ideas of Charles Lyell contributed to Darwin's thinking?
    A. There is variation within any population of organisms.
    B. Traits are passed down through the inheritance of acquired characteristics.
    C. A trait must be inherited to have any importance in evolution.
    D. There is an immense geological time scale.

18. The concept that within populations there is constant competition for food and other resources, was the idea of
    A. Charles Darwin.
    B. Charles Lyell.
    C. Thomas Malthus.
    D. A. R. Wallace.

19. Which of the following developed a theory of evolution by natural selection?
    A. Lamarck.
    B. A. R. Wallace.
    C. Erasmus Darwin.
    D. Lyell.

20. Which of the following is **not** a statement that Darwin would have made?
    A. There is biological variation within all species.
    B. The environment selects which traits are beneficial.
    C. Geographical isolation may lead to a new species.
    D. Traits that are acquired during an individual's lifetime are passed to the next generation.

21. Those individuals that produce more offspring, relative to other individuals in the population, are said to have greater
    A. fitness.
    B. selective pressure.
    C. variation.
    D. survival potential.

22. Forces in the environment which influence reproductive success are called
    A. k-selection.
    B. selective pressures.
    C. phyletic gradualism.
    D. differential reproduction.

23. Which of the following historical figures did **not** believe in the Fixity of Species?
    A. Lamarck.
    B. Linnaeus.
    C. Cuvier.
    D. Ray.

24. One of the best documented case of natural selection acting on non-human populations is
    A. starfish as keystone predators of mussels in the Pacific Northwest.
    B. mutualism involving sharks and remoras.
    C. industrial melanism involving peppered moths near Manchester, England.
    D. the symbiosis formed by cork sponges and hermit crabs.

25. What happened to the peppered moth population in England during the Industrial Revolution?
    A. There was a change in wing length due to the stability of the environment.
    B. There was a loss of functional wings due to a change in the environment.
    C. They became extinct because these moths could not adapt to the environment.
    D. There was a shift in body color from light to dark in this population.

26. Industrial melanism refers to
    A. a case of natural selection in Britain.
    B. Lamarck's example for the inheritance of acquired characters.
    C. Darwin's example for evolution by natural selection.
    D. Lyell's example of the "struggle for existence."

27. Differential net reproductive success refers to
    A. one individual leaving more offspring than all other individuals.
    B. the number of offspring that survive to reproduce relative to other individuals.
    C. an evolutionary shift in a trait.
    D. the development of new traits.

28. Darwin's explanation for evolution suffered from his inability to explain
   A. the role of variation in natural selection.
   B. the origins of variation.
   C. the effects of the environment.
   D. the immense time span that would be required.

29. Natural selection acts upon the _____ while _____ evolve.
   A. species; gene
   B. genus; family
   C. chromosome; cell
   D. individual; population

30. Charles Darwin was not familiar with the works of which of the following individuals?
   A. Lamarck.
   B. Malthus.
   C. Mendel.
   D. Lyell.

31. Which of the following statements is **true**?
   A. "Creation Science" is falsifiable.
   B. "Creation Science" and "Intelligent Design Theory" both invoke a supernatural creator.
   C. Evolutionary science asserts that its theories are absolute and infallible.
   D. "Creation Science" is amenable to modification based on hypothesis testing.

32. "Creation Science"
   A. asserts that its ideas are absolute and infallible.
   B. is not amenable to scientific testing and falsification.
   C. is religion, not science.
   D. All of the above.

SHORT ANSWER QUESTIONS (& PAGE REFERENCES)

1. What is the fixity of species? (p. 25)

2. Why was Lamarck important in the development of evolutionary thought? (pp. 29-30)

3. Why was the voyage of the *H.M.S. Beagle* so important for the development of Darwin's ideas? (pp. 34-36)

4. Why must a trait be inherited to have importance in natural selection? (pp. 37-38)

5. What were Darwin's weaknesses in understanding evolution? (p. 42)

ESSAY QUESTIONS (& PAGE REFERENCES)

1. Who were the most important pre-Darwinian figures and how did they contribute to the development of Darwin's evolutionary synthesis? (pp. 28-32)

2. Compare and contrast Darwin's natural selection to Lamarck's inheritance of acquired characteristics as competing mechanisms for explaining evolutionary change? (pp. 29; 35-38)

3. Why is "creation science" not scientific? (pp. 43-45)

ANSWERS, *CORRECTED STATEMENT* IF FALSE & REFERENCES TO TRUE/FALSE QUESTIONS

1. **TRUE**, p. 25

2. **FALSE**, p. 28, *Carolus Linnaeus* developed the system of classification that became the basis for taxonomy we still use today.

3. **FALSE**, pp. 29, The inheritance of acquired characteristics was an early mechanism of evolution proposed by *Lamarck*.

4. **TRUE**, pp. 31

5. **FALSE**, p. 31-31, *Thomas Malthus'* "Essay on the Principle of Population" greatly influenced Charles Darwin's view of the importance of competition in nature.

6. **FALSE**, p. 36, Charles Darwin and *Alfred Wallace* independently devised the idea of natural selection in the *mid-19th* century.

7. **TRUE**, p. 37.

8. **FALSE**, p. 37, Fitness, a measure of relative *reproductive success*, can be measured by an individual's *genetic* contribution to the *next generation*.

9. **FALSE**, p. 42, Darwin's *weaknesses* were his *inability* to explain the origins of variation and his *incomplete* understanding of the mechanism by which parents transmitted traits to their offspring.

10. **TRUE**, p. 44

34

Answers & References to Multiple Choice Questions

1. **B**, p. 25	17. **D**, p. 32
2. **A**, p. 27	18. **C**, p. 30-31
3. **B**, p. 28	19. **B**, p. 36-37
4. **C**, p. 28	20. **D**, pp. 37
5. **D**, p. 28	21. **A**, p. 37
6. **B**, p. 28	22. **B**, p. 38
7. **A**, p. 28	23. **A**, pp. 29
8. **B**, p. 29	24. **C**, pp. 38-39
9. **C**, pp. 29	25. **D**, pp. 38-39
10. **C**, pp. 29	26. **A**, pp. 38-39
11. **A**, p. 29	27. **B**, pp. 40-41
12. **C**, p. 29	28. **B**, p. 42
13. **C**, p. 29	29. **D**, p. 37-38
14. **B**, p. 29	30. **C**, p. 29-36
15. **B**, pp. 30	31. **B**, p. 44
16. **B**, p. 32	32. **D**, pp. 44-45

Concept Application Solution

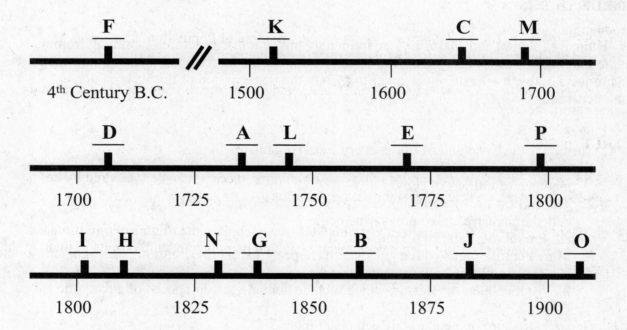

CHAPTER 3
THE BIOLOGICAL BASIS OF LIFE

LEARNING OBJECTIVES

After reading this chapter you should be able to
- describe the structure of a generalized cell (pp. 48-50).
- recognize the structure and function of DNA (pp. 50-52).
- understand the process of protein synthesis (pp. 53-56).
- explain the function of a gene (pp. 56-61).
- understand how a mutation occurs (pp. 61-63).
- recognize and understand the importance of chromosomes (pp. 64-66)
- understand what a karyotype is and why it is useful (pp. 66-67).
- understand the processes of mitosis and meiosis (pp. 67-69).
- recognize the evolutionary significance of meiosis (pp. 69-72).
- understand the basics of the new genetic technologies (pp. 73-74).
- recognize the impact of molecular technology upon forensic anthropology (pp. 76-78).

CHAPTER OUTLINE

Introduction

    Human evolution and adaptation are intimately linked to life processes stemming from the genetic functions of cells. This occurs in cell replication, in the translation of genetic information into products usable by the organism and finally into the transmission of this information to future generations.

I   CELLS
    A. The cell is the basic unit of life in every living organism.
       1. Complex multicellular life forms, such as plants and animals, (this means you too) are made up of billions of cells.
       2. The earliest life on earth, appearing by at least 3.7 billion years ago, were single celled organisms called prokaryote cells.
         a. Prokaryote cells lack a nucleus.
       3. More complex cells with a nucleus first appeared around 1.2 billion years ago.
         a. These cells are called eukaryote cells.
         b. Multicellular organisms, which include humans, are composed of eukaryotic cells.
    B. General structure of a eukaryotic cell (see Figure 3-2).
       1. Cells are three-dimensional structures made up of carbohydrates, fats, nucleic acids, and proteins.
       2. Cells contain several structures including a nucleus, cytoplasm and organelles.
       3. The cytoplasm is a semifluid within which the other structures are found.
       4. The nucleus is a discrete unit within the cell.
         a. It is surrounded by a nuclear membrane.
         b. The nucleus contains DNA (deoxyribonucleic acid) and RNA (ribonucleic acid).

5. There are numerous, functionally different organelles within the cell.
   a. Think about how you are comprised of organs.
      i) These work together to facilitate the function of you
      ii) These are basically analogous to the organelles in a cell.
6. Other organelles in the cytoplasm break down nutrients and eliminate waste, and make proteins.
7. Two important organelles are mitochondria and ribosomes
8. Mitochondria produce energy in the cell and have a distinct kind of DNA called mitochondrial DNA (mtDNA).
   a. mtDNA is similar to nuclear DNA but it is organized differently.
   b. mtDNA is significant in evolutionary studies and forensic examination.
9. Ribosomes are essential for protein synthesis.
C. There are two types of cells (somatic cells and gametes).
   1. Somatic cells are the cells of the body with the exception of the sex cells.
   2. Gametes are sex cells involved with reproduction.
      a. Egg cells are produced in female ovaries.
      b. Sperm are sex cells produced in male testes.
      c. A zygote is the union between a sperm and an egg.

II THE STRUCTURE OF DNA
A. The discovery of the properties of DNA in the early 1950's revolutionized biological science.
B. The structure and function of DNA is critical to cellular function and inheritance.
C. DNA is composed of two chains of nucleotides.
   1. A nucleotide consists of a sugar, a phosphate, and one of four nitrogenous bases.
   2. Nucleotides form long chains and the two chains are held together by chemical bonds formed by the bases.
   3. Together the chains form a double helix shape.
   4. The four bases of DNA are the key to how DNA works.
   5. Bases are paired (bonded) based on their chemically properties.
      a. This is essential to the ability of DNA to copy itself.
      b. Adenine (A) pairs with thymine (T).
      c. Guanine (G) pairs with cytosine (C).

III DNA REPLICATION
A. Organisms grow and repair themselves by cell multiplication and division.
B. In order for cells to do this DNA must be replicated (make copies of itself).
   1. This takes place in the cell nucleus.
C. The replication process:
   1. Enzymes break the bonds between the base pairs.
   2. The two separated nucleotide chains serve as templates for the formation of a new strand of nucleotides.
   3. Unattached nucleotides pair with the appropriate complementary nucleotide.
   4. The end result is two newly formed strands of DNA.
      a. Each new strand is joined to one of the original strands of DNA.
      b. The strands are identical to each other (and to the original).

IV PROTEIN SYNTHESIS

A. DNA directs protein synthesis (the production of proteins) within the cell.
   1. This is the most important function of DNA.

B. Proteins are the major structural components of the body.

C. Structure and function of proteins:
   1. Many proteins initiate and enhance chemical reactions.
   2. Proteins include substances like collagen, lactase, and insulin.
   3. Proteins are comprised of smaller molecules called amino acids.
      a. We say amino acids are the building blocks of proteins.
      b. There are 20 biologically important amino acids,
         i) 12 of these are produced within your cells.
         ii) The remaining 8 must come from your food.
      c. Each protein differs from the others based on the number and sequence of amino acids.

D. DNA is a recipe for making proteins.
   1. A triplet (3consecutive base pairs) in the DNA defines which amino acid is added to a sequence to form a protein.
   2. Protein synthesis takes place outside the nucleus at the ribosome.
   3. DNA is too large to pass through the membrane that surrounds the nucleus.
   4. The DNA message is modified into a form of RNA (transcription).
   5. Messenger RNA (mRNA) can pass through the nuclear membrane.

E. RNA is similar to DNA but different in 3 important ways.
   1. It is single stranded.
   2. It contains a different type of sugar.
   3. It contains the base uracil (U) which binds to thymine (T).

F. The mRNA molecules leaves the nucleus and travels through the cell to the ribosome.

G. The ribosome translates the mRNA message into groups of 3 bases (codons).
   1. Codons (3 consecutive base pairs of mRNA) are base pair triplets that code for a particular amino acid.

H. Another form of RNA, transfer RNA, (tRNA), is found in the cytoplasm.
   1. tRNA is bound to an amino acid and carries particular amino acids to the ribosome as required.

I. Ribosomes join the amino acids together to form a protein.

V WHAT IS A GENE?

A. The segment of DNA responsible for synthesizing a protein is a gene.
   1. A gene codes for the production of a polypeptide chain.
   2. The proteins composed of only a single polypeptide chain are produced through the actions of a single gene.
   3. Other proteins are made up of two or more polypeptide chains and require the action of two or more genes.

B. An alteration in the sequence of bases in a gene is called a mutation.
   1. This may interfere with the organism's ability to produce vital proteins.

C. Genes consist of exons and introns.
   1. DNA segments that code for specific amino acids are called *ex*ons.
      a. They are *ex*pressed.
   2. DNA sequences not expressed during protein synthesis are called *in*trons.
      a. They are *not in*volved in protein synthesis

38

VI . REGULATORY GENES

A.   Regulatory genes function to control the expression of other genes.
1. Example: DNA deactivation during embryogenesis.
2. Example: Bone cells lose the ability through deactivation by regulatory genes to produce stomach enzymes.

B. Homeobox or *Hox* genes are important regulatory genes
1. *Hox* genes direct the development of body plans and segmentation in utero.
2. Interact with other genes to determine the identity and characteristics of body segments.
a. Example: where limb buds will appear.
b. Example: development of the different types of vertebrae (spinal bones).
    i) Vertebrae of the neck (cervical), torso (thoracic) and lower back (lumbar) are unique and related to the specific function of the different areas of your spine.
3. Homeobox genes are highly conserved, meaning that that they have been maintained throughout much of evolutionary history.
4. Alterations in the behavior of homeobox genes may be responsible for some of the observed physical differences between closely related species like chimps and humans.

C. DNA is the universal building block of all life on earth.

VII MUTATION: WHEN A GENE CHANGES

A. A change in genetic material is called mutation.
B. An example of a mutation: sickle-cell hemoglobin (See also Chapter 4).
1. Hemoglobin (Hb) is a molecule on red blood cells that facilitates the transport of oxygen throughout your system.
2. Hb consists of four polypeptide chains, two alpha chains and two beta chains.
a.   Each beta chain is composed of 146 amino acids.
    i) This is 438 bases.
b. An error involving the 6th amino acid in the beta chain results in an abnormal hemoglobin (hemoglobin S or Hb^S).
3. (Hb^S) is caused by the substitution of one amino acid (valine) for another (the normally occurring glutamic acid) on the beta chain.
4. Abnormal hemoglobin does not distribute oxygen as efficiently as normal Hb.
5. This mutation results from the substitution of a single base.
a. CTC incorrectly replaced by CAC
b. This mutation is called a point mutation.
6. Sickle-cell anemia is a genetic condition in which the affected individual inherits the mutation from both parents.
a. When oxygen demands increase, the red blood cells become sickle shaped and the person goes into crisis.
b. Untreated sickle-cell anemia can be fatal.
7. Point mutations may be the most common and most important source of new variation.
8. For a mutation to be evolutionarily significant:
a. It must be passed on to offspring (must occur in a gamete).
b. It must be selected for by other evolutionary forces.

VIII CHROMOSOMES

A. Most of the time DNA exists as an uncoiled granular substance called chromatin.
B. During cell division the chromatin coils up to become chromosomes.
C. Chromosome structure:
   1. A chromosome is composed of a DNA molecule and associated proteins.
   2. During interphase (prior to cell division) chromosomes exist as single-stranded structures.
   3. During early cell division chromosomes consists of two strands of DNA.
      a. These two strands are joined together at a constricted region called the centromere.
      b. The two strands of DNA are because replication has occurred and one strand is an exact copy of the other.
D. Each species is characterized by a specific number of chromosomes.
   1. Humans have 46 chromosomes, chimps and gorillas both have 48.
   2. Chimp and gorilla DNA is packaged differently that human DNA.
E. Types of Chromosomes
   1. Chromosomes occur in pairs.
   2. One member of each pair of chromosomes is inherited from the father and one from the mother.
      a. Members of chromosome pairs are similar in size, position, and centromere position.
      b. They also carry genetic material that governs the same traits.
   3. All normal human somatic cells have 22 pairs of autosomes and 1 pair of sex chromosomes.
      a. To function normally humans must have a full complement of 23 pairs or 46 chromosomes.
   4. Autosomes carry genetic information that governs all physical characteristics except primary sex determination.
      a. The autosomal pairs are known as homologous pairs.
   5. The two sex chromosomes are the X and Y chromosomes.
      a. Genetically normal mammalian females have two X chromosomes.
      b. Genetically normal mammalian males have one X chromosome and one Y chromosome.
   6. Alleles are the different possible forms of genes at each genetic locus.

IX KARYOTYPING CHROMOSOMES

A. A photomicrograph that displays an individual's chromosomes is called a karyotype.
   1. Karyotypes are constructed from photographs taken through a microscope of chemically treated chromosomes (see Figure 3-19).
      a. Homologous chromosomes are matched up.
      b. Chromosomes are arranged by size, and centromere position.
   2. Karyotypes have numerous practical applications.
      a. They can be used in diagnosis of chromosomal disorders.
      b. They can also be employed in prenatal diagnoses.

3. Technological advances now allow us to identify the location of every chromosome on the basis of banding patterns.
   a. Karyotypes and banding patterns enable researchers to deduce relationships between different species.
   b. The chromosome patterns of humans, chimpanzees, and gorillas indicate a very close relationship between these three species.
   c. Today genomes can be compared directly so karotypes are used less often for this purpose.

X   CELL DIVISION
A. Prior to cell division the DNA replicates.
B. There are two types of cell division.
   1. Mitosis
      a. Cell division of body cells
   2. Meiosis
      a. Cell division that produces sperm and egg
C. Mitosis
   1. Cell division in somatic cells is called mitosis or simple cell division.
      a. Mitosis occurs during growth and development
      b. Mitosis occurs to repair and replace tissues.
   2. Steps in mitosis:
      a. The 46 double stranded chromosomes line up in the center of cell (see Fig. 3-20).
      b. The chromosomes are then pulled apart at the centromere.
      c. The separated chromosomes are pulled towards opposite ends of the cell; each separated chromosome is composed of one DNA molecule.
      d. The cell membrane pinches in and separates into two cells.
   3. Mitosis produces two daughter cells
      a. The cells are genetically identical to each other and the original cell.
   4. Not all somatic cells undergo mitosis
      a. It does not occur in red blood cells, adult nerve and brain cells, or in mature liver cells.
D. Meiosis
   1. Meiosis has two cell divisions (see Figures 3-21 and 3-22).
      a. Meiosis produces 4 daughter cells.
      b. Each daughter cell is unique
      c. Each daughter cell has half the original number of chromosomes
         i) One of each pair
   2. Specialized cells in the testes and ovaries undergo meiosis to become sperm and egg cells, respectively.
   3. Meiosis is a reduction division.
      a. Initially the sex cells have the original number (23 pairs in humans), or full complement, of chromosomes.
         i) Recall replication generates 23 double stranded pairs
      b. After the two dividing stages of meiosis takes place, the sperm and egg contain only half the normal complement of chromosomes (23 unpaired single stranded chromosomes).
      c. Reduction division allows one egg and one sperm to come together can create a zygote with 46 chromosomes.

41

4. Recombination, or crossing over occurs during the first division of meiosis:
   a. The paired chromosomes are together along the cell's equator.
   b. While paired chromosomes are together they exchange pieces of genetic material.
   c. Recombination increases the uniqueness of each chromosome.
5. As the cell divides members of each pair migrate to the opposite pole of the cell.
6. The first division results in two daughter cells with 23 randomly separated double stranded chromosomes.
7. The second division is similar to the process of mitosis
   a. The double stranded chromosomes line up along the center of both cells.
   b. The chromosomes are then pulled apart at the centromere.
   c. The separated chromosomes are pulled towards opposite ends of the cell; each separated chromosome is composed of one DNA molecule.
   d. The cell membrane pinches in and separates into two cells.
8. Meiosis results in 4 unique daughter cells with 23 single-stranded chromosomes (haploid).

E. The evolutionary significance of meiosis.
   1. Meiosis increases genetic variation in populations.
      a. Random assortment of chromosome pairs can create millions of different gametes.
      b. Random assortment insures that in every generation, the genetic deck is shuffled.
   2. Natural selection acts on hereditary variation in all populations.
      a. Without the genetic variation of meiosis, natural selection would have almost nothing to work with.
      b. Mutation is the only source of *new* genetic variation.
      c. However, in sexually reproducing species recombination produces new combinations of genetic information, providing additional material for natural selection to act upon.

F. Problems with meiosis.
   1. Incorrect meiosis can lead to abnormal fetal development.
      a. The failure of chromosomes to separate during meiosis is called nondisjunction.
         i) This can lead to a gamete with an incorrect number of chromosomes (22 or 24).
         ii) If an affected gamete fuses with a normal gamete this will result in a zygote with either 45 or 47 chromosomes.
            a) 45 = monosomy: only one of a chromosomal pair
            b) 47 = trisomy: three of a chromosomal pair
      b. Zygotes with the incorrect number of chromosomes may be spontaneously aborted.
   2. Examples of abnormal numbers of chromosomes:
      a. Trisomy 21 (Down syndrome) is caused by three copies of the 21st chromosome.
         i) Congenital problems associated with Trisomy 21 include mental impairment, heart defects, and susceptibility to respiratory infections.
         ii) Trisomy 21 is associated with advanced maternal age (over 35 years of age).
   3. Nondisjunction may also occur in the sex chromosomes resulting in other conditions (see Table 3-3).
      a. Many of these include impaired mental function, sterility, or death.

42

XI   NEW FRONTIERS

A. The field of genetics has revolutionized biological science.

B. Polymerase chain reaction (PCR), developed in 1986, makes it possible to produce and amplify multiple copies of small samples of DNA.
    1. This allows researchers to analyze and identify very small segments of DNA that otherwise would have been impossible without this new technology.
    2. For example, PCR has been used to isolate and amplify DNA from Neandertal fossils.
    3. DNA fingerprinting is another PCR application.
        a.   Used to identify remains of unidentified people in the September 11 attacks.

C. Recombinant DNA technology allows genes from one species to be transferred into another.
    1. One use of this technology is to enable bacteria to produce medically valuable human gene products such as insulin.
    2. Genetic manipulation has become controversial.
        a. genetically modified crops

D. Cloning research has been very controversial since 1997 and Dolly.
    1. 1960s the African toad was first cloned, now cloning is commonplace.
    2. Cloning is done by nuclear transfer.
        a. First an egg cell nucleus is removed.
        b. Somatic cell nuclear material is inserted from an adult animal.
        c. The egg is placed into a surrogates uterus.
        d. The surrogate gives birth to clone that is genetically identical to the adult donor of nuclear material.
    3. Cloning a primate has been more difficult that expected.

E. The single most important advance in genetics has been the progress made on the Human Genome Project.
    1. The goal is to sequence the entire human genome.
    2. The next goal is to determine which sections of DNA are functional.
        a.   In 2003, the remainder of the Human Genome Project was completed.
    3. As of September 2000, the genomes of over 600 other species (mostly microorganisms) have been completely or partially sequenced.
        a.   By December 2002 the mouse genome was completely sequenced.
        b.   In December 2003 a "rough draft" of the chimpanzee genome was announced.
        c.   Comparative genome analysis should provide a thorough assessment of the evolutionary relationships between humans and other primates.

KEY TERMS

alleles: alternate forms of a gene. Alleles occur at the same locus on homologous chromosomes and thus govern the same trait. However, because they are different, their action may result in different expressions of that trait. Synonym: gene.

amino acids: small molecules that are the basic building blocks of proteins.

autosomes: one of the pairs of chromosomes that determines traits other than sex.

centromere: the constricted portion of a chromosome. After replication, the two strands of a double-stranded chromosome are joined at the centromere.

chromatin: the loose, diffuse form of DNA seen during interphase. When condensed, chromatin forms into chromosomes.

43

chromosome: structures that are composed of DNA and protein, found in the nucleus of the cell, and are only visible during cell replication.

clone: an organism that is genetically identical to another organism.

codon: three nitrogenous bases (i.e., a triplet) found on the mRNA which complements three bases on a tRNA carrying a specific amino acid.

complementary: refers to the fact that certain bases in DNA and RNA always bind together. Cytosine always pairs with Guanine and, in DNA, Adenine always pairs with Thymine. In RNA Uracil replaces Thymine and pairs with Adenine.

cytoplasm: the region of a cell that is contained within the cell membrane, excluding the nucleus.

deoxyribonucleic acid (DNA): a double-stranded molecule that contains the genetic information.

diploid: the full complement of chromosomes of a species.

enzyme: specialized proteins that initiate and direct chemical reactions in the body.

gametes: sex cells, viz. ova (eggs) and sperm.

gene: a sequence of DNA nucleotides that code for a particular polypeptide chain.

genome: the complete genetic makeup of an individual or a species.

haploid: half the normal complement of chromosomes of a species. The haploid condition is characteristic of animal sex cells.

hemoglobin: a protein molecule that occurs in red blood cells and binds to oxygen molecules.

homeotic genes: regulatory genes that direct the development and segmentation of body plans.

homologous: the pair of chromosomes that carry genes for the same traits.

hormones: substances that are produced by specialized cells and that travel to other parts of the body, where they influence chemical reactions and regulate various cellular functions.

Human Genome Project: an international effort aimed at sequencing and mapping the entire human genome.

interphase: the portion of a cell's cycle during which metabolic processes and other cellular activities occur. DNA replication occurs during interphase.

karyotype: the chromosomal complement of an individual or that typical for a species. Usually displayed as a photomicrograph, often using special stains to highlight the bands or centromeres.

locus: position on a chromosome where a given gene occurs.

meiosis: specialized cell division in the reproductive organs which produce gametes. The gametes are haploid and are not identical.

messenger RNA (mRNA): a form of RNA, formed on one strand of the DNA, that carries the DNA code from the nucleus to the cytoplasm where protein synthesis takes place.

mitochondria: organelles found in the cytoplasm which produce cellular energy.

mitochondrial DNA (mtDNA): DNA in the mitochondria inherited only from the mother.

mitosis: cell division in somatic cells.

molecule: structure made up of two or more atoms.

mutation: a change in the sequence of bases coding for the production of a protein.

nondisjunction: the failure of homologous chromosomes to separate during meiosis.

nucleotide: the basic unit of DNA. A nucleotide consists of one of four nitrogenous bases, plus a sugar and a phosphate.

nucleus: a structure found in eukaryotic cells which contains chromosomal DNA.

organelle: a structure found in the cytoplasm that performs some physiological function.

point mutation: a mutation that results from the substitution of one nitrogenous base by another.

polymerase chain reaction (PCR): a method of producing thousands of copies of a DNA segment using the enzyme DNA polymerase.

polypeptide chain: a sequence of amino acids that may act alone or in combination as a functional protein.

proteins: three-dimensional molecules composed of amino acids that serve as structural components of animal bodies and as catalysts for biochemical reactions.

protein synthesis: the process by which proteins are produced from amino acids.

random assortment: the random distribution of chromosomes to daughter cells during meiosis; along with recombination, the source of variation resulting from meiosis.

recombinant DNA technology: artificial transfer of cells from one species to another.

recombination (crossing over): the exchange of genetic material between homologous chromosomes during meiosis.

replicate: to duplicate. How the DNA molecule makes copies of itself.

ribonucleic acid (RNA): a single-stranded molecule, similar in structure to DNA. The three types of RNA are essential to protein synthesis.

ribosome: a cytoplasmic organelle, made up of RNA and protein, where protein synthesis takes place.

sex chromosomes: in animals, those chromosomes involved with primary sex determination. The X and Y chromosomes.

sickle-cell anemia: a severe inherited disease that results from a double dose of a mutant allele, which in turn results from a single base substitution at the DNA level.

somatic cells: the cells of the body, excluding the cells involved with primary reproduction.

transcription: the formation of a messenger RNA molecule from a DNA template.

transfer RNA (tRNA): the form of RNA that binds to a specific amino acid and, during translation, transports them to the ribosome in sequence.

translation: the process of sequencing amino acids from a messenger RNA template into a functional protein or a portion of a protein.

zygote: a cell resulting from the fusion of a sperm and an egg (ovum).

MEDIA EXERCISES

1) Explore the official Human Genome Project suite of web sites sponsored by the U.S. Department of Energy (http://www.ornl.gov/sci/techresources/Human_Genome/home.shtml). What are some new medical applications that are being projected to grow out of this massive research effort? In this context, what are the ethical, legal and social issues involved with the HGE?

2) Google OMIM (Online Mendelian Inheritance in Man). Explore the site (which is a collection of over 10,000 genetic conditions—some the result of mutations) and consider typing in any of the genetic conditions mentioned in this chapter.

INFOTRAC

1) In *InfoTrac* do a keyword search on "Recombinant DNA or cloning" and then click the "Limit Search" button and add "ethics or debate" in the "by **entering a word** (or words)" box. Read a few of the articles that are listed on rDNA and/or cloning. What are the ethical challenges posed by these new technologies? Do you think that these obstacles can be overcome? Should they be?

CONCEPT APPLICATION

First, convert the following string of DNA bases into its complementary mRNA molecule. Next, translate the mRNA into a polypeptide chain of amino acids using Table 3-1 on p. 55 in your text. (Remember that mRNA is read in three-base words called codons).

    1. DNA bases: CAATATGGAAGCCGACTCACCCTAATT

    2. mRNA string: _

    3. amino acids: ____ ____ ____ ____ ____ ____ ____ ____ ____

A substitution point mutation has occurred to this genetic sequence. The third base was replaced by a "T". What is the ultimate effect of this genetic change on the resultant polypeptide chain? How does this illustrate the concepts of "redundancy" and "neutral mutations"?

    4. DNA bases: CA**T**TATGGAAGCCGACTCACCCTAATT

    5. mRNA string: _

    6. amino acids: ____ ____ ____ ____ ____ ____ ____ ____ ____

Now answer the True/False, Multiple Choice and Short Answer sample test questions. Following completion of the tests, correct them using the answers and textbook page references at the end of this Study Guide chapter. Note your strengths and weaknesses to guide your studying. Finally, answer the sample Essay Questions.

TRUE/FALSE QUESTIONS

If false, consider what modification would make the statement true.

1. Mitochondria and ribosomes are found within the nucleus of the cell.
   TRUE   ~~FALSE~~

2. Enzymes are specialized proteins that initiate and direct chemical reactions in the body.
   ~~TRUE~~   FALSE

3. The mRNA message transcribed from the DNA is read in 4-letter words called quadrates at the site of protein synthesis, the mitochondria.
   TRUE   ~~FALSE~~

4. Genes include both exons, DNA that codes for particular amino acids, and introns, non-coding DNA.
   ~~TRUE~~   FALSE

5. Sickle-cell anemia results from a chromosomal mutation causing a trisomy at the 15th chromosomal pair.   → point mutation
   TRUE   ~~FALSE~~

6. Humans have 48 chromosomes while chimps and gorillas only have 46.
   TRUE   ~~FALSE~~

7. A zygote is an illustration of the chromosomal complement of an individual or that which is typical for a species.
   ✓ karyotype   TRUE   ~~FALSE~~

8. Somatic cells have a full compliment of chromosomes while gametes have half.
   ~~TRUE~~   FALSE

9. Nondisjunction is a failure of chromosomes to separate during meiosis.
   ~~TRUE~~   FALSE

10. Recombinant DNA technology is a method for producing thousands of copies of a DNA segment using the enzyme DNA polymerase.
    TRUE   ~~FALSE~~

MULTIPLE CHOICE QUESTIONS

1. The discipline that links or influences the various subdisciplines of physical (biological) anthropology is
   A. genetics.
   B. cell biology.
   C. paleontology.
   D. primatology.

2. A cell that has its DNA enclosed by a nucleus is called a
   A. karyote cell.
   B. prokaryote cell.
   C. eukaryote cell.
   D. prion.

3. The two nucleic acids that contain the genetic information that controls the cell's functions are
   A. ribosomes and Golgi apparati.
   B. mitochondria and desmosomes.
   C. the endoplasmic reticulum and ribosomes.
   D. DNA and RNA.

4. Organelles found in the cytoplasm that contains their own DNA are the
   A. ribosomes.
   B. mitochondria.
   C. lysosomes.
   D. vacuoles.

5. Which of the following is **not** a gamete?
   A. sex cell.
   B. egg.
   C. sperm.
   D. skin cell.

6. A cell formed by the union of an egg and a sperm is called a
   A. gamete.
   B. zygote.
   C. neuron.
   D. ovum.

7. The smallest unit of DNA consists of one sugar, one phosphate, and one of four bases. This unit is called a
   A. sperm.
   B. nucleotide.
   C. nucleus.
   D. ribosome.

48

8. Researchers found that certain bases of the DNA macromolecule always pair. These bases are referred to as
    A. independently assorted.
    B. segregated.
    C. in equilibrium.
    D. complementary.

9. A parental chain of DNA provides the following template: AAT CGA CGT. Which of the following sequences of free nucleotides would pair with the parental template?
    A. TTA GCT GCA.
    B. AAT CGA CGT.
    C. GGC TAG TAC.
    D. UUA GCU GCA.

10. The end result of DNA replication is
    A. two identical strands of DNA.
    B. the fusion of the mother's DNA with the father's DNA.
    C. the formation of a mRNA molecule.
    D. the production of an amino acid molecule.

11. A type of protein which helps to enhance chemical reactions in the body is a(n)
    A. bone.
    B. muscle.
    C. enzyme.
    D. hemoglobin.

12. Proteins consists of chains of
    A. carbohydrates.
    B. lipids.
    C. amino acids.
    D. fatty acids.

13. Which of the following is **not** true about RNA?
    A. It is single stranded.
    B. Some forms of RNA are involved with protein synthesis.
    C. It has a different type of sugar than DNA has.
    D. It contains the base thymine.

14. The formation of a mRNA molecule from DNA is called
    A. transcription.
    B. translation.
    C. translocation.
    D. transformation.

15. The reading of mRNA by a ribosomes to produce protein is called
    A. transcription.
    B. translation.
    C. translocation.
    D. transformation.

16. A 3-base sequence of a mRNA molecule that determines one amino acid in a polypeptide chain is called a
    A. nucleotide.
    B. gene.
    C. codon.
    D. polymerase.

17. In protein synthesis all of the following occur **except**
    A. amino acids are initially bonded to specific tRNA molecules.
    B. amino acids are transported to the nucleus to bond with DNA molecules.
    C. the sequence of amino acids is determined by the codon sequence in mRNA.
    D. amino acids are bonded together to form a polypeptide chain.

18. What is the name of the molecule that binds to amino acids?
    A. messenger RNA (mRNA)
    B. ribosomal RNA (rRNA)
    C. transfer RNA (tRNA)
    D. mitochondrial DNA (mtDNA)

19. The following segment of mRNA contains the bases UUA CGC UGA. Which are the bases for the three tRNAs associated with this segment?
    A. UUA CGC UGA
    B. AAT GCG ACT
    C. AGU CGC AUU
    D. AAU GCG ACU

20. The sequence of DNA bases on the chromosome that code for a particular polypeptide chain is a(n)
    A. ribosome.
    B. amino acid.
    C. gene.
    D. polypeptide chain.

21. A single base substitution in the DNA causes a severe hemoglobin disorder in which oxygen stressed red blood cells collapse. This condition is
    A. sickle-cell anemia.
    B. Tay-Sachs disease.
    C. cystic fibrosis.
    D. hemolytic disease of the newborn.

50

22. A change in one base of a codon may produce a change in the hereditary information and is called a
   A. point mutation.
   B. chromosomal reversal.
   C. chromosomal inversion.
   D. synapsis.

23. What is the characteristic number of chromosomes in human somatic cells?
   A. 23
   B. 46
   C. 48
   D. 78

24. A genetically normal human female has
   A. 23 pairs of autosomes.
   B. 23 pairs of autosomes and two X chromosomes.
   C. 22 pairs of autosomes and two X chromosomes.
   D. 22 pairs of autosomes, one X chromosome, and one Y chromosome.

25. The end result of mitosis in humans is
   A. two identical "daughter" cells.
   B. four haploid cells.
   C. two cells with 23 chromosomes.
   D. two cells with mutations.

26. Which of the following is true for meiosis?
   A. It involves only one division which duplicates the parent cell exactly.
   B. It produces gametes.
   C. When a mutation occurs it affects only the individual.
   D. It has no effect on evolution.

27. The most important regulatory genes that control embryonic development of body plans and segmentation are know as
   A. homeobox genes.
   B. jumping genes.
   C. introns.
   D. 501 and 505 genes.

28. Which of the following is **not** an example of nondisjunction?
   A. Down syndrome
   B. Sickle-cell anemia
   C. Turner syndrome
   D. Trisomy X

29. If chromosomes or chromosome strands fail to separate during meiosis serious problems can arise. This failure to separate is called
    A. Turner's syndrome.
    B. nondisjunction.
    C. a monosomy.
    D. random assortment.

30. The multinational effort to sequence all of the genes of the human body is called
    A. UNESCO.
    B. cloning.
    C. polymerase chain reaction.
    D. Human Genome Project.

31. A process in which genes from the cell of one species are transferred to the cell of another species is known as
    A. the polymerase chain reaction.
    B. recombinant DNA technology.
    C. meiosis.
    D. protein synthesis.

SHORT ANSWER QUESTIONS (& PAGE REFERENCES)

1. List and briefly describe the functions of three different components of the animal cell. (p. 48-50)

2. What are the differences between DNA and RNA? (p. 49)

3. What is transcribed during protein synthesis and why? (p. 55)

4. What is the influence of regulatory genes in a developing organism? (p. 58)

5. How do the end-products of mitosis and meiosis differ? (pp. 67-71)

6. What is nondisjunction? (pp. 71-72)

ESSAY QUESTIONS (& PAGE REFERENCES)

1. What is a gene? Why are the concepts of exons and introns important in this regard? (pp. 56-58)

2. What is the evolutionary significance of meiosis? (pp. 69-70)

3. Why would it not be an exaggeration to say that this is the most exciting time in the history of evolutionary biology since Darwin published *On the Origin of Species*? (pp. 73-74)

ANSWERS, *CORRECTED STATEMENT* IF FALSE & REFERENCES TO TRUE/FALSE QUESTIONS

1. FALSE, p. 49, Mitochondria and ribosomes are found *outside of* the nucleus of the cell.

2. TRUE, p. 52.

3. FALSE, pp. 55-56, The mRNA message transcribed from the DNA is read in *3-letter* words called *codons* at the site of protein synthesis, the *ribosomes*.

4. TRUE, p. 57

5. FALSE, p. 61, Sickle-cell anemia results from a *point* mutation *affecting the beta chain for the allele that produces hemoglobin.*

6. FALSE, p. 64, Humans have *46* chromosomes while chimps and gorillas have *48*.

7. FALSE, pp. 66-67, A *karyotype* is the illustration of the chromosomal complement of an individual or that which is typical for a species.

8. TRUE, pp. 67-69

9. TRUE, pp. 71-72

10. FALSE, p. 73, *The Polymerase Chain Reaction* is a method for producing thousands of copies of a DNA segment using the enzyme DNA polymerase.

1. A, p. 48
2. C, p. 49
3. D, p. 49
4. B, p. 50
5. D, p. 50
6. B, p. 50
7. B, p. 51
8. D, p. 52
9. A, p. 52
10. A, pp. 52-53
11. C, p. 52
12. C, p. 54
13. D, p. 55
14. A, p. 55
15. B, p. 56
16. C, p. 56
17. B, pp. 53-56
18. C, p. 56
19. D, pp. 55-57 (see Figure 3-9)
20. C, p. 56
21. A, p. 61
22. A, p. 63
23. B, p. 64
24. C, p. 64
25. A, p. 67
26. B, p. 69
27. A, p. 58
28. B, pp. 71-72
29. B, p. 71
30. D, p. 74
31. B, p. 73

CONCEPT APPLICATION SOLUTION

mRNA molecule:

GUUAUACCUUCGGCUGAGUGGGAUUAA

Amino acids, Polypeptide chain:

Valine-Isoleucine-Proline-Serine-Alanine-Glutamic acid-Tryptophan-Aspartic acid-STOP

Mutated mRNA molecule:

GU**A**AUACCUUCGGCUGAGUGGGAUUAA

Resultant amino acids, Polypeptide chain:

Valine-Isoleucine-Proline-Serine-Alanine-Glutamic acid-Tryptophan-Aspartic acid-STOP

See "A Closer Look," point #3 on p. 54 for an explanation of redundancy and an illustration of neutral mutation.

CHAPTER 4
HEREDITY AND EVOLUTION

LEARNING OBJECTIVES

After reading this chapter you should be able to
- describe the principle of Mendelian inheritance (pp.82-85)
- understand the significance of dominance and recessiveness (p.83)
- discuss Mendel's Principles of Segregation and Independent Assortment (pp. 82-85)
- recognize the patterns of inheritance for autosomal dominant, autosomal recessive and sex-linked traits (pp. 88-91)
- discuss the importance of pleiotropy (pp. 95-96)
- discuss the interaction between genes and the environment (pp. 96-97)
- define biological evolution (pp. 97-99)
- describe the factors that produce and distribute genetic variation (pp. 99-103)
- discuss the role of natural selection in directing evolution (pp. 103-106)

CHAPTER OUTLINE

Introduction

In the last chapter the structure and function of DNA was presented. In this chapter we look at the principles of heredity, originally studied by Gregor Mendel. We close with the synthesis of Darwinism, Mendelianism, and genetics into the comprehensive modern theory of biological evolution.

I. **THE GENETIC PRINCIPLES DISCOVERED BY MENDEL.**
   A. Introduction
      1. Gregor Mendel (1822-1884) systematically explored the question of heredity.
      2. Mendel experimented with plants in the monastery garden.
      3. He considered how traits are passed to offspring.
      4. He explored how physical traits like color and height could be expressed in hybrids.
      5. He tracked seven different traits in garden peas.
         a. Each of these traits can only be expressed in two different ways.
            i. For example, trait of see shape has two expressions: round or wrinkled.
            ii. See Figure 4-3 p. 81.
      6. The basic principles that Mendel observed in pea plants apply to all biological organisms including humans.
      7. Mendel's work promoted two basic principles of inheritance.
   B. Segregation
      1. Mendel crossed purebred parental tall plants with purebred parental short plants (see Figure 4-4).
         a. All offspring (F_1 generation) were tall.
            i. One of the traits (short) disappeared.
         b. Plants of the F_1 generation were not medium-size as would be the case if blending inheritance was valid.

        i.   Blending was the expectation regarding inheritance of traits prior to the work of Mendel; offspring were thought to be a blend of the traits of the parents.

    c.   When the F_1 generation self-fertilized, a portion of the offspring exhibited the "lost" trait; they were short.

    d.   Mendel recognized a relationship between the two expressions of each trait he observed.

        i.   One as dominant and the other as recessive.

    e.   Within the offspring generation (F_2 generation), Mendel observed a ratio of 3 dominants (tall) to 1 recessive (short).

2.   The notion that the traits were controlled by two discrete units, which separate into different sex cells, is the principle of segregation.

    a.   Today we know that meiosis explains Mendel's principle of segregation.

C. Dominance and Recessiveness

1.   Mendel labeled the trait that disappeared in the F_1 generation, but reappeared in the F_2 generation, recessive.

2.   Mendel labeled the trait that was expressed in the F_1 generation dominant.

3.   Height in pea plants is controlled by 2 different alleles.

    a.   One allele is dominant and the other allele is recessive.

4.   When two copies of the same allele are present the individual is homozygous for that trait. Can be:

    a.   homozygous dominant, or

    b.   homozygous recessive.

5.   When the two alleles are different (one dominant and one recessive), the individual is heterozygous for that trait.

    a.   Synonymous with hybrid and carrier.

6.   Alleles are often symbolically represented with letters.

    a.   The dominant allele is often coded as a capital letter.

    b.   The recessive allele coded with a lowercase letter.

    c.   The combination of alleles is the genotype (genetic makeup) of an individual.

        i.   The phenotype is the outward expression (appearance) of ones genotype.

7.   A Punnett square can be used to represent different combinations of alleles.

    a.   A punnett square is a book keeping tool (see Figure 4-5).

8.   Punnett squares illustrate the genotype of crosses and possible genotypes of offspring.

    a.   Punnett squares demonstrate proportions of offspring for each genotype.

    b.   A punnett square does not indicate the number of each genotype that will be born.

D. Independent Assortment

1.   Mendel crossed plants to investigate whether there is a relationship between traits.

2.   He crossed plants that differed in their expressions of height and seed color.

    a.   Homozygous tall with yellow seeds crossed with homozygous short with green seeds.

    b. F_1 all plants dominant.

    c. F_2 generation all phenotypic combinations present.

        i.   See Figure 4-6.

3.Mendel showed that traits aren't necessarily inherited together.

    a.   Plant height and seed color are independent of each other.

56

4. This is Mendel's second principle; principle of independent assortment.
   a. The alleles that control plant height and seed color assort independently from one another during gamete production.
5. By chance Mendel did not use traits that were linked.
   a. Traits are linked if their loci are found closely located on the same chromosome.
      i. Linked traits cannot assort independently
   b. If Mendel had used linked traits his results would have been considerably different.
   c. Genes on the same chromosomes travel together during meiosis; consequently, they are not independent of one another and do not conform to the ratios predicted by independent assortment.

II. MENDELIAN INHERITANCE IN HUMANS

A. Mendelian traits are also called simple or discrete traits.
B. Mendelian traits are characteristics controlled by alleles at only one genetic locus.
   1. Over 18000 human traits are inherited by simple Mendelian principles.
   2. Most Mendelian traits are biochemical.
   3. Many genetic disorders are inherited in Mendelian fashion.
      a. Some genetic disorders are inherited as dominant traits.
         i. Affected individuals can be homozygous dominant or heterozygous.
      b. Some genetic disorders are inherited as recessive traits.
         i. Affected individuals will be homozygous recessive; two copies of the recessive allele.
         ii. Recessive conditions are associated often with a lack of an enzyme.
         iii. Heterozygotes for such disorders are not affected, but because they carry only one copy of the recessive allele.
            (i) These heterozygotes are often called carriers.
      c. Carrier parents have a 25% chance of having a homozygous recessive child.
C. Your bold type is another example of simple Mendelian inheritance.
D. The human ABO blood system
   1. There are 3 alleles: A, B, O (see Table 4-2).
      a. These alleles determine the kind of surface antigens on the red blood cell
      b. The A and B alleles are dominant to the O allele.
      c. The A and B alleles are codominant to one another and both traits are expressed together in the AB blood type.
         i. The allelic combination of AB is the heterozygote.
         ii. The heterozygote has a unique phenotype for codominant alleles.
   2. There are 4 phenotypes: A, B, AB, O
   3. There are 6 Genotypes: AA, AO, BB, BO, AB, OO
E. Misconceptions regarding dominance and recessiveness.
   1. Mendel assumed that in heterozygotes the recessive allele was inactive.
   2. Among carriers, recessive alleles can exert an effect at the biochemical level.
   3. Another misconception is that dominant alleles are more common, or that they are "stronger" or "better."
   4. Another misconception is that eye color is a simple trait.
      a. It is not as it is controlled by more than one locus.

F. Patterns of Inheritance
1. The principle technique used in human inheritance studies is the construction of pedigree charts.
    a. A pedigree chart illustrates the genotypes for members of families.
    b. Pedigree analysis helps determine whether a trait is Mendelian.
    c. Pedigree analysis helps determine the mode of inheritance.
        i. Six different modes of Mendelian inheritance are recognized.
        ii. The three most important are:
            (i) autosomal dominant.
            (ii) autosomal recessive.
            (iii) X-linked recessive.
    d. Standard symbols are utilized:
        i. squares represent males
        ii. circles represent females.
2. Autosomal dominant traits.
    a. These traits are governed by alleles located on autosomes.
    b. Pattern of inheritance:
        i. An individual will be affected with only allele.
            (i) Most affected individuals are heterozygotes.
        ii. Each affected individual has at least one affected parent.
        iii. These conditions do not skip a generation.
    c. There is no sex bias in autosomal dominant traits; equal numbers of males and females are affected.
    d. Another characteristic of autosomal dominance is that about one-half of the offspring of an affected parent are also affected.
3. Autosomal recessive traits.
    a. These traits are also controlled by loci located on the autosomes.
    b. Pattern of inheritance:
        i. An individual must have two recessive alleles to be affected.
        ii. Affected individuals often have two unaffected parents who are carriers.
            (i) These conditions will appear to skip generations
4. Sex-linked traits.
    a. These traits are governed by alleles located on the sex chromosomes.
    b. Most of the known sex-linked traits are governed by alleles on the X chromosome.
        i. Females have two X chromosomes
            (i) Will only express the trait with two alleles
            (ii) Females inherit the trait from affected fathers.
        ii. Males have one X and one Y chromosomes
            (i) Will express the trait with only one allele.
            (ii) Hemizygous
    c. Almost all affected people are males because males have only one X chromosome.
    d. One of the best-known sex-linked traits is hemophilia.
        i. Condition inhibits formation of a clotting factor in blood.
        ii. Most famous pedigree of hemophilia is from the English royal family.

58

III. NON-MENDELIAN INHERITANCE

A. Polygenic Inheritance.
1. Polygenic traits account for most of the observable variation in humans.
2. Polygenic traits are continuous traits governed by alleles at more than one genetic locus.
   a. Continuous traits show gradations.
      i. A series of measurable intermediate forms between two extremes.
      ii. Consider human height (see Figure 4-14).
      iii. Skin color is a polygenic trait, governed by perhaps 3-6 loci and at least 12 alleles.
3. Each locus in a polygenic trait contributes to the phenotype.
4. Because polygenic traits <u>are</u> continuous they can be treated statistically.
   a. The mean is a summary statistic which gives the average of a sample or population.
   b. A standard deviation measures within-group variation.
   c. Researchers are able to compare continuous traits between different populations to see if there are statistically significant differences.
   d. Mendelian characteristics are not as amenable to statistical analysis when compared to polygenic characters.
      i. Mendelian characteristics can be described in terms of frequencies within populations and compared between populations.
      ii. Mendelian characters can be analyzed for mode of inheritance from pedigree data.
      iii. Mendelian characters are valuable because the approximate or exact position of genetic loci for them is often known.
5. See At a Glance on pg. 95 for a comparison of Mendelian and Polygenic traits.

B. Pleiotropy
1. One single gene influences more than one trait.
   a. Probably the rule rather than the exception.
2. Phenylketonuria (PKU) is an example.
   a. Homozygous individuals don't produce a particular enzyme.
      i. This metabolic malfunction causes mental deficiencies.
         (i) The absence of this enzyme also results in low melanin production
         (ii) Affected individuals will have fair skin, hair, and blue eyes.

C. Mitochondrial Inheritance.
1. All cells contain mitochondria.
   a. Mitochondria are the energy converters of the body.
2. Every mitochondria has a ring shaped DNA molecule: mitochondrial DNA (mtDNA).
   a. mtDNA is distinct from nuclear DNA although the molecular structure and function are the same.
   b. All mtDNA is inherited from the mother.
   c. There is no meiosis and therefore only mutation can change mtDNA.
   d. Geneticists have used mutation rates of mtDNA to
      i. Investigate the evolutionary relationship between species.
      ii. Trace ancestral relationships within the human lineage.
      iii. Study genetic variability among individuals and populations.

IV. GENETIC AND ENVIRONMENTAL FACTORS

A. With respect to polygenic traits, the environment interacts with the genotype
1. The genotype sets limits and potentials for development.
   a. Many aspects of the phenotype are influenced by the genetic/environmental interaction.
   b. The environment influences many polygenic traits, such as height.
      i. Well-known study showed that Japanese immigrants to Hawaii were 3-4 inches taller than their parents.
B. Mendelian traits are less likely to be influenced by the environment.
1. Consider your blood type.
   a. It was fixed at fertilization.
   b. No environmental change can alter your blood type.
2. Even though polygenic traits are controlled by several loci and are more susceptible to environmental influences, they still obey Mendelian principles at the individual loci.

V. MODERN EVOLUTIONARY THEORY

A. Darwin, Wallace, and Mendel discovered essential mechanisms of evolution.
1. By the 1930s it was realized that natural selection and Mendelian genetics were complementary factors that explained evolution; the modern synthesis.
B. The Modern Synthesis partitioned evolution into two stages:
1. The production and redistribution of variation (inherited differences among individuals)
2. Natural selection acts on this variation.
   a. Individuals who posses favorable traits pass on more genes.
C. Evolution is a change in allele frequency from one generation to the next.
1. Allele frequencies are the percentage of alleles in a population at a particular time.
2. Allele frequencies are indicators of the genetic makeup of a population (gene pool).
3. Only populations evolve, individuals do not evolve over time.
D. Microevolution is small-scale inherited changes that occur over a short period within a species.
E. Macroevolution is large scale change requiring isolation and geological time which results in a new species.

VI. FACTORS THAT PRODUCE AND REDISTRIBUTE VARIATION

A. Mutation
1. If a gene is altered a mutation has occurred.
   a. A point mutation is a change in a single DNA base.
2. For a mutation to have any evolutionary significance it must occur in a sex cell.
3. Mutation rates for any given trait are quite low.
4. Mutation is the only way to produce "new" variation.
B. Gene Flow
1. Gene flow is the exchange of genes between populations.
   a. Can be one way or reciprocal.
2. Gene flow has been a consistent feature of hominin evolution and explains why speciation has been rare in humans.
   a. Gene flow can decrease between population variation.
   b. Gene flow can increase within population variation.

60

C. Genetic Drift
1. Random factor that is a function of population size.
    a. Drift has a greater effect in small populations.
2. A special case of genetic drift is called founder effect.
    a. A very small proportion of a population contributes alleles to the next generation.
        i. Small group moves to a new area.
        ii. Maintains reproductive isolation.
        iii. The genes from the small group, even if rare in the parent group, will increase in frequency in future generations of the founder group.
    b. When all members of the founder group have the same allele the allele is fixed.
    c. Loss of genetic diversity is called a bottleneck.
3. Genetic drift has probably played an important role in human evolution.
    a. Nevertheless, the effects of drift have been irregular and nondirectional.
4. Drift, along with gene flow, probably results in microevolutionary changes within a species.
    a. However, there is some evidence that our species experienced a genetic bottleneck in the last 100,000 to 200,000 years; if this is the case genetic drift would have played a very important role in our evolution.
D. Recombination.
1. Sexual reproduction is, in itself, a recombination, or reshuffling, of genetic material coming from two different parents.
2. Meiosis (crossing over) is the greatest source of variation.

VII. NATURAL SELECTION ACTS ON VARIATION
A. Natural selection acts on variation.
B. Without natural selection there is no direction to evolution.
C. Selection results in a change in allele frequency relative to specific environmental factors.
1. If the environment changes, selection pressures change also.
2. A shift in allele frequencies based on a change in environment is adaptation.
D. Hemoglobin S (Hb^S) is the best-documented case of natural selection in humans (see Chapter 2).
1. Hb^S results from a point mutation in the gene coding for the hemoglobin beta chain.
2. The mutation for Hb^S occurs in all human populations, but does not have a high frequency most places.
3. Inherited in a double dose (homozygous recessive) the individual will suffer the severe manifestations of sickle-cell anemia.
    a. The sickle-cell allele (Hb^S) has a frequency in some populations.
        i. West and central Africa
        ii. Greece and India.
    b. Higher frequencies of Hb^S occur where malaria is prevalent.
        i. Malaria has exerted enormous selection pressures on human populations.
        ii. Kills between 1-3 million people per year.
    c. Heterozygotes are much more resistant to malaria.
        i. Heterozygote system is not a supportive environment for the malarial parasite to reproduce.
        ii. Homozygous dominant (normal) will suffer from malaria more.

d. Heterozygous people are protected from malaria and are not as affected by sickle cell.
e. "Normal" individuals were more likely to have their reproductive success lowered due to malarial infections.

VIII. REVIEW OF GENETICS AND EVOLUTIONARY FACTORS
A. Evolution is the change in allele frequencies in a population.
1. A new allele can only arise through mutation.
2. An allele can increase in frequency in a small population due to genetic drift.
3. Migration of people is associated with genetic migration; i.e. gene flow.
4. Mutations must spread; this could occur in a small population through genetic drift.
5. Long-term evolutionary trends can only occur due to natural selection.

KEY TERMS

allele: the alternative form of a gene, often represented symbolically using a single letter.

allele frequency: the proportion of a particular allele to all the other alleles at a given locus in a population.

antigens: large molecules found on the surface of cells. Several different loci governing antigens on red and white blood cells are known. Foreign antigens provoke an immune response in individuals.

autosome: any of the chromosomes excluding the two sex chromosomes.

carrier: an individual who is a heterozygote for a recessive genetic disorder; the individual is unaffected.

codominance: both alleles are expressed in the phenotype.

continuous traits: traits which have measurable gradations between the two end points, such as height in humans.

discrete traits: traits which fall into clear categories, such as a purple flower vs. a white flower in a garden pea.

dominant: the genetic trait that is expressed in the heterozygous state.

evolution (modern genetic definition): a change in allele frequencies between generations.

founder effect: a type of genetic drift in which allele frequencies significantly differ in small populations that are taken from, or are remnants of, larger populations.

gene flow: exchange of genes between different populations of a species.

gene pool: total complement of genes shared by breeding members of a population

genetic drift: evolutionary changes in the gene pool of a small population due to chance (random factors).

gamete: a sex cell, in humans these are ova (eggs) and sperm.

genotype: the genetic makeup of an organism.

hemizygous: condition where there is only one allele present (on the X chromosome) instead of two.

heterozygous: the presence of two different alleles for a given genetic trait in an individual.

homozygous: the presence of two identical alleles for a given genetic trait in an individual.

hybrid: parents who are in some ways genetically dissimilar. This term can also be applied to heterozygotes.

linked: describing genetic loci or genes located on the same chromosome.

mean: a summary statistic which gives the average of a sample or of a population.

macroevolution: evolutionary changes on a large scale, encompassing many generations, and involving change above the species level.

Mendelian traits: traits that are inherited at a single locus on a single chromosome

microevolution: small, short-term changes in the gene pool of a population occurring over just a few generations.

mutation: an alteration in the genetic material (a change in the base sequence of DNA).

natural selection: the evolutionary factor that causes changes in the allele frequencies in populations due to differential net reproductive success of individuals. The force of evolution that gives direction in response to environmental factors.

pedigree chart: a diagram showing family relationships in order to trace the hereditary pattern of particular genetic traits.

phenotype: the physical expression of an organism's genotype

phenotypic ratio: the proportion of one phenotype to other phenotypes.

pleiotropy: a situation whereby several, seemingly unrelated, phenotypic effects are influenced by the action of a single gene.

point mutation: a chemical change in a single base of a DNA sequence.

population: a community of individuals, all of the same species, that occupy a particular area and breed among themselves.

polygenic: referring to traits that are influenced by genes at two or more loci.

principle of independent assortment: Mendel's principle that states that alleles for different traits sort independently during gamete formation

principle of segregation: the principle expounded by Mendel that alleles occur in pairs which separate (segregate) during gamete formation. At fertilization the full number of alleles is restored.

recessive: the genetic trait that is not expressed in a heterozygous state.

selective breeding: choosing plants/animals for specific qualities and mating them.

sex chromosome: the chromosomes that determine sex. In humans these are the X and Y chromosomes.

sickle-cell trait: a condition resulting from a point mutation of the gene coding for production of the beta-chain hemoglobin. A red blood cell with this trait is subject to collapse during periods of extreme stress or low blood oxygen levels.

standard deviation: a summary statistic which measures within-group variation.

variation (genetic): inherited differences between individuals. The basis of all evolutionary change.

zygote: union of two gametes.

MEDIA EXERCISES

1) Go online to the National Center for Biotechnology Information's "Online Mendelian Inheritance in Man" website (http://www.ncbi.nlm.nih.gov/entrez/query.fcgi?db=OMIM). Look to the left and click the link titled: "Search the Morbid Map". This will take you to a search page. In the "Search for" box, type one of the Mendelian traits listed in Table 4-1 on p. 70 of your text. For example, if you enter "Albinism" and click the "Find" button you will be taken to the database listing all of the Mendelian conditions that are associated with albinism. Click on a numbered hyper-link in the "Disorder" column to read more about the condition.

1) In *InfoTrac* do keyword searches on these three individuals who were central to the construction of the modern synthesis of evolutionary biology: Sewall Wright, Ernst Mayr and George Gaylord Simpson. Read an article on each that describes their major contributions.

CONCEPT APPLICATIONS

Punnett squares

Fill in the Punnett squares below to figure out the ABO blood type ratios for the next generation. In the box at left, the symbols represent an individual with blood type A (genotype is AO) crossed with an individual with blood type B (genotype is BO). What are the possible combinations of offspring? The box in the center are two individuals both with blood type AB (genotypes are AB, remember they alleles A and B are codominant). At right is a B blood type crossed with AB.

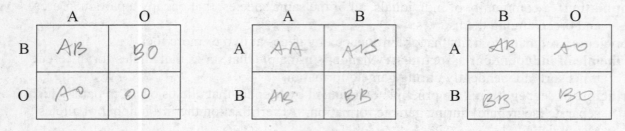

	A	O
B	AB	BO
O	AO	OO

	A	B
A	AA	AB
B	AB	BB

	B	O
A	AB	AO
B	BB	BO

Identify the phenotypic ratios of the blood types for each of the above squares.

Now fill in the Punnett square for one of Mendel's dihybrid cross experiments. Both parents are heterozygous for plant height ("T" is dominant for "Tall", "t" is recessive for "short") and seed shape ("R" is dominant for "Round", "r" is recessive for "wrinkled"). Each gamete in this example will have **2** alleles: one for plant height and one for seed shape. What are the possible phenotypes produced by this mating and what will the phenotypic ratios of the offspring be?

	TR	Tr	tR	tr
TR				
Tr				
tR				
tr				

Pedigree Chart for X-Linked Recessive Trait

The pedigree chart below illustrates a couple who had four children (a son and 3 daughters labeled 1-4). The mother is a carrier of an X-linked recessive trait (such as hemophilia) and her carrier status is indicated by the circle (indicating "female") enclosing a dot. The conditions of the couple's grandchildren are given: open shapes are unaffected individuals, carriers are the circle/dots and those afflicted with the genetic disease are indicated by the filled-in shapes. Given the grandparents' and grandchildren's conditions, figure out the conditions of the four offspring of the original pair (labeled 1-4 in the dotted shapes).

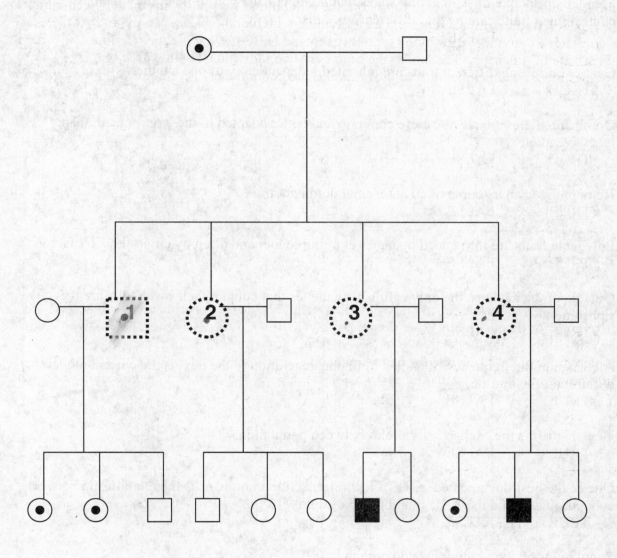

Now answer the True/False, Multiple Choice and Short Answer sample test questions. Following completion of the tests, correct them with the answers and textbook page references at the end of this Study Guide chapter. Note the areas in which you are strong and weak to guide you in your studying. Finally, answer the sample Essay Questions.

TRUE/FALSE QUESTIONS

If false, consider what modification would make the statement true.

1. Mendel's principle of segregation states that members of a pair of hereditary factors controlling a trait separate into different sex cells.
    TRUE   FALSE

2. Genes controlling different traits are inherited independently of one another.
    TRUE   FALSE

3. Dominant alleles are always more common and better adapted to the environment than recessive alleles.
    TRUE   FALSE

4. Hemophilia is an example of an autosomal dominant trait.
    TRUE   FALSE

5. Polygenic traits are influenced by genes at multiple loci and often by environmental factors.
    TRUE   FALSE

6. Outside of the nucleus, the only cellular organelles that contain their own DNA are the ribosomes.
    TRUE   FALSE

7. A change in the frequency of alleles from one generation to the next is the current modern definition of evolution.
    TRUE   FALSE

8. Genetic drift is the exchange of alleles between populations.
    TRUE   FALSE

9. One of the best-documented cases of natural selection in humans is the relationship between achondroplasia and the ABO blood group system.
    TRUE   FALSE

10. Populations evolve, individuals do not.
    TRUE   FALSE

MULTIPLE CHOICE QUESTIONS

1. In a cross between two purebred strains of garden peas Mendel found that in the offspring
    A. both traits were represented in the next generation.
    B. they were homozygous for the traits being studied.
    C. one of the traits disappeared.
    D. the traits were intermediate between the two parental traits.

2. Mendel used the term dominant for
    A. plants that were larger than others of the same variety.
    B. a trait that prevented another trait from appearing.
    C. a variety of pea plants that eliminated a weaker variety.
    D. a trait that "skipped" generations.

3. When Mendel crossed peas with Rr and Rr genotypes, the phenotypic ratio of the offspring
    was _____ (hint: you may want to use a Punnett square to figure this out)
    A. 1:1.
    B. 3:1.
    C. 1:2:1.
    D. 2:2.

4. Genes exist in pairs in individuals; during the production of gametes, the pairs are separated so that a gamete has only one of each kind. This is known as the
    A. principle of segregation.
    B. principle of independent assortment.
    C. mitosis.
    D. unification theory.

5. What physiological process explains Mendel's principle of segregation?
    A. mitosis.
    B. meiosis.
    C. metamorphosis.
    D. metastasis.

6. Which of the following is characteristic of dominant alleles?
    A. Dominant alleles are expressed in heterozygous genotypes.
    B. Dominant alleles are the alleles which are most common in a population.
    C. Dominant alleles always cause more serious defects than recessive alleles.
    D. Dominant alleles drive recessive alleles out of a population.

7. A trait which is inherited as a recessive is expressed in the
    A. homozygous recessive individual.
    B. homozygous dominant individual.
    C. heterozygous individual.
    D. codominant individual.

8. An alternative form of a gene is called a(n)
    A. nucleotide.
    B. locus.
    C. allele.
    D. epistasis.

9. Which of the following genotypes is homozygous?
    A. AB
    B. OO
    C. ABO
    D. BO

10. The principle of independent assortment states that
    A. a pair of genes segregates during the production of gametes.
    B. genes recombine in a predetermined way.
    C. the distribution of one pair of genes does not influence the distribution of other pairs of genes on other chromosomes.
    D. mutations come from independent sources.

11. A heterozygous genotype would be written as
    A. AA.
    B. Aa.
    C. aa.
    D. AA and aa.

12. Mendelian traits are
    A. influenced by alleles at only one genetic locus.
    B. controlled by alleles at multiple genetic loci.
    C. the product of several alleles on different chromosomes.
    D. only known for about 160 human traits.

13. When there are two different alleles present in a heterozygote and both of these alleles are expressed, this condition is called
    A. recessive.
    B. dominance.
    C. codominance.
    D. sex-linked.

14. Geneticists call the diagram that shows the matings that have taken place in a family, going back several generations, a
    A. karyotype chart.
    B. pedigree chart.
    C. genotype.
    D. syndrome.

15. Which of the following are modes of Mendelian inheritance?
    A. autosomal recessive
    B. autosomal dominant
    C. sex-linked
    D. all of the above

16. Which sex is more likely to suffer from X-linked recessive disorders such as hemophilia?
    A. females
    B. males
    C. males and females are equally likely
    D. neither sex

17. Polygenic traits are produced by the interaction between multiple genes and
    A. proteins.
    B. the environment.
    C. the sex chromosomes.
    D. recombination.

18. This ring-shaped DNA molecule is found outside of the nucleus and is transmitted exclusively through the maternal line.
    A. ribosomal DNA (rDNA)
    B. nuclear DNA (nDNA)
    C. mitochondrial DNA (mtDNA)
    D. all of the above

19. Polygenic traits can often be graphically illustrated as
    A. a normal curve.
    B. a simple indication of presence or absence.
    C. an ellipse.
    D. a 2-bin histogram.

20. The modern synthesis integrates Darwinian natural selection with
    A. paleontology.
    B. embryology.
    C. genetics.
    D. ecology.

21. The modern genetic definition of biological evolution is
    A. change.
    B. a change in allele frequency from one generation to the next.
    C. mutation.
    D. survival of the fittest.

22. Which of the following is the **only** evolutionary force that can create brand-new genetic variation within a population?
    A. mitosis.
    B. natural selection.
    C. mutation.
    D. recombination.

23. The introduction of alleles from one population into another population is known as
    A. genetic drift.
    B. gene flow.
    C. founder effect.
    D. bottleneck effect.

24. An example of gene flow would be
    A. the children of U.S. servicemen and Vietnamese women in Vietnam.
    B. the isolated Amish of Pennsylvania.
    C. the American colonization of Antarctica.
    D. a small hunting and gathering society in Siberia with little outside contact.

25. The force of evolution which is significant when small human populations become isolated is
    A. gene flow.
    B. mutation.
    C. genetic drift.
    D. random mating.

26. In 10th Century Norway, Eric the Red and his followers were banished for murders and general rowdiness. This small group, which had a higher representation of an allele that contributes to red-hair color than the rest of the population of Norway, sailed west and established a colony on Iceland. Within several centuries the colony had a population of several thousand, the majority of whom were red-heads. This would **best** be explained by
    A. gene flow.
    B. natural selection.
    C. mutation.
    D. founder effect.

27. In any sexually reproducing species both parents contribute genes to the offspring. This is
    A. mutation.
    B. genetic drift.
    C. recombination.
    D. natural selection.

28. The hemoglobin S allele
    A. is present only in "black" populations.
    B. reaches its highest frequencies in areas where malaria is present.
    C. is powerful enough to produce sickle-cell anemia in heterozygotes.
    D. originated in the first place by genetic drift.

29. The unit of evolutionary change is the
    A. family.
    B. individual.
    C. population.
    D. pedigree.

SHORT ANSWER QUESTIONS (& PAGE REFERENCES)

1. What is Mendel's principle of segregation? (pp. 82-83)

2. Describe three Mendelian traits manifested in humans. (p. 86, Table 4-1)

3. Why does hemophilia affect males more often than females? (p. 91)

4. What are the differences between polygenic and pleiotropic traits? (pp. 93-96)

5. What is founder effect? (pp. 101-103)

ESSAY QUESTIONS (& PAGE REFERENCES)

1. Describe one of Mendel's pea plant experiments. How do the results illustrate the principles of segregation and independent assortment? (pp. 81-84)

2. What is the modern genetic definition of evolution? In this context, define and state the significance of the following terms: population, allele frequency, microevolution and macroevolution. (pp. 97-99)

3. What are the factors that produce and redistribute genetic variation? (pp. 99-103)

71

ANSWERS, *CORRECTED STATEMENT* IF FALSE & REFERENCES TO TRUE/FALSE QUESTIONS

1. TRUE, p. 83

2. TRUE, p. 84

3. FALSE, p. 88, Dominant alleles are *not* always more common and *may or may not be* better adapted to the environment than recessive alleles.

4. FALSE, p. 91, Hemophilia is an example of a *sex-linked* trait.

5. TRUE, pp. 93-94

6. FALSE, p. 96, Outside of the nucleus, the only cellular organelles that contain their own DNA are the *mitochondria*.

7. TRUE, p. 98

8. FALSE, p. 100, *Gene flow* is the exchange of alleles between populations.

9. FALSE, pp. 104-106, One of the best-documented cases of natural selection in humans is the relationship between *malaria* and *hemoglobin S*.

10. TRUE, p. 99

ANSWERS & REFERENCES TO MULTIPLE CHOICE QUESTIONS

1. **C**, pp. 82-83		17. **B**, p. 96
2. **B**, p. 83		18. **C**, pp. 50, 96
3. **B**, p. 84		19. **A**, pp. 93-94
4. **A**, p. 83		20. **C**, p. 97
5. **B**, p. 83		21. **B**, p. 98
6. **A**, pp. 83-84		22. **C**, p. 99
7. **A**, p. 83		23. **B**, p. 100
8. **C**, pp. 83-84		24. **A**, p. 100
9. **B**, p. 87		25. **C**, pp. 100-103
10. **C**, pp. 84-85		26. **D**, pp. 101-103
11. **B**, p. 84		27. **C**, p. 103
12. **A**, p. 86		28. **B**, pp. 104-105
13. **C**, p. 87		29. **C**, p. 107
14. **B**, p. 89		
15. **D**, pp. 89-91		
16. **B**, p. 91		

CONCEPT APPLICATION SOLUTIONS

Punnett Squares

	A	O
B	AB	BO
O	AO	OO

	A	B
A	AA	AB
B	AB	BB

	B	O
A	AB	AO
B	BB	BO

Square 1 - ¼ Blood Type AB : ¼ Blood Type B : ¼ Blood Type A : ¼ Blood Type O
Square 2 - ¼ Blood Type A : ½ Blood Type AB : ¼ Blood Type B
Square 3 - ¼ Blood Type AB : ½ Blood Type B : ¼ Blood Type A

	TR	Tr	tR	tr
TR	TTRR	TTRr	TtRR	TtRr
Tr	TTRr	TTrr	TtRr	Ttrr
tR	TtRR	TtRr	ttRR	ttRr
tr	TtRr	Ttrr	ttRr	ttrr

Dihybrid cross:
    9/16 Tall/Round : 3/16 Tall/wrinkled : 3/16 short/Round : 1/16 short/wrinkled

Pedigree Chart for X-Linked Recessive Trait

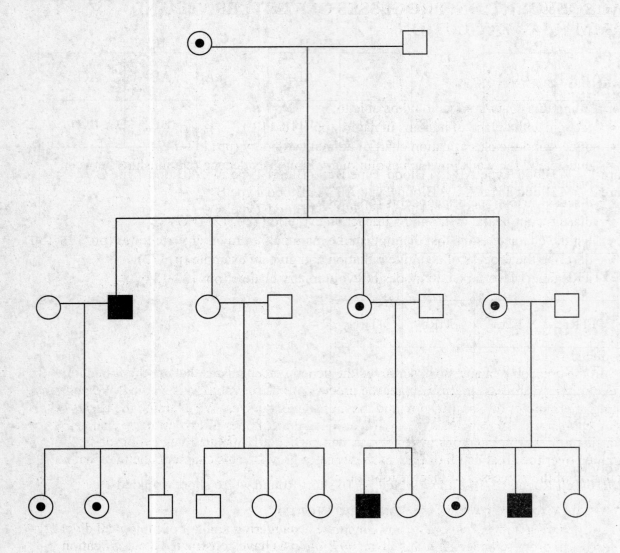

CHAPTER 5
MACROEVOLUTION: PROCESSES OF VERTEBRATE AND MAMMALIAN EVOLUTION

LEARNING OBJECTIVES

After reading this chapter you should be able to:
- recognize the place of humans in nature (pp. 110-112)
- understand the classification chart of animal taxonomy (pp. 111-112)
- understand the ways in which evolutionary biologists deduce relationships between organisms (pp. 113-118)
- discuss various species concepts (pp. 118-122)
- discuss continental drift and its impact on evolution (pp. 126-127)
- list the characteristics that distinguish the mammals from other vertebrates (pp. 128-130)
- describe the process of adaptive radiation and give an example (p. 132)
- understand the tempo and modes of evolutionary change (pp. 133-134)

CHAPTER OUTLINE

Introduction

    In the preceding chapters we surveyed the genetic mechanisms that are the foundation of the evolutionary process. In this chapter the process of macroevolution is studied. We begin by looking at principles of classification and the meaning of species. We examine the basics of geological history, the principles of classification, and the modes of evolutionary change. A synopsis of the key innovations in vertebrate, and particularly mammalian, evolution is examined over the great depth of time of these major groups. This chapter concludes with a discussion of the processes of macroevolution.

I   **THE HUMAN PLACE IN THE ORGANIC WORLD**
    A. The living and extinct organisms constitute a staggering amount of biological diversity.
       1. In order to understand this diversity biologists have constructed a classification system.
       2. The classificatory system organizes life into convenient groupings.
         a. This helps to reduce the complexity.
         b. These groupings indicate evolutionary relationships.
    B. The place of humans in nature.
       1. Review Figure 5-1; classification chart of the Animalia Kingdom.
       2. This hierarchical system organizes diversity into categories.
       3. It illustrates evolutionary and genetic relationships.
       4. Multicellular organisms that move about and ingest food are members of the Animalia kingdom.
       5. Humans belong to this kingdom and to the Chordata Phylum.
         a. Animals that possess a nerve cord, a stiff supporting rod along the back, and
         b. gill slits (at some stage of development).

6. Humans belong to the Subphylum Vertebrata.
    a. These animals are characterized by a vertebral column.
    b. Vertebrates have a well developed brain.
    c. Vertebrates have paired sensory structures for sight, smell, and balance.
7. Vertebrates are divided into six classes: bony fishes, cartilaginous fishes, amphibians, reptiles, birds and mammals.
8. Humans and our closest relatives the primates are placental mammals and are members of the Primates Order.

II PRINCIPLES OF CLASSIFICATION

A. The field that specializes in delineating the rules of classification is taxonomy.
    1. One criterion for classifying organisms is physical similarities.
    2. This is how Linnaeus classified organisms.
B. Taxonomy
    1. Similarities must reflect evolutionary descent to be useful for classification.
    2. Structures that are shared through descent from a common ancestor are called homologies.
        a. Seemingly major evolutionary modifications in structure could occur from relatively minor genetic changes.
        b. For example, just a few Hox regulatory genes control forelimb development in vertebrates.
        c. Basic genetic regulatory mechanisms have been maintained relatively unchanged for hundreds of millions of years.
    3. Structures in organisms that have a similar function, developed independently, and are not the result of common descent, are called analogies (analogous structures).
        a. Homoplasy is the process by which similarities can develop in different groups of organisms.
        b. Analogies can develop through homoplasy in unrelated organisms.
C. Constructing classifications and interpreting evolutionary relationships
    1. There are two major approaches for the interpretation of evolutionary relationships and classifications.
        a. Evolutionary systematics is the more traditional approach.
        b. Cladistics is more recently favored among many anthropologists.
    2. There are similarities in both approaches.
        a. Both attempt to trace evolutionary relationships and construct classifications.
        b. Both recognize that organisms must be compared using specific characters and that some characters are more informative than others.
        c. Both focus exclusively on homologies.
    3. There are important differences between the two approaches.
        a. They differ in how characters are chosen.
        b. They differ in which groups are compared.
        c. They differ in how the results are interpreted and incorporated into evolutionary explanations.
    4. Cladistics specifies the kinds of homologies that are useful.
        a. Some homologous characters are more informative than others.
            i. Characters or traits that are shared due to a remote common ancestor are called ancestral traits.

76

      b. Ancestral traits don't supply enough information to make evolutionary interpretations of relationships between groups.

   5. Cladistics attempts to identify clades: groups of related organisms.

      a. Derived characteristics are traits of interests to cladists.

         i. Traits that are diagnostic of a particular lineage and differ from the ancestral form are derived traits.

        ii. Shared derived traits are the most informative as they are shared by all members of a group, but were not seen before the evolution of the group.

      b. Cladists use cladograms which do not include time.

   6. Traditional evolutionary systematics uses phylogenetic trees to illustrate evolutionary relationships.

      a. Phylogeny attempts to discern ancestor-descendant relationships; cladistics does not.

   7. In practice, most physical anthropologists and other biologists combine the two approaches.

   8. See Figure 5-3 for an illustration of ancestral and derived characteristics in passenger cars and trucks.

III   **DEFINITION OF SPECIES**

  A. The most basic level of taxonomic classification is the species.

  B. How are species defined?

   1. Biological Species Concept

   2. Recognition Species Concept

   3. Ecological Species Concept

   4. Phylogenetic Species Concept

  C. The biological species concept is the one preferred by most zoologists.

   1. Species are groups of individuals that are capable of interbreeding yet are reproductively isolated from other such groups.

   2. Geographic isolation can lead to reproductive isolation and the accumulation of genetic differences through time.

  D. The Recognition Species Concept focuses on mate recognition.

   1. The key aspect of species is the ability of individuals to identify members of their own species for purposes of mating.

  E. The Ecological Species Concept emphasizes that speciation is the result of different habitats.

   1. Species is a group of organisms who exploit a single ecological niche.

  F. The Phylogenetic Species Concept is based on an identifiable parental pattern of ancestry.

  G. Speciation is the process by which new species evolve from earlier species.

  H. Processes of Speciation.

   1. Biologists have hypothesized that speciation could occur in three different ways:

      a. Allopatric speciation

      b. Parapatric speciation

      c. Sympatric speciation.

   2. Allopatric speciation is by far the most widely accepted view of speciation.

      a. This model requires complete reproductive isolation within a population, leading to the development of species that are separated from the ancestral population.

3. Parapatric speciation requires only partial reproductive isolation.
   a. A hybrid zone would form between the two partially isolated populations.
4. Sympatric speciation does not require any geographic isolation and is not well supported by contemporary evidence.
5. A fourth type, instantaneous speciation, has been documented in plants but is unlikely to occur often (if at all) in animals.
   a. Rapid chromosomal alterations generate reproductive barriers.
6. These various approaches are not mutually exclusive and could be profitably used in combination to help us better understand species.

I. Interpretation of species and other groups in the fossil record
1. Our goal is to make meaningful biological statements when we assign taxonomic names.
2. What do the names used in taxonomic classification mean in evolutionary terms?
3. All sexually reproducing populations contain variation.
   a. Individual variation exists.
   b. Age-dependent variation exists.
      i. In humans and apes, there is a difference in the number of adult teeth vs. deciduous teeth.
      ii. It would be a mistake to not recognize that members of the same species may have different numbers of teeth at different ages; otherwise two species would be described when there should only be one.
   c. Sex based variation exists.
      i. Sexual dimorphism exists to varying degrees and refers to differences between males and females.
      ii. This can be a confounding factor when describing a species; males and females may have different structural traits and may be interpreted as two species.

J. Recognition of Fossil Species
1. The minimum biological category that we would like to assign fossil primates to is the species.
   a. Do fossil species meet the criteria for the modern Biological Species Concept?
   b. We obviously cannot observe their behavior or the outcomes of their matings, so we cannot know for certain.
2. Our only way of understanding variation in fossil species is through reference to living species.
3. What is the biological significance of the variation we see in fossils?
   a. Variation can be accounted for by individual qualities, age, and sex differences
      i. This type of variation is referred to as intraspecific (within the species).
   b. Variation can represent differences between reproductively isolated groups.
      i. This variation is significant enough to warrant designation as more than one species, i.e., interspecific variation (between species).
4. How do paleontologists differentiate between intraspecific and interspecific variation?
   a. To make the choice, we must use living species as models.
   b. If the amount of morphological variation observed in fossil samples is consistent with the amount of variation within a modern species, then we should not split our sample into more than one species.

     c. One serious problem with fossil species is that not only is there variation across space, but there is also variation through time.
        i. Even more variation is possible in paleospecies because individual specimens may be separated by thousands, perhaps millions, of years.
        ii. Standard Linnaean taxonomy is designed to account for the variation present at a particular time (in living species) and, basically, describes a static situation (no change, or evolution, occurring).
     d. "Splitters" claim that speciation occurred frequently during hominin evolution
        i. They will identify numerous species.
     e. "Lumpers" assume that speciation was less common.
        i. They assume variation is intraspecific and recognize fewer hominin species.
  K. Recognition of Fossil Genera
    1. The next higher level of taxonomy above the species is the genus.
    2. The classification of fossils at the genus level presents its own set of problems.
     a. In order to have more than one genus there must be at least two species.
    3. One definition of a genus is a group of species more closely related to each other than they are to species from another genus.
     a. This definition can be very subjective.
    4. Another definition of a genus is a number of species that share the same broad adaptive zone.
     a. An adaptive zone is indicative of a general ecological lifestyle more basic than the particular ecological niches characteristic of species.
     b. This ecological definition is more useful for applying to fossil genera.
     c. Teeth are the most often preserved parts and they are excellent ecological indicators.
    5. Classification by genus can be well served by incorporating cladistic analysis.
     a. Members of the same genus should all share a suite of derived characters.

IV   VERTEBRATE EVOLUTIONARY HISTORY: A BRIEF SUMMARY
  A. In addition to the great diversity of life, evolutionary biologists must also contend with vast periods of time.
  B. Geologists have formulated the geological time scale to organize time.
    1. The geological time scale is a hierarchical approach to managing time.
     a. Large time spans are divided into eras.
     b. Eras are divided into periods.
     c. Periods are divided into epochs.
    2. Delineations between the time divisions coincide with global events.
    3. Check out A Closer Look: Deep Time on page 128.
  C. There are three geological eras: the Paleozoic, Mesozoic, and Cenozoic.
  D. Continental drift
    1. The position of the earth's continents has dramatically shifted during the last several hundred million years.
     a. This process is called continental drift.
    2. Continental drift is explained by the theory of plate tectonics which posits that the earth's crust is a series of gigantic and colliding plates.

3. In the late Paleozoic the earth's continents constituted a single land mass, the colossal continent called Pangea.
   a. In the early Mesozoic Pangea began to break up forming a southern "supercontinent" Gondwanaland (consisting of modern South America, Africa, Antarctica, Australia, and India).
   b. The northern continent was called Laurasia, consisting of North America, Europe, and Asia.
   c. By the end of the Mesozoic (ca. 65 m.y.a.), the continents were beginning to assume their current positions.
4. The evolutionary ramifications of continental drift were profound.
   a. The evolutionary history of vertebrates was profoundly influenced by geographical events.
   b. Groups of land animals became geographically isolated from one another.

E. The Paleozoic
   1. See Figure 5-9 for a list of Paleozoic periods and major events.
   2. The earliest vertebrates are present in the fossil record early in the Paleozoic, around 500 million years ago (mya.).
   3. Later in the Paleozoic, several varieties of fishes, amphibians and reptiles appeared.
   4. At the end of the Paleozoic (ca. 250 mya.) several types of mammal-like reptiles are present, likely including the ancestors of modern mammals.

F. The Mesozoic
   1. During this era, the reptiles underwent an adaptive radiation, (rapid expansion into a variety of ecological niches).
   2. Dinosaurs dominated the landscape.
   3. The first mammals are known from fossil traces during the Mesozoic.
   4. The placental mammals do not appear until late in the Mesozoic, around 70 mya
   5. See Figure 5-9 for a list of Mesozoic periods and major events.

G. The Cenozoic
   1. The Cenozoic is divided into two periods.
      a. The Tertiary lasts for approximately 63 million years.
      b. The Quaternary begins 1.8 m.y.a. and continues to the present.
   2. The Cenozoic era is most commonly divided into seven epochs of the Cenozoic.
      a. Paleocene, Eocene, Oligocene, Miocene, Pliocene, Pleistocene, Holocene.

V   MAMMALIAN EVOLUTION
   A. After the dinosaur extinctions mammals underwent an adaptive radiation in which they filled a wide variety of ecological niches.
      1. This mammalian diversification was so successful that the Cenozoic is sometimes referred to as the Age of Mammals.
      2. Mammals and birds replaced reptiles as the dominant terrestrial vertebrates.
   B. Factors contributing to the mammalian success:
      1. The cerebrum of the mammalian brain expanded, in particular the neocortex which controls higher brain functions, came to comprise the majority of brain volume.
         a. This increase in brain size led to a greater ability to learn and a general flexibility of behavior in mammals.
      2. Longer more intense period of growth and development.
      3. Internal prenatal development.

4. Mammals give birth to live young.
5. Mammals have different forms of teeth.
   a. This is called heterodonty.
   b. Mammals have four basic types of teeth
      i. Incisors are used for cutting.
      ii. Canines function in grasping and piercing.
      iii. Premolars are used for crushing and grinding.
      iv. Molars are used for crushing and grinding.
   c. Teeth are particularly important in paleontology because there is a disproportionate representation of teeth in the fossil record.
      i. The enamel that covers the teeth is the hardest substance in the body.
6. Mammals are homeothermic; this means that mammals are able to regulate and maintain a constant body temperature.
   a. Associated with homeothermy is endothermy, the ability to generate body heat by muscle action.
   b. These processes allow mammals to be active during colder times.

VI   THE EMERGENCE OF MAJOR MAMMALIAN GROUPS
   A. There are three major subgroups of living mammals: monotremes, marsupials, and placental mammals.
   B. Monotremes are egg-laying and are extremely primitive.
   C. Marsupials give birth to immature young who finish development in an external pouch (marsupium).
   D. Placental mammals develop over long periods of time in utero nourished via a placenta.
      1. Allows the central nervous system to develop more completely in the fetus.
      2. The placenta is a structure that prevents the mother's immune system from rejecting the fetus.
      3. Mammals also have the "bond of milk" between the mother and the offspring.
         a. This period of association between the mother and the offspring provides more time for neural structures to form.
         b. It is not sufficient that the young mammal has a brain capable of learning; mammalian social systems provide youngsters with ample learning opportunities.

VII   PROCESSES OF MACROEVOLUTION
   A. Adaptive radiation
      1. Adaptive radiation is the evolutionary process by which a species undergoes expansion and diversification in response to new ecological niches.
      2. An adaptive radiation will occur if the species, or group of species, has:
         a. an adaptive potential, and
         b. available ecological niches to occupy.
      3. Examples of adaptive radiation:
         a. Early reptiles were amphibian water dwellers.
            i. With evolution of water tight eggs, gradually reptiles became fully terrestrial and a wide array of niches opened up.
            ii. Reptiles diversified in an adaptive explosion.
         b. The rapid advancement of placental mammals during the early Cenozoic.

B. Generalized and Specialized Characteristics
   1. The adaptive potential of a particular trait is related to its characteristics.
   2. A generalized characteristic is adapted for many functions.
   3. A specialized characteristic is limited to a narrow set of ecological functions.
C. Modes of evolutionary change
   1. Until recently, it was thought that microevolutionary changes accumulating over time will result in macroevolution, or speciation.
      a. In the last 20 years, this view has been seriously challenged.
      b. Many researchers now accept that macroevolution can only be partly explained by microevolutionary factors.
D. Gradualism vs. Punctuated Equilibrium
   1. See Figure 5-14 page 134.
   2. The traditional view of evolution, as put forth by Darwin, is called phyletic gradualism.
      a. According to gradualism, evolution works by gradual changes accumulating over vast periods of geologic time.
      b. There should be a series of intermediate, or transitional, forms in any line.
      c. The reason that such forms are rarely found is attributed to the incompleteness of the fossil record.
   3. The concept of punctuated equilibrium challenges the idea of gradualism.
      a. Punctuated equilibrium posits that species may persist for long periods with little or no change.
         i. A period of "stasis" comes to an end with a "spurt" of speciation.
      b. Punctuated equilibrium does not challenge that evolution has occurred; it challenges the mode and tempo of gradualist evolution.
      c. Rather than long periods of gradual change, this alternate view postulates long periods of no change, punctuated only occasionally by sudden bursts of speciation.
      d. Speciation events and the longevity of these transitional species are so short that they are not preserved in the fossil record.
   4. Evidence indicates that both gradualism and punctuated equilibrium have occurred.
      a. Even within some lineages, the pace of evolution can speed up or slow down.
      b. Environmental changes that influence the pace and direction of natural selection likely also influence speciation.

KEY TERMS

adaptive radiation: the rapid expansion and diversification of an evolving group of organisms into a variety of new ecological niches.

allopatric: a speciation model emphasizing physical barriers that produce reproductive isolation between populations.

analogies: similarities between organisms based strictly on common function with no assumed descent from a common ancestor (e.g. the wings of an insect and the wings of a bat).

ancestral (primitive): referring to a character that reflects the initial condition within a lineage.

biological species concept: a group of interbreeding individuals isolated from other such groups.

classification: the ordering of organisms into categories, such as phyla, orders, and families to show evolutionary relationships.

Cenozoic: the geological era during which primate evolution occurred. It encompasses the last 65 million years.

Chordata (chordates): the phylum of the animal kingdom that includes the vertebrates.

clade: a group of organisms sharing a common ancestry.

cladistics: an approach to taxonomy that groups taxa based on shared derived characteristics.

cladogram: a chart showing evolutionary relationships as determined by cladistic analysis. It is based solely on interpretation of shared derived characters. No time component is indicated, and ancestor-descendant relationships are not inferred.

continental drift: the movement of continents on sliding plates of the earth's surface. This has resulted in dramatic movement of the earth's land masses over time.

derived (modified): referring to a characters that reflects specialization within a lineage and are more informative than primitive traits about evolutionary relationships between organisms.

ecological niches: the positions of species within their physical and biological environment.

ecological species concept: a group that shares a single ecological niche.

endothermic: able to produce heat within the body by means of metabolic processes of cells (mainly muscle cells). Birds and mammals are living endothermic animals.

epochs: categories of the geological time scale; subdivision of periods.

evolutionary systematics: a traditional approach to classification (and evolutionary interpretation) in which presumed ancestors and descendants are traced in time by analysis of homologous characters.

genus: a group of closely related species.

geological time scale: the organization of earth history into eras, periods, and epochs.

Gondwanaland: the southern continents that broke off of Pangea. Gondwanaland (a.k.a. Gondwana) included South America, Africa, Antarctica, Australia, and India.

heterodont: having different kinds of teeth specialized for different functions.

homologies: similarities between organisms based on descent from a common ancestor (e.g. the bones in the wing of a bird and the bones in the arm of a human).

homoplasy: separate evolutionary development of similar characteristics in different groups of organisms.

homeothermy: the ability to maintain a constant body temperature. Through physiological feedback mechanisms heat generated through endothermy is either dissipated or retained within the normal range of body temperature for the species.

interspecific: refers to between two or more species.

intraspecific: refers to within one species.

Laurasia: the northernmost continents that had been part of Pangea. Laurasia included North America, Europe, and Asia.

Metazoa: the multicellular animals, a major division of the animal kingdom. The metazoa are all of the animals except the sponges.

modified: see derived.

neocortex: the outer layer of brain tissue of the cerebrum, which has expanded during the evolution of the vertebrates, particularly in primates, and most especially in humans. The neocortex is associated with high mental functions.

paleospecies: groups of fossil organisms that are assigned to the same species.

Pangea: the supercontinent that included all of the present-day continents. Pangea began to break up in the early Mesozoic.

phyletic gradualism: the evolutionary concept, first postulated by Charles Darwin, that evolutionary change takes place slowly with slight modifications in each generation.

phylogenetic species concept: splitting many populations into separate species based on identifiable parental pattern of ancestry.

phylogenetic tree: a chart showing evolutionary relationships as determined by phylogenetic systematics. It contains a time component and infers ancestor-descendant relationships.

placental: a type of mammal that grows fetuses internally.

primitive: see ancestral.

punctuated equilibrium: the evolutionary concept that there are long periods in the history of a species in which no change takes place (stasis) followed by a quick spurt of evolutionary change (speciation).

recognition species concept: a groups whose individuals recognize each other as potential mates.

sexual dimorphism: differences in physical characteristics between males and females of the same species.

shared derived trait: referring to a character shared in common by two forms and considered the most useful for making evolutionary interpretations.

speciation: the process by which new species are produced from earlier species. The most important mechanism of macroevolutionary change.

theropods: small- to medium-sized dinosaurs that lived on the ground and may have been ancestral to birds.

vertebrates: animals with bony backbones; includes fishes, amphibians, reptiles, birds, and mammals.

MEDIA EXERCISES

1) To see a colorful and fascinating animation of continental drift and seafloor spreading documenting the breakup of Pangea (ca. 200 m.y.a. to the present), go to http://www.scotese.com/sfsanim.htm. After the animation loads, click and drag your cursor across the image from left to right (as fast or as slowly as you'd like) to "playback" 200 million years of earth history!

2) If you dare, take a journey into the mysterious world of systematics at the University of California's Museum of Paleontology (http://evolution.berkeley.edu/evolibrary/article/phylogenetics_01). Follow the links to learn more about phylogenetic systematics.

3) Discover the history of life by taking a virtual tour through the University of California Museum Paleontology exhibit halls (http://www.ucmp.berkeley.edu/historyoflife/histoflife.html). Check out their "History of Life Through Time" (http://www.ucmp.berkeley.edu/exhibit/phylogeny.html) and "Tour of Geologic Time" (http://www.ucmp.berkeley.edu/exhibit/geology.html) links.

CONCEPT APPLICATION

Use the "Events" labeled A-K below to fill in the Geological Time Scale table. (The first two are filled in to give you a head-start…)

A. The first placental and marsupial mammals	G. The "Great Age of Dinosaurs"
B. The "Age of Fish"	H. Trilobites abound
C. Human ancestors spread around the world	I. Mammal-like reptiles
D. First air-breathing animals	J. Modern mammals diversify
E. Modern insects diversify	K. The first egg-laying mammals
F. First fish	

ERA	PERIOD	BEGAN M.Y.A.	EVENT
CENOZOIC	Quaternary	1.8	C
	Tertiary	65	J
MESOZOIC	Cretaceous	136	
	Jurassic	190	
	Triassic	225	
PALEOZOIC	Permian	280	
	Carboniferous	345	
	Devonian	395	
	Silurian	430	
	Ordovician	500	
	Cambrian	570	

Now answer the True/False, Multiple Choice and Short Answer sample test questions. Following completion of the tests, correct them with the answers and textbook page references at the end of this Study Guide chapter. Note the areas in which you are strong and weak to guide you in your studying. Finally, answer the sample Essay Questions.

TRUE/FALSE QUESTIONS

If false, consider what modification would make the statement true.

1. Structures that are shared by species on the basis of descent from a common ancestor are called homoplasies.
   TRUE   FALSE

2. Cladistics is an approach to classification that seeks to make rigorous evolutionary interpretations based solely on analyses of derived characters.
   TRUE   FALSE

3. Evolutionary systematics is the most basic process of macroevolution wherein a new species evolves from a prior species.
   TRUE   FALSE

4. Most speciation is allopatric.
   TRUE   FALSE

5. A group of closely related species is known as a paleospecies.
   TRUE   FALSE

6. Due to continental drift, the positions of landmasses have shifted dramatically during earth's history.
   TRUE   FALSE

7. During the Paleozoic Era, the dinosaurs were preeminent.
   TRUE   FALSE

8. Mammals are heterodont and give birth to live young.
   TRUE   FALSE

9. The diversification of mammals in the Cenozoic is an excellent example of adaptive radiation.
   TRUE   FALSE

10. Punctuated equilibrium states that evolutionary change proceeds by long periods of stasis interrupted by rapid periods of change.
    TRUE   FALSE

MULTIPLE CHOICE QUESTIONS

1. Humans are
   A. animals.
   B. vertebrates.
   C. chordates.
   D. all of the above.

2. The scientific discipline that specializes in establishing rules of classification is
   A. paleontology.
   B. stratigraphy.
   C. homology.
   D. taxonomy.

3. The traditional approach to classifying organisms is based upon similarities in
   A. physical structure.
   B. analogies.
   C. diet.
   D. ecology.

4. Bats have wings that allow them to fly. So do birds and insects. Similarities such as wings in different animals that are based on independent functional adaptation
   A. must mean they have a recent common ancestry.
   B. are called homologies.
   C. are called analogies.
   D. are always primitive traits.

5. Humans and apes have certain characteristics in common such as a broad sternum, a Y-5 cusp pattern on the molars, and the lack of a tail. Since these features are not found in monkeys and strepsirhines these characteristics are
   A. analogies.
   B. primitive traits.
   C. shared derived traits.
   D. general traits.

6. A major difference between a paleospecies and a biological species is that a paleospecies
   A. is more variable.
   B. adds a temporal component.
   C. is not yet extinct.
   D. is static.

7. Closely related species are grouped together in a
   A. paleospecies.
   B. subspecies
   C. genus.
   D. family.

8. Which of the following is **not** a species concept?
    A. Biological Species Concept
    B. Hybrid Species Concept
    C. Recognition Species Concept
    D. Ecological Species Concept

9. _____ speciation requires complete reproductive isolation, leading to the formation of a new species geographically separated from its ancestral population.
    A. Allopatric
    B. Sympatric
    C. Parapatric
    D. all of the above

10. In the early Mesozoic, Pangea broke into two large continents, Gondwana and Laurasia. Laurasia consisted of the present day continents of
    A. South America and Africa.
    B. South America, Africa, and Australia.
    C. South America, Africa, Australia, India, and Antarctica.
    D. North America, Europe, and Asia.

11. Continental drift has affected the evolution of organisms by
    A. forming water barriers.
    B. affecting long-term rainfall patterns.
    C. decreasing the opportunities for gene flow.
    D. all of the above

12. During the Mesozoic the dominant terrestrial life forms were
    A. crossopterygians.
    B. amphibians.
    C. reptiles.
    D. birds.

13. Which of the following is **not** one of the mammalian innovations that have led to their success?
    A. deriving body warmth from the sun.
    B. heterodonty.
    C. live birth to young.
    D. endothermy.

14. The primary advantage of heterodont dentition is that it
    A. allows the animal to defend itself more efficiently.
    B. allows for processing a wide variety of foods.
    C. opens up news ways of interacting with potential mates.
    D. allows the animal to grab prey that it could not catch otherwise.

15. The vast majority of fossil material that is available from most vertebrates, including primates, consist of
    A. pelves.
    B. humeri and other arm bones.
    C. femurs, which are the largest bones in any vertebrate.
    D. teeth.

16. The group of mammals that reproduce by laying eggs and generally have more primitive traits than other mammals are the
    A. monotremes.
    B. marsupials.
    C. placentals.
    D. eutherians.

17. An important aspect of *in utero* development is the specialized tissue that provides for fetal nourishment during a prolonged gestational period.. This specialized tissue is the
    A. placenta.
    B. lymphatic system.
    C. hard-shelled egg.
    D. human lymphatic antigen.

18. After birth a young mammal has a period of neural development coupled with learning. This period of close association between the young mammal and its mother is known as the
    A. rehearsal period.
    B. placental connection.
    C. biosocial perspective.
    D. "bond of milk".

19. Small- to medium-sized ground-living dinosaurs that may have been ancestral to birds are
    A. mammal-like reptiles.
    B. theropods.
    C. monotremes.
    D. all of the above.

20. A chart depicting evolutionary relationships containing a time component and implying ancestor-descendant relationships is called a(n)
    A. cladogram.
    B. taxonomy.
    C. phylogenetic tree.
    D. evolutionary time scale.

21. A group of interbreeding individuals that are reproductively isolated from other such groups defines the
    A. Ecological Species Concept.
    B. Biological Species Concept.
    C. Recognition Species Concept.
    D. Phylogenetic Species Concept.

22. Which of the following has **not** been proposed as a speciation process?
    A. allopatric.
    B. pseudopatric.
    C. parapatric.
    D. instantaneous.

23. Which of the following is the smallest division of the geological time scale?
    A. eon
    B. era
    C. period
    D. epoch

24. Which of the following was **not** part of Gondwana?
    A. South America
    B. India
    C. Europe
    D. Antarctica

25. Which of the following is not a mammalian tooth type?
    A. incisor
    B. premolar
    C. postcanine
    D. molar

26. The type of mammal in which young develop in their mother's pouch are
    A. marsupials.
    B. monotremes.
    C. placentals.
    D. ectotherms.

28. A human hand is relatively _____ compared to a bat wing or a dolphin flipper.
    A. analogous
    B. generalized
    C. specialized
    D. punctuated

29. There are two bird species on a Midwestern prairie that look very much alike physically and are probably descended from a common ancestor. During courtship, however, the males of one species stands on one leg while looking at the female. The males of the second species uses both feet to drum on the prairie floor. The females will only mate with those males who behave appropriately during courtship. This is an example of
    A. parallel evolution.
    B. convergent evolution.
    C. behavioral isolation.
    D. geographical isolation.

90

30. The fossil record of many marine invertebrates shows long periods where there is very little change in species. New species appear geologically suddenly without the occurrence of any transitions. These observations best support the idea of
   A. convergent evolution.
   B. punctuated equilibrium.
   C. phyletic gradualism.
   D. small microevolutionary changes that lead to transspecific evolution.

31. A relatively rapid expansion and diversification of life forms into new ecological niches is known as
   A. adaptive radiation.
   B. punctuated equilibrium.
   C. phyletic gradualism.
   D. convergent evolution.

SHORT ANSWER QUESTIONS (& PAGE REFERENCES)

1. What is the difference between homology and analogy? (pp. 112-113)

2. Name three ways that have been hypothesized for speciation to occur. (pp. 122-123)

3. What is continental drift? (p. 126)

4. How do mammals differ from reptiles? (pp. 128-131)

5. What is adaptive radiation? (p. 132)

ESSAY QUESTIONS (& PAGE REFERENCES)

1. What are the differences between the traditional evolutionary systematic and newer cladistic approaches in trying to reconstruct evolutionary relationships between species? (pp. 113-118)

2. Compare and contrast the Biological, Recognition and Ecological Species Concepts. (pp. 118-122)

3. Compare and contrast phyletic gradualism versus punctuated equilibrium with respect to the mode and tempo of evolution. (pp. 133-134)

ANSWERS, *CORRECTED STATEMENT* IF FALSE & REFERENCES TO TRUE/FALSE QUESTIONS

1. **FALSE**, p. 113, Structures that are shared by species on the basis of descent from a common ancestor are called *homologies*.

2. **TRUE**, pp. 113-114

3. **FALSE**, p. 119, *Speciation* is the most basic process of macroevolution wherein a new species evolves from a prior species.

4. **TRUE**, p. 122

5. **FALSE**, p. 125, A group of closely related species is known as a *genus*.

6. **TRUE**, p. 126

7. **FALSE**, p. 127, During the *Mesozoic* Era, the dinosaurs were preeminent.

8. **TRUE**, p. 130

9. **TRUE**, p. 132

10. **TRUE**, p. 133

ANSWERS AND REFERENCES TO MULTIPLE CHOICE QUESTIONS

1. **D**, pp. 110-112
2. **D**, p. 112
3. **A**, p. 112
4. **C**, p. 113
5. **C**, p. 117
6. **B**, p. 124
7. **C**, p. 125
8. **B**, pp. 118-122
9. **A**, pp. 122-123
10. **D**, p. 126
11. **D**, pp. 126-127
12. **C**, p. 127
13. **A**, p. 130
14. **B**, p. 130
15. **D**, p. 130
16. **A**, p. 130
17. **A**, p. 131
18. **D**, p. 131
19. **B**, p. 116
20. **C**, p. 117
21. **B**, p. 118
22. **B**, pp. 118-122
23. **D**, p. 126
24. **C**, p. 126
25. **C**, p. 130
26. **A**, pp. 130-131
27. **B**, pp. 132-133
28. **C**, p. 119
29. **B**, p. 133
30. **A**, p. 132

CONCEPT APPLICATION SOLUTION

ERA	PERIOD	BEGAN M.Y.A.	EVENT
CENOZOIC	Quaternary	1.8	C
	Tertiary	65	J
MESOZOIC	Cretaceous	136	A
	Jurassic	190	G
	Triassic	225	K
PALEOZOIC	Permian	280	I
	Carboniferous	345	E
	Devonian	395	B
	Silurian	430	D
	Ordovician	500	F
	Cambrian	570	H

93

CHAPTER 6
SURVEY OF THE LIVING PRIMATES

LEARNING OBJECTIVES

After reading this chapter you should be able to
- list the general primate characteristics (pp. 141-144)
- describe the influence of the arboreal environment on primate evolution (pp. 145-148)
- locate where primates live geographically (pp. 146-148)
- describe the teeth and diet of primates (pp. 148-150)
- describe the major forms of locomotion found among primates (pp. 150-151)
- explain how taxonomic classification reflects biological relationships (pp. 151-153)
- name the major groupings within the strepsirhine and haplorhine suborders (pp. 153-169)
- discuss primate conservation challenges facing primatologists today (pp. 169-175)

CHAPTER OUTLINE

Introduction

By studying our closest mammalian relatives we can better understand our own evolution and behavior. We can also help to conserve the fragile primate species. The comparative approach is taken in this chapter to describe physical and behavioral characteristics in the approximately 230 primate species alive today. In this chapter, we will discuss the taxonomy of the living primates and also note general characteristics of each group of primates.

I   **PRIMATE CHARACTERISTICS**
   A. Primates share many characteristics with other placental mammals.
     1. Some of these include: body hair, long gestation, live births, mammary glands, teeth types, endothermy, large brain, capacity for learning.
   B. Recall the primates are an order within the mammalian class and as such share some features.
   C. Primates are quite generalized.
     1. They retain many ancestral mammalian traits that other mammals have lost.
   D. Because primates are generalized mammals they cannot be defined by one or two common traits.
     1. There are a group of features that characterize most primates.
     2. These characteristics are divided up into 4 categories.
       a. Limbs and locomotion
       b. Diet and teeth
       c. Senses and the brain
       d. Maturation, learning and behavior
     3. These are often referred to as evolutionary trends.
       a. The degree of expression varies between species
       b. They are a combination of ancestral (A) and derived (D) traits.

E. Limbs and locomotion
1. Primates exhibit a tendency toward an erect posture, especially in the upper body (D).
    a. whether sitting, leaping, or standing.
2. Flexible, generalized limb structure which does not necessitate a particular form of locomotion (A).
3. Primate hands and feet possess a high degree of prehensility (grasping ability) (D).
    a. the retention of five digits on hand and feet (A).
    b. An opposable thumb and, in most species, a divergent and partially opposable great toe (D).
    c. Primates possess nails on most digits (D).
    d. Primates have tactile pads enriched with sensory nerve fibers at the ends of digits, which enhance the sense of touch (D).
F. Diet and teeth
1. Primates, for the most part, lack dietary specializations and tend to eat a wide variety of foods.
    a. Primates tend to be omnivorous (A).
2. Primates possess generalized dentition (A).
    a. Associated with absence of dietary specialization.
G. The senses and the brain
1. Primates rely heavily on vision and less on olfaction than other mammals (D).
    a. This is associated with evolutionary changes in the skull, brain, and eye.
        i)   See A Closer Look on pp. 144-145.
    b. Color vision in all diurnal primates. Nocturnal primates lack color vision.
    c. Depth perception or stereoscopic vision
        i)   Eyes are positioned in the front of the skull, providing over-lapping fields of vision (known as binocular vision).
        ii)   Visual information from each eye is transmitted to the visual centers in both hemispheres of the brain.
        iii)   Visual information is organized into three-dimensional images by specialized structures in the brain (D).
2. Primates have a decreased reliance on the sense of smell (olfaction) (D).
3. The primate brain has expanded in size and has become increasingly complex (D).
H. Maturation, learning, and behavior
1. A more efficient means of fetal nourishment; the placenta (D).
2. Longer periods of gestation, fewer numbers of offspring, delayed maturation, and elongation of the entire life span (D).
3. Greater dependence on flexible, learned behavior (D).
4. Primates tend to live in social groups. Males are permanent members of many primate social groups, a situation unusual among mammals (D).
5. Primates tend to be diurnal (active during the day) (D).

II   **PRIMATE ADAPTATIONS**
A. Primate anatomical traits evolved as adaptations to environmental circumstances.
B. Primate characteristics can (traditionally) be seen as adaptations to arboreal living (the arboreal hypothesis).
1. The primate adaptive niche is the trees.

2. Primates found food in the trees which eventually led to an omnivorous diet and generalized dentition.
3. Arboreal stresses led to increased reliance on vision and grasping hands and feet.

C. The visual predation hypothesis
   1. The visual predation hypothesis is an alternative to the arboreal hypothesis.
      a. Visual predators have forward facing eyes.
   2. Forward-facing, close-set eyes and grasping hands enabled early primates to judge distance when grabbing for insects.
   3. Early primates may have adapted to shrubby undergrowth and the lowest tiers of the forest canopy where they hunted insects and small prey.

D. The angiosperm radiation hypothesis.
   1. This perspective suggests that basic primate traits developed in conjunction with the rise of flowering plants.
   2. Primate traits may have arisen in relation to fruits, flowers, and seeds.
      a. The primate features of vision, grasping, omnivory provide the tactile and visual discrimination necessary to feed on small angiosperms.

E. These hypotheses are not mutually exclusive explanations.
   1. Many primate features may have begun in non-arboreal settings.
   2. Nevertheless, primates did move into the trees and, if they did have characteristics that evolved in another setting, they were suited for life in the trees.

F. Geographical distribution and habitats
   1. Most living nonhuman primates live in the tropical or semitropical areas of the New and Old Worlds.
   2. See Figure 6-3 on pp. 146-147.

G. Diet and teeth
   1. Primates are generally omnivorous and this is reflected in their generalized dentition.
   2. Although the majority of primate species emphasize some food items over others, most eat a combination of fruit, leaves and insects.
      a. Some get animal protein from birds and amphibians.
      b. Some primates (capuchins, baboons, bonobos and especially chimpanzees) occasionally kill and eat small mammals.
      c. Some monkeys are more specialized and subsist mostly on leaves.
   3. Dietary generalists have an advantage in that they can find a food source (if not one, then a substitute).
      a. This is particularly important in marginal environments.
      b. The downside of generalization is the competition with more specialized animals.
      c. Specialization can be dangerous in marginal environments.
   4. Most primates have four types of teeth.
      a. Incisors and canines function in biting and cutting.
      b. Premolars and molars are used for crushing and grinding.
   5. A dental formula describes the number of each type of tooth that typifies a species.
      a. A dental formula is presented as a series of numbers (indicating the number of each type of tooth in a quarter of the mouth).
      b. A dental formula may appear in a fraction format with the numerator as the number of teeth in half the upper jaw, and the denominator as half the number of teeth in the lower jaw.
      c. A dental formula is read in the following order: incisor(s), canine(s), premolar(s), and molar(s).

96

d. Old World Anthropoids have a dental formula of 2.1.2.3.
    i) 2 incisors, 1 canine, 2 premolars, and 3 molars.
    ii) The primitive dental formula for all placental mammals is 3.1.4.3.
6. Primates, as well as other mammals, have fewer teeth than the primitive mammalian condition because of evolutionary trends in those lineages.
H. The primate dentition is characterized by a lack of dental specialization.
1. Unlike carnivore or herbivore specialists, primates possess low, rounded cusps that enable them to process most foods.
I. Locomotion
1. Almost all primates are, to some degree, quadrupedal - using all four limbs in their locomotion.
    a. Many primates use more than one form of locomotion, a product of their generalized limb structure.
    b. The majority of quadrupedal primates are arboreal, but terrestrial quadrupedalism is also fairly common.
    c. Limb ratios of animals can be indicative of locomotion form.
        i) The limbs of terrestrial quadrupeds are approximately equal in length, with forelimbs being 90 percent as long as hind limbs.
        ii) In arboreal quadrupeds, forelimbs are proportionately shorter than hind limbs.
2. Vertical clinging and leaping is found in many lemurs and tarsiers.
    a. VCL movers hold on while tightly flexed lower limbs are used to propel them.
3. Brachiation (arm swinging) is a suspensory form of locomotion.
    a. Anatomical modifications of the shoulders allow humans and apes to brachiate.
    b. Only the small gibbons and siamangs of Southeast Asia use this exclusively.
    c. Brachiators are characterized by:
        i) arms much longer than their legs.
        ii) a short stable lumbar spine.
        iii) long curved fingers.
        iv) reduced thumbs.
    d. These features are found in the great apes, though today none of them are brachiators.
    e. Brachiator characteristics have been inherited by the great apes from their ancestors who were either brachiators or climbers.
    f. Some monkeys that use a combination of leaping with some arm swinging are termed semibrachiators.
4. An aid to locomotion is a prehensile tail.
    a. Among the primates prehensile tails are found only among the New World monkeys.
    b. A prehensile tail is like a fifth hand.
5. Knuckle walking is observed in some gorillas, bonobos, and chimpanzees.
    a. This modified quadrupedalism has weight supported on back surface of bent fingers.

III   PRIMATE CLASSIFICATION
A. See Figure 6-7 (p. 152) for a primate taxonomic classification.
B. In taxonomic systems organisms are organized into increasingly specific categories.

1. All of the primates are grouped together in the Order Primates.
2. This primate order is subdivided into two suborders: Strepsirihini and Haplorhini.
   a. The Strepsirihini include lemurs and lorises.
      i) By grouping these primates together an evolutionary statement is implied – the lemurs and lorises are more closely related to each other than they are to any other primates.
   b. The other suborder, Haplorhini, includes tarsiers, monkeys, apes, and humans.
3. At each taxonomic level finer distinctions are made ending at the species level.
   a. Classifications organize diversity into categories and illustrates evolutionary and genetic relationships between species and groups of species.
C. Genetic evidence
   1. Primate classification is in a transition state due to advances in molecular biology.
   2. By looking at physical traits it is possible to overlook the effects of separate evolutionary history.
   3. Direct comparisons between the genes is possible given the number of species whose genomes have been sequenced.
   4. This comparative genomics approach gives a more accurate picture of evolutionary and biological relationships.
   5. In 2005 a complete draft sequence of the chimp genome was published.
      a. Comparative studies reveal the number of nucleotide changes that have taken place between species.
      b. Geneticists can calculate how long ago these changes took place.
   6. Genetic analysis shows that humans are most closely related to chimps.
      a. The DNA sequences are 98.4% to 99.4% identical.
      b. The chimp human split has been put at 6-7 mya based on molecular information.
   7. Humans have more noncoding DNA than any other primates (that have been studied).
      a. This is being investigated to determine what makes us different from our closest relatives.

IV   A SURVEY OF THE LIVING PRIMATES
   A. Strepsirhini suborder (lemurs and lorises)
      1. Lemurs and lorises are the most primitive of the primates.
         a. More similar anatomically to early mammalian ancestors than are other primates.
      2. Primitive characteristics include:
         a. Greater reliance on olfaction compared to the other primates.
            i) This is reflected in the moist rhinarium at the end of the nose and the relatively long snout.
            ii) Strepsirhines mark their territories with scent.
         b. Strepsirhines have more laterally placed eyes.
         c. Differ in reproductive physiology; shorter gestation and maturation periods.
      3. Many strepsirhines possess a dental specialization called the "dental comb."
         a. This structure is formed by forward-projecting lower incisors and canines.
         b. The dental comb is used in both feeding and grooming.
      4. Strepsirhines also retain a grooming claw on the second toe.
   B. Lemurs
      1. Lemurs are found only on the island of Madagascar and several nearby islands off the east coast of Africa.

98

a. Diversified into numerous and varied ecological niches without competition from higher primates.
b. Lemurs became extinct elsewhere in the world.
2. Characteristics of lemurs
a. Body size ranges from 5 inch long (mouse lemur) to 3 feet long (indri).
b. Larger lemurs are diurnal and exploit a wide variety of vegetable foods ranging from fruit to leaves, buds, bark, and shoots.
c. Smaller lemurs are nocturnal and insectivorous (insect-feeding).
3. There is great variation in lemur movement and behavior.
a. Many are arboreal but some are more terrestrial (ring-tailed lemur).
b. Some arboreal forms are quadrupedal, while others, such as the sifaka, are vertical clingers and leapers.
c. Some species (e.g. ring-tailed lemurs and sifakas) live in groups of 10 to 25 animals, including males and females of all ages.
d. Others live in family groups (e.g. indri).
e. Most of the nocturnal species are solitary.
C. Lorises
1. Lorises resemble lemurs.
a. Lorises are nocturnal which enabled survival in mainland areas without competing with monkeys.
b. Loris superfamily consists of 2 major groups: lorises and galagos.
2. Found in tropical forests and woodlands of India, Sri Lanka, Southeast Asia, and Africa (app. eight species of lorises).
3. Found in forests and woodlands of sub-Saharan Africa (Six to nine galago, or bushbabies, species).
4. Characteristics of lorises
a. Locomotion
    i) Lorises employ a slow cautious climbing form of quadrupedalism.
    ii) Galagos are active vertical clingers and leapers.
b. Diet
    i) Some lorises are almost completely insectivorous.
    ii) Others supplement their diet with combinations of fruit, leaves, gums, and slugs.
c. These animals frequently forage alone.
    i) Ranges overlap and females frequently form associations for foraging or in sharing the same sleeping nest.
    ii) They park their infants in trees while they forage.
D. Both lemurs and lorises represent the same general primate adaptive level.
a. Both groups practice grasping and climbing abilities.
b. Vision not completely stereoscopic.
c. Color vision is not as developed as in anthropoids.
d. These animals have longer life spans compared to other similar-sized mammals.
    i) Life spans range from 14-19 years.
E. Haplorhines (tarsiers, monkeys, apes and humans)
1. The suborder divided into two infraorders: Anthropoidea and Tarsiformes
F. Tarsiers
1. Tarsiers are highly specialized nocturnal insectivores.
a. Five recognized species.

        b. Found in the islands of Southeast Asia.
        c. Inhabit a wide range of forest types.
        d. The basic social pattern appears to be a family unit consisting of a mated pair and their offspring.
    2. Tarsiers were traditionally classified in the same suborder as lemurs and lorises (prosimian suborder).
    3. Tarsiers exhibit a combination of anatomical traits not seen in other primates.
        a. Have enormous eyes, each one being about the size of its brain.
    4. Tarsiers exhibit suite of Anthropoid like characteristics
        a. Now classified in the suborder with the anthropoids.
G. Anthropoids
    1. Infraorder consisting of Monkeys, apes and humans.
    2. Anthropoid characteristics (compared to strepsirhines).
        a. A larger average body size.
        b. Larger brains both in absolute size and in relation to body size.
        c. Reduced reliance on the sense of smell.
        d. Increased reliance on vision with forward-facing eyes placed at the front of the face.
        e. Greater degree of color vision.
        f. Bony plate at the back of the eye socket.
        g. Blood supply to the brain different from that of prosimians.
        h. Both halves of the mandible are fused at the midline.
        i. More generalized dentition.
        j. Internal female reproductive anatomy is different from the strepsirhine condition.
        k. Longer gestation and maturation periods.
        l. Increased parental care.
        m. More mutual grooming.
    3. Monkeys represent about 85% of all primate species.
    4. Monkeys are divided into two groups (parvorders): New World monkeys and Old World monkeys.
H. New World Monkeys
    1. Parvorder: platyrhini
        a. Found in a range of arboreal environments in Mexico, Central and South America.
    2. Wide range of sizes, diet, and ecological adaptation.
    3. New World monkeys are almost exclusively arboreal.
    4. All species, with the exception of the owl monkey, are diurnal.
    5. One characteristic that distinguishes the New World monkeys from the Old World monkeys is the shape of the nose.
        a. New World monkeys have broad noses with nostrils that face outward.
        b. New World monkeys are placed in the infraorder Platyrrhini (meaning "flat-nosed").
        c. Old World monkeys have narrower noses with downward facing nostrils.
        d. Platyrrhine means flat-nosed and catarrhine, means downward-facing nose.
    6. Platyrrhines are represented by three families: Pithecidae, Cebidae, and Atelidae.
        a. The new world monkeys are a single superfamily, the Ateloidea.
        b. Primarily found in central America and South America, there are 70 species.
        c. Wide range of variation in diet, locomotion, and adaptations.
            i) Range in size from less than one pound to approximately 20 lbs.

100

        d. Almost exclusively arboreal.

        e. Marmosets and tamarins (cebidae species) are the smallest.

            i)   Have nails instead of claws

            ii) Mostly insectivorous but some eat tree gum and fruit.

            iii) Live in family groups composed of mated pairs, or a female and two adult males, plus the offspring: Polyandry.

                a) Males are heavily involved with infant care.

7. New World Monkeys range in size from 1.5 pounds to 22 pounds.

    a. Diet varies, with most eating a combination of fruit and leaves supplemented by insects.

    b. Most are quadrupedal.

        i)   Spider monkeys are semibrachiators.

        ii)   Muriquis, spider, and howler monkeys have prehensile tails.

    c. Most live in groups of both sexes and all ages.

    d. Some form monogamous pairs with their subadult offspring.

I. Old World monkeys – the most widely distributed primate except for humans.

1. Old World monkeys are found from sub-Saharan Africa to the islands of Southeast Asia.

    a. Habitats range from tropical forests to semiarid desert and even extend to seasonally snow-covered highland forests in northern Japan.

2. General characteristics of Old World monkeys.

    a. The locomotor pattern of most Old World monkeys is quadrupedal.

    b. They are primarily arboreal, although some have adapted to life on the ground.

    c. Spend a good deal of time feeding, sleeping, and grooming.

    d. Old World monkeys have hardened areas of skin called ischial callosities that serve as sitting pads.

3. All of the Old World monkeys belong to one family, the Cercopithecidae, which is divided into two subfamilies, the cercopithecines and the colobines.

4. Cercopithecines

    a. Cercopithecines are more generalized than the colobines.

    b. Cercopithecines have an omnivorous diet.

        i)   Eat almost anything: fruit, seeds, leaves, grasses, tubers, etc.

    c. "Cheek pouched monkeys"

        i)   Have cheek pouches that enable them to store food while foraging.

    d. Geographical distribution

        i)   Most cercopithecines are found in Africa.

        ii)   A number of species of macaques are also found in southern Asia and India.

5. Colobines

    a. These animals are mostly leaf eaters.

        i)   "leaf eating monkeys"

    b. Geographical distribution

        i)   Mostly in Asia but some, like the colobus, are found in Africa.

        ii)   Langurs are found in Asia and proboscis monkeys on Borneo.

6. Locomotor behavior in Old World monkeys.

    a. Guenons, macaques, and langurs are arboreal quadrupeds.

    b. Baboons and macaques are terrestrial quadrupeds.

    c. Colobus monkeys practice semibrachiation and leaping.

7. Many Old World monkey species show a marked difference in size or shape between the sexes.
   a. Called sexual dimorphism is pronounced in terrestrial species such as baboons and patas monkeys.
8. Females of several species exhibit pronounced cyclical changes of the external genitalia.
   a. This hormonally initiated period is called estrus.
9. Old World monkeys have several types of social organization.
   a. Colobines tend to live in small groups that contain only one or two adult males.
   b. Savanna baboons and most macaques live in large groups containing adults of both sexes and offspring of all ages.
   c. Monogamy not common among mammals, but is seen in langur and guenon species.
J. Old and New World monkeys: a case of homoplasy
1. New World and Old World monkeys have followed separate evolutionary paths for the last 40 million years.
   a. Once believed that they had evolved from separate prosimian lineages.
   b. Currently we think that both groups originated in Africa from a monkey-like ancestor.
   c. New World monkeys would have reached South America, then an island continent, by "rafting" (floating on chunks of land that break off from mainland areas and float on currents to another landmass) as described in Chapter 9 (see A Closer Look p. 357).
2. The evolutionary principle of Homoplasy explains the similarities between New World and Old World monkeys (See Chapter 5, p. 113).
   a. Results from geographically distinct populations responding to similar environmental pressures.
K. Hominoids (apes and humans)
1. The superfamily Hominoidea includes the "lesser" apes (family Hylobatidae: gibbons and siamangs) and the great apes and humans (family Homininae).
2. Hominoid characteristics that distinguish them from monkeys include:
   a. Larger body size (gibbons and siamangs are exceptions).
   b. Absence of a tail.
   c. Shortened trunk (the lumbar area is relatively shorter and more stable).
   d. Arms that are longer than legs.
   e. Differences in position and musculature of the shoulder joint (adapted for suspensory locomotion).
   f. More complex behavior.
   g. More complex brains and enhanced cognitive abilities.
   h. Increased period of infant development and dependency.
L. Gibbons and siamangs
1. Gibbons and siamangs are found in the tropical areas of southeast Asia.
2. They are the smallest of the apes - gibbons weigh 13 pounds and siamangs 25 pounds.
3. Gibbons and siamangs have anatomical features adapted for brachiation that include
   a. Extremely long arms.
   b. Curved fingers.
   c. Reduced thumbs.
   d. Powerful shoulder muscles.

4. The highly specialized locomotor adaptations may be related to feeding behavior while hanging beneath branches.
5. Diet is composed largely of fruit with supplements of leaves, flowers and insects.
6. The primary social unit is a male-female pair with their dependent offspring.
   a. Members of pair have been observed mating with other individuals.
   b. Males are very involved with the rearing of the offspring.
   c. Lesser apes are territorial and defend their territories with elaborate siren-like whoops and "songs."

M. Orangutans (*Pongo pygmaeus*) belong to the subfamily Ponginae.
1. Orangutans are represented by two subspecies
2. Highly endangered, today they are found only in heavily forested areas of Borneo and Sumatra.
3. They are almost completely arboreal and are slow, cautious, fourhanded climbers.
   a. Sometimes they travel quadrupedally on the ground.
4. They are large animals (males = 200 pounds, females = 100 pounds) with pronounced sexual dimorphism.
5. Orangutans lead rather solitary lives though females are accompanied by a dependent offspring.
6. They are principally frugivorous (fruit-eating).

N. Gorillas (*Gorilla gorilla*) belong to the subfamily Gorillinae.
1. Gorillas are the largest of the living primates and are confined to forested regions of central and western Africa.
2. There are four recognized subspecies although one of these (Western lowland) may be distinct enough to qualify as a separate species.
3. Gorillas exhibit marked sexual dimorphism, males can weigh up to 400 pounds, females 200 pounds.
4. Because of their large size gorillas are primarily terrestrial employing a semi-quadrupedal posture called knuckle-walking.
5. Gorillas live in groups that usually consist of a large silverback male, a few adult females, and their subadult offspring.
   a. Both females and males leave their natal group as young adults.
   b. Females join other groups.
   c. Males may live alone or may join other males before eventually forming their own group.
6. All gorillas are almost exclusively vegetarian.
   a. Their diets consist primarily of leaf, pith and stalks.

O. The subfamily Homininae consists of common chimps, bonobo chimps and humans.
1. Chimpanzee species and subspecies are in the tribe Panini and the Pan genus.

P. Chimpanzees (*Pan troglodytes*)
1. Chimpanzees are the found in patches throughout equatorial Africa.
2. Chimpanzees anatomically resemble gorillas in many ways particularly in limb proportions and upper body shape.
   a. Both locomote by knucklewalking
   b. Chimps spend more time in the trees.
   c. Chimps are smaller than orangutans and gorillas but they are sexually dimorphic though not to the degree seen in the orangutans and gorillas.
3. Locomotion includes quadrupedal knuckle-walking on the ground and suspensory behavior (including brachiation, especially among younger chimps) in the trees.

4. Chimpanzees eat fruits, leaves, insects, nuts, eggs, berries, and small mammals.
    a. Chimps have been observed hunting small mammals, including monkeys, bushpigs and antelope.
5. Chimpanzees live in large, fluid communities of between 10 and 100.
    a. The core of chimp communities is bonded (related) males who stay in their birth (natal) group.
    b. Not all members are together at a single time; they are often dispersed into foraging parties.
    c. Females frequently forage alone or in the company of their offspring.
6. In many chimpanzee communities, females leave their natal group.
    a. This action likely reduces the risk of mating with male relatives.
7. Chimps for strong social bonds that last a long time.
Q. Bonobos (*Pan paniscus*)
1. This species of chimpanzee is found in an area south of the Zaire River in the Democratic Republic of the Congo.
2. Bonobos are the least studied of the chimpanzees and differ in several ways.
    a. They have been called "pygmy chimpanzees."
    b. Bonobos are less stocky, have longer legs relative to arms, smaller heads, and dark faces.
3. Bonobo behavior:
    a. Bonobos are more arboreal than chimpanzees.
    b. They are less aggressive among themselves.
    c. Like chimps they live in fluid communities.
    d. Bonobos exploit many of the same foods as chimps, including occasional meat from killing small mammals.
4. The core of bonobo society is male-female bonds.
    a. This may be due to bonobo sexuality in which copulations are frequent and occur throughout the female's estrous cycle.
    b. Bonobos use sexual behaior to diffuse tense situations.
R. Humans (*Homo sapiens*)
1. Humans are the only living representatives of habitually bipedal hominins (members of the Hominini tribe).
2. Our primate heritage is evident in:
    a. our anatomy
    b. our genetic makeup
    c. many behavioral aspects
    d. dependence on vision
    e. decreased reliance on olfaction.
    f. flexible limbs and grasping hands.
    g. Humans are omnivorous, and are adapted to digesting a wide range of foods.
3. Human cognitive abilities are unique.
    a. These abilities are the result of increases in brain size and other neurological changes.
4. Humans are completely dependent on culture and cultural innovations.
5. Another unique characteristic of our species is the development of spoken language.
    a. Certain neurological and anatomical structures developed only in the human lineage.

104

      b. Apes can communicate with symbols so our ability to use language derives from our ape heritage.

    6. Humans differ from other primates in that they are habitual bipeds.

      a. Bipedal locomotion has required significant structural modifications of the pelvis and the limbs.

V   ENDANGERED PRIMATES

A. Three main factors threaten endangered primate species.

    1. Habitat destruction; most primates live in tropical rain forests that are being logged or destroyed for their natural resources or for farm land.

    2. Human predation.

    3. Live capture for export or local trade.

B. In 2000 Miss Waldron's red colobus was declared extinct.

    1. This is the first primate declared extinct in the 21st century.

C. Human population growth is at the root of primate endangerment.

    1. Ninety percent of all primates live in the tropical forests of Africa, Asia, and Latin America.

    2. These nations, with an estimated 1.5 billion people, are suffering from a fuel-wood shortage leading to forest destruction.

    3. In Brazil the rainforest used to cover almost 400,000 square miles. Today only 7% remains.

    4. Loss of rainforests to short term economic gain is a major disaster.

    5. In Sierra Leone the rainforest covered 15,000 square miles, now less than 530 square miles remain.

D. Primates have also been live captured for zoos, biomedical research, and the exotic pet trade.

    1. Live capture has declined dramatically in recent years.

    2. The implementation of the Convention on Trade in Endangered Species of Wild Flora and Fauna (CITES) in 1973 has made a difference.

    3. By August 2005 169 countries have signed this treaty.

E. Hunting of primates

    1. The slaughter of forest animals now accounts for the loss of tens of thousands of primates annually.

    2. A multimillion dollar trade in Bushmeat rapidly developed in the 1990's.

      a. Most extreme in Africa.

    3. In South America the hunting of monkeys is decimating populations.

    4. In China and Southeast Asia the live capture and trade of primates continues.

      a. Primate body parts figure in the practice of traditional medicine.

F. Disease Impacts

    1. West African countries of Gabon and the Republic of Congo are home to 80% of remaining great apes.

      a. From 1983 to 2000 population declined by 50%.

    2. Decrease due to hunting and disease: Ebola

    3. Reportedly 5000 gorillas died of ebola

    4. Populations may not be able to survive this rapid decrease in numbers

G. Mountain Gorillas are one of the most endangered primate species

    1. Their population numbers 700

2. In January 2007, 10 mountain gorillas were slaughtered in a refuge park.
   a. They were killed to rid them from the area where charcoal is manufactured.
H. Conservation Efforts
1. Many developing countries have designated areas as national parks or biological reserves.
2. Private international efforts are aimed at curbing the "bushmeat" trade.
3. It is only through such practices and through educational programs that many primate species have any chance at escaping extinction.

KEY TERMS

adaptive niche: the entire way of life of an organism: where it lives, what it eats, how it obtains food, etc.

amino acid sequencing: a molecular technique in which amino acid sequences in proteins are mapped. They can then be compared between species in order to deduce evolutionary relationships.

anthropoid: any of the members of the primate infraorder Anthropoidea. This suborder includes the monkeys, apes, and humans.

arboreal: living in the trees.

arboreal hypothesis: the view that primate characteristics, such as stereoscopic vision and grasping hands, are the result of evolutionary adaptation to arboreal habitats.

Atelidae: the family of New World monkeys that includes the howlers and spider monkeys.

Ateloidea: the superfamily of New World monkeys.

auditory bulla: a bony structure surrounding the middle-ear cavity that is partially formed from the temporal bone.

binocular vision: vision that results from forward facing eyes, hence overlapping visual fields. Binocular vision is a requirement for stereoscopic vision.

brachiation: a form of suspensory locomotion involving arm swinging. Found mainly among the apes.

bushmeat: term used for primates and other game that are killed for food.

Cebidae: the family of New World monkeys that includes the capuchin, squirrel, and marmoset monkeys.

Cercopithecidae: the one taxonomic family of the Old World monkeys.

cercopithecines: the subfamily of Old World monkeys that includes the baboons, macaques, and guenons.

colobines: the subfamily of Old World monkeys that have evolved anatomical specializations in their teeth and in a large sacculated stomach for consuming a diet of leaves.

Convention on Trade in Endangered Species of Wild Flora and Fauna (CITES): a treaty aimed at the conservation of endangered organisms. This treaty has been signed by 87 nations.

cusps: the elevated portions (bumps) on the chewing surfaces of premolar and molar teeth.

dental formula: a morphological formula that gives the number of each kind of tooth for one-quarter of the mouth for a mammal. If the upper and lower dentition is different the dental formula will be presented for one-half of the mouth.

derived: refers to specialization found within a particular evolutionary lineage.

diurnal: an animal that is active during the day.

DNA hybridization: a molecular technique in which two single strands of DNA from two different species are combined to form a hybrid molecule of DNA. Evolutionary relationships can be deduced from the number of mismatched base pairs between the two strands of DNA.

estrus: period of sexual receptivity in female mammals that corresponds with ovulation. It differs from menstruation, the condition found in human females, in that the endometrial lining is reabsorbed rather than shed.

evolutionary trends: overall characteristics of an evolving lineage, such as the primates. Such trends are useful in helping categorize the lineage as compared to other lineages.

frugivorous: a diet that consists mainly of fruit.

Haplorhines: the suborder, haplorhini, that includes the anthropoids and the tarsiers.

Hominoidea: the primate superfamily that includes apes and humans.

Hylobatidae: gibbons and siamangs.

intelligence: mental capacity; ability to learn, reason, or comprehend and interpret information, facts, relationships, meanings, etc.

ischial callosities: a pad of callused skin over the bone of the ischial tuberosity (a part of the pelvic bone) that serves as a sitting pad in Old World monkeys and gibbons.

lumbar: lower back

macaques: group of Old World monkeys that are distributed widely across Africa and Asia.

midline: the hypothetical line that divides the right from the left half of the body.

morphology: the form (size, shape) of anatomical structures. This can include the entire organism.

natal group: the group in which animals are born and raised.

neocortex: the recently evolved portions of the brain that control higher thinking.

nocturnal: an animal that is active during the night.

omnivorous: a diet consisting of many different food types.

polyandry: one female and more than one male social group.

postorbital bar: a ring of bone that encloses the eye sockets in the primate skull.

postorbital plate: a plate of bone at the back of the eye orbit in primates.

prehensility: grasping by hands, feet (and some tails) in primates.

primates: members of the mammalian order Primates. This includes prosimians, monkeys, apes and humans.

primatologist: a scientist that studies the biology of primates, including primate evolution.

primitive: in evolutionary terms, an organism that is most like the ancestor from which its lineage was derived. A more general member of its group. In primates the prosimians are the most primitive members.

quadrupedal: using all four limbs to support the body during locomotion. This is the basic mammalian (and primate) form of locomotion.

rhinarium: the moist, hairless pad at the end of the nose seen in most mammalian species.

sensory modalities: different sensory perceptions of the environment (e.g. sight, touch, taste…)

sexual dimorphism: differences in physical features between males and females of the same species. Examples among primates include larger body size of males (baboons, gorillas among others) and larger canine teeth in males (baboons and chimpanzees are representative).

specialized: traits that have evolved to perform a particular function. Particular specialized traits are found in a specific lineage and serve to elucidate evolutionary relationships.

stereoscopic vision: a condition, due to binocular vision, in which visual images are superimposed upon one another. This is interpreted by the brain and results in the perception of depth or three-dimensional vision.

Strepsirhine: any of the members of the primate suborder strepsirhini. This suborder includes lemurs and lorises.

territorial: protecting all or part of a resource area.

MEDIA EXERCISES

1) Take an online visit to the wonderful Primate Info Net (http://pin.primate.wisc.edu/index.html) hosted by the Wisconsin Regional Primate Research Center of the University of Wisconsin – Madison. Click on the "AV Resources" button on the left and you are taken to the site's audiovisual archives. From there you can browse through the primate world of sight and sound. Listen to numerous primate vocalizations (the gibbon "songs" and howler "howls" are particularly cool), and view hundreds of images of primates stored in their fully searchable online slide collection.

2) Learn more about the 2007 slaughter of great apes that occurred in Virunga Volcanoes Conservation Area. Use an internet search engine to discover articles written about the disaster.

INFOTRAC

1) In *InfoTrac* do a keyword search on "primate extinction." Read a couple of articles and summarize what is currently being done to prevent specific species of endangered primates from going extinct.

CONCEPT APPLICATION

Fill in the 19 numbered blanks in the simplified primate taxonomy below with the 19 lettered choices provided.

A. ischial callosities	K. stereoscopic vision and prehensility
B. species include *troglodytes* and *paniscus*	L. dental comb shared with lorises
C. reliance on olfaction more than other primates	M. bigger, brainier than prosimians
D. largest eyes among the primates	N. language, reliance on culture
E. acrobatic ape brachiators	O. means "flat-nosed"
F. not nearly as ferocious as popularly perceived	P. suspensory locomotion
G. all have a 2-1-2-3 dental formula	Q. bipedalism
H. includes the galagos, or bushbabies	R. only found on Borneo and Sumatra
I. some can hang by their tails	S. tarsiers, monkeys, apes and humans
J. the great apes	

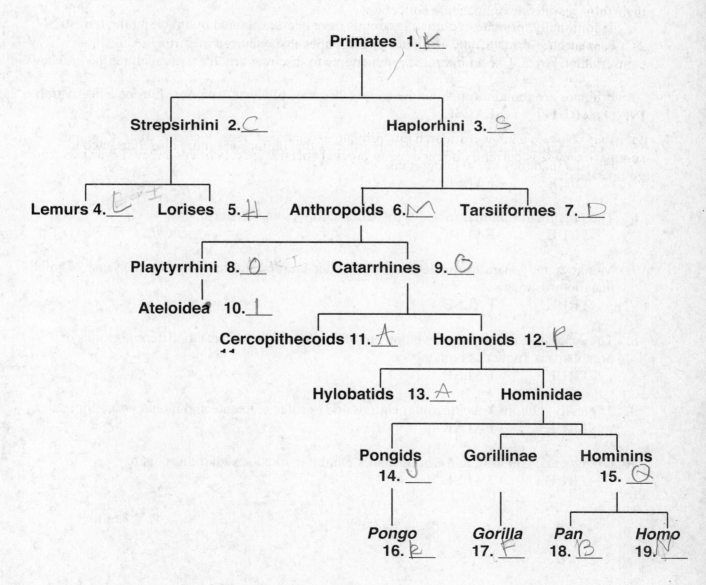

Primates 1. K

Strepsirhini 2. C   Haplorhini 3. S

Lemurs 4. L or I   Lorises 5. H   Anthropoids 6. M   Tarsiiformes 7. D

Playtyrrhini 8. O or I   Catarrhines 9. G

Ateloidea 10. I

Cercopithecoids 11. A   Hominoids 12. P

Hylobatids 13. A   Hominidae

Pongids 14. J   Gorillinae   Hominins 15. Q

Pongo 16. R   Gorilla 17. F   Pan 18. B   Homo 19. N

109

Now answer the True/False, Multiple Choice and Short Answer sample test questions. Following completion of the tests, correct them with the answers and textbook page references at the end of this Study Guide chapter. Note the areas in which you are strong and weak to guide you in your studying. Finally, answer the sample Essay Questions.

TRUE/FALSE QUESTIONS

If false, consider what modification would make the statement true.

1. Compared to most mammals, primates are quite specialized.
   TRUE   **FALSE**

2. Primates are characterized by binocular (overlapping) vision and stereoscopic vision (depth perception).
   TRUE   **FALSE**

3. Traditionally, primate evolutionary trends have been explained by invoking the terrestrial adaptation -- primates are adapted to a life on the ground.
   TRUE   **FALSE**

4. Primates are found throughout the temperate zones of North America, Europe and Australia.
   TRUE   **FALSE**

5. Genetic and biochemical analyses have shown that chimps are more closely related to humans than they are to orangutans.
   TRUE   **FALSE**

6. The prosimian suborder includes the lemurs, lorises and tarsiers.
   TRUE   **FALSE**

7. Monkeys are generally smaller-bodied, smaller-brained and rely more on the sense of smell than do prosimians.
   TRUE   **FALSE**

8. The separate evolutionary development of similar characteristics in different groups of organisms is known as homoplasy.
   TRUE   **FALSE**

9. Typically gibbons knuckle-walk, chimps and gorillas brachiate and monkeys are bipedal.
   TRUE   **FALSE**

10. Orangutans, Gibbons, and Chimpanzees exhibit marked sexual dimorphism.
    TRUE   **FALSE**

110

MULTIPLE CHOICE QUESTIONS

1. Which of the following is **not** an evolutionary trend of primates?
   A. Increasing reliance on the sense of smell.
   B. A tendency for most species to be active during the day, i.e. diurnal.
   C. A trend towards omnivory.
   D. A tendency to develop color vision.

2. Primate evolutionary trends developed because most primates
   A. spend their lives in the trees.
   B. spend their lives on the ground.
   C. eat meat.
   D. are bipedal.

3. Binocular vision in primates results in
   A. color vision.
   B. dichromatic vision.
   C. panoramic vision.
   D. stereoscopic vision.

4. The dental formula 2-1-2-3 corresponds to what order of teeth?
   A. molar, pre-molars, canines, incisors.
   B. premolars, incisors, molars, canines.
   C. canines, premolars, incisors, molars.
   D. incisors, canines, premolars, molars.

5. All Old World monkeys, apes and humans share which of the following features?
   A. tails
   B. 2-1-2-3 dental formula
   C. arms that are relatively longer than their legs
   D. all of the above

6. The tarsier has a dental formula of 2-1-3-3/1-1-3-3. How many incisors does a tarsier have?
   A. 2
   B. 3
   C. 4
   D. 6

7. On which of the following continents would you **not** find any non-human primates living in the wild?
   A. Australia
   B. Asia
   C. Africa
   D. South America

111

8. Which of the following statements is correct?
    A. Most apes are arboreal quadrupeds.
    B. Terrestrial quadrupeds generally have much longer arms compared to their legs.
    C. Brachiators have longer hind limbs than forelimbs.
    D. Prehensile tails are only found in some New World monkeys.

9. A form of locomotion found among some of the smaller lemurs and tarsiers is
    A. knuckle-walking.
    B. quadrupedalism.
    C. vertical clinging and leaping.
    D. bipedalism.

10. In what part of the world would you find a primate that has huge eyes, is exclusively carnivorous and is a spectacular clinger and leaper?
    A. South America.
    B. Africa.
    C. Madagascar.
    D. the islands of Southeast Asia.

11. In the traditional taxonomy, tarsiers are classified with the _____, since we now know that they share a more recent common ancestor with the _____.
    A. insectivores; rodents
    B. haplorhines; anthropoids
    C. New World monkeys; Old World monkeys
    D. gibbons; lemurs

12. Strepsirhini are considered to be the most primitive of the primates. What does "primitive" mean in evolutionary biology?
    A. anatomically more similar to the ancestor
    B. poorly adapted
    C. inferior
    D. evolved later in time

13. In which type of primate would you find a "dental comb?"
    A. Old World Monkey.
    B. New World Monkey.
    C. lemur.
    D. gibbon.

14. Lemurs are found exclusively in
    A. Borneo.
    B. India.
    C. Madagascar.
    D. Sri Lanka.

15. Why are lemurs so diverse compared to lorises?
    A. Lemurs evolved much earlier than did lorises.
    B. Lemurs were isolated from competition with higher primates.
    C. Lemurs are much more geographically widespread.
    D. Lemurs live exclusively on the ground.

16. Which of the following traits is/are characteristic of the ring-tailed lemur?
    A. dental comb
    B. post-orbital bar
    C. a rhinarium
    D. all of the above

17. Which of the following is **not** true of tarsiers?
    A. They are nocturnal.
    B. They are insectivorous.
    C. The live in large social groups.
    D. They can rotate their heads almost 180°.

18. Which of the following is **not** characteristic of anthropoids?
    A. a bony plate that encloses the orbit
    B. relatively shortened gestation period
    C. a relatively larger brain
    D. increased parental care

19. The only nocturnal anthropoid is the
    A. baboon.
    B. chimpanzee.
    C. howler monkey.
    D. owl monkey.

20. Which of the following is **not** true regarding New World monkeys?
    A. Some species have prehensile tails.
    B. Their nostrils face downward.
    C. Almost all species are arboreal.
    D. They include marmosets, spider monkeys and howler monkeys.

21. Which of the following structures are found in cercopithecines?
    A. ischial callosities
    B. prehensile tail
    C. claws
    D. dental comb

113

22. The term "sexual dimorphism" refers to
    A. differences in size and structure between males and females.
    B. differences in behavior between males and females.
    C. differences in reproductive physiology between males and females.
    D. parallel evolution between males and females of different species.

23. The period of sexual receptivity in non-human, female primates is called
    A. estrus.
    B. menarche.
    C. menstruation .
    D. hylobates.

24. New World monkeys and Old World monkeys have been geographically separated for a minimum of 30 million years, yet they are clearly recognizable as monkeys. This is an example of the evolutionary principle of
    A. reciprocal evolution.
    B. homoplasy.
    C. evolutionary reversal.
    D. Dollo's Law.

25. Which of the following hominoids demarcate their territories by sound?
    A. gibbons and siamangs.
    B. orangutans.
    C. gorillas.
    D. Humans.

26. A frugivore is standing in front of a vending machine. Which item will he select?
    A. Koala Brother's Eucalyptus Cough Drops.
    B. Rainbow Fruit Bar.
    C. Rigney's Chewing Gum.
    D. Rip Tyle's Chocolate-Covered Ants.

27. Which of the following statements are accurate in describing chimpanzees?
    A. They are exclusively insectivorous.
    B. They live in monogamous family units.
    C. They are almost always bipedal on the ground.
    D. They occasionally hunt and eat young monkeys.

28. In what way do bonobos differ from chimpanzees?
    A. They are more terrestrial than chimps.
    B. Their have relatively larger heads.
    C. Their legs are relatively longer.
    D. They have larger body sizes.

114

29. The prime-age male that dominates gorilla social groups is known as
    A. a redtail.
    B. a silverback.
    C. a blackback.
    D. the big Kahuna.

30. Which of the following statements regarding the comparison of human and chimpanzee DNA sequences is **not** true?
    A. Humans, genetically speaking, are most closely related to chimpanzees.
    B. Coded DNA sequences are 98.4% - 99.4% identical between humans and chimpanzees.
    C. DNA sequence differences range between 2.7% - 6.4%.
    D. It is estimated that chimanzee and human lineages diverged between 9 and 10 mya.

31. Which of the following is **not** a reason that many nonhuman primates are endangered?
    A. habitat destruction for logging, mining, and agriculture uses
    B. hunting for food and commercial products
    C. live capture for either the exotic pet trade or biomedical research
    D. establishment of biological reserves

32. In 1973, the implementation of what international agreement caused a dramatic decline in live capture of non-human primates?
    A. NASA
    B. OPFOR
    C. CITES
    D. UNESCO

SHORT ANSWER QUESTIONS (& PAGE REFERENCES)

1. Describe five features that can be used to distinguish primates from other mammals. (pp. 142-144)

2. Describe three different modes of primate locomotion. (pp. 150-151)

3. What do the coded primate DNA sequences that have been identified and studied tell us about chimp and human evolutionary relationships? (p. 153)

4. How do apes differ from monkeys? (pp. 156-162)

5. In what ways are chimps and gorillas similar? How do they differ? (pp. 164-167)

ESSAY QUESTIONS (& PAGE REFERENCES)

1. Compare and contrast the traditional arboreal hypothesis for the evolution of the primates to the visual predation hypothesis. (pp. 147-148)

2. Why do some primate taxonomists classify tarsiers as strepsirhines while others refer to them as haplorhines? (Figure 6.7, p. 152, and Appendix A)

3. What are the major challenges facing primate conservationists? What approaches to primate conservation appear to be the most promising? (pp. 169-175)

ANSWERS, *CORRECTED STATEMENT* IF FALSE & REFERENCES TO TRUE/FALSE QUESTIONS

1. **FALSE**, p. 141, Compared to most mammals, primates are considered generalized because they have retained several ancestral mammalian traits that many other mammals have lost over time

2. **TRUE**, p. 143

3. **FALSE**, p. 145, Traditionally, primate evolutionary trends have been explained by invoking the *arboreal* adaptation -- primates are adapted to a life *in the trees*.

4. **FALSE**, pp. 146-148, Primates are found throughout the *subtropical and tropical* zones of *South America, Africa and Asia.*

5. **TRUE**, p. 153

6. **TRUE**, pp. 152-153

7. **FALSE**, p. 156, Monkeys are generally *larger*-bodied, *larger*-brained and rely *less* on the sense of smell than do prosimians.

8. **TRUE**, p. 162

9. **FALSE**, pp. 162, 165, 169, Typically gibbons *brachiate*, chimps and gorillas *knuckle-walk* and *humans* are bipedal.

10. **FALSE**, pp. 163-167, Orangutans and gorillas exhibit marked sexual dimorphism while chimpanzees are less sexually dimorphic in comparison.

ANSWERS & REFERENCES TO MULTIPLE CHOICE QUESTIONS

1. **A**, p. 142		17. **C**, p.156
2. **A**, pp. 145-146		18. **B**, pp. 156-157
3. **D**, p. 143		19. **D**, p. 162
4. **D**, p. 149		20. **B**, p. 159
5. **B**, p. 149		21. **A**, p. 160
6. **D**, p. 156		22. **A**, p. 160
7. **A**, pp. 146-148		23. **A**, pp. 160-161
8. **D**, pp. 150-151		24. **B**, p. 162
9. **C**, p. 151		25. **A**, pp. 162-163

10. **D**, p. 156	26. **B**, p. 164
11. **B**, p. 156	27. **D**, p. 167
12. **A**, p. 153	28. **C**, p. 168
13. **C**, p. 154	29. **B**, p. 165
14. **C**, p. 154	30. **D**, p. 153
15. **B**, p. 154	31. **D**, pp. 169-175
16. **D**, pp. 144-145	32. **C**, p. 171

CONCEPT APPLICATION SOLUTION

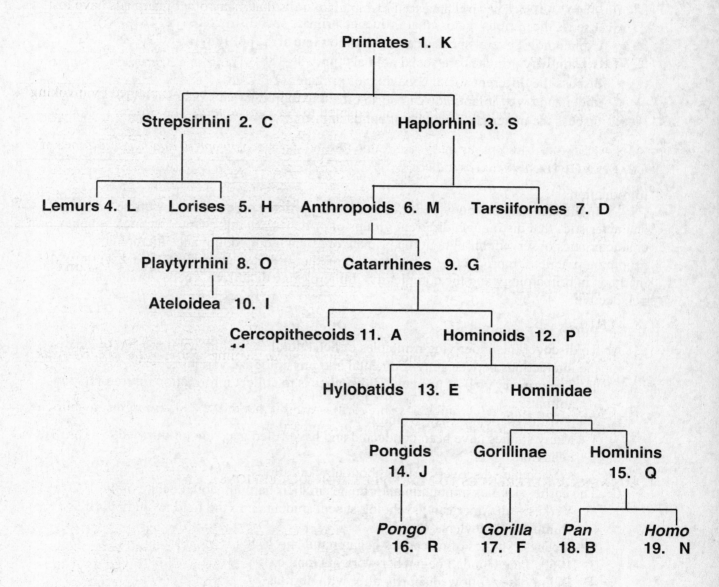

Primates 1. K

Strepsirhini 2. C   Haplorhini 3. S

Lemurs 4. L   Lorises 5. H   Anthropoids 6. M   Tarsiiformes 7. D

Playtyrrhini 8. O   Catarrhines 9. G

Ateloidea 10. I

Cercopithecoids 11. A   Hominoids 12. P

Hylobatids 13. E   Hominidae

Pongids 14. J   Gorillinae   Hominins 15. Q

Pongo 16. R   *Gorilla* 17. F   *Pan* 18. B   *Homo* 19. N

117

CHAPTER 7
PRIMATE BEHAVIOR

LEARNING OBJECTIVES

After reading this chapter you should be able to:
- understand why anthropologists study nonhuman primate behavior (pp. 179-180)
- understand the importance of behavioral ecology in explaining the evolution of primate behavior (pp. 180-181)
- discuss the various factors that influence primate social structure (pp. 181-185)
- explain how several species can live in the same area (pp. 185-186)
- explain why primates are social animals (pp. 186-188)
- discuss the different social behaviors of primates (188-195)
- understand why infanticide can be an effective reproductive strategy (pp. 197-199)
- discuss the maternal and paternal bonds in primate societies (pp. 199-201)

CHAPTER OUTLINE

Introduction

In the last chapter you were introduced to the primate order and some of the biological characteristics that distinguish different groups of primates. In this chapter we look at behavioral characteristics observed throughout the primate order including dominance hierarchies, grooming practices, reproductive strategies and mother-infant relationships. We discuss field methods in primatology and the complexity of interpreting data from a behavioral ecology perspective.

I   PRIMATE FIELD STUDIES
A.   To discover the underlying principles of behavioral evolution, we first need to identify the interactions between environmental and physiological variables.
   1.   The primary goal of primate field studies is to collect information on free-ranging animals.
B.   Wild primates are not easy to study.
   1.   Many studies have been conducted and have filled gaps in our knowledge of primate behaviors
      a. Each new discovery brings about new questions.
C.   The earliest studies of nonhuman primates in their natural habitat began in the 1920s.
   1.   Yerkes – an American psychologist sent students into the field to study gorillas, chimps, and howlers.
   2.   Japanese studies of macaques beganin the late 1940s.
   3.   1960s Jane Goodall began her work at Gombe.
   4.   Dian Fossey followed shortly after with gorillas.
   5.   Birute Galdikas also began research on orangutans in Borneo.
   6.   These initial studies were largely descriptive.
D.   Some early studies of baboons related aspects of social structure and individual behavior to ecological factors.

118

1. Most early work emphasized male behavior.
2. In the 1970s and 1980s attention focused on females and their influence on the group.

E. Currently, primate studies focus on social behaviors.
1. aim to discern the costs and benefits of group living,
2. and to recognize the advantages and disadvantages of specific behaviors to individuals.

F. Behavioral research is done within an evolutionary framework.
1. Recently, genetic techniques have been applied to behavioral questions as well.

II THE EVOLUTION OF BEHAVIOR

A. Scientists study primate behavior from within an ecological and evolutionary framework.
1. They focus on the relationship between behavior (group and individual), the natural environment, and various physiological traits of the species under investigation.
2. This approach is known as behavioral ecology.
3. Behaviors are environmental adaptations.

B. Behavioral ecology looks at the evolution of behavior through natural selection
1. Behavioral ecology views behavior as a phenotypic expression.
2. Individuals whose behavioral phenotypes increase reproductive fitness will pass on their genes at a faster rate than others.

C. A criticism of this approach is the idea that a specific behavior is the result of a single gene.
1. Nor does it suggest that behaviors that are influenced by genes can't be modified through learning.

D. Among insects and lower vertebrates behavioral patterns are largely under genetic control.
1. Among primates and humans most behavior results from learning.
2. In higher organisms some behaviors are influenced by gene products, such as hormones.
3. Increased levels of testosterone have been shown to increase aggressive behavior in many non-human species.

E. Behavioral genetics is the study of how genes influence behavior.
1. This is a relatively new field and we currently are not sure of how much influence genes have on the behavior of primates.
2. Behavior is a highly complex trait and is the product of interactions between genetic and environmental factors.
3. There is considerable variation in behavioral plasticity between species.
4. The behavioral limits and potentials of species are set by genes, ecological settings, and evolutionary history.

F. Today one of primatology's major goals is determining how behaviors influence reproductive fitness and how ecological factors have influenced behaviors.

G. Some factors that influence social structure:
1. Body size
   a. Body sizes range from 2.5 oz. (mouse lemur) to 260 lbs (male gorilla)
   b. Larger animals require relatively less food than smaller animals because they have a smaller surface area to mass ratio.

2. Basal metabolic rate (BMR)
   a. BMR is the rate at which energy is used by the body at rest to maintain all bodily functions.
   b. The BMR is closely tied to body size: larger animals have relatively slower metabolisms than smaller ones and therefore need relatively less energy.
   c. Smaller primates (with higher BMR) require higher energy foods while larger ones can subsist on lower quality leaf and pith.
3. Diet
   a. Primatologists studying the relationship between diet and behavior consider the benefits in terms of energy (calories) against the costs (energy expended) of obtaining and digesting food items.
   b. While most primates eat a wide variety of foods they tend to focus on some foods over others
      i)   Small-bodied primates focus on high-energy foods.
      ii) Large-bodied species don't necessarily need to.
   c. Some colobine monkeys (OWM) have evolved specializations of the gut to aid their digestion of leaf.
   d. A duplicated gene in two langur species (OWM) has been identified that produced an enzyme that helps digestion of leaf.
4. Distribution of resources
   a. Different primate food sources are distributed in various ways.
   b. Leaves can be abundant and found throughout the forest and can support large groups.
   c. Fruits and nuts are seasonally available and occur in patches.
   d. The availability of food resources impacts the size of feeding groups.
   e. The distribution of water also impacts primate groups.
5. Predation
   a. Primates are vulnerable to many types of predators.
   b. Primate responses depend upon body size, social structure and predator type.
   c. Predation pressure influences group size
      i)   Among small bodied primates, if predation pressure is high large groups are advantageous.
6. Relationships with other, non-predatory species
   a. Many primates associate with other primate and non-primate species.
   b. These groupings may aid in predator avoidance.
   c. In habitats where multiple primate species reside, the primates will exploit different resources.
7. Dispersal
   a. Among most mammal species, members of one sex leave the natal (birth) group around the time they reach sexual maturity.
   b. This influences many facets of primate life.
   c. One common theme in dispersal is that those individuals who leave usually find mates outside their natal group.
   d. Two possible explanations for dispersal are
      i)   reduced competition for mates and
      ii) decreased likelihood of close inbreeding.

120

    e. The philopatric sex remains in their natal group.
        i)   Males tend to leave their natal groups more than females.
    f. Philopatry is beneficial as it enables some to form close, long-term relationships with kin of the same sex and to get to know group members very well.
    g. This would have selected for increased social intelligence over time in primate evolution.

8. Life histories
    a. Life history traits typify developmental stages of a given species and influence potential reproductive rates.
    b. These traits have important influences on primate social life and structure.

9. Strategies
    a. Strategies are behaviors that increase individual reproductive fitness.
        i)   They can influence group dynamics.
    b. These strategies are products of natural selection.
        i)   No conscious planning or motivation on the animal's part is implied.

10. Distribution and types of sleeping sites
    a. Most primates sleep in trees and their nesting distribution reflects both social structure and predator avoidance.

11. Activity patterns
    a. Almost all anthropoids are diurnal but many prosimians are nocturnal.

12. Human activities
    a. Virtually all wild non-human primate groups are influenced in one way or another by human activity.

13. Types of Nonhuman Primate Social Groups
    a. A Closer Look (p. 184).
    b. Primatologists observing groupings of primates have noted the predominance of five major forms of social organization.
        i)   One male (unimale), multifemale group
        ii)   Multimale and multifemale group
        iii)   Monogamous pair
        iv)   Polyandry
        v)   Solitary

III   SYMPATRIC SPECIES

A. Sympatric species are different species that occupy the same areas.
    1. Strategies allow for a way to maximize access to resources (i.e. food) while reducing competition between species.

B. Five monkey species have been studied in detail in the Kibale Forest of western Uganda.
    1. Species studied: black-and-white colobus, red colobus, mangabey, blue monkey, redtail monkey.
    2. Species differ in overall size, behavior, and food choices.
        a. This reduced competition for resources.
    3. Primate species are exceedingly flexible regarding group composition.
    4. Omnivores move about more and are more spatially dispersed than folivores.
    5. Omnivores have an indirect relationship between body size and group size and a direct relationship between body size and homerange size.

6. Female sexual swelling exists in those species that live in multimale multifemale groups.
7. Feeding, spacing, group residence, dispersal, and reproductive strategies (see p. 195) may differ between males and females of the same species.

IV   **WHY BE SOCIAL?**
   A. The majority of primates reside in groups.
   B. Although group living exposes members to competition for resources there must be advantages over not living alone.
   C. Likely predator avoidance is a major factor in why primates live in groups.
     1. Multimale-multifemale groups (larger in size) are advantageous in areas where predation is high.
       a. increased chances of seeing and escaping predators.
   D. Polyspecific associations also reduce predation by gathering different species together and sharing defense and detection of predators.
   E. Another explanation of primate sociality is that larger social groups can outcompete smaller groups of conspecifics (same species).

V   **PRIMATE SOCIAL BEHAVIOR**
   A. There are several well documented strategies that serve to maintain group cohesion.
   B. Dominance
     1. Dominance hierarchies impose a degree of order within the group.
     2. Dominant animals have priority access to resources (e.g. food and mates) and dominate inferior individuals.
     3. Many primatologists think that the primary benefit of dominance is increased reproductive success of high-ranking males and females.
       a. Not true in all cases as lower-ranking males sometimes mate successfully.
         i) Among male orangutans arrested development of secondary sex characteristics reduced competition with adult males.
     4. Increased reproductive success is also postulated for high-ranking females.
     5. An individual's rank is not permanent and can change throughout life.
       a. One's status is dependent upon many factors which may include some of the following:
         i) sex, age, level of aggression, time spent in group, intelligence, motivation and mother's social position.
         ii) Status is learned.
     6. Gestures and behaviors are used to indicate dominance and subordination.
     7. Young primates learn how to negotiate through social interactions by early contact with their mother and exposure to their peers' behavior.
   C. Communication
     1. All animals are capable of expression (i.e. communication) via a range of means that include olfactory, gestural, behavioral, or vocal.
     2. Communication is a necessary component of group living.
     3. Communication may be intentional or unintentional (autonomic).
       a. Examples of autonomic communication include body posture, raised body hair or enhanced body odor.

      b. Examples of intentional communication include Facial expressions, vocalizations, intense staring and branch shaking.

   4. A full range of emotions are communicated between primates.

      a. Threat gestures might include a quick yawn to expose canines or bobbing back and forth in a crouched position.

      b. Submission is indicated by a crouched position or by presenting the hindquarters.

      c. Reassurance can take the form of touching, patting, hugging or holding hands.

      d. Grooming serves to indicate submission or reassurance also.

      e. Play face is associated with play and the fear grin indicates fear and submission.

      f. Vocalizations are used to inform others that predators may be present or that food is present.

      g. Displays serve to communicate emotional states.

      h. Mounting is used to express dominance and is a ritualized behavior (an exaggerated display)

   5. Communication is learned.

      a. Think about the use of body language and/or gestures in your non verbal communication.

  D. Aggressive and affiliative interactions

   1. Affiliative interactions promote group cohesion.

      a. Affiliative behaviors reduce levels of aggression.

      b. Most affiliative behaviors involve physical contact.

   2. Aggressive interactions can lead to group disruption.

      a. Conflict within a group is often caused by competition for resources, such as mating partners or food.

      b. Conflicts may not always be resolved peacefully.

   3. A certain amount of aggression can also serve to maintain order in a population.

   4. Conflict resolution through reconciliation is important for primates.

   5. Common affiliative behaviors

      a. Reconciliation, consolation, simple amicable interactions between friends and relatives.

   6. Grooming is one of the most important affiliative behaviors among primates.

      a. Grooming is hygienic and pleasurable and has been observed in a variety of contexts.

      b. For example, mothers may groom infants, males may groom females (and vice versa), subordinates can groom dominants, and friends might groom friends.

   7. Reconciliation takes a number of forms

      a. Hugging, kissing, grooming.

   8. Primates may form alliances and coalitions

      a. These bonds may last a lifetime and are an important component of primate social life.

VI REPRODUCTION AND REPRODUCTIVE STRATEGIES

  A. As in most mammalian species, female primates are sexually receptive at certain hormonally dictated intervals.

   1. Females are sexually receptive (i.e. fertile) only when they are in estrus

   2. Visual cues to a female's sexual readiness include swelling and changes in color of the skin around the genital area.

123

B. Permanent bonding between males and females is uncommon among non-human primates.
   1. In some species, temporary relationships for mating purposes (consortships) have been observed.
      a. Seen in savanna baboons and chimpanzees.
      b. Male and female bonobos may mate even when the female is not in estrus.
   2. Such behavior may increase the reproductive success of both parties.
      a. The female also gains care and protection from the consort male.
C. Reproductive strategies
   1. The goal of both sexes is to produce and rear to adulthood as many offspring as possible.
      a. K-selection refers to the production of a few young with a large investment of parental care.
      b. r-selection refers to the production of many offspring with little parental care.
   2. Primates are among the most K-selected mammals.
      a. Enormous investment is necessary to raise a primate as they develop slowly.
      b. The mother generally carries most of the burden both before and after birth.
   3. Finding food and mates, avoiding predators, and caring for and protecting young are difficult.
   4. Males and females employ different strategies to meet these challenges.
   5. Metabolic demands on females due to pregnancy, lactation and dependent care are enormous.
   6. The best strategy for females is to maximize available resources
      a. They aggressively protect food resources and territories.
   7. It is to the advantage of the male to secure as many mates and produce as many offspring as possible.
D. Sexual selection
   1. Darwin described a type of natural selection that operates on one sex of a species.
   2. Male competition for mates or mate choice by females is the selective agent.
      a. One of the best recognized example is the brightly colored male peacock.
         i) Female birds frequently select males with vividly colored plumage.
         ii) Selection has thus increased the frequency of the alleles that influence color in those species.
      b. Sexual selection in primates is most apparent in polygynous groups due to greater competition between males for mates.
      c. Such selection has led to numerous dimorphic traits such as body size, canine size, etc.
         i) Males of many primate species are larger than females and have larger canines.
         ii) Species that live in pairs exhibit little to no sexual dimorphism.
   3. The degree and type of sexual dimorphism can be indicative of the social structure of the group.
E. Infanticide as a reproductive strategy?
   1. Infanticide (killing of infants) has been observed in several primate species.
      a. Redtail monkey, red colobus, blue monkey, savanna baboon, howler, orangutans, gorillas, and chimpanzees.

2. This may seem counterproductive for the species as a whole but individuals seek to maximize their own fitness not the fitness of the group.
3. It is associated with the take over of a social group by a new male.
4. As studied among the Hanuman langur monkeys, a newly dominant male will often attempt to kill the nursing infants in the group.
5. If the infanticidal male is successful, the mother who just lost her infant ceases to lactate and becomes sexually receptive within 2-3 months.
6. This system benefits the infanticidal male because he does not have to wait for the females to wean their offspring.
    a. If he did wait, he would be unlikely to sire any offspring because male tenure in harems is only 2-3 years and he would be supplanted before any of his offspring were weaned.
    b. If he was supplanted by an infanticidal male, he would likely not contribute any genes to the next generation because all of his offspring would be at risk of attack from the new male.
7. Alternate hypotheses for these observations have been promoted.
    a. These include competition for resources, aberrant behavior caused by human overcrowding, and inadvertent death by conflict.
8. However, recent studies of the behavior of chacma baboons and DNA from Hanuman langurs independently support the infanticide explanation.

VII MOTHERS, FATHERS, AND INFANTS

A. The basic social unit among all primates is the female and her dependent offspring.
    1. Except in those species in which monogamy or polyandry occurs, males do not participate in rearing offspring.
B. Mother-infant bond
    1. There appear to be innate factors that predispose a female to care for her infant.
    2. This is in part learned, so it requires that she (the mother) was raised normally as an infant.
C. Monkeys and apes raised with no mother don't know how to care for an infant.
    1. This was demonstrated by the famous Harlow experiments
        a. Those raised with a cloth covered surrogate mother formed attachments.
        b. Those raised with no mother were incapable of forming lasting attachments with other monkeys.
D. Monkeys reared in isolation were denied opportunities to learn the rules of social and maternal behavior.
E. Field work also supports the importance of mother-infant bonding.
F. In some monogamous and polyandrous species adult males are involved in the care of offspring.
G. Alloparenting is a term used for the parent like behavior of individuals whom are not the parent of the infant.
        a. Alloparenting is beneficial as it increases the potential for adoption of the young if their mother dies and also provides training for young females for motherhood.

KEY TERMS

affiliative: friendly relations between individuals.

agonistic: aggressive or defensive social interactions.

alloparenting: individuals other than the parents take care of infants.

autonomic: involuntary physiological responses.

behavior: any organismal response to a stimulus.

behavioral ecology: the study of the evolution of behavior, emphasizing the role of ecological factors as agents of natural selection.

communication: any act that conveys information to another individual.

consortships: temporary relationship between one adult male and an estrous female.

conspecifics: members of the same species.

core areas: a portion of a home range where reliable resources are found such as food, water and sleeping trees.

dispersal: members of one sex leave the natal group at puberty.

displays: physical movements that convey an emotional state.

diurnal: active during the day.

dominance hierarchies: systems of social organization wherein individuals are ranked relative to one another based on priority access to food and sex.

ecological: the relationship between organisms and all aspects of their environment.

estrus: period of sexual receptivity in female mammals (except humans) correlated with ovulation.

free-ranging: non-captive animals living in their natural habitat.

grooming: picking through fur to remove dirt, parasites or any other material that may be present.

home-range: the geographic area, usually permanent, exploited by an animal or social group for food, water and sleeping areas.

inclusive fitness: the total contribution of an individual's genes to the next generation, including those genes shared by close relatives.

infanticide: the killing of infants.

K-selected: a reproductive strategy wherein the individuals produce fewer offspring but increase parental investment of care, time and energy.

life history traits (or strategies): characteristics of developmental stages that influence reproductive rates.

matrilines: groupings of females who are all descendants of one female.

metabolism: chemical processes at the cellular level that release energy from nutrients for the body to use.

monogamous pair: a mated pair and its young.

natal group: the group in which an individual is born.

nocturnal: active at night.

philopatric: remaining in one's natal group or home range as an adult.

physiology: the physical and chemical phenomena involved with the functions and activities of an organism or any of its various parts

plasticity: capacity to change.

polyandry: one female with multiple males.

presenting: a subordinate animal presents his/her rear to a dominant animal.

126

reproductive strategies: behavioral patterns that contribute to an individual's reproductive success, i.e., producing and successfully rearing to adulthood as many offspring as possible.

ritualized behaviors: behaviors removed from their original context and sometimes exaggerated to convey information.

r-selected: a reproductive strategy wherein individuals produce many offspring and provide relatively little parental investment of care, time and energy.

sexual dimorphism: physical differences between males and females of a single species. This is most commonly associated with an overall difference in size.

sexual selection: a type of natural selection operating on one sex. It may be the result of males competing for mates or female preference in choosing sexual partners.

social grooming: grooming done for pleasure. Common among primates and reinforces social relationships.

social structure: the composition, size and sex ratio of a group of animals.

strategies: behaviors favored by natural selection that increase individual reproductive success.

sympatric: two or more species who live in the same area.

territory: the part of the home range that animals will defend.

MEDIA EXERCISES

1) Are you interested in a potential career in primatology? Primate Info Net, the excellent web site you visited last chapter (http://pin.primate.wisc.edu/index.html), has contributions from professionals in the field discussing what it takes to forge a career studying primates. Read what Dr. Kevin Hunt (Indiana University) has written concerning field research in primatology (http://pin.primate.wisc.edu/edu/careers/hunt.html) or what Helena Fitch-Snyder of the Zoological Society of San Diego's Center for the Reproduction of Endangered Species (CRES) has to say about zoo careers (http://pin.primate.wisc.edu/edu/careers/fitch.html).

2) Primate Info Net also has a comprehensive list of resources concerning primate behavior and ecology (http://pin.primate.wisc.edu/aboutp/behavior/index.html). Browse through the categories listed and click on a few of the hyperlinks under "Social Behavior" to learn more about non-human primate behavior from the researchers themselves.

3) Consider exploring the internet for video footage of primate culture. Recent documentation of monkey culture has been observed in South America. See if you can find evidence of primate culture.

4) Consider the practice of primate observation. Much of what we know of primates has been learned by the scientific study of primates: observations conducted over extended periods of time. Think about the use of the scientific method to investigate an aspect of primate behavior. Take an online visit to the wonderful Primate Info Net hosted by the Wisconsin Regional Primate Research Center of the University of Wisconsin – Madison. (http://pin.primate.wisc.edu/callicam/observing.html) Review the information on primate observation and then click on the link to the *callicam* and begin your own observation. Identify a primate by his/her specimen number and follow it for a period of time. How does it interact with others? How does it move about the enclosure?

CONCEPT APPLICATION

You are a primatologist who has just been awarded a grant to study a newly discovered monkey (*Colobus azures*) living in equatorial Africa. Before you leave for the field, you need to decide on what you want to learn in the six months that you plan to stay in the jungle. Based on the reading in your chapter, outline at least four different questions about this new primate that you wish to answer. To get you started, here is the first question.

> *I. Interspecies interactions:*
> *A. What other species are located in the same field site as the Colobus azures?*
> *1. Do the other species interact with C. azures?*
> *2. Are the other primate species predators of C. azures?*

Now answer the True/False, Multiple Choice and Short Answer sample test questions. Following completion of the tests, correct them with the answers and textbook page references at the end of this Study Guide chapter. Note the areas in which you are strong and weak to guide you in your studying. Finally, answer the sample Essay Questions.

TRUE/FALSE QUESTIONS

If false, consider what modification would make the statement true.

1. The primary goal of primate field studies is to collect information on captive animals that are generally influenced by human activity.
   TRUE   **FALSE**

2. The study of the evolution of behavior, emphasizing the role of ecological factors as agents of natural selection is known as behavioral ecology.
   TRUE   **FALSE**

3. Infanticide by Hanuman langur males may increase their chances of successfully reproducing.
   TRUE   **FALSE**

4. The sex that transfers out of its natal group is known as the philopatric sex. In most primate species the philopatric sex is male.
   TRUE   **FALSE**

5. Many (but not all) primatologists postulate that the primary benefit of dominance is the increased reproductive success of the individual.
   TRUE   **FALSE**

6. Aggressive interactions pertain to amicable associations between individuals. Aggressive behaviors, such as grooming, reinforce social bonds and promote group cohesion.
   TRUE   **FALSE**

128

7. Behaviors that are removed from their original context and sometimes exaggerated to covey information are known as ritualized behaviors.

   TRUE   FALSE

8. In most primate species, sexual behavior is not tied to the female's reproductive cycle, with females sexually receptive to males at any time throughout the cycle.

   TRUE   FALSE

9. R-selection is a type of natural selection that operates only on one sex within a species and results from competition for mates.

   TRUE   FALSE

10. Alloparenting is a common behavior in many primate species in which individuals other that the parent(s) hold, carry and interact with infants.

    TRUE   FALSE

MULTIPLE CHOICE QUESTIONS

1. Jane Goodall is renowned for her field study of
   A. mountain gorillas in Rwanda.
   B. lemurs in Madagascar.
   C. chimpanzees in Tanzania.
   D. orangutans in Borneo.

2. Studies of free-ranging primates
   A. in their natural habitats has become a focus of anthropology.
   B. is generally very challenging because most are arboreal and can move swiftly through dense vegetation.
   C. are not necessarily uninfluenced by human activities.
   D. all of the above

3. Characteristics or developmental stages that influence reproductive rates of individuals are
   A. dominance hierarchies.
   B. life history traits.
   C. K-selected.
   D. polyandrous.

4. Among primates, _____ can be viewed as adaptive responses to environmental demands.
   A. behaviors
   B. blood types
   C. dental formulas
   D. all of the above

5. One of the underlying assumptions of behavioral ecology is that
    A. intelligent organisms can manipulate their environment.
    B. the various components of ecological systems evolved together.
    C. social structures are completely independent of ecological structures.
    D. the distribution of sleeping sites determines a species activity pattern.

6. The social structure of a given primate species is influenced by
    A. distribution of food resources.
    B. the types of predators inhabiting the environment.
    C. relationships with other sympatric primate species.
    D. all of the above

7. Where predation pressure is high we generally find group composition to be
    A. multimale/multifemale.
    B. one male harem.
    C. polyandrous.
    D. solitary.

8. Savannah baboons are an excellent example of
    A. monogamous pair social structure.
    B. solitary social structure.
    C. multimale/multifemale social structure.
    D. one male harem social structure.

9. The excellent example of a solitary, insectivorous, nocturnal forager is the
    A. loris.
    B. Diana monkey.
    C. gibbon.
    D. all of the above

10. The detailed study of monkeys in the Kibale Forest of Uganda reveals that
    A. colobus, mangabeys and red-tailed monkeys all follow a similar pattern in exploiting the environment.
    B. all monkeys eat the same foods.
    C. male and female reproductive strategies are identical.
    D. there is little correlation between social organization and feeding strategies.

11. The sympatric species studied in the Kibale Forest of Uganda
    A. differ with regard to anatomy.
    B. differ with regard to behavior.
    C. differ with regard to dietary preference.
    D. all of the above

12. In the Kibale study
    A. omnivores are more mobile than folivores.
    B. the smallest omnivores live in the smallest groups.
    C. omnivore population density is greater than that for folivores.
    D. all of the above

13. A primate's basal metabolic rate and diet are both greatly influenced by the animal's
    A. position in their group's dominance hierarchy.
    B. vulnerability to predation.
    C. body size.
    D. home range.

14. Unlike in primates, the behavior of insects is
    A. primarily innate.
    B. learned.
    C. culturally transmitted.
    D. none of the above

15. In primates, we know that behavior must be viewed as a product of
    A. complex interactions between genetic and environmental factors.
    B. the long-term evolution of instinct.
    C. only learned behaviors passed from generation to generation.
    D. all of the above.

16. Among non-human primates a polyandrous social group would include
    A. one female with two males
    B. one male with one female
    C. one male with two females
    D. none of the above

17. Which of the following do **not** prey on primates?
    A. Bears
    B. Eagles
    C. Humans
    D. Other primates

18. Group living in primates
    A. increases protection from predators.
    B. increases the ability to compete for resources with conspecific groups.
    C. increases protection against infanticidal males.
    D. all of the above.

19. The philopatric sex
    A. does not reproduce.
    B. protects the group from predators
    C. remains in the natal group.
    D. transfers out of the natal group.

20. Dispersal in primate behavior refers to
    A. food distribution in the home range.
    B. the manner in which males and females exploit the environment.
    C. spreading seeds to germinate.
    D. one sex leaving the natal group.

21. Dominance hierarchies
    A. increase aggression and fighting within a group.
    B. have no apparent function in social groups.
    C. provide a degree of order in social groups.
    D. are limited to adult males.

22. Dominance hierarchies
    A. likely give dominant males and females a reproductive advantage.
    B. do not result in dominant females having priority access to food.
    C. are found only in monogamous and solitary primates.
    D. are permanent and inflexible.

23. Unintentional modes of communication among primates (including humans) might include
    A. enhanced body odor ("fear sweat").
    B. raised body hair ("goose bumps").
    C. body posture.
    D. all of the above.

24. Which of the following is not a threat gesture among nonhuman primates?
    A. a quick yawn to expose canines
    B. an intense stare
    C. bobbing back and forth
    D. mounting

25. Displays
    A. communicate an emotional state.
    B. reassure others in the group.
    C. console others.
    D. all of the above

26. Affiliative behaviors
    A. are amicable associations between individuals.
    B. defuse potentially dangerous situations.
    C. promote group cohesiveness.
    D. all of the above

27. Grooming
    A. rarely occurs in primate social groups.
    B. often causes aggression between primate individuals.
    C. is only a hygienic activity.
    D. none of the above

28. Primate reproductive strategies (compared to other mammals)
    A. are similar for males and females.
    B. are K-selected.
    C. are r-selected.
    D. none of the above

29. Sexual selection
    A. is a type of natural selection.
    B. operates on only one sex.
    C. is the result of competition for mates.
    D. all of the above

30. Which of the following does **not** need to be demonstrated before the behavioral ecological explanation for infanticide in primates is accepted?
    A. Infanticidal males do not kill their own offspring.
    B. Infanticidal males are larger than non-infanticidal males.
    C. Infanticidal males mate with the female whose offspring he killed and fathers her infant.
    D. None of the above.

31. In which of the following species do males intervene on behalf of their own offspring significantly more often than they would for unrelated juveniles during disputes?
    A. gibbons
    B. marmosets
    C. savanna baboons
    D. tamarins

32. Mothering among primates appears to be
    A. completely innate.
    B. of minor importance in the development of offspring.
    C. dependent on a normal experience with one's own mother.
    D. all of the above

133

33. Alloparenting
   A. is not as common in primates as in other mammals.
   B. may help young females train for motherhood.
   C. does not often occur since female primates are extremely possessive of their offspring.
   D. is the adoption of an orphan primate by a female of another primate species.

SHORT ANSWER QUESTIONS (& PAGE REFERENCES)

1. What are the goals of primate field studies? (pp. 179-180)

2. Describe three different kinds of primate social groups. ("A Closer Look," p. 184)

3. What is the difference between autonomic and deliberate forms of primate communication? (pp. 190-192)

4. What are the various functions of grooming in primate societies? (pp. 190, 194-195)

5. Explain the difference between K-selection and r-selection. (p. 196)

ESSAY QUESTIONS (& PAGE REFERENCES)

1. Why is the field of behavioral ecology particularly well-suited to study primate behavior? (pp. 180-181)

2. How are dominance hierarchies in primates organized and what functions do they serve for individuals and primate groups? (pp. 188-190)

3. How and why do male and female reproductive strategies differ? (pp. 195-199)

ANSWERS, *CORRECTED STATEMENT* IF FALSE & REFERENCES TO TRUE/FALSE QUESTIONS

1. **FALSE**, p. 179, The primary goal of primate field studies is to collect information on *free-ranging* animals that are generally *uninfluenced* by human activity.

2. **TRUE**, p. 180.

3. **TRUE**, p. 197.

4. **FALSE**, pp. 183-184, The sex that *remains in* its natal group is known as the philopatric sex. In most primate species the philopatric sex is *female*.

5. **TRUE**, p. 189

6. **FALSE**, p. 194, *Affiliative* interactions pertain to amicable associations between individuals. *Affiliative* behaviors, such as grooming, reinforce social bonds and promote group cohesion.

7. **TRUE**, p. 192

8. **FALSE**, p. 195, In most primate species, sexual behavior is ~~not~~ tied to the female's reproductive cycle, with females sexually receptive to males *only when they are in estrus*.

9. **FALSE**, p. 196, *Sexual selection* is a type of natural selection that operates only on one sex within a species and results from competition for mates.

10. **TRUE**, p. 201

ANSWERS AND REFERENCES TO MULTIPLE CHOICE QUESTIONS

1. **C**, p. 179	10. **D**, pp. 185-186	19. **C**, p. 183	28. **B**, p. 196
2. **D**, pp. 179-180	11. **D**, p. 186	20. **D**, p. 183	29. **D**, p. 196
3. **B**, p. 184	12. **A**, p. 186	21. **C**, p. 188	30. **B**, p. 198
4. **A**, p. 188	13. **C**, p. 182	22. **A**, p. 189	31. **C**, p. 201
5. **B**, p. 180	14. **A**, p. 180	23. **D**, p. 190	32. **C**, p. 199
6. **D**, pp. 182-185	15. **A**, p. 180	24. **D**, p. 190	33. **B**, p. 201
7. **A**, p. 183	16. **A**, pp. 184, 199	25. **A**, p. 191	29. **D**, p. 196
8. **C**, pp. 186-187	17. **A**, p. 183	26. **D**, pp. 192-193	
9. **A**, p. 184 (A Closer Look)	18. **D**, p. 187	27. **D**, pp. 190, 194	

CONCEPT APPLICATION SOLUTION

I. Interspecies interactions:

    A. What other species are located in the same field site as the Colobus azures?

    1. Do the other species interact with C. azures?

    2. Are the other primate species predators of C. azures?

II. Intraspecific interactions

    A. What type of social behavior, if any, characterizes C. azures?

        1. What are the group sizes in my field site?

        2. How many males and females are in the area?

        3. How many offspring are in each group?

        4. How many offspring are there per parent?

III. Reproduction

    A. Do males and females copulate regularly or cyclically?

        1. Are these monkeys promiscuous, monogamous, polygynous, etc.

IV. Dominance

    A. Is there sexual dimorphism between males and females.

        1. Can we quantify the level of dimorphism?

    B. How is dominance established in the group?

    C. Are there two clear male and female hierarchies?

As you can see the list of questions can go on and on. It is important to think about science in terms of questions that we can answer based on observation or experimentation. This is what makes primatology a science.

CHAPTER 8
PRIMATE MODELS FOR THE EVOLUTION OF HUMAN BEHAVIOR

After reading this chapter you should be able to:
- describe characteristics that liken humans to, and distinguish humans from other primates (pp. 209-210)
- discuss the index of encephalization and its importance in brain evolution (pp. 210-214)
- give an overview of language studies done with nonhuman primates (pp. 214-217)
- discuss the basics of neurobiology and its relationship to the perception and production of speech and gestural language (pp. 218-221)
- discuss the evidence for nonhuman primate cultural behavior (pp. 221-228)
- discuss the motivation and advantages of aggressive interactions among nonhuman primates and the hypotheses regarding the evolution of human intergroup conflicts (pp. 228-231)
- explain altruism in an evolutionary context (pp. 231-232)
- understand why humans are part of a biological continuum (pp. 232-233)

CHAPTER OUTLINE

Introduction

In the last chapter the major theoretical models for the evolution of behavior in primates and the underpinnings of behavioral ecology were discussed. Additionally, the behavioral patterns and strategies of primates in regard to social groups were presented. In this chapter the relationship between body size and brain size, language capabilities, nonhuman primate cultural behaviors, aggressive interactions, affiliation, altruism and cooperation are explored. The adaptive significance of these relationships and what this might imply about human evolution are addressed. The chapter ends with a discussion of the primate continuum.

I.   HUMAN ORIGINS AND BEHAVIOR
  A. Certain behavioral attributes set humans apart from other primates.
    1. Culture became our strategy for coping with challenges
  B. Although we share 98% of our DNA coding sequences with chimpanzees, several anatomical features distinguish us from these apes:
    1. Humans have different limb proportions.
    2. Humans have flatter faces.
    3. Humans have smaller teeth.
    4. Most importantly, human brains are absolutely and relatively larger.
      a. Anatomical differences are the results of changes in regulatory genes that guide development.
      b. These alterations may be the most important factor in speciation.
  C. Nevertheless, chimpanzees and humans are sufficiently similar to identify shared derived traits that indicate a common ancestor

1. Our shoulders are anatomically similar to apes but different from monkeys.
2. Human hands are less derived than ape hands, and are therefore more similar to the hands of a generalized cercopithecine monkey.

D. Therefore, we should not limit behavioral and anatomical comparisons to our closest relatives (chimpanzees) but could profitably expand our reference sample to other primates (including monkeys).

E. Selective pressures such as environmental factors selected for anatomical and behavioral changes in hominins that separated them from hominoids responding to other selective pressures

F. Anthropologists study and compare patterns and the adaptive significance of nonhuman primate and human behaviors as a means of explaining the evolution of human behavior.
1. Several species have been chosen for comparison based on behavioral ecology and biological relatedness

II. BRAIN AND BODY SIZE

A. Relative brain size – the proportion of body size accounted for by the brain – clearly differentiates humans from other primates.
1. Brain size and body size are closely correlated.
2. Proportional brain size is more important than absolute brain size.
3. The "index of encephalization" is the predictable relationship between body and brain size in a species.
   a. The degree of encephalization is used to estimate brain size for any given body size.
4. Modern humans are much more encephalized than early members of the genus *Homo* and the primitive hominins, the australopithecines.
5. The degree of encephalization is that must be explained as a unique and central component of recent human evolution.

B. Allometry (scaling) refers to the differential proportions among various anatomical structures.
1. Allometric comparisons have become increasingly more important in understanding contemporary primate life history and adaptations
2. It is more appropriate to emphasize the relative size of certain structures in the brain than to compare brain size among species.
3. Compared to reptile brains that have a small cortex, primate brains have a relatively expanded neocortex that makes up 80% of total brain volume and is capable of dealing with much more complex sensory stimuli.

C. Timing of brain growth is also important.
1. Nonhuman primates – brain grows most rapidly immediately before birth.
2. In humans rapid brain growth continues for at least the first year after birth.

D. The metabolic costs of a large brain must be compensated for by benefits.
1. Larger brains wouldn't have evolved if they did not offer some advantage.

E. Various hypotheses have been proposed for the evolution of large brains in primates.
1. Social brain hypothesis
   a. Proposes that primate brains coevolved, increasing in relative size and complexity, with social group living.

138

      b. Social living requires primates to negotiate complex relationships including dominance hierarchies, competition, alliance formation, friendships, and avoidance of certain individuals.

      c. Intelligence evolved to solve physical problems (finding food, predator avoidance) and to analyze and use social information.

   2. Another suggestion is that increasing reliance upon meat during hominin evolution allowed for brain size expansion.

      a. The brain is a very metabolically expensive organ and requires relatively more calories than any other organ system.

      b. Meat (a rich source of calories, proteins, and fats) would meet the nutritional demands of a lineage in which relatively large brains were becoming important.

      c. Negotiating the sharing of kills within the social group would have also selected for greater cognitive complexity.

      d. Comparison of human and chimpanzee genomes show that several genes responsible for producing enzymes for animal protein metabolism have changed over time for both species.

      e. As chimpanzee and human lineages diverged, selection favored enzyme mutations that enabled some hominins to digest meat more efficiently.

III. **LANGUAGE**

  A. The development of language was one of the most significant events in human evolution.

  B. Nonhuman primates do not use language the same way humans do.

   1. Studies have demonstrated that several nonhuman primates use distinct vocalizations that have specific references.

  C. Humans use language – a set of written and/or spoken arbitrary symbols that refer to concepts, people and objects.

   1. Human language, as a mode of communication, is an open system

  D. Humans and apes differ in the anatomy of the vocal-tract and the language-related structures in the brain.

  E. Language has always been considered a uniquely human achievement; however, different apes have demonstrated varying degrees of human-like language capabilities.

  F. Humans are not the only species to have the capacity for some degree of symbolic thought and complex communication

   1. Washoe, an infant female chimpanzee, learned ASL (American Sign Language for the deaf). Washoe later deliberately taught a chimp named Loulis some signs.

   2. Sara, another chimpanzee, learned to recognize plastic chips as symbols for objects.

   3. Chimps at the Yerkes Regional Primate Center were able to communicate using a computer with symbols imprinted on the keyboard.

   4. Koko, a female gorilla uses more than 500 signs of ASL, and communicated regularly via sign language with Michael, a male gorilla, who was also involved in the same study.

   5. Chantek, a male orangutan, learned to sign in reference to objects that were not present.

   6. Chimpanzees have shown that they can use symbols to categorize unfamiliar objects into classes.

7. Kanzi, an infant male bonobo, spontaneous acquisition and use of language and symbols at the age of 2½ years was significant in regards to the criticism that apes must be "taught" to use symbols while human children acquire language through exposure

G. The manner in which chimpanzees are introduced to language influences their ability to understand the representational value of symbols.

IV. THE EVOLUTION OF LANGUAGE

A. The ape studies provide clues concerning the origins of human language.
1. It is significant that great apes use gestures for communication in the wild.
2. It is possible that the last common ancestor also had these predispositions.
3. We need to identify the factors that enhanced the adaptive significance of these abilities in our own lineage, and explore why these pressure didn't operate to the same degree in our closest relatives.

B. Human language developed through the reorganization and elaboration of preexisting brain structures that allowed for the possibility of language acquisition.
1. The neurological changes that enhanced language development in humans would not have happened if early hominins had not already acquired the behavioral and neurological foundations that made them possible.
2. Language developed due to selective pressure that favored the ability of early humans to precisely and efficiently communicate.

C. For most humans the language center of the brain is "lateralized" in the left hemisphere of the brain
1. Broca's area
   a. Is located in the motor cortex of the left frontal lobe, and is involved with the production of speech
   b. When speaking, information is sent to Broca's area where it is organized specifically for communications.
2. Wernicke's area
   a. Is located in the left temporal lobe, and is involved in the perception of speech
   b. It is an association area that lies near structures involved in the reception of sound
3. The perception and production of speech involves much more than these two areas.
   a. The use of written language requires additional neurological structures.
   b. Information relating to all senses is eventually combined and relayed to Broca's area where it is translated for speech production.

D. MRI images of greater ape brains show similar lateralization of the areas equivalent to the language areas
1. In humans, these areas have been suggested as being important for the development of gestural language.
2. Greater apes show some gestural handedness especially when combined with vocalizations.

E. Specialization of auditory centers of the left hemisphere for language may have preceded the evolutionary divergence of humans and apes and therefore have a long evolutionary history.

140

F. The recent identification of the FOXP2 gene may provide more clues to the origins of language.
   1. The human FOXP2 gene influences the embryological development of brain circuitry related to language.
   2. When mutations affect this gene, the afflicted human has severely impaired speech and language capabilities.
   3. The human FOXP2 gene product differs by only two amino acids from the homologous gene of apes.
   4. FOXP2 is the first gene to influence language development and may have played a role in the development of language capacities in humans.

V.   **PRIMATE CULTURAL BEHAVIOR**
   A. Most biological anthropologists feel that it is appropriate to use the term culture in referring to nonhuman primates as well as humans.
      1. The term "cultural primatology" is frequently now being used.
   B. Most aspects of culture are uniquely human; however primates share certain behavioral patterns.
   C. Cultural behavior is learned and passed on from one generation to the next.
      1. Young primate infants learn appropriate behaviors, and cultural traditions emerge from mother-offspring learning.
      2. Humans deliberately teach their young while it appears that most nonhuman primates do not.
      3. Young nonhuman primates and humans acquire a large amount by knowledge through observation.
   D. The earliest reported cultural behavior among nonhuman primates concerned macaques from Japan.
      1. Imo began washing her sweet potatoes in seawater rather than freshwater before eating them.
      2. Within 3 years, other macaques were washing potatoes in seawater.
   E. Orangutans in 6 areas performed 19 behaviors (including food procurement) that showed sufficient regional variation to be classified as cultural variants.
   F. Tool use was once thought to be only a human endeavor; however, this behavior is not unique to humans as other animals (including non-primates) have been observed using tools
      1. Tool use is most elaborate among primates.
   G. Chimpanzees exhibit more complex forms of tool use than any other nonhuman primate.
      1. Chimpanzee tools include termite fishing sticks, leaf sponges, twigs as toothpicks, sticks for digging, and stones as nutcrackers and weapons.
      2. Inferences regarding nonhuman primate intelligence can be made from the modification/preparation of natural objects for use as tools.
         a. The activity implies planning and forethought.
         b. They must have a preconceived idea of what the finished product needs to be in order for the tool to be useful.
      3. Chimpanzees have also been observed to use tools to catch small prey
         a. Small branches are modified into spears for use.

141

4. Tool use enhances the chimpanzees' ability to exploit resources.
H. Chimpanzees exhibit regional variation in their types and methods of tool use and dietary preferences.
   1. Regional patterns in tool use and food preferences that are not related to environmental variation are reminiscent of the cultural variations characteristic of humans.
I. Capuchin monkeys have also been observed to consistently use tools and exhibit elements of cultural behavior.
   1. Many tool use behaviors parallel those observed among chimpanzees.
J. Eight criteria for cultural behaviors in nonhuman species were presented by primatologist William McGrew. They are as follows:
   1. Innovation – new pattern is invented or modified.
   2. Dissemination – pattern is acquired (via imitation) by another from an innovator.
   3. Standardization – pattern is consistent and stylized.
   4. Durability – pattern is performed without the presence of a demonstrator.
   5. Diffusion – pattern spreads from one group to another.
   6. Tradition – pattern persists from innovator's generation to the next
   7. Nonsubsistence – pattern transcends subsistence
   8. Naturalness – pattern is shown in absence of direct human influence.
   9. Capuchins meet the first six criteria, and all criteria are met by at least some chimpanzees in some instances.
K. Kanzi, a captive male bonobo, learned to produce sharp-edged stone flakes by throwing a stone onto a concrete floor. He later learned (via imitation) from a human teacher to strike two stones together to produce stone flakes.
L. Culture has become the environment in which modern humans live.
M. Evolution is not directed towards producing humans.
   1. Such a view is termed anthropocentric.
   2. Nonhuman primate behaviors that have been recently documented by humans are not newly-developed in our nonhuman primate relatives.

VI. AGGRESSION
A. Primate land use and defense
   1. The home range is where groups of primates live permanently
   2. Within the home range is the core area (territory)
   3. Core areas contains the highest concentration of predictable resources, and are defended against intrusion.
   4. Portions of the home range may overlap with that of one or more groups, however territories do not overlap
B. Not all primates are territorial
   1. Territoriality is associated with species whose ranges are sufficiently small to permit patrolling and protection
C. Chimpanzee territoriality is atypical for primates; however males are particularly intolerant of strangers and will fiercely defend their territory and resources.
   1. Chimpanzee intergroup interactions typically include some form of aggressive behavior
   2. Lethal aggression is relatively common between groups of chimpanzees, and has been reported among red colobus monkeys, and spider monkeys

3. Chimpanzees frequently travel to peripheral areas outside (or overlapping) their home range, and will occasionally enter another groups territory.
    a. Before entering a peripheral area chimpanzees will hoot and display to see if any other animals are around.
4. Male chimpanzees (sometimes accompanied by one or two females) patrol their territory borders.
    a. When patrolling, they travel silently in compact groups.
    b. Chimpanzee border patrols that have resulted in brutal attacks of outnumbered individuals from neighboring communities.
5. Beginning in 1974, at least five unprovoked brutal attacks by groups of chimpanzees on one chimpanzee were witnessed in Gombe.
    a. Additional cases of intergroup aggression in and around Gombe have been observed between 1993 - 2002
6. Although chimpanzees clearly engage in lethal attacks, the number of observed incidents is low

D. Humans and chimpanzees are the only known mammalian species where lethal and unprovoked aggression occurs between conspecific groups.
1. Primatologists have focused on aggression between groups of conspecifics and how that behavior helps to explain human aggression.
2. In chimpanzees and most traditional human cultures males are philopatric and have strong affiliative bonds between adult males of the same group.
3. In most conflicts involving females the attacks are not fatal.
4. The apparent benefit to lethal aggressive behavior seems to be acquisition of mating partners and food.

E. Similarities in aggressive male behavior suggest a common evolutionary background.
1. Shared patterns of strife between populations may be a predisposition that chimpanzees and early hominins inherited from a common ancestor.

VII. AFFILIATION, ALTRUISM, AND COOPERATION
A. Some affiliative behaviors appear to be examples of care giving or compassion.
1. Little Bee, a Gombe chimpanzee, brought food to her dying mother.
2. Chimpanzees have also been observed shooing flies and grooming dying relatives.

B. Altruism
1. Altruism refers to behaviors that benefit others with some risk or sacrifice to the performer.
2. Protecting dependent offspring is the most basic of altruistic behaviors.
3. Among primates, recipients of altruistic acts may include individuals who aren't offspring and who may not even be closely related to the performer.
4. Adoption is another form of altruism that is common among chimpanzees and has been reported for capuchins, macaques, and baboons.

C. Kin selection hypothesis
1. Individuals are more likely to perform risky behaviors for the benefit of a relative who shares genes with the performer.
2. The individual may enhance his or her reproductive success as the relative may reproduce and therefore pass on genes that both individuals shared.

D. Reciprocal altruism hypothesis
   1. When the recipient of an altruistic act reciprocates at a later time.
   2. Coalitions and alliances are forms of reciprocal altruism
   3. Although reciprocal altruism occurs, it has yet to be explained and therefore requires further testing.
E. Group selection hypothesis
   1. An individual may act altruistically to benefit other group members because it is to the performer's benefit that the group survives.
   2. If the altruist dies, his or her genes will be passed on in the group.
   3. According to natural selection, individual reproductive success is enhanced by acting selfishly.
   4. Supporters of group selection argue that natural selection works on both the individual level and the species level.

VIII. THE PRIMATE CONTINUUM
A. Humans are part of a biological continuum with other animals, and are also part of a behavioral continuum with the nonhuman primates.
B. Therefore, differences in many human and chimpanzee behaviors are differences in degree, not kind (differences are primarily quantitative and not qualitative).
C. It is important to recognize that our behaviors are extensions of our hominin and primate ancestry.

KEY TERMS

affiliation: friendly relations between individuals.

allometry (scaling): the relative growth of a part of an organism in relation to the entire organism.

altruism: helping another individual at some risk or cost and no direct benefit to oneself.

anthropocentric: interpreting nonhuman traits and behaviors from the perspective of human values and experiences. Viewing humans as the most important entity in the world.

anvil: surface on which an object is placed prior to being struck by another object

biological continuum: traits and behaviors that continuously grade into one another in such a way that characteristics (of organisms that are related through common ancestry) cannot be parsed into discrete categories.

Broca's area: an area of the brain responsible for the production of speech.

conserved: maintained unchanged over evolutionary history.

conspecifics: members of the same species.

core areas (territories): areas within the home range where the highest concentration of reliable resources are found that animals will defend.

cortex: the brain layer responsible for interpreting sensory inputs.

cultural behavior: learned behaviors used to adapt to the natural environment that are passed on from generation to generation.

encephalization: a predictable relationship between brain size and body size.

home range: a geographic area where a primate group remains permanently.

lateralized: localized to one side of the brain. Functional specialization of the brain's hemispheres for specific activities.

motor cortex: the areas of the brain's cortex responsible for movement. In humans movement of the mouth, larynx and tongue for language production are located in this area of the brain.

neocortex: more recently evolved portion of the cortex involved in higher mental functions.

philopatric: remaining in one's natal group.

scaling: (see **allometry**)

social intelligence: the ability to assess a social situation before acting and storing information related to social interactions.

territory: (see **core areas**)

Wernicke's area: an area of the brain responsible for perception of speech.

MEDIA EXERCISES

1) Revisit Primate Info Net's comprehensive list of resources concerning primate behavior and ecology (http://pin.primate.wisc.edu/aboutp/behavior/index.html). Under the heading "Learning (Language, problem solving, tool use)" click on a few of the hyper-links to learn more about some of the famous "language-using" apes discussed in the chapter such as Koko, Chantek and Kanzi. Review these sites critically, focusing on the question of whether or not apes have been demonstrated to master human-like language.

CONCEPT APPLICATION

Go to the Emory University Living Links web site: (http://www.emory.edu/LIVING_LINKS/av.html) and click on the link under Video clips called *Living Links video "Chimpanzee Conflict"*. Watch the short video narrated by Dr. De Waal. In the text you learned about both aggressive and affiliative behavior in primates. How do chimps show aggressive behavior that is threatening but not harmful and threatening and harmful? How are conflicts resolved between juveniles? How do adults show reconciliation with each other?

Now answer the True/False, Multiple Choice and Short Answer sample test questions. Following completion of the tests, correct them with the answers and textbook page references at the end of this Study Guide chapter. Note the areas in which you are strong and weak to guide you in your studying. Finally, answer the sample Essay Questions.

TRUE/FALSE QUESTIONS

If false, consider what modification would make the statement true.

1. When studying behavior we should limit comparisons of our behavior to that of chimpanzees.
   TRUE   FALSE

2. The use of language is a unique human achievement that sets humans apart from the rest of the animal kingdom.
   TRUE   FALSE

3. Primate brains have a much smaller neocortex than reptiles.
   TRUE   FALSE

4. Modern humans have a brain size that is expected for a primate of similar body size.
   TRUE   FALSE

5. Work with captive apes has confirmed that they can learn to interpret visual signs and use them in communication.
   TRUE   FALSE

6. Non-human primates have the capacity for culture, learned behaviors that are transmitted from generation to generation.
   TRUE   FALSE

7. Lethal, unprovoked aggression between groups of conspecifics is only known to occur among chimpanzees.
   TRUE   FALSE

8. The adoption of orphaned infants, reported in macaques, baboons and chimpanzees, is an example of anthropocentrism.
   TRUE   FALSE

9. Chimpanzee use stone tools in West Africa to break open nuts and hard-shelled fruits.
   TRUE   FALSE

10. Many of our behaviors are elaborate extensions of those of our hominin ancestors and close primate relatives.
    TRUE   FALSE

146

MULTIPLE CHOICE QUESTIONS

1. Primate
   A. neurological complexity is generally reduced when compared with other mammals.
   B. neurological complexity is increased compared with other mammals.
   C. instinctive behaviors are more important than learned behaviors.
   D. none of the above

2. Modern human behavior
   A. does not reflect patterns seen in other primates.
   B. is predominantly learned.
   C. is genetically inherited.
   D. all of the above.

3. Viewing human behavior from a biological perspective
   A. concludes that all human behaviors are unique in the animal kingdom.
   B. may help to explain how certain behavior patterns may have evolved.
   C. is wrong because we are cultural beings.
   D. ignores the plasticity of human behavior.

4. Which of the following do we **not** share with chimpanzees?
   A. shoulder structure
   B. short, more stable lower backs
   C. 98% of our DNA
   D. reduced thumbs and elongated fingers

5. The predictable relationship between body and brain size is known as the index of
   A. neuronal excess.
   B. cranial capacity.
   C. encephalization.
   D. none of the above.

6. The portion of the brain that processes sensory inputs and controls higher mental functions is
   A. the brainstem.
   B. the medulla.
   C. the hypothalamus.
   D. the neocortex.

7. Compared to other organs, the human brain is energetically and metabolically
   A. much more expensive.
   B. less expensive.
   C. equally expensive.
   D. variable depending upon the activity.

147

8. An explanation for the increase in the relative size and complexity of primate brains suggests that living in _____ was responsible for this evolutionary change.
    A. trees
    B. social groups
    C. tropical grasslands
    D. isolation from conspecifics

9. The addition of what foodstuff to the diet probably contributed to the evolution of the larger and more complex hominin brain?
    A. fruit
    B. leaf
    C. insects
    D. meat

10. Vervet monkey communication
    A. confirmed the belief that primate vocalizations could not reference external events.
    B. is limited to scent marking and autonomic displays.
    C. includes specific alarm calls for different categories of predators (air, tree or ground).
    D. all of the above

11. Apes do not speak because
    A. they lack the intelligence.
    B. their vocal tract anatomy and language centers of the brain are different from ours.
    C. they have nothing to say.
    D. none of the above

12. Sara is a chimpanzee who
    A. learned ASL from her mother.
    B. learned to recognize plastic chips as symbols for various objects.
    C. spontaneously began signing after observing others.
    D. taught an infant chimp ASL.

13. Koko
    A. is a female lowland gorilla.
    B. has learned over 500 signs of ASL.
    C. communicated with a male gorilla named Michael using ASL.
    D. all of the above

14. Kanzi
    A. is an orangutan who learned how to make bone and wooden tools.
    B. is a Ugandan nature preserve that is home to 300 lowland gorillas.
    C. is a bonobo who spontaneously learned language through observation.
    D. none of the above

15. Ape language experiments
    A. show that apes are not capable of symbolic thought.
    B. may suggest clues to the origins of human language.
    C. show that all ape species have the same understandings of symbols and the objects they represent.
    D. have no value in assessing the evolutionary relationship between humans and apes.

16. In most humans the language centers of the brain
    A. include Broca's area.
    B. are located in the right hemisphere.
    C. are localized in the cerebellum.
    D. all of the above

17. The study of comparative brain structure
    A. is a very simple task.
    B. indicates that absolute brain size is the only important factor in the development of language.
    C. suggests that reorganization of neurological structures is most important in the development of language.
    D. demonstrates that human brains are simply enlarged monkey brains.

18. Nonhuman primate culture
    A. is innately inherited from one generation to the next.
    B. is uniform between different groups within the same species.
    C. is learned through observation.
    D. includes regional variation in predator alarm calls.

19. A famous example of nonhuman primate cultural behavior is
    A. the Japanese macaque named Imo who taught her peers to wash sweet potatoes and separate grain from sand in sea water.
    B. the orangutan named Lana who learned ASL.
    C. the gorilla named Francine who learned how to say five spoken words in English.
    D. the bonobo named Bob who learned how to play the kazoo.

20. Which of the following tool uses have **not** been seen among free-ranging chimpanzees?
    A. termite fishing
    B. leaf sponging
    C. sweet potato washing
    D. tooth picking

21. Kanzi has shown abilities in all but which of the following areas?
    A. problem-solving capabilities
    B. cooperative hunting
    C. tool manufacturing
    D. goal-directed activities

149

22. A portion of the home range that is actively protected is known as the group's
    A. territory.
    B. biological continuum.
    C. allometry.
    D. conspecifics.

23. Chimpanzee border patrollers
    A. loudly display at their community's borders.
    B. are relaxed and playful during patrols.
    C. may attack a lone chimp from a neighboring community.
    D. are looking for other groups to join in the food quest.

24. When female macaques and baboons band together in aggressive encounters with other
    groups of females
    A. fatalities almost always result.
    B. are unusual because most primate group conflicts are between members of the
       opposite sex.
    C. they are usually the result of competition for resources.
    D. none of the above

25. The principle benefit to chimpanzees who engage in lethal attacks appears to be acquisition
    of
    A. mating partners.
    B. sleeping sites.
    C. territory.
    D. affiliative relationships with male relatives in neighboring communities.

26. Affiliative behaviors
    A. are most common when there is competition for resources.
    B. enhance group cohesiveness.
    C. are rare among primates.
    D. often include aggressive displays.

27. Conspecific refers to
    A. cooperative hunters.
    B. a mating pair.
    C. members of the same species.
    D. those who remain in their natal community.

28. Altruistic behaviors
    A. are always aggressive in nature.
    B. never result in the helping of one animal by another.
    C. are absent in free-ranging primates.
    D. benefit another individual at some potential cost or risk to oneself.

150

29. Which of the following may reflect kin selection?
    A. Adoption of orphaned infants by older siblings among chimpanzees.
    B. Helping a family member rather than a non-family member.
    C. Enhancing one's own reproductive success by helping a family member.
    D. all of the above

30. Which of the following have lead to the awareness that humans are part of a biological continuum with other primates?
    A. neurological processes
    B. the need for close bonding and physical contact
    C. dependence on learning
    D. all of the above

SHORT ANSWER QUESTIONS (& PAGE REFERENCES)

1. What is encephalization? (p. 210)

2. How is the FOXP2 gene involved in the evolution of human language? (pp. 220-221)

3. Name three ways that apes have been taught to communicate symbolically. (pp. 216-217)

4. Describe three chimpanzee tools and how they are used. (pp. 223-225)

5. How is altruism explained evolutionarily? (pp. 231-232)

ESSAY QUESTIONS (& PAGE REFERENCES)

1. How do the ape language studies demonstrate similarities between human and ape language capabilities? How do they illustrate ape limitations in this regard? (pp. 214-221)

2. Do chimpanzees have culture? What do field studies on chimp tool-usage, diet and hunting have to contribute to the resolution of this issue? (pp. 221-225)

3. How is chimpanzee and human inter-group aggression unique amongst mammals? What explanations have been offered to explain this troubling similarity? (pp. 228-231)

ANSWERS, CORRECTED STATEMENT IF FALSE & REFERENCES TO TRUE/FALSE QUESTIONS

1. **FALSE**, p. 209, We should include many primate species in our comparisons because the selective pressures that acted on ancestral primates played a role in human evolution also.

2. **FALSE**, pp. 215-216, Work with captive apes has modified our view about the capacity of nonhuman primates to use language

3. **FALSE**, p. 211, Primate brains have a much *larger* neocortex than reptiles.

4. **FALSE**, p. 210, Modern humans have a brain size *well beyond* that expected for a primate of similar body size.

5. **TRUE**, pp. 216-217

6. **TRUE**, p. 211

7. **FALSE**, pp. 228-231, Lethal, unprovoked aggression between groups of conspecifics is known to occur among *red colobus monkeys, spider monkeys, chimpanzees and humans*.

8. **FALSE**, p. 231, The adoption of orphaned infants, reported in macaques, baboons and chimpanzees, is an example of *altruism*.

9. **TRUE**, p. 225

10. **TRUE**, p. 233

ANSWERS AND REFERENCES TO MULTIPLE CHOICE QUESTIONS

1. **B**, pp. 210-211	7. **A**, pp. 211, 213	13. **D**, p. 216	19. **A**, pp. 221-222	25. **A**, p. 230
2. **B**, p. 208	8. **B**, pp. 211	14. **C**, p. 217	20. **C**, pp. 223-225	26. **B**, p. 220
3. **B**, p. 208	9. **D**, pp. 213-214	15. **B**, p. 218	21. **B**, pp. 217, 227	27. **C**, p. 220
4. **D**, p. 209	10. **C**, pp. 214-215	16. **A**, p. 218	22. **A**, p. 228	28. **D**, p. 231
5. **C**, p. 210	11. **B**, p. 216	17. **C**, p. 218	23. **C**, pp. 228-229	29. **D**, p. 232
6. **D**, p. 211	12. **B**, p. 216	18. **C**, p. 221	24. **C**, p. 230	30. **D**, p. 233

CONCEPT APPLICATION SOLUTION

How do chimps show aggressive behavior that is threatening but not harmful and threatening and harmful? *The alpha chimp in the video uses a ball and screams to draw attention to himself and intimidate the other chimps. He runs around the enclosure slapping objects and just avoiding contact with other chimps. This is an example of non-harmful threatening. Threatening harmful behavior includes outright attacks with hitting, slapping and biting. Injuries occur often during these types of encounters but seem to heal quickly.*

How are conflicts resolved between juveniles? *Juveniles often play-fight as they learn the rules of their group. Occasionally play-fights may turn into more serious altercations. In most cases, the fights are resolved between the two juvenile but sometimes adults intervene. Usually mothers intervene but sometimes the alpha male becomes involved and in the case of the video chooses sides to end the battle.*

How do adults show reconciliation with each other? *Chimpanzees reconcile after fight to maintain group cohesion. One individual will seek forgiveness but getting into submissive postures and presenting the hand to the forgiver. Sometimes one chimp will put their hand into the other chimps mouth to show trust on both sides. A chimp's jaws can easily bite the fingers off of a rival.*

CHAPTER 9
OVERVIEW OF THE FOSSIL PRIMATES

LEARNING OBJECTIVES

After reading this chapter you should be able to:
- discuss the taxonomic classification of Mesozoic era primates (pp. 237-240)
- list the Cenozoic era epochs and the associated fossil primate groups and evolutionary events important in primate origins (p. 240)
- discuss the Archaic primate semiorder plesiadapiforms (pp. 241-242)
- define and characterize euprimates (pp. 242-243)
- list and discuss adapoid family divisions and the evolution of lemurs and lorises (pp. 242-247)
- discuss the taxonomically diverse omomyoids and their relationship to modern tarsiers (pp. 249-250)
- discuss fossil Eocene anthropoids and understand the difficulties associated with their classification (250-252)
- list and discuss the Old and New World Oligocene primate fossils (pp. 253-256)
- list the primate fossils and discuss the diversification of cercopithecoids and hominoids during the Miocene (pp. 256-268)

CHAPTER OUTLINE

Introduction

This chapter introduces you to the large array of extinct fossil primate forms and focuses on exploring the relationships between strepsirhines and haplorhines in order to understand our own evolutionary history. The identification of retained primitive skeletal features (pentadactyly) and highly derived traits – such as orthograde (upright) body position and forward facing eyes – allows us to organize fossil primate forms into meaningful groups which facilitates the exploration of our evolution. Modern primates share some characteristics with early mammals, and the differentiation of unique primate features seen in the fossil record from those traits seen in distantly related mammals is the initial step in recognizing our own beginnings. As we move through time into the present, the traits that link early primates to modern forms are discussed.

I. **BACKGROUND TO PRIMATE EVOLUTION: LATE MESOZOIC**
   A. The Age of Mammals began following extinction of the dinosaurs at the end of the Mesozoic era (Cretaceous-Tertiary).
   B. Mammals were left to diversify and explore the vacant ecological niches.
   C. During the Cretaceous period, primates began to diverge from closely related mammalian lineages.
      1. These closely related "sister" lineages are categorized as Euarchonta.
      2. The supergroup Euarchonta is designated for sister orders of tree shrews, flying lemurs (colugos), and primates.

II PRIMATE ORIGINS

A. The Cenozoic era is the time period during which most primate evolution occurred and is divided into 7 epochs.
   1. Paleocene (65-55.8 mya) – first archaic primates (plesiadapiforms).
   2. Eocene (55.8-33 mya) – first euprimates – early strepsirhines and haplorhines.
   3. Oligocene (33-23 mya) – early catarrhines (precursors to monkeys and apes emerge).
   4. Miocene (23-5.3 mya) - monkeys and apes emerge (first humanlike creatures appear).
   5. Pliocene (5.3-1.8 mya) – early hominins diversify.
   6. Pleistocene (1.8-0.01 mya) – early *Homo* develops.
   7. Holocene (0.01 mya – present) – modern humans.
B. Disparity in dates regarding primate emergence is due to difficulty in reconciling molecular and morphological evidence for the key time of evolutionary divergence.
   1. Approaches using molecular and morphological data allow us to date the divergences of primates and Euarchonta from the last common ancestor sometime between 90-65 mya.

III MADE TO ORDER: ARCHAIC PRIMATES

A. Fossil evidence indicates that between 65-52 mya a major radiation of archaic primates (plesiadapiforms) occurred.
B. Currently plesiadapiforms are taxonomically classified as a primate semiorder that is separate from the later euprimates.
C. The majority of Plesiadapiform fossils have been found in North America.
D. Six families of plesiadapiforms are recognized. Three of which are:
   1. Purgatoriidae
   2. Plesiadapidae
   3. Carpolestidae
E. Family purgatorridae
   1. This family includes the oldest recognized archaic primate genus *Purgatorius*.
   2. Members of this genus are believed to have been about the size of modern rats.
   3. At least 2 (possibly 4) species lived in the American Northwest during the Paleocene (65 mya), which may indicate an origin in the late Cretaceous.
F. Family Plesiadapidae
   1. This family was among the more successful plesiadapiform groups.
   2. They were chipmunk- to marmot-sized mammals with large rodent-like incisors.
      a. The incisors did not grow continuously and did not self-sharpen which suggests a vegetative diet. .
   3. The best-known genus *Plesiadapis* of this family probably originated in North America, and later colonized Europe prior to extinction.
G. Family Carpolestidae ("fruit stealer")
   1. They were common in North America and Asia during the Paleocene, however, they were not as successful as the Plesiadapidae.
   2. They were mouse- to rat-sized mammals with enlarged incisors.

154

3. A nearly complete skeleton of *Carpolestes* was discovered in the Clarks Fork Basin in Wyoming.
   a. The post-cranial elements indicate adaptation to an arboreal environment.
      i. They had opposable first toes with nails instead of claws.
      ii. They had no adaptation for leaping.

IV   EOCENE PRIMATES (55.8-33 MYA)
  A. Plesiadapiforms gradually become extinct and are replaced by euprimates in North America, Europe, and Asia during this epoch.
    1. The euprimates have recognizably modern derived primate traits suggestive of adaptation to a warm climate with year-round rainfall and lush forests.
      a. Forward-facing eyes
      b. Greater encephalization
      c. Post-orbital bar
      d. Nails instead of claws
      e. Opposable big toe
    2. The Eocene was a time of rapid diversification for all mammals (not just primates).
    3. Two main branches of Euprimates include the superfamilies Adapoidea and Omomyoidea.
      a. Adapoidea – primitive lemur-like primates.
      b. Omomyoidea – primitive tarsier- or galago-like primates.
    4. Fossil evidence indicates that the earliest euprimates engaged in a rapid westward dispersal with Asia as the possible geographical origin
  B. Lemur-like Adapoids
    1. Adapoids include more than 35 genera and share the primitive dental formula of 2.1.4.3.
      a. They are the most primitive primate group and the best known of the Eocene strepsirhines.
    2. Adapoids are subclassified into 5 families based on biogeographical distinctions. The most prominent of these are the …
      a. Notharctids of North America
      b. Adapids of Europe
      c. Amphipithecids of Asia
    3. Notharctids (North America)
      a. *Cantius* is the earliest notharctid, known primarily from North America.
      b. Skeletal remains indicate that this was a small- to medium-sized diurnal creature that foraged during the day.
         i. They were probably quadrupedal leapers.
         ii. Dentition indicates they were probably frugivores.
    4. Adapids (Europe)
      a. Appeared near the end of the Eocene and quickly became extinct.
      b. The phylogeny for this group is poorly understood, however they most likely emigrated from Asia.
      c. *Adapis* is the best known genus from this family.
         i. *Adapis* was the first nonhuman fossil primate named.

   ii. They may have had a dental comb.

   iii. They were slow, arboreal quadrupeds and most likely foraged for leaves during the day.

 5. Amphipithecids (Myanmar and Thailand)

  a. They had generally been accepted as a dead-end lineage living during the Eocene with no Oligocene relatives.

   i. A recent fossil discovery in Pakistan has challenged this notion.

  b. The amphipithecids are an example of convergent evolution as their "anthropoid" traits are homoplasies and not shared derived traits.

   i. Amphipithecids developed dental patterns similar to anthropoids due to exploiting the same dietary niches.

   ii. Amphipithecid mandibles and postcranial skeletons indicate that they were slow-moving specialized adapoids that exploited an arboreal niche.

C. Evolution of True Lemurs and Lorises

 1. Modern lemurs anatomically resemble adapoids because of retained ancestral traits; however, adapoid fossils do not show specialized development of a dental comb.

  a. There is no clear evolutionary relationship between Eocene adapoids and later lemurs and lorises

  b. The evolution of lemurs and other strepsirhines is of interest due to their taxonomic relationship to all other primate lineages.

   i. data related to their initial emergence and radiation and be used to determine subsequent primate divergence dates.

 2. Lorisoids (lorises and galagos) are the earliest examples of strepsirhine primates

  a. Fossil lorisoids have been found in late Eocene deposits of the Fayum Depression in Egypt

   i. A late Eocene fossile appears to have a dental comb which may indicate that it is a stem galagid

   ii. Lorises and galagos likely diverged by the end of the middle Eocene.

 3. Stem strepsirhines from the African mainland likely colonized Madagascar to give rise to crown lemuriforms.

  a. Colonization likely occurred by the crossing of the Mozambique Channel or unintentional rafting on debris; this would indicate that lemurs have never existed outside of Madagascar.

  b. Several extinct subfossil lemurs have been found on Madagascar; many of which were much larger than modern lemurs.

   i. They were mostly arboreal, possibly diurnal, and filled ecological niches not shared by extant lemurs.

  c. *Archaeolemur* more closely resembled a monkey with a fused mandible, bilophodont molars, and a sulcul (grooved) brain pattern.

  d. *Megaladapis* had a body build like that of a gorilla, was approximately 170 lbs., and is the best known of the giant lemurs.

   i. This species became extinct once forests were cleared for farming.

   ii. The monkey-like skeletal morphology of both *Archaeolemur* and *Megaladapis* are suggestive of evolutionary convergence.

      e. Subfossil lemur discoveries indicate that 16 species have become extinct within the past 2000 years.

D. Tarsier-like Omomyoids

    1. Omomyoids are more taxonomically diverse than adapoids, and are characterized by:

        a. 1.1.3.3. dental formula,

        b. large orbits,

        c. small snouts.

    2. Earlier omomyoids are more generalized than later ones, and may be ancestral to all later haplorhines (tarsiers, New and Old World Monkeys, apes, and humans).

    3. The genus *Teilhardina* are found on 3 continents.

        a. Related *Teilhardina* species indicate that the oldest (most primitive) members were from Asia, and the youngest were from North America.

           i. This supports a westward migration of euprimates from Asia, through Europe, and eventually to North America.

          ii. A recent fossil discovery in Mississippi may challenge this theory.

    4. *Shoshonius* (North America) and *Necrolemur* (Europe) are Eocene omomyidae fossils thought to be closely related to the tarsier based on large convergent eye orbits and portions of the ear.

        a. *Necrolemur's* tibia and fibula may have been fused, and the calcaneus may have been elongated.

           i. These features in modern tarsiers enable them to leap; however many researchers believe the similarities in skeletal morphology are not shared derived traits.

        b. The position of the olfactory part of the brain links Eocene omomyoids with tarsiers.

E. Evolution of True Tarsiers

    1. Fossil tarsiers have been recovered from Egypt, China, and Thailand.

    2. The morphology indicates that modern tarsiers retained their Eocene anatomy.

    3. Biomolecular studies indicate that the 5 extant tarsier species diverged in the Miocene.

F. Eocene and Oligocene Early Anthropoids

    1. Recent molecular evidence indicates that anthropoid primates probably emerged separately from adapoids and omomyoids around 77 mya.

        a. However, fossil anthropoids from 77 mya have not been discovered.

    2. *Algeripithecus* (50 mya - middle Eocene) is the earliest undisputed fossil anthropoid.

        a. This fossil from Africa has more derived anthropoid characteristics and is 3 million years older than the earliest potential anthropoid ancestors found in Asia.

    3. Most of our Eocene and Oligocene anthropoid fossils come from the Fayum Depression in Egypt.

        a. *Biretia* (37 mya) represents the most complete remains of an early African anthropoid and was placed into the extinct superfamily Parapithecoidea.

           i. *Biretia* was a small primate (weighing under 1 pound).

   ii. Has the dental morphology typical of a basal (most primitive) anthropoid.

   iii. Molar tooth roots indicate large eye orbits which suggest this primate was nocturnal.

  b. *Catopithecus* (35 mya) possessed anthropoid features (complete postorbital closure) and some derived catarrhine features (2.1.2.3. dental formula).

   i. *Catopithecus* genera is from the family Oligopithecidae.

  c. Current molecular and biogeographical data agree that anthropoids had an African origin.

V OLIGOCENE PRIMATES

 A. Over 1,000 Old World primate fossils have been found in the Fayum Depression in Egypt; these represent a paleontological record of a rich primate ecosystem.

 B. True Anthropoids

  1. Stem Primates of this epoch are classified into one of 3 families:

   a. Oligopithecids

   b. Parapithecids

   c. Propliopithecids.

  2. Oligopithecids are among the earliest anthropoid primates.

   a. *Catopithecus* is classed as the earliest catarrhine based on anthropoid features (complete postorbital closure) and a derived 2.1.2.3. dental formula.

  3. Parapithecids are the most abundant of the Oligocene fossils and belong to the genus *Apidium*.

   a. *Apidium* was a small arboreal quadruped (about the size of a squirrel) and adept at leaping and springing.

   b. 2.1.3.3. dental formula indicates that *Apidium* appeared before Old and New World anthropoids diverged.

   c. The dentition indicates that *Apidium* ...

    i. May be an early ancestor of platyrrhines (New World anthropoids).

    ii. Probably ate fruit and seeds

    iii. May have lived in polygynous social groups (one male/multiple females and offspring) – due to large degree of sexual dimorphism in canine size.

   d. We know about parapithecid cranial anatomy due to the discovery of a complete skull of the genus *Parapithecus* (a close relative of *Apadium*).

  4. Propliopithecids include the most significant Fayum fossil *Aegyptopithecus*.

   a. *Aegyptopithecus* is the proposed ancestor of Old World monkeys and apes and humans, and ...

    i. was roughly the size of a howler monkey (13-18 pounds)

    ii. had considerable sexual dimorphism

    iii. had a 2.1.2.3. dental formula (shares the derived catarrhine dental formula)

    iv. was most likely a short-limbed, robust slow-moving arboreal quadruped (primitive catarrhine).

      b. *Aegyptopithecus'* skull was small with a relatively small brain size.
         i. Indicates that encephalization must have evolved independently within the 2 anthropoid parvorders (Platyrrhini and Catarrhini)

C. Early Platyrrhines: New World Anthropoids
  1. The first New World primates date to 27 mya.
  2. Genus *Branisella,* found in Bolivia, are the earliest platyrrhine fossils (late Oligocene).
     a. Were small frugivorous monkeys (~ 2 pounds)
     b. It is so primitive that it is not placed into any living platyrrhine lineage.
     c. It may represent a remnant of the first platyrrhine radiation.
     d. Molecular evidence indicates living platyrrhines converge on a 20 million years old shared ancestor.
  3. Genus *Homunculus* ("miniature human") – appears in the middle Miocene.
     a. A cranium dated to 16.5 mya was discovered in Argentina.
  4. *Branisella* and *Homunculus* fossils provide clues to the earliest New World radiation and primate colonization of South America.
     a. It is likely that the first anthropoids came to the New World during the late Eocene (45 – 35 mya).
     b. Molecular evidence puts the Old World- New World monkey divergence between 50 and 35 mya.
  5. There are several hypothesis regarding the platyrrhine migration to/arrival in South America.
     a. Atlantic "rafting" - A transatlantic voyage would have required the crossing of an oceanic barrier.
        i. South America was an island continent until 5 mya.
        ii. Platyrrhines most likely floated across the Atlantic Ocean from Africa to South America on natural vegetation mats.
        iii. The closer proximity of South America and Africa during the Eocene supports this theory.
     b. North American migration and Antarctic migration route theories.
        i. A North American tarsier-like omomyoid journeyed to South America giving rise to the platyrrhines.
        ii. Alternatively, platyrrhines could have migration by passing through the Antarctic – Africa south to Antarctica to South America.

VI   MIOCENE PRIMATES
A. Diversification of the anthropoids occurred throughout the Miocene
B. Monkeying Around
  1. There are 2 families of Cercopithecoids (Old World Monkeys)
     a. victoriapithecids (extinct)
     b. cercopithecids (extant)
  2. Victoriapithecidae represent the earliest lineage leading to modern Old World monkeys.
     a. Found in North and East Africa as early as 19 mya, they predate the split between colobines and cercopithecines at 16 mya.
     b. May represent the LCA of living OW monkeys or may be a sister group.

  c. *Victoriapithecus* is the best known victoriapithecid.
    i. It was a small monkey, probably a terrestrial quadruped that exhibits colobine and cercopithecine features.
    ii. It had bilophodont molars (like all living OW monkeys), suggesting a diet of hard fruits and seeds.
 3. Cercopithecines and colobines had replaced the victoriapithecids by 12 mya.
 4. True colobine fossils are found in African deposits that date to ~ 9mya.
  a. These were smaller (8-9 pounds) than most extant colobines.
  b. They radiated into Europe and Asia.
 5. The subfamily Cercopithecinae includes macaques and baboons.
  a. Fossil macaques resemble other fossils and living macaques indicating their ancestral morphology has been retained for 5 million years.
  b. Biomolecular evidence indicates that *Macaca* diverged from *Papio* (modern baboons) about 10 mya.
 6. In East Africa, the baboon-like *Theropithecus* was the dominant cercopithecine genus of the Plio-Pleistocene.
  a. The hands and teeth indicate they were grass eaters.
  b. This genus includes fossil remains of the largest monkey that ever lived (225 pounds).
  c. By the middle Pleistocene, all species of *Theropithecus* became extinct except for *Theropithecus gelada*.
    i. Competition with *Papio* may have been a factor in their extinction.
C. Aping Monkeys
 1. Continental drifting caused the early Miocene to be warmer and wetter than the Oligocene, resulting in rainforests and woodlands as the dominant African environments.
 2. Molecular evidence indicates that monkeys and apes diverged ~ 27 mya.
 3. The first ape-like fossils anatomically resemble monkeys except in dentition.
  a. Superfamily proconsuloidea are commonly called "dental apes" because of the Y-5 patter on their molars.
  b. Proconsuloid fossils come from East Africa.
    i. They varied in size from 22 – 110 pounds.
    ii. They had diverse locomotor patterns from suspensory locomotion to arboreal and ground quadrupedalism.
 4. The best known proconsuloid is the genus *Proconsul* (20-17 mya). They …
  a. ranged in size from 10 -150 pounds,
  b. were frugivores,
  c. had a generalized cranium with a Y-5 molar pattern,
  d. retained adaptations for quadrupedal locomotion,
  e. occupied a wide range of habitats (rainforest – open woodlands),
  f. may not have had a tail.
    i. This indicates this hominoid characteristic had an ancient origin.
    ii. May place them outside Hominoidea as the lack of tail was due to convergence.
 5. Superfamily Pliopithecoidea date to the early Miocene, but
  a. They are more primitive than all other catarrhines, and small-bodied

b. Around 19 mya African Pliopithecids were the first catarrhines to leave Africa to colonize Asia and Europe.
   i. The discovery of genus *Lomorupithecus* (earliest pliopithecoid) found in Uganda supports this notion.
6. *Pliopithecus* is the best known pliopithecid from Europe.
   a. A robust mandible suggests a diet of leaves.
   b. Postcrania suggest it was a suspensory locomotor.
   c. Lacked a prehensile tail.
   d. They became extinct during the Pliocene.

D. True Apes
   1. True apes belong to superfamily Hominoidea and appear during the middle Miocene (16 mya).
   2. Best known Hominoidea genus is *Kenyapithecus* which …
      a. was a large-bodied terrestrial quadruped
      b. was possibly the first hominoid adapted to live on the ground (specialized humerus, wrist, and hand adaptations)
      c. was probably a knuckle-walker.
      d. had dentition more similar to extant great apes than *Proconsul.*
   3. West Side Story: European Radiation
      a. Hominoids left Africa ~16 mya to colonize Africa, and colonized Asia ~15 mya.
      b. *Dryopithecus* is the best known middle Miocene (~12-9 mya) hominoid found in southern France and northern Spain.
         i. *Dryopithecus* had long arms, hands, and fingers suggesting the ability to brachiate
         ii. Dentition imply a diet of fruit and leaves.
         iii. Was a highly arboreal species.
      c. *Ouranopithecus* is a late Miocene (9.6 – 8.7 mya) discovered in Greece.
         i. An abundance of fossils were deposited during a prehistoric flood.
         ii. It shares many features with extant African great apes including …
         iii. Large brow ridges
         iv. Wide interorbital distance
         v. Powerful jaws with small canines and thick molar enamel.
         vi. Sexual dimorphism comparable to the modern gorilla.
   4. East Side Story: Asian Radiation
      a. Asian hominoid fossils date to the middle and late Miocene
      b. *Sivapithecus* fossils have been discovered in India and Pakistan.
         i. *Sivapithecus* was a large (70-150 pounds) arboreal ape with facial characteristics resembling modern orangutans which include …
         ii. concave facial profile
         iii. broad zygomatics
         iv. projecting maxilla and incisors.
         v. Postcranial morphology incates *Sivapithecus* was an arboreal quadruped (unlike hominoids)
      c. *Gigantopithecus* ("gigantic ape) was a decendent of *Sivapithecus* from the late Miocene through the Pleistocene.

161

d. Two species of *Gigantopithecus* have been discovered.
e. *Gigantopithecus blacki* (2 mya), the Chinese species, is known from 4 mandibles and 1,500 isolated teeth.
    i. *Gigantopithecus blacki* was likely the largest primate ever, estimated as weighing more than 800 pounds and standing 9 ft. tall fully erect.
    ii. *Gigantopithecus blacki*'s small incisors and canines, thick premolar and molar enamel suggests a diet of tough fibrous vegetation.
    iii. *Gigantopithecus blacki* became extinct during the Middle Pleistocene (~ 200,000 ya).
f. *Gigantopithecus giganteus* (8.5 mya) from India and Pakistan was about half the size of *blacki*.
g. *Lufengpithecus*, found in southern China, dates to 9-5 mya.
    i. Was a medium-sized ape with an estimated weight of 110 pounds.
    ii. It is known from one of the most complete fossil ape assemblages including 5 crania, 41 mandibles, and over 650 teeth.
    iii. It is considered to be a stem orangutan based on narrow interorbital distance, ovoid orbits, and projecting incisors.
    iv. It existed in an environment created by the uplift of the Himalayas and they survived until 5 mya.
h. Teeth recovered from Pleistocene cave sites in southern China indicate that there may have been 3 distinct great ape lineages in Asia
    i. *Gigantopithecus*
    ii. *Pongo*
    iii. *Lufengpithecus*

E. Evolution of Extant Hominoids
  1. Hylobatids: The Lesser Apes
    a. Molecular data indicates the gibbon- great ape split occurred 15 -18 mya, and radiation of hylobatids (lesser apes) occurred 10.5 mya.
    b. Discovery of the small-bodied stem hylobatid *Yuanmoupithecus* supports this date.
    c. Pliopithecoids had been considered a possible gibbon ancestor; however, they share numerous primitive features with Oligocene catarrhines such as
        i. the lack of a tubelike middle ear
        ii. small tail
        iii. elbow joint morphology
    d. Gibbon radiation to Malaysia and Sumatra began 10.5-9 mya in China.
        i. In Sumatra, gibbons differentiated into two taxa including modern *Hylobates* which eventually dispersed into Borneo and Java 5-3 mya.
  2. The African Great Apes
    a. Molecular data indicates the gorillas diverged from humans and chimpanzees between 9-8 mya, and divergence of humans and chimpanzees occurred between 6-5 mya.
    b. After migration out of Africa, hominoids disappear from the fossil record ~13mya, and reappear (as *Chororapithecus*) around 10.5-10 mya.
        i. This may be due to Eurasian fossil apes migrating back to Africa as colobine monkeys were leaving.

162

      ii. *Ouranopithecus* (9.6-8.7 mya) from Greece was thought to be a stem African ape/human ancestor.

   c. *Chororapithecus* (10.5-10 mya) is the oldest African fossil genus representative of a large-bodied ape in eastern Africa following the "ape gap"

      i. Dental morphology indicates an adaptation to a fibrous diet.

      ii. If these genus is a gorilla ancestor (to the exclusion of humans) this would indicate divergence at 11-10mya (contrary to molecular data).

   d. *Nakalipithecus* (9.9-9.8 mya) from Kenya is thought to be the LCA of African great apes and humans

      i. Body size and dentition indicate a terrestrial lifestyle.

      ii. This genus shares many features with *Ouranopithecus*, and morphological similarities may indicate an ancestor-descendant relationship.

   e. Relationships among these 3 fossil great apes appear to indicate an African origin (rather than Eurasian) for the living African apes.

   f. Fossil chimpanzee teeth dating to ~500,000 ya found near Lake Baringo, Kenya may represent the only fossils belonging to the genus *Pan*

      i. These teeth are more similar to *Pan troglodytes* than *Pan paniscus*.

3. Asia's Lone Great Ape

   a. Orangutan ancestry is well documented.

   b. Current evidence indicates that *Sivapithecus* gave rise to *Gigantopithecus* (before 9 mya) and to *Lufengpithecus*, and finally to *Pongo* (orangutans) in the late Miocene.

   c. Biomolecular evidence shows that the orangutan lineage split from the African ape/human common ancestor – 14 mya.

   d. The relationship between *Sivapithecus* and *Pongo* is based on cranial similarities

   e. *Lufengpithecus* appears to have a closer relationship to *Pongo* based on postcranial similarities.

KEY TERMS

basal: most primitive

bilophidont: refers to molar teeth that have 4 cusps, oriented in 2 parallel rows.

catarrhine; member of Catarrhini, a parvorder of Primates, one of the 3 major divisions of the suborder Haplorhini, consisting of Old World monkeys and apes.

crown group: all of the taxa that come after a major speciation event. The members possess the clade's shared derived traits.

dental ape: an early ape that resembles a monkey postcranially, but apes dentally.

dental formula: a numerical shorthand sequence that specifies the number and type of tooth found in one quadrant of either the upper or lower jaw.

endocast: a solid impression of the inside of the skull.

Eurarchonta: the superorder designated for the sister orders of tree shrews, flying lemurs, and primates.

euprimate: true primate.

haplorhines: members of the primate suborder Haplorhini, which includes tarsiers, monkeys, apes, and humans.

last common ancestor (LCA): the final evolutionary link between two related groups.

paleoprimatologist: anthropologists specializing in the study of the nonhuman primate fossil record.

platyrrhines: members of Platyrrhini, a parvorder of Primates, one of the 3 major divisions of the suborder Haplorhini, consists of only New World monkeys.

postcranial: refers to all or part of the skeleton not including the skull; the portion of the body behind (or beneath) the head.

orthograde: an upright body position.

sagittal crest: a ridge of bone that runs down the middle of the cranium.

semiorder: the taxonomic category above suborder and below order.

sister groups: two new clades that result from the splitting of a single common lineage.

stem group: all of the taxa in a clade before a major speciation event. They do not often have the shared derived traits found in the crown group.

strepsirhines: members of the primate suborder Strepsirhini, which includes lemurs and lorises

subfossil: bone not old enough to have become completely mineralized as a fossil.

superorder: a taxonomic group ranking above and order and below a class or subclass.

terrestrial: living and locomoting primarily on the ground.

Y-5 molar: 5 cusped molar with grooves running between 5 cusps forming a Y shape. Characteristic of hominoids.

zygomatics: cheekbone.

MEDIA EXERCISES

1) Learn more about Eocene and Oligocene fossil primates at the Duke University Lemur Center, Division of Fossil Primates, Click on the Interactive Learning link and explore the images and text at http://www.fossils.duke.edu/index.html.

2)To learn more about the largest primate to have every lived, go to http://www.uiowa.edu/~bioanth/giganto.html.

3) Digital technology is revolutionizing the way paleontologists work. Check out a 3d version of the early Texas fossil *Rooneyia* at http://www.digimorph.org/specimens/Rooneyia_viejaensis/.

CONCEPT APPLICATIONS

1) The best way to grasp the similarities and differences between the skeletons of prosimians, monkeys, and apes is to see them side by side. Go to http://www.eskeletons.org/ and use the skeletal comparison tools to visual the morphology that was discussed in the chapter.

2) On the eSkeleton Project web site click on the Comparative anatomy link. Choose the Common marmoset and the human. Chose dentition in step 2 and then choose a view.

How to the teeth vary in these groups? Do they differ in the number of teeth? Now choose the ruffed lemur and human, choose cranium, and choose a ventral view. How do the eye orbits differ between these two species?

Now answer the Multiple Choice, True/False and Short Answer sample test questions. Following completion of the tests, correct them with the answers and textbook page references at the end of this Study Guide chapter. Note the areas in which you are strong and weak to guide you in your studying. Finally, answer the sample Essay Questions.

TRUE/FALSE QUESTIONS

If false, consider what modification would make the statement true.

1. The sister groups that fall into the superorder Euarchonta are tree shrews, flying lemurs, and primates.
   TRUE   FALSE

2. The fossil primate semiorder called plesiadapiforms are known mainly from North America.
   TRUE   FALSE

3. The only shared derived characteristic that links Euprimates to Paleocene plesiadapiforms is an upright posture.
   TRUE   FALSE

4. Derived characteristics that Eocene euprimates have that Paleocene plesiadapids lack include forward facing eyes, greater encephalization, and opposable thumbs.
   TRUE   FALSE

5. Subfossil lemurs are found all over southern Africa.
   TRUE   FALSE

6. The most productive region for finding Eocene and Oligocene anthropoid fossils is the Fayum Depression in northern China.
   TRUE   FALSE

7. Although there are several competing theories about how anthropoids arrived in the New World, the theory that is the best supported is the Atlantic "rafting" theory.
   TRUE   FALSE

8. Fossil and living members of the cercopithecine genus *Theropithecus* are known for their peculiar diet of grass.
   TRUE   FALSE

9. The best known pliopithecoid from Europe, *Pliopithecus*, possessed a prehensile tail which allowed it to brachiate effortlessly in the high tree tops.
   TRUE   FALSE

10. After their migration into Asia and Europe, hominoids disappear from the African fossil record around 13 mya, and do not reappear until the late Miocene.
    TRUE   FALSE

MULTIPLE CHOICE QUESTIONS

1. Two of the most important "derived" traits of primates are
   A. Pentadactyly and bilophodonty.
   B. Orthograde body position and forward facing eyes.
   C. Bipedalism and orthognathism.
   D. Elongated snout and color vision.

2. The first primate-like mammals (plesiadapiforms) appear in the _____ at _____ mya.
   A. Paleocene, 65.
   B. Eocene, 55.8.
   C. Oligocene, 33.
   D. Miocene, 23.

3. The Paleocene plesiadapiform called *Carpolestes* revealed what derived primate-like postcranial feature?
   A. Primate dental pattern.
   B. Finger and toe nails instead of claws.
   C. Encephalization.
   D. Long finger and toe bones.

4. All the taxa in a clade prior to a major speciation event is called a
   A. Crown group.
   B. Superorder.
   C. Sister group.
   D. Stem group.

5. Which of the following is not a characteristic of euprimates?
   A. Forward facing eyes.
   B. Greater encephalization.
   C. homoplasy.
   D. A postorbital bar.

6. The lemur-like adapoids are divided into five families. Which of these families is found in North America?
    A. Notharctids.
    B. Adapoids.
    C. Amphipithecids.
    D. Pliopithecids.

7. Amphipithecids had similar dental features to anthropoids but these features were not derived from the same ancestor. This is called
    A. The last common ancestor.
    B. homology.
    C. homoplasy.
    D. ancestral.

8. Why did so many species of lemurs go extinct around 2000 years ago?
    A. Sea levels rose and the lemurs drowned.
    B. The climate changed and the environment became unusable.
    C. Monkeys rafted to Madagascar and out-competed lemurs.
    D. Humans came and changed the available environment.

9. Which genus is not a member of the Omomyoid family?
    A. *Teilhardina.*
    B. *Biretia.*
    C. *Shoshonius*
    D. *Necrolemur*

10. Which living species of primate has a body plan that has essentially stayed the same since the Eocene?
    A. *Tarsius.*
    B. *Eosimias.*
    C. Gibbons.
    D. *Colobus.*

11. Which of the following is not a characteristic of lemuriformes?
    A. Dental comb.
    B. Grooming claw.
    C. Unfused frontal bone.
    D. Fused mandible.

12. Which of the following is not true about *Apidium*?
    A. They had a dental formula of 2.1.3.3.
    B. They probably appeared after Old and New World anthropoids diverged.
    C. They were small arboreal quadrupeds.
    D. They probably lived in polygynous social groups.

13. The most significant propliopithecid fossil genus, *Aegyptopithecus*, had a dental pattern that was the same as all Old World anthropoids. What is that pattern?
    A. 1:1:3:3.
    B. 2:1:2:3
    C. 2:1:3:3.
    D. 1:2:3:3

14. Molecular anthropologists's conservative estimate of the divergence point between catarrhines and platyrrhines is at _____ mya.
    A. 43.
    B. 55.
    C. 65.
    D. 90.

15. Which of the following is not a general New World monkey characteristic?
    A. Sideways facing nostrils.
    B. Ring-like ear hole with no tube.
    C. Grasping tail.
    D. Dental formula of 2:1:2:3.

16. Which genus of Miocene primate represents the earliest fossil evidence of Old World monkeys?
    A. *Theropithecus*.
    B. *Aegyptopithecus*.
    C. *Homunculus*.
    D. *Victoriapithecus*.

17. Why are proconsuloids considered dental apes?
    A. Their bodies are apelike but their teeth are bilophont.
    B. Their postcranial skeleton look monkey-like but their teeth look apelike.
    C. Molecular evidence from teeth date these fossils to the age of the apes.
    D. Proconsuloid teeth are specialized for grass eating.

18. Which of the following is not a general ape characteristic?
    A. Bilophodont molars.
    B. Broad nose and palate.
    C. Large body size .
    D. No tail.

19. Why is *Ouranopithecus* important to researchers interested in African ape origins?
    A. Similarities in facial morphology between African apes and *Ouranopithecus* indicated that *Ouranpithecus* migrated back to Africa.
    B. There is evidence of rafting across the Mediterranean.
    C. The postcranial of *Ouranopithecus* is adapted to long distance travel.
    D. *Ouranpithecus* is not important to these researchers.

168

20. The larger arboreal ape *Sivapithecus* from the Asian Radiation of hominoids in the Miocene resembles which of the living great apes in facial morphology but not body morphology?
    A. Gorilla.
    B. chimpanzee.
    C. orangutan.
    D. Bonobos.

21. How do scientists know that the Miocene ape *Gigantopithecus* from Asia weighed as much as 900 pounds?
    A. There is extensive postcranial evidence.
    B. From four lower jaws and several hundred teeth.
    C. *Gigantopithecus* did not weigh that much.
    D. *Gigantopithecus* has only been found in Africa.

22. When in time do molecular anthropologists put the gibbon-great ape split?
    A. 15-18 mya.
    B. 20-22 mya.
    C. 24-26 mya.
    D. 30-32 mya

23. In 2005, at Lake Baringo, Kenya, researchers discovered 500 kya fossil teeth of what great ape genus?
    A. *Ouranopithecus*.
    B. *Pan*.
    C. *Pongo*.
    D. *Hylobates*

24. Which of the following groups are considered anthropoids?
    A. Lemurs.
    B. Lorises.
    C. Adapids.
    D. Platyrrhines

SHORT ANSWER QUESTIONS (& PAGE REFERENCES)

1. The lemur-like adapoids are the most primitive primate group. This group of early primates has a dental formula of 2:1:4:3. What do these numbers stand for? (p. 149)

2. Why does *Archeolemur*'s skull resemble a monkey's skull? (p. 247)

3. List at least 3 general anthropoid characteristics. (p. 251)

4. Explain what a Y-5 molar pattern is. (p. 261)

169

5. Based on Fig. 9-19 which genus of extinct primate is considered the last common ancestor of both great apes and catarrhines? (p. 260)

ESSAY QUESTIONS (& PAGE REFERENCES)

1. Briefly describe the morphological characteristics of the Paleocene primate-like mammals. (pp. 241-242)

2. How do researchers distinguish between euprimates and the primate-like mammals of the Paleocene? (pp. 242-243)

3. Humans are the only living indigenous North American. Briefly describe at least two early North American primates. (pp. 213-214).

4. How do scientists think that New World monkeys got to South America? (pp.255-257).

5. Why is there so little evidence of the early ancestry of modern great apes? (pp. 267-268).

ANSWERS, *CORRECTED STATEMENT* IF FALSE & REFERENCES TO TRUE/FALSE QUESTIONS

1. **TRUE**, p. 237

2. **TRUE**, p. 241

3. **FALSE**, pp. 241-242, Currently, finger and toe nails are the only shared derived trait that links Euprimates to plesiadapiforms.

4. **TRUE**, p. 242

5. **FALSE**, p. 247, Subfossil lemurs are only found on the island of Madagascar.

6. **FALSE**, p. 252, The Fayum is productive but it is in Africa not China.

7. **TRUE**, pp. 256-257

8. **TRUE**, pp. 259

9. **FALSE**, p. 262, *Pliopithecus* did not have a prehensile tail.

10. **TRUE**, p. 267

ANSWERS & REFERENCES TO MULTIPLE CHOICE QUESTIONS

1. **B**, p. 236	9. **B**, pp. 249-252	17. **B**, p. 261
2. **A**, p. 241	10. **A**, p. 250	18. **A**, p. 258
3. **B**, p. 242	11. **D**, p. 251	19. **A**, p. 267
4. **D**, p. 237	12. **B**, p. 253	20. **C**, p.264
5. **C**, p. 242	13. **B**, p. 254	21. **B**, p. 265
6. **A**, p. 245	14. **A**, p. 255	22. **A**, p. 266
7. **C**, p. 245	15. **D**, p. 254	23. **C**, p. 267
8. **D**, p. 247	16. **D**, p. 258	24. **D**, p. 253

CONCEPT APPLICATIONS SOLUTIONS

The marmoset and human have very different teeth. Marmoset teeth are pointed and sharp. They are good for crunching on bugs and extracting sap from trees. Human teeth are more generalized with some teeth being sharp for cutting and tearing and other flat for grinding. The orbital area of lemurs and humans vary widely. Lemur eye orbits are not closed off in the back like in humans. This is an ancestral trait. The closed off orbits is a derived trait of anthropoids.

171

CHAPTER 10

PALEOANTHROPOLOGY: RECONSTRUCTING EARLY HOMININ BEHAVIOR AND ECOLOGY

LEARNING OBJECTIVES

After reading this chapter you should be able to:

- list defining characteristics of a hominin (pp. 274-275)
- discuss what mosaic evolution is and the mosaic nature of human evolution (p. 275)
- explain how and why paleoanthropology is a multidisciplinary science (pp. 279-282)
- discuss the significance of Olduvai Gorge to paleoanthropology (pp. 282-283)
- compare relative dating techniques to chronometric techniques (pp. 283-289)
- list and describe the types of early hominin sites found at Olduvai (pp. 289-290)
- describe the purposes of experimental archaeology (pp. 290-293)
- review theories explaining the origins of hominin bipedalism (pp. 296-299)

CHAPTER OUTLINE

Introduction

We have seen in previous chapters that humans are primates and we share our evolution and even much of our behavior with other primates. At some point, however, our ancestors went off in a separate direction from the other primates to become the unique species we are today. Some primitive hominoids may have begun this process as long as 10 million years ago, but after 5 mya there is definite hominin fossil evidence in East Africa. One of the factors influencing hominin evolution was their behavior, once again emphasizing the biocultural nature of human evolution. This chapter looks at how scientists deduce early human behavior and the methods used by paleoanthropologists.

I   DEFINITION OF HOMININ
  A. Modern humans and our hominin ancestors are distinguished from our closest relatives by
     a number of characteristics.
     1. The earliest evidence of hominins are dental and cranial remains from the Miocene.
     2. Dental remains don't solely identify hominins and are not distinctive of later stages of human evolution.
  B. Various researchers have pointed to certain characteristics as being significant (at some stage) for hominins:
     1. bipedal locomotion.
     2. large brain size.
     3. tool-making behavior.
  C. Mosaic evolution.
     1. Consult Figure 10-1 p. 275.
     2. All of the above mentioned characteristics did not evolve simultaneously.

3. The evolutionary pattern in which different features evolve at different rates is called mosaic evolution.
4. The defining characteristic of hominins is bipedal locomotion.
   a. The evolution of bipedalism predates other hominin characteristics such as brain development and toolmaking behaviors.
   b. Skeletal evidence for bipedal locomotion is the only truly reliable indicator of hominin status.
D. Hominins are members of the Hominini tribe.
   1. See Figure 10-2 p. 276
   2. The great apes are not a monophyletic group (i.e. they do not make up a coherent evolutionary group that shares a single common ancestor.
   3. This taxonomic system emphasizes the very close relationship between humans and African apes (especially the chimpanzees and bonobos).
   4. As such, the term hominid, once commonly used to refer to humans only, now includes all great apes and humans.
      a. Traditional taxonomic use of the term hominid is synonymous with the current use of the term hominin.
E. Biocultural evolution: the human capacity for culture.
   1. The most distinctive behavioral feature of modern humans is our extraordinary elaboration and dependence on culture.
   2. Culture integrates an entire adaptive strategy involving cognitive, political, social and economic components.
      a. The material culture, tools and other items, is but a small portion of this cultural complex.
   3. The record of earlier hominins is almost exclusively comprised of material culture, especially residues of stone tool manufacture.
      a. Thus, it is difficult to learn anything about the earliest stages of hominin cultural development before the regular manufacture of stone tools, around 2.6 mya
      b. Without such evidence we cannot know exactly the behavior of the earliest hominins.
      c. Likely hominins used other types of tools (such as sticks) made of soft, perishable materials before they constructed stone tools
      d. Review A Closer Look: What was Doing at Olduvai and the Other Plio-Pleistocene Sites? (pp. 278-279).
   4. The fundamental basis for human cultural success relates directly to cognitive abilities.
      a. Humans display cognitive abilities in a complexity several orders of magnitude beyond that of other animals.
      b. Care must be taken to recognize the manifold nature of culture and to not expect it always to contain the same elements across species or through time.
      c. We know that the earliest hominins did not regularly manufacture stone tools.
         i. The earliest members of our lineage date back to approximately 7-5 mya
         ii. These early hominins may have carried objects such as naturally sharp stones or stone flakes, parts of carcasses and pieces of wood.
         iii. At the least, we expect them to have displayed these behaviors to the same degree as what is found in living chimpanzees.

d. Hominins, by 6 mya (possibly 7 mya) had one crucial advantage; they were bipedal and could easily carry objects.

e. Over the millions of years of hominin evolution, numerous components interacted, but they did not all develop simultaneously.

   i. As cognitive abilities developed, so did more efficient means of communications and learning.

   ii. As a result of neural reorganization, more elaborate tools and social relationships also emerged.

   iii. This selection for greater intelligence in turn selected for further neural elaboration.

f. These mutual dynamics are at the very heart of hominin biocultural evolution.

II THE STRATEGY OF PALEOANTHROPOLOGY

A. Recovering and interpreting the clues left by early hominins is central to paleoanthropology.

  1. Paleoanthropology is a diverse, multidisciplinary field that seeks to reconstruct the dating, anatomy, behavior and ecology of our ancestors.

    a. Review Table 10-1 on p. 280 for a list of the related disciplines.

B. Site survey

  1. An area will be surveyed usually by Geologists and Paleoanthropologists to identify potential hominin sites.

  2. Technology like satellite images and aerial photography may aid in the search.

  3. Vertebrate paleontologists may be involved in this early work as they can:

    a. Help find fossil beds containing fauna.

    b. Give quick estimates of the geological age of a site based on faunal remains.

C. More extensive site surveys are conducted after potential hominin sites are identified.

D. Archaeologists often participate in the search for hominin material traces.

E. Evidence of hominin presence can consist of bones or material items referred to as artifacts

  1. Artifacts are remains left behind that provide behavioral clues of early hominin activities.

    a. The modification of stone indicates the activities of hominins and provides us with a preserved record of human activity.

     i. Stones are transported from one place to another.

     ii. Stones are used for a number of things such as throwing projectiles, cutting tools, or simply for use in windbreaks.

     iii. The oldest artifact sites now documented are from the Gona and Bouri areas of northeastern Ethiopia, dating to 2.5 mya.

    b. Organic materials used as tools are typically not preserved in the archaeological record, therefore prior to stone tool usage we have no record of the earliest stages of hominin cultural modifications.

F. Coordinated research projects are crucial to paleoanthropology.

  1. Fieldwork is a costly endeavor requiring hundreds of thousands of dollars.

  2. Projects are headed by an archaeologist or physical anthropologist.

    a. Field crew members survey for bones and artifacts.

    b. They collect soil, pollens, and rock samples during their searches.

G. Laboratory analysis is a long and detailed component of paleoanthropology.
   1. Back in the lab, materials are cleaned, sorted and labeled.
      a. Animal and plant remains can help reconstruct the paleoecology
      b. Paleoecological analysis can help in reconstructing early hominin diet.
         i. Palynology (the study of fossil spores, pollen and other microscopic plant parts).
      c. Taphonomy (the study of the deposition of bones and other materials) is a part of such investigations as it indicates the formation processes and context of the site.
   2. The paleoanthropologist synthesizes the conclusions from each component of the investigation to discern the nature of the site and its connection to human evolutionary history.
      a. Dates for the site.
         i. Geological, paleontological, geophysical data
      b. Paleoecology of the site.
         i. Paleontological, palynological, geomorphological, and taphonomic data
      c. Archaeological traces of behavior
      d. Anatomical evidence from hominin remains.
   3. Analyses of the above aid in the determination of the kind of creature that may have been our direct ancestor (or a very close relative).
   4. Primatologists may contribute information comparing humans and contemporary nonhuman primates.
   5. Cultural anthropologists and ethnoarchaeologists may contribute ethnographic information on the behavior of more recent humans, particularly the ecological adaptations of contemporary hunter-gatherer groups exploiting roughly similar environmental settings as reconstructed for a hominin site.
   6. The end results is the production of a more complete and accurate understanding of human evolution.

III **PALEOANTHROPOLOGY IN ACTION - OLDUVAI GORGE**
   A. The greatest abundance of paleoanthropological information concerning the behavior of early hominins comes from Olduvai Gorge, Tanzania.
      1. First "discovered" by an early twentieth century butterfly catcher.
      2. Continuous excavations of the area were done by Louis and Mary Leakey between 1935 and 1984; others continue their work.
   B. Olduvai is located on the eastern branch of the Great Rift Valley of Africa.
      1. It is a steep-sided valley with a deep ravine that resembles a miniature Grand Canyon.
      2. Olduvai is part of the Serengeti Plains, and extends for 25 miles in length.
      3. The semi-arid pattern of modern Olduvai is believed to be similar to most of the past environments preserved there over the last two million years.
      4. The surrounding countryside is a grassland savanna
         a. The geological processes associated with the formation of the Rift Valley makes Olduvai extremely important to paleoanthropological investigation.
         b. Three results of geological rifting are most significant:
            i. faulting (earth movement) exposes geological beds near the surface normally hidden by hundreds of feet of accumulated sediments.

175

      ii. active volcanic processes cause rapid sedimentation, which yields excellent preservation of bone and artifacts.

      iii. volcanic activity provides a wealth of radiometrically datable material.

C. The greatest contribution of Olduvai to paleoanthropological research is the establishment of an extremely well documented and correlated sequence of geological, paleontological, archeological and hominin remains over the last two million years.

   1. A well-established geological context is the foundation of all paleoanthropological research.

      a. Hominin sites can be accurately dated relative to other sites in the Olduvai Gorge by cross-correlating with marker beds that have established dates.

   2. Paleontological evidence includes more than 150 species of extinct animals including:

      a. fish, turtles, crocodiles, pigs, giraffes, horses, birds, rodents and antelope.

      b. Analyses of these remains provide clues to the ecological conditions experienced by the earliest humans.

         i. These remains tell us a great deal about the ecological conditions and early human habitats at Olduvai.

   3. The archeological sequence is well documented for the last two million years.

      a. The earliest hominin site is from around 1.85 million years ago.

      b. Additionally, there is a well developed stone tool kit called the Oldowan which includes choppers and some flake tools.

      c. The Oldowan tradition continues into later beds, being somewhat modified into what is called Developed Oldowan.

      d. Partial remains of several fossilized hominins have been recovered at Olduvai that range in time from the earliest occupation to fairly recent *Homo sapiens*

         i. This includes the discovery of the *Zinjanthropus* skull ("Zinj") discovered by Mary Leakey in 1959.

         ii. Review "A Closer Look: Discovery of *Zinjanthropus* and the Beginnings of Modern Paleoanthropology" p. 284.

IV   DATING METHODS

A. An essential objective of paleoanthropology is establishing a chronological framework of sites and fossils (i.e., how old are they?)

B. The two types of dating methods used by paleoanthropologists are relative dating and chronometric (absolute) dating.

C. Relative dating

   1. Relative dating tells you which object is older or younger than another object, but not by how much in actual years.

   2. One type of relative dating is based on stratigraphy which is the study of the sequential layering of deposits.

      a. Stratigraphy is based on the principle of superposition, i.e., that the lowest stratum (layer) is the oldest and higher strata are more recent.

      b. Problems associated with stratigraphic dating include:

         i. Earth disturbances such as volcanic activity, river activity, mountain building, or even modern construction activities by humans, can shift strata making it difficult to reconstruct the chronology.

176

  ii. The time period of the formation of a particular stratum (i.e., how long the layer took to accumulate) is not possible to determine with much accuracy.

3. Fluorine analysis is another relative dating method; however it can only be used on bones.

 a. Groundwater seeps and deposits fluorine into the bone during the fossilization process.

 b. The longer a bone is in the earth, the more fluorine it will contain.

  i. Bones deposited at the same time should contain the same amount of fluorine.

  ii. This method was used to expose Piltdown hoax.

 c. Fluorine analysis is only useful with bones found at the same location.

  i. The amount of fluorine in groundwater is based on local conditions and varies from one area to another.

  ii. Therefore, comparing bones from different localities is not possible.

 d. Actual ages of artifacts and strata cannot be obtained from relative techniques.

D. Chronometric (absolute) dating.

1. Chronometric dating provides an estimate of age in years and is based on radioactive decay.

 a. Certain radioactive isotopes of elements are unstable and they decay to form an isotope of another element.

 b. This decay occurs at a constant rate but the rate varies for different elements.

  i. By measuring the amount of disintegration in a particular sample, the number of years it took for the amount of decay may be calculated.

2. The time it takes for one-half of the original amount of the isotope to decay into another isotope is referred to as the half-life.

3. Potassium/argon (K/Ar) dating involves the decay of potassium into argon gas.

 a. K/Ar has a half-life of 1.25 billion years.

 b. It has been used extensively to date materials in the 1-5 million year range.

 c. The $^{40}Ar/^{39}Ar$ method is a more accurate variant of the potassium/argon technique.

  i. It allows analysis of smaller samples.

  ii. It reduces experimental error.

  iii. It has been used on a wide variety of hominin fossil sites.

  iv. It can date a much wider range than K/Ar, even up to modern times.

 d. Both K/Ar and $^{40}Ar/^{39}Ar$ techniques can only be done on rock matrix; they will not work on organic material such as bone.

4. The best type of rock to perform K/Ar dating on is volcanic rock.

 a. When the lava is laid down in its molten state the argon gas present is driven off.

 b. After solidification any argon that has been trapped in the rock is the result of potassium decay.

 c. To obtain the date of the rock, it is reheated and the escaping argon gas is measured.

5. Carbon-14 is a radiometric method commonly used by archaeologists.

 a. Carbon-14 has a half-life of 5730 years.

 b. This method can be used to reliably date organic materials younger than 40,000 years.

6. Thermoluminescence is a technique used to directly date inorganic artifacts.
   a. Relies on the principle of radiometric decay.
   b. Heated artifacts give off beta particles trapped in the rock.
   c. Particles emit a glow called thermoluminescence.
   d. Researchers reheat the artifact to 500° C and calculate the age from the displaced beta particles.
   e. Can be used on flint tools from hominin sites and ceramic from prehistoric sites.
7. Uranium series dating and electron-spin resonance dating.
   a. Uranium series relies on radioactive decay of short-lived uranium isotopes.
   b. ESR measures released electrons- used on dental enamel.
8. No dating method is absolutely precise.
   a. Chronometric analyses provide approximate dates with standard deviations that provide a time range.
   b. Review "A Closer Look: Chronometric Dating Estimates" and "At a Glance: Relative and Chronometric Dating" p.287.
E. Application of dating methods: examples from Olduvai.
   1. Olduvai has some of the best-documented chronology for any hominin site in the Lower or Middle Pleistocene.
   2. Potassium-Argon method is a valuable dating technique in East Africa.
   3. *Zinjanthropus* ("Zinj") (OH 5) was dated potassium-argon to ~1.79 million years.
      a. Due to potential sources of error, K/Ar dating must be cross-checked using other independent methods.
   4. Fission-track dating
      a. Most important techniques for cross-checking K/Ar determinations.
      b. Uranium-238 decays at a constant rate through spontaneous fission, which leaves microscopic tracks in crystals.
      c. By counting tracks (i.e., the fraction of uranium atoms that have fissioned) the age of a mineral can be estimated.
      d. One of the earliest uses of uranium-238 dating was at Olduvai, which yielded a date of 2.30 (±.28) mya, compatible with the K/Ar dates.
   5. Another important method of cross-checking dates is paleomagnetism.
      a. This technique is based on the constantly shifting magnetic pole of the earth.
      b. The earth's magnetic field, currently oriented in a northern direction, periodically shifts.
      c. Paleomagnetic dating involves taking samples of sediment that contains magnetically charged particles.
         i. Magnetically charged particles orient towards the magnetic pole, and will be oriented towards the direction of the magnetic pole that existed when they were incorporated into rock.
         ii. Thus these particles serve as a "fossil compass."
      d. The paleomagnetic sequence is compared against the K/Ar dates to check accuracy.
   6. Faunal correlation (biostratigraphy) is another method for cross-checking dating methods.
      a. The presence of particular fossil pigs, elephants, etc. in areas where dates are known can be used to extrapolate an approximate age by noting which genera and species are present in areas that are not otherwise possible to date.

178

7. Because each dating technique has problems, it is important to use several methods in conjunction with one another in order to cross-check the results.

V **EXCAVATIONS AT OLDUVAI**
   A. Olduvai provides a cross section of 2 million years of history.
   B. Olduvai has provided several dozen hominin sites.
      1. An incredible amount of paleoanthropological information has come from these excavated areas.
      2. There has been much controversy over the interpretation of the types of early hominin activity at various sites.
         a. These sites have been interpreted as
            i. Campsites
            ii. The result of nonhuman activity
            iii. Cache areas for tools
            iv. The activities of gatherer/scavengers

VI **EXPERIMENTAL ARCHAEOLOGY**
   A. We can learn more about our ancestors by understanding how they made and used tools.
   B. Stone tool (lithic) technology
      1. Stone is the most common residue of prehistoric cultural behavior.
         a. Blanks are nodules of stone that fracture in controlled ways
         b. The smaller piece struck off of a stone is called a flake, the larger remaining portion is the core
      2. Early hominins probably also used sticks and egg shells which are not preserved in the fossil record.
      3. The Oldowan is the earliest known stone tool industry.
         a. Olduwan choppers were once thought to be the central component of a lithic assemblage.
         b. Reanalysis has shown that the choppers were just by-products of flake production.
      4. Knapping (manufacturing stone tools) is a complex learned skill.
      5. The objective in tool making is to produce a usable cutting surface.
      6. Direct percussion means hitting a core with a hammer stone to produce a flake.
      7. Tools flaked on both sides are called bifacial.
      8. Tiny blades called microliths are found in the uppermost beds at Olduvai (circa 17,000 y.a.)
      9. Pressure flaking is a manufacturing method that utilizes a pointed piece of bone or antler pressed against the stone to make thin microliths.
      10. Ancient tools show signs of microwear which may indicate how they were used.
      11. Microscopic pieces of organic material found on the edges of stone implements called phytoliths may also reveal how tools were employed.
   C. Analysis of bone
      1. Experimental archaeologists are also interested in how bones were altered by early humans and natural forces.
      2. Taphonomy is a branch of paleoecology that is concerned with the study of how natural factors influence bone deposition and preservation.
         a. Lab experiments have shown how water influences bone at archaeological sites.

179

b. These studies also provide insight into how tools were employed for butchering and breaking bone.

VII RECONSTRUCTION OF EARLY HOMININ ENVIRONMENTS AND BEHAVIOR

A. Paleoanthropologists are interested in how early hominins evolved and why the process occurred the way it did.
   1. They develop scenarios based on evidence to interpret past behavior; however, scenarios are not testable.
B. Environmental explanations for hominin origins
   1. The earliest hominins do not appear until the late Miocene or the very early Pliocene (7-5 mya.)
      a. Anthropologists are interested in the environmental conditions and the general ecological patterns that help to explain the origins of the first hominins.
   2. Environment determinism.
      a. It is a common misconception that a single environmental change is related to a major adaptive change in a type of organism.
         i. Environment change X produced adaptation Y in a particular organism.
         ii. Environmental determinism grossly underestimates the true complexity of the evolutionary process
   3. When early hominins were diverging from the other ape lineages some major ecological changes may be been occurring in Africa.
   4. For most of the Miocene, Africa was generally tropical but became cooler and drier at the end of the Miocene.
   5. The earliest evidence of hominin diversification comes from eastern and central Africa.
   6. Stable carbon isotopes are produced by plants in differing proportions depending on temperature and aridity.
      a. Animals eat the plants and stable carbon isotopes in the bones provide a signature of the general type environment.
   7. One model of the past environment postulates that as climates grew cooler in East Africa 12-5 mya …
      a. Forest became less continuous.
      b. Forest "fringe" habitats and transitional zones between forests and grasslands became more widespread.
      c. In transitional environments some hominoids used the drier and some the wetter environments.
      d. Further adaptive strategies would have followed
         i. bipedalism
         ii. increased tool use
         iii. dietary specialization
         iv. changes in social organization
   8. Our knowledge of the factors influencing the appearance of the *earliest* hominins is limited.
   9. Evolutionary pulse theory

180

a. Elizabeth Vrba of Yale University studying faunal remains in South African sites, hypothesized that climatic shifts may have played a central role in stimulating hominin evolutionary development at key stages.

10. Sites in Java, Indonesia reveal that the flora and fauna may have enticed hominins out of Africa.

11. Researchers have shown that early humans were adaptively flexible and may not have been forced to change or move based on the environment.

C. Why did hominins become bipedal?

1. Bipedal locomotion was the most fundamental adaptive shift among the early members of our family.

2. Environmental influences would have to occur *before* documented evidence of well-adapted bipedal behavior.

3. The major shift in locomotion would have to have been at the end of the Miocene.

4. Hominins come to the ground to seize the opportunities offered in more open habitats.

5. Successful terrestrial bipedalism made possible the further adaptation to more arid open territory.

6. Bipedalism was not a sudden transformation.

7. Like terrestrial nonhuman primates, early hominins would have sought safety at night in the trees.

8. The primary influences claimed to have stimulated the shift to bipedalism include:
   a. the ability to carry objects and offspring,
   b. hunting on the savanna,
   c. gathering seeds and nuts,
   d. feeding from bushes,
   e. a better view of open country to spot predators,
   f. long-distance walking,
   g. and provisioning by males of females with dependent offspring.

9. Jolly scenario
   a. Seed-eating hypothesis uses the feeding behavior and ecology of gelada baboons as an analogy for early hominins.
      i. Seed eating is an activity that requires keen hand-eye coordination with bipedal shuffling improving the efficiency of foraging.
   b. Early hominins are thought to have adapted to open country and bipedalism as a result of their primary adaptation to eating seeds and nuts.

10. Lovejoy scenario.
    a. This scenario combines presumed aspects of early hominin ecology, feeding, pair bonding, infant care, and food sharing.
    b. Lovejoy's scenario has 3 assumptions:
       i. The earliest hominins had offspring that were as K-selected as other large-bodied hominoids.
       ii. Hominin males ranged widely and provisioned females and their young which remained more attached to a home base.
       iii. Males paired monogamously with females.

11. There are several critiques of these scenarios.

a. Jolly's seed-eating hypothesis predictions relating to size of the back teeth in most early hominins are met, but
   i. The proportions of the front teeth in many forms aren't what we'd expect to see in a committed seed eater.
b. Lovejoy – the evidence that appears to contradict the male-provisioning scenario is that all early hominins were quite sexually dimorphic.
   i. There should not be such dramatic differences in body size between males and females.
   ii. Notions of food sharing, home bases, and long-distance provisioning are questioned by more controlled interpretations of the archaeological record.

12. Falk's radiator hypothesis
   a. Suggests that an upright posture put severe constraints on brain size.
   b. Falk hypothesizes that new brain-cooling mechanisms must have coevolved with bipedalism.
   c. Requirements for better brain cooling would have been particularly marked as hominins adapted to open-country ground living on the hot savanna
   d. This theory helps explain the relationship of bipedalism to later brain expansion, and also explains why only some hominins became encephalized.

13. Attempts to interrelate lines of evidence, the application of contemporary primate models, and predictions concerning further evidence form paleoanthropological contexts can help us to better understand and test information in the paleontological record.

KEY TERMS

absolute dating techniques: see chronometric dating techniques.

accuracy: refers to how close a measured quantity is to the true value of what is being measured. Generally, the true value is represented by a standard.

artifacts: material remnants of hominin behavior, usually of made of stone or, occasionally, bone, early in the archaeological record.

association: what is found with an artifact or archeological trace.

biostratigraphy: dating method based on evolutionary changes within an evolving lineage.

blank: a stone suitably sized and shaped to be further worked into a tool.

chronometric dating: dating techniques that gives an estimate in actual number of years, based on radioactive decay (i.e. absolute dating).

context: the environmental setting where an archaeological trace is found.

core: stone from which flakes are removed.

culture: extrasomatic adaptations to the environment.

direct percussion: striking a core with another stone to remove flakes.

environmental determinism: oversimplified interpretation linking simple environmental change directly to major evolutionary shifts in organisms.

faunal analysis: see biostratigraphy.

feature: in archaeology, an immovable residue of human occupation, such as an ash pit.

flake: sharp-edged fragment removed from a core.

fluorine analysis: a relative dating technique in which the amount of fluorine deposited in bones is compared. Bones with the most fluorine are the oldest.

geomorphology: changes in the form of the earth, such as rifting of land, mountain building, development of ravines and canyons, etc.

half-life: in chronometric dating, the amount of time that it takes for one-half of the original (parent) isotope to decay into its daughter isotope.

knappers: stone tool makers.

lithic: referring to stone tools.

microliths: small stone artifacts struck from narrow blades.

microwear: diagnostic, microscopic use-wear patterns on the edges of stone tools.

monophyletic group: a coherent evolutionary group that shares a single common ancestor.

mosaic evolution: the evolutionary pattern in which different characteristics evolve at different rates.

multidisciplinary: refers to research involving mutual contributions and cooperation of experts from various scientific fields.

paleoecology: the study of fossil communities and environments.

paleomagnetism: dating methods based on the earth's shifting magnetic poles.

paleontology: the recovery and study of ancient organisms.

palynology: the study of fossil spores, pollen and other microscopic plant parts.

phytoliths: microscopic, glassy structures found in the cells of many plants.

precision: refers to the closeness of repeated measurements of the same quantity to each other.

pressure flaking: a flake-removal method that presses a bone or antler point against a core.

principle of superposition: in a stratigraphic sequence, the lower layers were deposited before the upper layers.

protohominin: the earliest members of the hominin lineage. No fossils of this hypothetical group have yet been found.

relative dating: a type of dating in which objects are ranked by age. Thus, some objects can be said to be older than other objects, but no actual age in years can be assigned.

scenarios: general, speculative reconstructions produced from various scientific data.

stable carbon isotopes: produced in plants in differing proportions depending on environmental conditions.

stratigraphy: study of the sequential layering of deposits.

taphonomy: the study of how bones and other materials came to be buried and preserved as fossils.

thermoluminescence (TL): technique for dating certain archaeological materials, such as stone tools.

MEDIA EXERCISES

1) Are you interested in experiencing paleoanthropology in action? Then perhaps you should check out a paleoanthropological field school. Here are a couple of those that are available:

- Koobi Fora Field School, northwestern Kenya (administered jointly by Rutgers U. & the National Museums of Kenya), found at http://www.rci.rutgers.edu/~kffs/.
- Hadar Paleoanthropology Field School (administered by the Institute of Human Origins, University of Arizona), found at http://www.public.asu.edu/~kreed/Hadar.htm.

2) Go to http://www.leakeyfoundation.org/audio/, click on *Mary Leakey (Human Origins, 1980)* and listen to Mary Leakey speak about Olduvai paleontology.

CONCEPT APPLICATION

Answer the following questions that refer to the vertical profile (cross-section) of a paleoanthropological site on the next page.

1) What chronometric method was likely used to date the volcanic layers that are labeled "1.0 mya" and "50,000 ya"?

2) Put the three skulls labeled "X, Y & Z" in the correct chronological order, from youngest to oldest. Approximately how old are skulls "X, Y & Z"?

3) The teeth on the right side are most likely associated with which skull? Why?

4) Which two of the three fireplaces (labeled "1, 2 & 3") are most likely the same approximate age? What chronometric technique would you use to verify your answer?

5) Can you use the same technique on the other fireplace? Why or why not?

6) Which two of the three sets of limb bones (labeled "A, B & C") are most likely the same approximate age? What dating technique would you use to verify your answer?

7) What geological event can probably account for the difficulty in interpreting this site's stratigraphy?

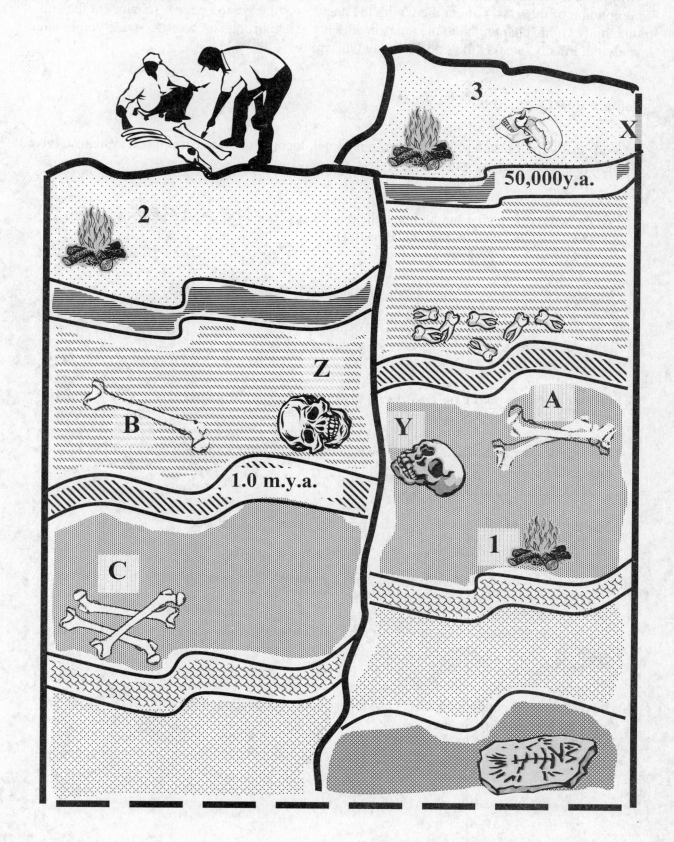

Now answer the True/False, Multiple Choice and Short Answer sample test questions. Following completion of the tests, correct them with the answers and textbook page references at the end of this Study Guide chapter. Note the areas in which you are strong and weak to guide you in your studying. Finally, answer the sample Essay Questions.

TRUE/FALSE QUESTIONS

1. Mosaic evolution states that the hominin dental, locomotor and neurological systems evolved at remarkably uniform rates.
   TRUE   FALSE

2. When compared with other animals, the most distinctive behavioral feature of humans is our extraordinary reliance on biological instinct.
   TRUE   FALSE

3. Modern paleoanthropologists work independently of other scientists.
   TRUE   FALSE

4. Olduvai Gorge is located in Ghana, in western Africa.
   TRUE   FALSE

5. Potassium-argon dating only works on organic material, like charcoal.
   TRUE   FALSE

6. Biostratigraphy is the dating method based on the constantly shifting nature of the earth's magnetic pole,
   TRUE   FALSE

7. The thin-edged fragment removed from another rock is called a core.
   TRUE   FALSE

8. Vrba's evolutionary pulse theory suggests a gradual evolutionary change in hominin species.
   TRUE   FALSE

9. The most fundamental adaptive shift in hominin evolution was the development of a large brain.
   TRUE   FALSE

10. Lovejoy's seed-eating hypothesis used the feeding behavior and ecology of lemurs as an analogy for early hominins.
    TRUE   FALSE

MULTIPLE CHOICE QUESTIONS

1. Evolution in which structures evolve at different rates is termed
   A. convergent evolution.
   B. parallel evolution.
   C. mosaic evolution.
   D. punctuated equilibrium

2. Human evolution can be characterized as
   A. parallel.
   B. convergent.
   C. homologous.
   D. mosaic.

3. Which of the following is an aspect of material culture that could be a vestige of the earliest hominins?
   A. a fragment of a stone tool
   B. cognitive abilities
   C. economic systems
   D. social systems

4. Initial surveying and locating potential hominin sites is the primary task of
   A. physical anthropologists.
   B. geologists.
   C. paleoecologists.
   D. archaeologists.

5. The primary task of an archeologist at a paleoanthropological site is to
   A. search for hominin "traces."
   B. reconstruct the ancient environment of the site.
   C. establish the relationships of any fossil humans recovered.
   D. perform dating techniques to establish the time period.

6. The earliest documented artifact sites are
   A. Laetoli at 3.4 mya
   B. Gona and Bouri at 2.5 mya
   C. Olduvai at 1.85 mya
   D. Taung at 1 mya

7. The archeological setting where an artifact is found is called the
   A. microlith.
   B. context.
   C. quarry site.
   D. monolith.

187

8. Which of the following does a paleoanthropologist **not** use in the concluding stages of a site interpretation?
    A. information pertaining to dating.
    B. paleoecology.
    C. information from linguists.
    D. anatomical evidence from hominin remains.

9. The paleoanthropologist who discovered the famous "Zinj" skull at Olduvai was
    A. Louis Leakey.
    B. Mary Leakey.
    C. Jane Goodall.
    D. Meg Weigel.

10. The earliest stone tool industry found at Olduvai is called the
    A. Acheulean.
    B. Chellean.
    C. Oldowan.
    D. Developed Oldowan.

11. Which of the following statements is **not** correct?
    A. Earth disturbances may shift geological strata and the objects within them.
    B. Fluorine analysis can only be done on bones that come from the same location.
    C. Chronometric dating techniques are absolutely precise.
    D. Chronometric techniques are based on the phenomenon of radioactive decay.

12. A disadvantage to fluorine analysis is that it
    A. can only be done on volcanic beds.
    B. can only be done on bones found in the same area.
    C. is not effective for materials older than 50,000 years.
    D. has a range of error of 12,000 years.

13. Chronometric techniques are based on
    A. radioactive decay.
    B. superposition.
    C. stratigraphy.
    D. the works of Oldowan Kanobe.

14. A half-life
    A. differs for the isotopes of different elements.
    B. is the amount of time it takes for all of the original amount of an isotope to decay.
    C. is set at 5,730 years for K/Ar.
    D. All of the above.

15. The dating technique used extensively in paleoanthropology for the time period 1-5 mya is
    A. uranium-238.
    B. carbon-14.
    C. fluorine analysis.
    D. potassium-argon.

16. Chronometric dates are accompanied with a
    A. standard deviation.
    B. mean.
    C. analysis of covariance.
    D. regression slope.

17. If you found a fossil in East Africa and you suspected that it might be over a million years old, what type of dating technique would you use to obtain an actual date?
    A. Carbon-14 dating
    B. Biostratigraphy
    C. argon-argon
    D. stratigraphy

18. Several different dating techniques are used to cross-check the age of a paleoanthropological site because
    A. no single one is perfectly reliable by itself.
    B. sources of error differ in the various techniques.
    C. sampling error, contamination and experimental error can cause imprecision.
    D. All of the above.

19. A thin-edged fragment removed from a core stone during tool making is called a
    A. chunk.
    B. flake.
    C. knapper.
    D. microlith.

20. A stone tool that is flaked on one side only is called a
    A. biface.
    B. half-tool.
    C. uniface.
    D. blank.

21. Knappers are
    A. thin-edged fragments.
    B. stones reduced by flake removal.
    C. those who flake stone tools.
    D. another word for hammerstones.

22. Microwear refers to
    A. microscopic changes on the edges of stone tools.
    B. microscopic structures in the cells of many plants.
    C. clothing associated with our smaller hominin ancestors.
    D. a method of removing flakes from a core.

23. The study of how natural factors influence bone deposition and preservation is
    A. osteology.
    B. paleontology.
    C. petrology.
    D. taphonomy.

24. Environmental determinism refers to
    A. a single large environmental change producing a major adaptive change in a species.
    B. the environment influencing a species' evolutionary path.
    C. the destiny of a species being determined by its environment.
    D. a cause and affect relationship that exists between the environment and extinction.

25. The appearance of new species in Africa has been linked to
    A. increased rainfall.
    B. seasonal stability.
    C. periodic episodes of aridity.
    D. glacial advances in the northern and southern portions of the continent.

26. Which of the following has **not** been suggested as a factor that may have influenced the initial evolution of hominin bipedality?
    A. carrying objects, such as tools and infants
    B. seed and nut gathering
    C. the beginnings of agriculture
    D. hunting

27. Owen Lovejoy proposed that _____ was critical in the origins of bipedality in early hominins.
    A. seed eating
    B. visual surveillance
    C. feeding from bushes
    D. male provisioning

28. The most fundamental adaptive shift among early hominins was
    A. sleeping in trees.
    B. hunting.
    C. making tools.
    D. becoming bipedal.

SHORT ANSWER QUESTIONS (& PAGE REFERENCES)

1. What is mosaic evolution? (p. 275)

2. What is the difference between relative and chronometric dating? (pp. 283-287)

3. What is the difference between a flake and a core? (p. 290)

4. What is taphonomy? (pp. 281, 292-293)

ESSAY QUESTIONS (& PAGE REFERENCES)

1. How and why is paleoanthropology a multidisciplinary field? (pp. 279-282)

2. What is experimental archaeology and how does it help us understand early hominin behavior? (pp.290-292)

3. Compare and contrast Jolly's seed-eating hypothesis with Lovejoy's provisioning model of hominin origins. (pp. 298-299)

ANSWERS, *CORRECTED STATEMENT* IF FALSE & REFERENCES TO TRUE/FALSE QUESTIONS

1. **FALSE**, p. 275, Mosaic evolution states that the hominin dental, locomotor and neurological systems evolved at *markedly different* rates.

2. **FALSE**, p. 277, When compared with other animals, the most distinctive behavioral feature of humans is our extraordinary reliance on *culture*.

3. **FALSE**, pp. 279-280, Modern paleoanthropologists work *cooperatively with many* other scientists.

4. **FALSE**, p. 282, Olduvai Gorge is located in *Tanzania, in eastern* Africa.

5. **FALSE**, p. 285-286, Potassium-argon dating only works on *volcanic* material, like *lava*.

6. **FALSE**, p. 288, *Paleomagnetism* is the dating method based on the earth's shifting magnetic pole.

7. **FALSE**, p. 290, The thin-edged fragment removed from another rock is called a *flake*.

8. **FALSE**, p. 295, Vrba's evolutionary pulse theory suggests *major climatic shifts* caused changes in hominin species.

9. **FALSE**, p. 296, The most fundamental adaptive shift in hominin evolution was the development of *bipedal locomotion*.

10. **FALSE**, p. 298, *Jolly's* seed-eating hypothesis used the feeding behavior and ecology of *gelada baboons* as an analogy for early hominins.

ANSWERS AND REFERENCES TO MULTIPLE CHOICE QUESTIONS

1. **C**, p. 275
2. **D**, p. 275-276
3. **A**, p. 277
4. **B**, p. 280
5. **A**, p. 280
6. **B**, p. 280
7. **B**, p. 281

8. **C**, p. 281
9. **B**, p. 283
10. **C**, p. 290
11. **C**, pp. 285-289
12. **B**, p. 285
13. **A**, p. 285
14. **A**, p. 285-286

15. **D**, p. 285
16. **A**, p. 287
17. **C**, p. 285-287
18. **D**, p. 285-287
19. **B**, p. 290
20. **C**, p. 291
21. **C**, p. 291

22. **A**, p. 292
23. **D**, p. 292
24. **A**, p. 294
25. **C**, p. 294-295
26. **C**, p. 296-299
27. **D**, p. 298
28. **D**, p. 296

CONCEPT APPLICATION SOLUTIONS

1) **What chronometric method was likely used to date the volcanic layers that are labeled "1.0 mya" and "50,000 y.a."?** *Potassium-argon or better yet the $^{40}Ar/^{39}Ar$ method, particularly for the 50,000-year-old layer.*

2) **Put the three skulls labeled "X", "Y" & "Z" in the correct chronological order, from youngest to oldest. Approximately how old are skulls "X", "Y" & "Z"?** *"X" is younger than "Z" is younger than "Y". "X" is less than 50,000 years old, "Z" is between 50,000 and 1,000,000 years old and "Y" is older than 1,000,000 years.*

3) **The teeth on the right side are most likely associated with which skull? Why?** *They are most likely associated with skull "Z" because they are both from the 2nd stratum, or layer.*

4) **Which 2 of the 3 fireplaces (labeled "1", "2" & "3") are most likely the same approximate age? What chronometric technique would you use to verify your answer? Can you use the same technique on the other fireplace? Why or why not?** *Fireplaces "3" and "2" are from the topmost layer so they are probably closest in age. Carbon-14 would be best to apply to these two fireplaces because this layer is younger than 50,000 years. Carbon-14 could not be applied to the Fireplace "1" because that layer is older than 1,000,000 years, well beyond the limits of the method.*

5) **Which 2 of the 3 sets of bones ("A", "B" & "C") are most likely the same approximate age? Which dating technique would you use to verify your answer?** *Limb bones "A" and "C" are possibly the same age because they are both found beneath the million-year-old volcanic layer. The fluorine method could check if the bones are similar to each other in age.*

6) **What geological event can probably account for the difficulty in interpreting this site's stratigraphy?** *An earthquake likely caused the faulting in the section that raised the right side in relation to the left.*

192

CHAPTER 11
HOMININ ORIGINS IN AFRICA

LEARNING OBJECTIVES

After reading this chapter you should be able to:
- list the major attributes of bipedalism (pp. 302-304)
- discuss the evidence for the earliest African hominins (pp. 310-313)
- discuss the importance of *Australopithecus* discoveries from Laetoli and Hadar (pp. 313-317)
- recognize the more derived species that resided in Africa from 2.5 to 1.2 mya (pp. 317-321)
- explain why identification of the earliest members of the *Homo* genus is problematic (pp. 321-323)
- note the significance of the "Taung baby" fossil (pp. 320-321)
- understand the approach for interpreting fossil remains (pp. 323-325)
- discuss adaptive patterns in early hominins (pp. 326-327)

CHAPTER OUTLINE

Introduction

In this chapter, we look at the evidence for the most ancient hominins and then we review the large collections of early hominins recovered from East and South Africa encompassing the period from 7 mya to 1 mya Analysis of these several specimens has led paleoanthropologists to conclude that bipedalism represents the primary functional adaptation that best distinguishes the hominin lineage. This chapter also explores the difficulties in trying to interpret this vast array of fossil material. We will look at the broader areas of interpretation where a general consensus can be found and end with the more specific interpretations of proposed evolutionary relationships.

I   **THE BIPEDAL ADAPTATION**
  A. Efficient bipedalism among primates is found only among hominins.
  B. The process of bipedal walking can be summarized as follows:
    1. To walk bipedally a human must balance on the "stance" leg while the "swing" leg is off the ground.
    2. During normal walking, both feet are simultaneously on the ground only about 25% of the time.
  C. Structural/anatomical modifications for bipedalism
    1. Review relevant figures in Appendix A for illustrations of comparative skeletal anatomy.
    2. To maintain a stable center of balance many drastic anatomical modifications in the basic primate quadrupedal pattern are required.
    3. The most dramatic changes occur in the hominin pelvis and its associated musculature.

a. The hominin pelvis is shorter and broader than the quadruped.
    i. A quadruped has vertically elongated pelvic bones that are positioned more posteriorly (towards the back).
b. This configuration helps to stabilize the line of weight transmission from the lower back to the hip joint.
c. The broader two sides of the pelvis produces a basin-shaped structure that helps to support the abdominal organs.
4. Several key muscles that act on the hip and leg, changing their mechanical function are positioned differently in the bipedal pelvis.
    a. The gluteus maximus, the major muscle in bipedal walking is the largest muscle in humans (but not so in quadrupeds).
        i. The gluteus maximus is a powerful extensor (pulls it to the rear) of the thigh and provides additional force, particularly during running and climbing.
        ii. In quadrupeds the gluteus maximus pulls the leg more laterally (to the side).
5. Bipedalism impacts other musculoskeletal areas of the body.
    a. See A Closer Look pp: 306-307.
    b. The foramen magnum in bipeds is located under the cranium so that the head balances on the spine.
        i. This arrangement also removes the need for robust neck muscles to hold the head erect.
    c. Spinal curves (S shaped in bipeds) help to maintain the center of gravity by transmitting the weight of the upper body over the hips.
    d. A longer hindlimb in bipeds increases the stride length
    e. In bipeds, the femur is angled inward toward the knees which brings the feet under the body.
    f. The big toe is realigned so that it is in line with the other toes, losing its opposability.
        i. A longitudinal arch develops which helps to absorb shock and adds a propulsive spring.
6. For these major anatomical changes to have been selected for, there must have been a tremendous selective advantage to bipedalism.
    a. It bears repeating that we do not know what conditions led to bipedalism.
    b. The various ideas of what led to bipedalism should be considered scenarios rather than hypotheses.
    c. We do not have sufficient data to test any of these ideas.
D. Form follows function in structural modifications, exemplified by bipedalism.
    1. During evolution, organisms do not undergo significant structural change (i.e., form) unless these changes assist individuals in a functional capacity.
    2. Evolutionary changes such as bipedalism do not occur at once, but likely evolve over a fairly long period of time.
E. Hominin bipedalism is habitual and obligate.
    1. Habitual bipedalism means that hominins move bipedally as their standard and most efficient mode of locomotion.
    2. Obligate bipedalism means that hominins cannot locomote efficiently in any other manner.

194

3. When examining the earliest hominins it is crucial to identify those anatomical features that indicate bipedalism and to what degree these organisms were committed to bipedalism.
   a. All of the major structural features required for bipedalism are seen in early hominins from Africa (by at least 4 mya).
   b. In particular, the pelvis shows dramatic remodeling to support weight in a bipedal stance.
   c. Other structural changes seen in the earliest relatively complete postcranial hominin remains from Africa (after 4 mya) confirm the pattern seen in the pelvis.
      i. The vertebral column shows the same curve as in modern humans.
      ii. The lower limbs were as long as in modern humans (although the arms were longer than in modern humans).
      iii. The carrying angle of weight support from the hip to the knee was also very similar to modern humans.
4. Early hominin foot structure is known from fossils found in both South and East Africa.
   a. Fossils from Sterkfontein site in South Africa consist of four connecting bones of the ankle and big toe.
      i. These specimens indicate that the heel and longitudinal arch were well adapted for a bipedal gait.
   b. Some paleontologists suggest, however, that the great toe was divergent, unlike the pattern seen in later hominins.
      i. This would have aided the foot in grasping; enabling early hominins to more effectively exploit arboreal habitats.
      ii. This type of foot would not have been as efficient as a stable platform during bipedal locomotion.
   c. The evidence from East Africa supports this conclusion.
   d. Consequently, some researchers believe that early hominins were not necessarily obligate bipeds.
      i. They believe that these early humans spent considerable amount of time in the trees.
      ii. Nevertheless, all the early hominins that have been identified from Africa are thought by most researchers to have been both habitual and obligate bipeds.

II   FINDING EARLY HOMININ FOSSILS
A. Paleoanthropology relies upon the discovery and recovery of fossil material.
   1. This is a time consuming process that requires expertise and perhaps a bit of luck.
B. Evidence of the earliest hominins can be found in Africa.
   1. Early fossil hominins have been found in Africa over the past 80 years primarily from East and South African locations.
C. East African sites are located along the Great Rift Valley.
   1. This region is over 2000 miles long and was formed by geological shifting between tectonic plates.
   2. Discoveries have been made in Ethiopia, Kenya, and Tanzania.
D. South African sites have yielded evidence of early hominins.
   1. First finds came from South Africa.

2. South Africa fossils are imbedded in breccia making archaeological recovery fossils difficult.
3. The geological circumstances found in East Africa produce a clearer stratigraphic than South Africa.
   a. There is a better association with hominin finds in the East.
   b. Sites in the east are easier to date chromometerically.
   c. In the east, fossils are easier to find because of the geography.

III **EARLY HOMININS FROM AFRICA**
A. Refer to Appendix C: Summary of Early Hominin fossil finds from Africa, pp: 517-521.
B. Various hominins lived in Africa dating back to app. 7 mya.
   1. Paleoanthrpologists accept the existence of 6 genera.
      a. Pre-australopiths
      b. Australiopths
      c. Early *Homo*
C. Pre-australopiths (7.0-4.4 mya)
D. *Sahelanthropus* genus
   1. Remarkable new discovery in Chad (at the site of Toros-Menalla) this century.
      a. Surprising finds because it is located central not southern or eastern Africa.
   2. These new discoveries may push back the timing of hominin origins to 7 million
      a. It was dated biostratigraphically to approximately 7 mya.
      b. This dating method is not as specific as others.
   1. The age of this fossil puts it 1 million years earlier than any of the other proposed early hominins.
   2. The morphology of this skull is unusual, with a unique combination of characteristics.
      a. It had a small brain, no large than a modern chimp's.
      b. However, it had massive browridges like later hominins.
      c. Its teeth were also unlike apes and more similar to hominins.
      d. The upper canine is reduced and is worn down from the tip like hominins.
   3. This fossil was regarded as a brand new form of hominin by its discoverers and was given the new binomial: *Sahelanthropus tchadensis*.
   4. Other researchers have debated this fossil's significance and its hominin status is still in question because no associated skeletal remains that indicate bipedalism have yet been found.
      a. Foramen magnum location is intermediate between apes and later hominins.
E. *Orrorin* genus
   1. Areas in Kenya (Tugen Hills) have yielded early fossils.
   2. Tugen Hills - 6 mya
      a. The fossil remains consist of a few teeth and bits of lower jaw and near complete postcranial elements.
      b. Clearly bipedal hominins.
F. *Ardipithecus* genus
   1. Middle Awash area of Ethiopia date to 5.8-5.2 mya
      a. Fragmentary remains including mostly teeth, a jaw fragment, and a few pieces of limb skeleton.
   2. *Ardipithecus* from Aramis (Ethiopia) date to 4.4 mya

a. the group of fossils from this site are the oldest substantial collection of hominins.
3. Remains of 50 individuals recovered
   a. Including jaws, teeth, partial crania and upper limb bones.
   b. In addition, 40% of a single skeleton was recovered in 1995.
   c. As of now, however, this specimen has not yet been fully scientifically described.
4. What makes researchers think that it is a hominin?
   a. The foramen magnum is positioned further forward than in quadrupeds.
   b. Features of the humerus suggest that the forelimb was not weight-bearing.
   c. The provisional interpretation from this evidence is that these specimens were bipeds.
5. Tim White and his co-workers have suggested that the Aramis hominins be assigned to a new genus and species, *Ardipithecus ramidus*.
   a. The thin enamel caps on the molars of *Ardipithecus* contrast to the thicker enamel caps typical for hominins.
   b. The basis for this recognition of a new genus is that these specimens are much more primitive than *Australopithecus* (the other hominin genus closest to this time period).
   c. The environment associated with *Ardipithecus* is more forested than later hominin sites.
G. Australopiths (4.2-1.2 mya)
   1. Composed of two closely related genera: *Australopithecusand Paranthropus*.
   2. The australopiths represent two major subgroups:
      a. An earlier (4.2-3 mya) more primitive collection of species.
      b. Later (since 2.5 mya), more derived species.
   3. Several morphological attributes are shared by all australopiths:
      a. All bipedal
      b. All have small brains
      c. All have large teeth (especially back teeth) with thick enamel.
I. Earliest come from East Africa: from northern Kenya and date to 4.2-3.0 mya.
   1. Very early hominins with primitive traits like sectorial lower first premolars and small openings for the ear canal.
      a. Assigned to the species *Australopithecus anamensis*.
J. *Australopithecus afarensis*
   1. Several hundred specimens of 60 to 100 individuals have been removed from Laetoli (in Tanzania) and Hadar.
      a. Forty-percent of an *Australopithecus afarensis* female, nicknamed "Lucy," was recovered from Hadar in 1974.
      b. This is one of the two most complete hominin skeletons dating before 100,000 years ago.
   2. Thousands of footprints representing 20 different kinds of animals were found at Laetoli.
      a. Several hominin footprints were also found including a trail 75 feet long made by 2 or 3 individuals.
      b. Analysis of the tracks indicate one individual was 4' 9" and the other was 4' 1".
      c. We know for certain that there were bipedal hominins walking in East Africa at this time.

197

3. *A. afarensis* is more primitive than any of the later species of *Australopithecus*.
   a. By "primitive" it is meant that *A.afarensis* is less evolved in any particular direction than are the later occurring hominin species.
4. *A. afarensis* shares more primitive features with other early hominoids and living apes than do later hominins.
5. The teeth of *A. afarensis*, for example, are quite primitive.
   a. The canines are often large, pointed teeth that overlap.
   b. The lower first premolar is semisectorial (i.e., it provides a shearing surface for the upper canine).
   c. The tooth rows are parallel.
6. The cranial parts that are preserved also exhibit several primitive hominoid features.
   a. Cranial capacities are difficult to estimate but they seem to range from 375 cm^3 to 500 cm^3.
   b. It may be that the smaller cranial capacities are for females and the larger cranial capacities are for males.
   c. One thing that is certain is that *A. afarensis* had a small brain; the mean for the species is probably 420 cm^3.
7. Postcrania
   a. Relative to the lower limbs, the upper limbs of *A. afarensis* are longer than in modern humans.
      i. This is also a primitive hominoid condition.
      ii. This does not mean that the arms were longer than the legs.
   b. Wrist, hand, and foot bones show several differences from modern humans.
8. Stature has been estimated
   a. *A. afarensis* was shorter than modern humans.
   b. There appears to have been considerable sexual dimorphism.
      i. Females were between 3.5 to 4 feet tall.
      ii. Males could have been up to 5 feet tall.
      iii. *A. afarensis* may have been as sexually dimorphic as any living primate.
9. New find of a mostly complete 3-year-old *A.afarensis* skeleton announced in 2006.
   a. The infant comes from the same geological horizon as Hadar.
   b. First well preserved immature individual early than 100,000 years.
   c. Perhaps mixed locomotion: infant probably a biped with capacity to climb trees.
K. *A. afarensis* likely ancestral to all later hominins.
L. Later More Derived Australopiths (2.5-1.2 mya)
   1. *Australopithecus* and *Paranthropus* contemporaneous with early *Homo* species.
   2. *Paranthropus* species are most derived
      a. Relatively small cranial capacities (ranging from 510-530 cm^3) compared to later hominins.
      b. Very large, broad faces.
      c. Massive back teeth and lower jaws.
      d. Individuals possess a sagittal crest associated with muscle attachment sites.
   3. The earliest representative of the *Paranthropus* is WT 17000 ("the black skull").
      a. With a cranial capacity of 410 cm^3 WT 17000 has the smallest definitely ascertained brain volume of any hominin yet found.
      b. WT 17000 also has other primitive traits reminiscent of *A. afarensis*, that include:

    c. a compound crest in the back of the skull.

    d. a projecting upper face.

    e. the upper dental row that converges in back.

    f. WT 17000 is a mosaic of primitive traits and very derived traits.

    g. WT 17000 has been placed in a separate *species, Paranthropus aethiopicus.*

4. By 2 mya., even more derived members of the robust lineage were on the scene in East Africa.

    a. East African *Paranthropus* individuals are robust in teeth and jaws

    b. *Paranthropus boisei.*

5. *Paranthropus* in South Africa.

    a. Dates 2-1.2 mya

    b. Similar to cousin in east Africa, but distinct enough to warrant *Paranthropus robustus.*

        i. relatively small cranial capacities (the average is 530 cm^3).

       ii. large, broad faces.

      iii. Megadont back teeth

    c. What happened to *Paranthropus*?

        i. Not seen after 1 mya.

6. Also in South Africa, discoveries at four sites have been made of *Australopithecus africanus.*

    a. Earliest discovery of all hominins in Africa was of this species

    b. Dart published discovery of child from Taung quarry as ancient member of hominin family tree.

        i. Dart observed several features that suggested that this child was a hominin.

       ii. The foramen magnum was farther forward than in modern apes (although not as far forward as in modern humans).

      iii. The slope of the forehead was not as receding as in apes.

      iv. The milk canines were exceedingly small and the first molars were large, broad teeth.

       v. In all respects this fossil resembled a hominin rather than a pongid with the glaring exception of the very small brain.

    c. Once dated as far back as 3.3 mya.

    d. More recently dated to 2.5-2 mya.

M. Early *Homo* (2.4-1.4 mya)

  1. The earliest appearance of our genus, *Homo*, may be at the time of *Paranthropus*.

  2. The earliest evidence of *Homo* may be skull and jaw fragments dating from 2.4-2.3 mya. in Kenya and Ethiopia.

  3. In the 1960s, Leakey proposed a larger brain hominin: *Homo habilis*

  4. *Homo habilis* at Olduvai ranges in time from 1.85-1.6 mya

  5. *H. habilis* differs from *Australopithecus* in cranial capacity and cranial shape.

    a. The average cranial capacity for *H. habilis* is estimated at 631 cm^3 compared to 520 cm^3 for *Paranthropus*.

    b. Compared to australopithecines, *H. habilis* has larger front teeth relative to back teeth and narrower premolars.

199

6. When L. S. B. Leakey named these specimens *Homo habilis* (meaning "handy man")
   a. It inferred that *Homo habilis* was the early Olduvai toolmaker.
   b. By calling this group *Homo*, Leakey was arguing for at least two separate branches of hominin evolution in the Plio-Pleistocene.
   c. implied that they were our ancestors.

N. From the available evidence, it appears that one or more species of early *Homo* were present in East Africa by 2.4 mya
   1. They would have developed in parallel with at least one line of hominins.
   2. These hominin lineages lived contemporaneously for at least one million years.
   3. After this time the australopithecine lineage became extinct.

IV   INTERPRETATIONS: WHAT DOES IT ALL MEAN?

A. Fossil data are the foundation of human evolutionary research.
B. Paleoanthropologists number fossil specimens in an attempt to keep designations neutral.
   1. Formal naming comes later.
   2. Using taxonomic nomenclature implies an interpretation of fossil relationships.
C. The interpretation of hominin evolutionary patterns follows several steps:
   1. Select and survey a site.
   2. Excavate the site and recover fossil hominins.
   3. Designate fossils with specimen numbers for clear reference.
   4. Clean, prepare, study and describe the fossils.
   5. Compare fossil variation.
   6. Assign formal, taxonomic names to the fossils.
D. What became of the populations that are represented by the fossils?
   1. Interesting to decide why some evolved and others became extinct.
E. Continuing uncertainties -- taxonomic issues
   1. Paleoanthropologists are concerned with making biological interpretations of variation found in the hominin fossil record.
      a. As new fossils are found this becomes more complex.
   2. However, at the species-level very little consensus can be found.
      a. Evolution is not a simple process.
      b. Disputes and disagreements are bound to arise.
   3. One particularly difficult obstacle is the varied combination of anatomical characteristics seen in early members of the hominin family.

V   SEEING THE BIGGER PICTURE: ADAPTIVE PATTERNS OF EARLY AFRICAN HOMININS

A. The early hominin fossil record is characterized by several different genera and a number of species.
   1. Speciation seems to have been quite common during this time period.
      a. Apparently, the australopithecine species had relatively restricted ranges and this may have led to the higher likelihood of speciation due to the effects of genetic drift.
   2. Australopithecines were at least partially arboreal, although the robust species may have been a bit less so compared to earlier forms.

200

3. Except for early *Homo*, there is very little evolutionary trend of increased body size or marked encephalization.
   a. From *Sahelanthropus* the brain size was no more than that in chimpanzees.
   b. Close to 6 million years later, relative brain size increased by no more than 10-15%.
   c. There is no absolute association of any of these hominins with patterned stone tool manufacture.
4. All of these early African hominins show an accelerated developmental pattern different from modern humans.
   a. This apelike development is also seen in some early *Homo* .
B. Finally, research has shown that australopithecines grew and developed rapidly, similar to modern apes, and quite unlike the slower pace of modern human growth and development.

KEY TERMS

australopith: a causal term to refer to any species that belong to the *Australopithecus* genus.

australopithecine: the common name for members of the genus *Australopithecus*. Originally this term was used as a subfamily designation. North American researchers no longer recognize this subfamily, but the term is well established in usage.

Australopithecus: a genus of Plio-Pleistocene hominin characterized by bipedalism, a relatively small brain and large back teeth.

endocast: a solid impression of the inside of the skull, showing the size, shape, and some details of the surface of the brain.

foramen magnum: the large opening at the base of the cranium through which the spinal cord passes and where the vertebral column joins the skull.

gracile: referring to smaller, morelightly built body/anatomical structure.

gracile australopithecine: the South African species, *Australopithecus africanus*, that is more lightly built than the stouter species inhabiting the same area.

habitual bipedalism: refers to the usual mode of locomotion of the organism. Used in reference to humans in the text, there are other habitual bipedal animals (e.g., large terrestrial flightless birds and kangaroos), although many hop rather than walk.

hominins: popular form of Homininae, the family to which modern humans belong; includes all bipedal hominoids back to the divergence from African great apes.

Homo habilis: a species of early *Homo*, well known in East Africa, but also perhaps from other regions.

line of weight transmission: the line over which a significant weight load is carried.

"Lucy": a female *Australopithecus afarensis* for which 40 percent of the skeleton was recovered.

morphological: referring to the form and structure of organisms.

obligate bipedalism: refers to the fact that the organism cannot use another form of locomotion efficiently.

os coxa: the structure that consists of three bones (fused together in the adult) that, together with another os coxa and the sacrum, constitutes the pelvis. It is also referred to as the coxal by some anatomists and as the innominate bone by an earlier generation of anatomists.

Plio-Pleistocene: referring to the Pliocene and first half of the Pleistocene epochs (~5-1 mya) during which hominins began to diversify.

postcranial: the skeleton not including the skull.

Pre-australopith: refers to any species that dates to or existed before the genus *Australopithecus*

robust: referring to large, heavily built body/anatomical structure.

robust australopithecine: any of the three species of *Australopithecus* that are characterized by larger back teeth relative to front teeth, a more vertical face, and often a sagittal crest.

sagittal crest: a ridge of bone running along the midline (i.e., sagittal plane) of the cranium. The temporalis muscle, used in chewing, attaches to the sagittal crest in those mammals that possess this structure.

sectorial premolar: a premolar with a bladelike cutting edge that sections food by shearing against the cutting edge of the upper canine. The shearing action also sharpens both teeth.

MEDIA EXERCISES

1) Check out "Becoming Human: Paleoanthropology, Evolution and Human Origins," a "broadband documentary experience" that lets you "journey through the story of human evolution" (http://becominghuman.org/). This site is produced and maintained by The Institute of Human Origins of Arizona State University and is a great supplement to your studies.

2) Go to the Leakey Foundation website (http://www.leakeyfoundation.org) and click on media, then audio archives. Select Don Johanson (Lucy and the First Family, 1981). You will hear about one of the most famous paleoanthropological finds from the person who led the expedition. Realize the interpretations he will recite are approximately 30 years old.

INFOTRAC

1) In *InfoTrac*, do keyword searches on, "*Ardipithecus*", "*Sahelanthropus*" and "*Orrorin*" to read articles in the scholarly and popular press about the newest members of our family tree. Do the popular reviews of the scientific literature always agree about their interpretations of the new hominins phylogenetic placement?

CONCEPT APPLICATION

Match the choices with the correct letter in this diagram comparing Chimpanzee and human skeletal and muscle morphology.

A._____

B._____

C._____

D._____

E._____

Choices:
Knee, Hamstring muscles, Hip Joint, Gluteus maximus, ilium.

(a) Human   (b) Chimpanzee

The diagram above illustrates a human and chimpanzee standing erect (Figure 11-4 p. 304). Observe the differences in the size and location of the two major muscles depicted in the diagram? Think too about differences in the shape of the chimpanzee pelvis compared to that of the human. Consult A Closer Look: Major Features of Bipedalism image (c), for a front (anterior) comparative view of the human and ape pelves.

Assess your bipedal stance. Stand erect with both feet flat on the floor. Extend one foot as you do to begin a stride. Move this leg through your stride and think about which part of this foot will hit the ground first. Also consider the leg muscles that have been involved in this process. What has your other leg done? How has your weight shifted as you moved the first leg through the stride? What portion of the other leg is the last to remain on the surface as you continue to walk? Remember we do not have an opposable toe. Consider too the prints that you have left on the ground (toe, heel and full foot) during this process. Consult A Closer Look: Major Features of Bipedalism image (f), for a comparative view of the foot print of a human and an ape.

The following page consists of a table that you can list and note attributes of the major species that comprise the hominin fossil record. Complete cells in the table and use it as a study guide to keep track of the specimens.

203

Species	Location	Date	Phylogenetic position	Morphological features	Cultural aspects	Teeth features	Cranial capacity
Sahelanthropus tchadensis	West Africa Near complete skull, teeth Found 2002	~7 mya	Possible hominid potentially earliest	Small brain and canines Ape like skull Foramen magnum	N/a		
Orrorin tugenesis							
Ardipithecus ramidus							
Australopithecus anamensis							
Australopithecus afarensis							
Australopithecus africanus							
Paranthropus aethiopicus							
Paranthropus robustus							
Paranthropus. boisei							
Homo habilis							
H. rudolfensis							

Now answer the True/False, Multiple Choice and Short Answer sample test questions. Following completion of the tests, correct them with the answers and textbook page references at the end of this Study Guide chapter. Note the areas in which you are strong and weak to guide you in your studying. Finally, answer the sample Essay Questions.

TRUE/FALSE QUESTIONS

If false, consider what modification would make the statement true.

1. Walking on two legs has been described as "the act of almost falling repeatedly."
   TRUE   FALSE

2. The earliest hominin recently discovered in Chad in West Central Africa, is assigned to the genus *Australopithecus*.
   TRUE   FALSE

3. When compared to our quadrupedal relatives, the most dramatic changes arising from bipedalism are in the hominin pelvis.
   TRUE   FALSE

4. Two of the most extraordinary discoveries of *Australopithecus afarensis* were the footprint trail at Laetoli and the "Lucy" skeleton from Hadar.
   TRUE   FALSE

5. "The black skull" is important because it documents the initial presence of "gracile" australopithecines in South Africa at 4.5 mya
   TRUE   FALSE

6. Early *Homo* from Olduvai Gorge and Koobi Fora are distinct from contemporary robust australopithecines in cranial size, cranial shape and tooth proportions.
   TRUE   FALSE

7. Raymond Dart's most important contribution to paleoanthropology was the announcement, description and interpretation of the Taung child as an early hominin ancestor that he named *Australopithecus africanus*.
   TRUE   FALSE

8. Important South African australopithecine sites include Koobi Fora and Olduvai Gorge.
   TRUE   FALSE

9. Given recent analyses, *Orrorin* is widely recognized as the earliest firmly established hominin.
   TRUE   FALSE

10. Early hominins are believed to be exclusively terrestrial; never occupying an arboreal location.
    TRUE   FALSE

205

MULTIPLE CHOICE QUESTIONS

1. Efficient bipedalism as the primary form of locomotion is seen only in
    A. Australopithecines.
    B. hominins.
    C. Great Apes.
    D. *Paranthropus*.

2. Which of the following is not a major feature of hominin bipedalism?
    A. Development of curves in the human vertebral column.
    B. The "straightening" of the human fingers from the curved condition found in the apes.
    C. The forward repositioning of the foramen magnum underneath the cranium.
    D. The modification of the pelvis into a basin-like shape.

3. What does a divergent big toe indicate about the locomotion and behavior of a primate?
    A. is the common ancestor of the lemurs and lorises.
    B. The primate
    C. The primate is an obligate biped.
    D. The primate uses an arboreal environment at least some of the time.

4. Which of the following is not part of the os coxae?
    A. ilium
    B. ischium
    C. scaphoid
    D. pubis

5. A foot that is highly capable of grasping and climbing is less capable as a stable platform during bipedal locomotion. This is because anatomical remodeling is limited by functional
    A. contingencies.
    B. constraints.
    C. paradoxes.
    D. drift.

6. Which of the following hominins was **not** recently discovered and given a new taxonomic name?
    A. *Orrorin*
    B. *Ardipithecus*
    C. *Sahelanthropus*
    D. *Australopithecus afarensis*

7. Which of the following is **not** true about *Sahelanthropus*?
    A. it dates to close to 7 mya
    B. it was discovered in the Great Rift Valley of East Africa
    C. it had a small cranial capacity, estimated between 320-380 cm3
    D. it had massively built, huge browridges

206

8. What hard evidence from Laetoli demonstrates that hominins were bipedal by 3.5 mya.?
   A. a complete fossilized foot skeleton
   B. fossilized footprints imprinted in volcanic tuff
   C. the forward position of the foramen magnum on the Laetoli cranium
   D. a short and broad fossil hominin pelvis fragment

9. Which of the following sites have yielded fossil remains of *Australopithecus afarensis*?
   A. Hadar
   B. Laetoli
   C. Swartkrans
   D. both A & B

10. Which of the following was found at Hadar?
    A. "the black skull"
    B. Taung child
    C. "Lucy"
    D. All of the above were found at Hadar.

11. Which of the following is **not** a characteristic of *Australopithecus afarensis*?
    A. small stature
    B. small brain, averaging around 420 cm^3
    C. upper limbs are longer, relative to lower limbs
    D. the teeth are quite similar in size to those of modern humans

12. The earliest species of robust australopiths is
    A. *Paranthropus boisei*.
    B. *Paranthropus robustus*.
    C. *Paranthropus aethiopicus*.
    D. *Australopithecus africanus*.

13. WT 17000 ("the black skull") is an excellent example of mosaic evolution because is possesses
    A. a very small cranial capacity.
    B. a very broad face and a huge sagittal crest.
    C. a projecting upper face.
    D. All of the above

14. Early *Homo* is distinguished from the australopithecines largely by
    A. larger cranial capacity.
    B. shorter stature.
    C. larger back teeth.
    D. the presence of a chin.

207

15. Which of the following is true with respect to early *Homo*?
    A. these hominins were more closely related to the South African australopithecines than to the East African australopithecines.
    B. there may be two separate branches of hominin evolution in the Plio-Pleistocene.
    C. these were tool-making species at Olduvai.
    D. both B and C.

16. Which of the following australopithecine species is found in South Africa?
    A. *Paranthropus boisei*
    B. *Australopithecus afarensis*
    C. *Paranthropus robustus*
    D. *Paranthropus aethiopicus*

17. Raymond Dart's claim that *Australopithecus africanus* was a hominin was rejected by many of his contemporaries because they expected early members of the human family to have
    A. long faces, stabbing canines, and small brains.
    B. large brains.
    C. manufactured stone tools.
    D. apelike jaws and teeth, small brains.

18. Compared to *A. africanus*, *P. robustus*
    A. was larger, weighing up to 300 pounds (about the size of a gorilla).
    B. had smaller grinding teeth (molars).
    C. had a sagittal crest and larger back teeth.
    D. probably was more arboreal.

19. The sagittal crest present in the robust australopithecines functions as
    A. additional buttressing protecting the skull from heavy blows.
    B. a structure used in head-butting during competition for females.
    C. additional surface area for attachment of a large temporalis muscle.
    D. an area where brain expansion occurred.

20. The species-level distinctions of the African Plio-Pleistocene hominins
    A. are fairly clear.
    B. are the subject of ongoing disputes.
    C. are being resolved through dating.
    D. require immediate splitting.

21. *Australopithecus anamensis*
    A. is more primitive than later australopiths.
    B. is represented by two almost complete skeletons.
    C. some researchers believe it may be ancestral to later australopiths.
    D. A & C

22. The key issue with early *Homo* is
    A. dating.
    B. determining whether or not it was an obligate biped.
    C. evaluating its arboreal capabilities.
    D. interpreting the observed variation as being either intraspecific or interspecific.

23. Basal hominins may include
    A. *Sahelanthropus*, *Ardipithecus* and *Orrorin*.
    B. *Australopithecus afarensis*.
    C. *Australopithecus africanus*.
    D. the robust australopithecines.

24. Which of the following evolutionary forces may have played an important role in the divergence of hominin species with restricted ranges and small population sizes?
    A. Gene flow.
    B. Genetic drift
    C. Sexual selection
    D. mutation.

SHORT ANSWER QUESTIONS (& PAGE REFERENCES)

1. How does a hominin's pelvis differ from an ape's? (pp. 306-307)

2. What are the features that define *Sahelanthropus* as a hominin? (p. 311)

3. What features (and evidence) indicate that A. afarensis is a hominin? (pp. 314-317)

4. How does WT 17000 "the black skull" illustrate the concept of mosaic evolution? (p. 319)

5. What is the functional significance of the sagittal crest as observed in certain hominin species? (p. 319)

ESSAY QUESTIONS (& PAGE REFERENCES)

1. What features of *Ardipithecus* from Ethiopia make it a hominin? (pp. 311-313)

2. Compare and contrast human versus ape skeletons focusing on the differences that reflect bipedal versus quadrupedal locomotion. (pp. 306-307)

3. What are the traits that link the *Paranthropus* fossils from East and South Africa (pp. 319-320)

4. Discuss the controversy concerning early *Homo* from East Africa (pp. 321-323)

5. Why are the taxonomic and phylogenetic status' of *Ardipithecus, Orrorin* and *Sahelanthropus* controversial? (pp. 310-313)

Answers, *Corrected Statement* if False & References To True/False Questions

1. TRUE, p. 303

2. FALSE, pp.311-312, The earliest hominin from Chad is assigned to the genus Sahelanthropus.

3. TRUE, pp. 303-305

4. TRUE, p. 314-315

5. FALSE, p.319, "The black skull" is important because it documents the initial presence of "*robust*" australopithecines in *East* Africa at *2.5 mya*

6. TRUE, p. 322

7. TRUE, p. 320

8. FALSE, pp. 314-320, Important South African australopithecine sites include *Sterkfontein and Swartkrans*.

9. TRUE, p. 311, *Orrorin* is widely recognized as the earliest definitive hominin.

10. FALSE, pp. 304-305, Early hominins likely exploited arboreal habitats in a limited fashion for safety and protection, etc.

Answers and References to Multiple Choice Questions

1. **B**, pp. 302-305	9. **D**, pp. 314-317	17. **B**, p. 320
2. **B**, pp. 302-305	10. **A**, p. 314	18. **C**, p. 319
3. **D**, p. 305	11. **D**, p. 315	19. **C**, p. 319
4. **C**, p. 303	12. **C**, p. 319	20. **B**, pp. 321-322
5. **B**, p. 305	13. **D**, p. 319	21. **D**, pp. 313-314
6. **D**, pp. 310-314	14. **A**, p. 322	22. **D**, pp. 321-322
7. **B**, pp. 310-311	15. **D**, p. 322	23. **A**, pp. 310-311
8. **B**, p. 314	16. **C**, p. 320	24. **B**, p. 326

Concept Application Solution

See page 304 in your textbook.

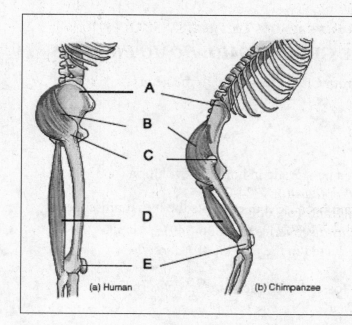

A. **Illium**

B. **Gluteus maximus**

C. **Hip joint**

D. **Hamstring muscles**

E. **Knee**

Choices:
Knee, Hamstrings, Hip Joint, Gluteus maximus, ilium.

(a) Human   (b) Chimpanzee

The diagram illustrates a human and chimpanzee standing bipedally.
What are the two muscles depicted in the diagram? *Gluteus maximus and hamstring. Realize that these are not the only muscles involved in bipedalism.*

What do you notice about the position of the two muscles in the diagram? *The attachment surface of the gluteus maximus in humans is farther in back of the hip joint than in a chimpanzee standing bipedally. Conversely, in chimpanzees, the hamstrings are farther in back of the knee.*

What do you notice about the shape of the chimpanzee pelvis compared to that of the human? *The chimpanzee pelvis is elongated and narrow compared to the human pelvis. The human pelvis distributes weight differently as it carries weight on two legs not four. The shape is associated with the position of the femur (thigh bone) under the body and the position and movement of the numerous muscles that facilitate obligate bipedalism.*

When you walk *your toe is the last to leave the ground (toe off) and the heel is the first to strike the ground (heel strike).*

CHAPTER 12
THE EARLIEST DISPERSAL OF THE GENUS *HOMO*: *HOMO ERECTUS* AND CONTEMPORARIES

LEARNING OBJECTIVES

After reading this chapter you should be able to:
- understand why *Homo erectus* represents a new grade in hominin evolution (p. 331)
- describe the physical characteristics of *H. erectus* (pp. 334-336)
- discuss who were the earliest African emigrants (pp. 338-340)
- present an historical overview of *H. erectus* discoveries (pp. 336-349)
- understand the technological advances reflected in the tool kit of *H. erectus* (pp. 350-351).
- present a regional overview of the major fossil discoveries of *H. erectus* (p. 354).

CHAPTER OUTLINE

Introduction

In the previous chapters we looked at early hominin evolution by examining fossils assigned to *Australopithecus* and early *Homo*. In this chapter we focus on *Homo erectus*, believed by most to be the ancestor of modern *Homo sapiens*. All aspects of this extinct hominin species are investigated, including its geographic and temporal distribution, physical characteristics, history of discovery, variation exhibited by African and Asian forms and the technological advances made by this very significant hominin species over the approximately 1.5 million years of its existence.

I   A NEW KIND OF HOMININ
   A. Specimens of H.*erectus* have been found in East Africa, China, Java and Europe.
     1. Discoveries date back to the 19th century
     2. Some think these regional discoveries represent more than one species
       a. Fossils from early African sites are called *Homo ergaster* by some
     3. Undoubtedly they are closely related.
   B. H. *erectus* is viewed as a grade of evolution.
     1. A grade is an evolutionary grouping that shows a similar adaptive pattern.
       a. A grade indicates similar adaptations, it does not imply shared ancestry.
     2. The increases in body size, changes in limb proportions, etc., indicate that this grade was more human in pattern than earlier hominins.

II   THE MORPHOLOGY OF *HOMO ERECTUS*
   A. Homo *erectus* lived in many different environments, nevertheless share common physical traits.
   B. Body size
     1. "Nariokotome Boy" shows that body size was larger than earlier hominins.
       a. Projected adult height of nearly 6'.

2. Adults are estimated to have weighed well over 100 pounds.
3. Average adult height is estimated at 5'6".
4. *H. erectus* was quite sexually dimorphic as indicated by the East African specimens.
5. Their skeletons were very robust, meaning that their bones were quite thick.
C. Brain size
   1. *Homo erectus* brain size ranges from 750 to 1250 cm^3.
      a. The mean for the species is about 900 cm^3.
      b. Remember early Homo was only about 500 cm^3
   2. Although *H. erectus* had bigger brains than any earlier hominins, this species was still considerably less encephalized than modern humans.
D. Cranial shape
   1. See Figure 12-2.
   2. The skull of *H. erectus* is distinctive in shape and size.
   3. *H. erectus* has thick cranial *bones*.
   4. *H. erectus* exhibit large browridges (supraorbital tori) and nuchal tori.
      a. Tori is an area where bone is built up so it appears large and pronounced.
      b. Supra orbital means above the orbit.
      c. Nuchal refers to the posterior (back) of the skull where the nuchal muscles attach.
   5. There is little development of a forehead with the skull receding from the brow area.
   6. The maximum breadth is low, below the ear opening.
   7. Most specimens also have a sagittal keel.
      a. This is a slight build up of bone along the midline of the skull from front to back.

III **THE FIRST *HOMO ERECTUS*: HOME ERECTUS FROM AFRICA**
A. *H. erectus* likely first appeared in East Africa.
   1. *By* 1.8 mya well dated sites in Kenya.
   2. Very quickly migrated to eastern Europe (by 1.75 mya) and Indonesia (by 1.6 mya).
B. Likely 2-1.8 mya in East Africa an early *Homo* form evolved into *H. erectus*.
C. The most significant Homo *erectus* from East Turkana is an almost complete skull that dates close to 1.8 mya
   1. Its cranial capacity is almost 850 cm^3.
   2. A specimen of interest also from East Turkana has a cranial capacity of 691 cm^3
      a. Extreme sexual dimorphism for this species could make this a female
D. A significant find from West Turkana is the near complete skeleton of a young boy.
   1. WT 15000 was found at a site known as Nariokotome in August 1984.
   2. It is the most complete *Homo erectus* skeleton ever found and dates to 1.6 mya.
      a. WT 15000 was a boy about 8 years old and stood 5'3".
      b. WT 15000's adult cranial capacity would have been over 900 cm^3.
E. A discovery in 1960 by Louis Leakey at Olduvai Gorge in Tanzania.
   1. OH 9 dates to 1.4 mya. and has a cranial capacity is estimated at 1,067 cm^3.
      a. OH 9 has the largest cranial capacity of African *H. erectus* and the largest browridges of any fossil hominin yet discovered.
      b. Has thin cranial bones.
      c. Some place this in a separate species, *Homo ergaster*.
F. A female pelvis was discovered recently.
   1. It dates to 1.3 mya. and is first female pelvis found.

2. Wide birth canal such that *erectus* babies may have been as large as modern babies.
 a. Perhaps *H. erectus* brain growth before birth was rapid like us, but
 b. *H. erectus* brain growth after birth was much slower than us.
G. A mostly complete cranium dating to 1 mya was recently discovered at Daka in the Middle Awash of Ethiopia.
 1. Its morphology resembles Asian *H. erectus* leading its discoverers to reject the idea of two different species in Africa and Asia.

IV **WHO WERE THE EARLIEST AFRICAN EMIGRANTS?**
A. *H. erectus* appears less than 2 mya in Africa and then appears in three different geographic locations.
 1. Currently accepted that *H. erectus* evolved in East Africa, and migrated rapidly across the old world.
B. The Dmanisi hominins were discovered in what is now the Republic of Georgia in eastern Europe.
 1. These fossils are dated to ~1.75 mya
 2. In some respects the Dmanisi crania are similar to *H. erectus*.
  a. Long low braincase, wide base, and sagittal keeling.
 3. Other characteristics are more similar to early *Homo*
  a. Less-robust and thinner browridge, projecting lower face, relatively large upper canine.
 4. Dmanisi crania have a smaller brain size than *H.* erectus (600-780 cm^3)
 5. The most remarkable discovery is a fourth skull that is nearly complete found in 2002.
  a. Older adult male who had only one tooth when he died.
   i. This is very rare in such ancient hominins.
   ii. He lived for several years with no teeth.
  b. This individual must have had assistance from his group.
 6. Researcher have also found some tools
  a. Tools are like the olduwan industry from Africa.
  b. Site predates the Acheulian tool industry commonly associated with *H. erectus*.
 7. Recent discoveries of post cranial bones indicate additional unique qualities of the Dmanisi hominins.
  a. Height is estimated to range from 4'9" to 5'5"
   i. Much shorter than *H. erectus*.
  b. Body proportions are more like erectus and modern sapiens than earlier hominins.
C. Dmanisi discoveries raise several questions:
 1. Was *Homo erectus* the first hominin to leave Africa or did an earlier form get out even earlier?
 2. Did hominins require a large brain and sophisticated stone tool culture to disperse out of Africa?
 3. Was the large, robust body build of *H. erectus* a necessary adaptation for the initial occupation of Eurasia?
D. Dmanisi fossils are small, but have key H. erectus features and would have been skilled travelers even without advanced tools or a large brain.

E.   The Dmanisi fossils suggest that the first hominins to leave Africa were possible small early form of *H. erectus*.

F.   It is possible that there were two early migrations out of Africa.

    1.   The first exodus gave rise to the small Dmanisi hominins

    2.   A second gave rise to the Asian populations of *H. erectus*.

V   HOMO *ERECTUS* FROM INDONESIA

A.   Eugene Dubois, a Dutch anatomist, went to Sumatra with the Dutch East India Army to look for the "missing link."

    1.   In 1891 he unearthed a skullcap and the next year a femur near Trinil in central Java.

B.   *Homo erectus* from Java

    1.   Six sites from central and eastern Java have yielded fossil hominins.

    2.   Attaining reliable dates is a problem, in part, because of the complexity of Javanese geology.

        a.   Generally accepted that the fossils belong to Early or Middle Pleistocene.

        b.   Most date between 1.6 and 1 mya

            i.   There is a wide range of dates from as early as 1.8 to as late as 27, 000.

    3.   At Ngandong 11 individuals were recovered.

        a.   Dates between 50,000 and 25,000 years old.

        b.   This are controversial but it appears that *H. erectus* survived very late in Indonesia.

    4.   If the Ngandong dates are correct it would make *Homo erectus* contemporary with *Homo sapiens*.

    5.   At Sangiran Dome over 80 different fossils have been found.

        a.   Specimens have thick cranial vaults, sagittal keels, browridges, and nuchal tori.

            i.   Traits are slightly more pronounced than in African *H. erectus*.

        b.   Large cranial capacities from 813 to 1059 cm^3.

        c.   Evidence indicates lived on river banks, in shadow of erupting volcanoes (like Africa).

VI   *HOMO ERECTUS* FROM CHINA

A.   Excavations began in the 1920's and later that decade a skull was found that was clearly an early hominin.

B.   Zhoukoudian site near Beijing, (then Peking).

    1.   Fossilized bonbes were long know in the region such that "Dragon bones," (ancient mammal fossils), were used as medicine and aphrodisiacs by the Chinese people.

    2.   Fossil skull found in 1929 was from a juvenile and was thick, low, and relatively small.

    3.   Zhoukoudian *Homo erectus is l*argest collection of *H. erectus* material found anywhere.

        a.   Site dates between 670,000 and 410,000 year ago.

    4.   Includes 14 skullcaps, other cranial pieces, and more than 100 isolated teeth.

        a.   Few postcranial bones.

        b.   This unusual pattern of preservation has been considered to be evidence of cannibalism and the work of giant hyenas.

5. Casts were made of the fossils which were subsequently lost at start of WWII and have never been seen again.
6. More than 40 *H. erectus* individuals (adult males, females and children) have been found.
7. Cranial features include the supraorbital torus and the nuchal torus.
   a. The skull has thick bones, sagittal keel, a protruding face and is widest at the bottom.

C. Cultural Remains
1. More than 100,000 artifacts have been unearthed.
   a. Early tools are crude and shapeless become more refined through time.
   b. Common tools were choppers, scrapers, burins, and awls
   c. Hunter-gatherer diet of hunted deer and horse, and gathered fruits, berries, eggs, seeds, herbs and tubers.
      i.   Some say H. erectus were hunters
      ii. Some say h. erectus remains are the result of hyena activity.
2. Recent work has questioned whether or not *H. erectus* even lived in the Zhoukoudian cave.
   a. These researchers claim that most of the evidence suggests that giant hyenas were responsible for the bone accumulations.
   b. Other researchers are also skeptical about the famous claims of fire use by *H. erectus* in the cave.
3. New research reveals that the "hearths" of Zoukoudian were in fact not hearths at all.
   a. There is no evidence of wood being burned
   b. The cave (accessible only via a vertical entry) was probably more of a trap than a home for hominins.

D. Other Chinese sites
1. Lantian site dates to 1.15 mya
   a. Remains of two female Homo *erectus* crania.
   b. Associated with fire-treated pebbles and flakes, as well as ash.
2. Two badly distorted crania were discovered in Yunxian in 1989 and 1990.
   a. Dated to 580-800 kya.
   b. A reassessment of the fauna and paleoenvironment of the site indicates that *H. erectus* employed relatively primitive hunting methods.
      i.   Hunted old and small prey
3. The Hexian cranium was discovered in 1980.
   a. A close relationship is postulated between the *H. erectus* from Hexian and Zhoukoudian.
   b. Date to 190,000 (some say 400,000)

E. Asian crania from Java and China are similar
   1.*H. erectus* lived in Asia much longer than in Africa
   2.Nonetheless there is geographic variation in this species.

216

VII ASIAN AND AFRICAN *HOMO ERECTUS*: A COMPARISON

A. East African *H. erectus* and those fossils from China and Java demonstrate a considerable degree of variation.

B. Is this variation intraspecific or indicative of more than one species?

   1. African *H. erectus* finds display several differences from the Javan and Chinese fossils.

   2. The crania of the East African specimens have thinner cranial bones than those found in the Asian representatives.

   3. Some scientists would argue that the African and Asian *H. erectus* finds should be classified as separate species.

     a. These scientists refer to the African specimens as *H. ergaster*.

     b. In support of this position, the newly published early dates from Java suggest that the African and Asian populations may have had a separate history for more than one million years.

   4. However, most paleoanthropologists consider *H. erectus* to have been a widespread single species that accommodated a considerable range of intraspecific variation.

     a. Discoveries at Daka do not support the view of a separate species.

VIII LATER *HOMO ERECTUS* FROM EUROPE

A. Evidence of *H. erectus* has been recently found in Spain and Italy.

B. These European sites do not exhibit the antiquity of other sites (Dmanisi).

C. Several caves in the Atapuerca region of northern Spain have yielded fossils that appear to be contemporaries of *H. erectus*.

   1. Sima del Elefante cave site dates to 1.2 mya

     a. Partial jaw with a few teeth

     b. Appears similar to the Dmanisi material.

     c. Stone tools like olduwan also found at this site.

   2. Gran Dolina in Spain

     a. Dates to ~850-780,000 years ago

     b. The Spanish scientists have named these fossils a new species: *H. antecessor*.

       i. The material is very fragmentary, so whether it is accurate to assign a new species name is not clear.

   3. A skull from Ceprano, central Italy, is the best evidence yet of true *Homo erectus* in western Europe

     a. Provisional dating is between 800-900 kya.

   4. After 400 kya the European fossil hominin record becomes much more abundant.

     a. This abundance leads to more variation and more room for debate.

     b. Some of the later "premodern" specimens have been considered early *H. sapiens* or another species.

IX TECHNOLOGICAL TRENDS IN *HOMO ERECTUS*

A. Across its distribution, it appears that *H. erectus* is associated with two tool industries.

   1. The species began using the Olduwan (associated with early *Homo*)

   2. And we believe *H. erectus* developed their own technology: Acheulian.

     a. Acheulian tool industry spread from Africa after 1.4 mya and became standard.

3. Acheulian tool kit characterized by a biface also called a hand axe.
   a. has a flatter core and is worked on two sides.
B. The Acheulian hand axe was an all-purpose tool for more than a million years.
   1. It has been found in Africa, parts of Asia and later in Europe.
   2. Recently, reports of Acheulian bifaces found in China dating to 800,000 y.a. have expanded the Acheulian tool kit to the full geographic range of H. *erectus*.
   3. With the Acheulian culture we find evidence that raw materials were transported across the landscape.
      a. Transport suggests forethought and planning (not seen with respect to Olduwan).
   4. Widespread evidence for butchering exists.
      a. Cut marks on bone often overlay carnivore tooth marks.
         i. This suggests the bones were scavenged and then processed by hominins.
   5. *Homo erectus* were most likely consuming 80% of their daily calories from plant materials.
      a. This practice is consistent with that of modern hunter-gatherers.

X **SEEING THE BIG PICTURE: INTERPRETATIONS OF *HOMO ERECTUS***
A. In the past it was accepted that H. erectus was able to emigrate out of Africa owing to advanced tools and a more modern anatomy.
B. Recent discoveries indicate that this is too simple and interpretation.
C. Some of the earliest emigrants due not exhibit the full suite of *H. erectus* characteristics.
   1. The recent discoveries at Dmanisi have thrown into question the tidy assumption that increased brain and body size of *Homo erectus* allowed this hominin species to first migrate out of Africa.
   2. Perhaps there were multiple early migrations, the first represented by the smaller-brained forms found at Dmanisi.
      a. This initial migration may have been ultimately unsuccessful in evolutionary terms.
   3. The second, but typical *H. erectus* was successful in colonizing much of the Old World.
D. Are recently proposed species names such as *H. ergaster* and *H. antecessor* justified?
   1. *Fo*r most scholars, the jury is still out, but recent finds, at Daka for example, indicate that *H. erectus* encompasses morphology seen in Asia and Africa.
   2. The separate species label for Soanish sites it not yet clearly established.
E. Nevertheless most scholars agree that *Homo erectus* was the first hominin species to embrace culture as a strategy of adaptation.
   1. Therefore, it is with this species that we can begin to talk of human (rather than just hominin) evolution.

KEY TERMS

Acheulian: a tool technology from the lower and middle Pleistocene characterized by bifacial tools usually made of stone.
artifacts: objects or materials made or modified for use by hominins
biface: a stone tool consisting of a core stone worked on both sides.
encephalization: the relationship between brain size and overall body size

grade: a grouping of organisms sharing a similar adaptive pattern.

morphology: refers to the form or shape of anatomical structures or an entire organism.

Nariokotome: also known as WT 15000. Refers to an almost complete skeleton of a 12 year old boy from West Lake Turkana in Kenya classified as *H. erectus*.

nuchal torus: large bony buttress at the rear of the skull

Pleistocene: the epoch of the Cenozoic dating from 1.8 mya to 10,000 y.a. characterized by continental glaciations of the northern latitudes. Frequently referred to as the "Age of Glaciers" or the "Ice Age."

postcranial: refers to the skeleton with the exclusion of the skull (cranium). Literally implies beyond the cranium-as in quadrupeds where body is after the skull.

supraorbital torus: heavy browridge.

Zhoukoudian: A village near Beijing famous for a cave that has yielded rich fossil remains of *H. erectus*.

MEDIA EXERCISES

1) A wonderfully informative website on Chinese paleoanthropology has been created and maintained by Dr. Dennis A. Etler, titled "The Fossil Evidence for Human Evolution in China" (http://www.chineseprehistory.com/). The site includes a picture gallery of fossils ranging from late Miocene hominoids, through Chinese *H. erectus*, to the first modern humans from China (http://www.chineseprehistory.com/pics1.htm).

INFOTRAC

1) In *InfoTrac* do a keyword search on "*Dmanisi*" to read a *National Geographic* article written by Josh Fischman on the recent discovery of the early fossils from Georgia. After reading the article, what can this site tells us about the way of life of some of our earliest European ancestors?

CONCEPT APPLICATION

1) One of the most fascinating and difficult tasks a paleoanthropologist faces is trying to explain how our hominin ancestors behaved in the past. In Chapter 12, we see a number of examples of how bones and stones have allowed researchers to make educated guesses about the behavior of *H. erectus* and *erectus*-like bipeds. Using your text, find at least two examples that exemplify hominin behavior from the bones and artifacts found at archaeological sites. Hint: Figure 12-6 on page 339 shows an early hominin that survived into old age. What does this say about the group with which this individual lived?

2) Now answer the True/False, Multiple Choice and Short Answer sample test questions. Following completion of the tests correct them with the answers and textbook page references at the end of this Study Guide chapter. Note the areas in which you are strong and weak to guide you in your studying. Finally, answer the sample Essay Questions.

TRUE/FALSE QUESTIONS

If false, consider what modification would make the statement true.

1. Current interpretations view the first hominin migrations out of Africa taking place between 500,000-250,000 years ago.
     TRUE   FALSE

2. Evidence of *H. erectus* like hominins have recently been found in caves in Spain and Italy.
     TRUE   FALSE

3. Brain size in *H. erectus* ranges from 750-1250 cm^3 with an average of around 900 cm^3.
     TRUE   FALSE

4. Eugene Dubois discovered the first *H. erectus* fossils in Java in the early 1890s.
     TRUE   FALSE

5. Zhoukoudian, a very important *H. erectus* site, is a cave located in the country of Java.
     TRUE   FALSE

6. WT 15000 is significant because it is the most complete *H. erectus* skeleton yet discovered.
     TRUE   FALSE

7. The site of Dmanisi, in the Republic of Georgia, is important because the hominin fossils found there are the youngest of all *H. erectus* finds, dating to 200,000 y.a.
     TRUE   FALSE

8. The Acheulian cultural tradition is characterized by bifacially worked core tools, such as hand axes and cleavers.
     TRUE   FALSE

9. A synthesis of *H. erectus* sites, indicates that the earliest occupants used Olduwan tools and later sites evidence the use of Acheulian toolkits.
     TRUE   FALSE

10. The first hominin species to wholeheartedly embrace culture as an adaptive strategy was *H. erectus*.
     TRUE   FALSE

MULTIPLE CHOICE QUESTIONS

1. Currently, it is believed that hominins first left Africa
   A. close to 2 mya
   B. due to a geologic catastrophe.
   C. around 500,000 y.a.
   D. and went directly to North and South America.

2. Some scholars refer the African forms of *H. erectus* to a different species called
   A. *H. ergaster*.
   B. *H. habilis*.
   C. *H. antecessor*.
   D. *H. neanderthalensis*.

3. The hominin crania from Dmanisi, Republic of Georgia, are
   A. dated to 1.75 mya
   B. smaller-brained than typical *H. erectus*.
   C. associated with a more primitive stone tool culture than most *H. erectus*.
   D. All of the above.

4. Fossil remains from the Gran Dolina site in northern Spain
   A. may be the oldest hominins in Western Europe.
   B. are agreed by all paleoanthropologists to represent *H. erectus*.
   C. are the oldest fossils of *H. sapiens*.
   D. are evidence of *H. habilis* in Europe.

5. A grouping of organisms that share a similar adaptive pattern defines a
   A. grade.
   B. clade.
   C. species.
   D. family.

6. Compared to australopithecines and modern humans, *H. erectus* limb bones were
   A. shorter.
   B. longer.
   C. less robust.
   D. more robust.

7. The Pleistocene lasted
   A. approximately 100,000 years.
   B. longer than the Miocene.
   C. more than 1.75 million years.
   D. until 3.5 million years ago.

8. Compared to earlier hominins, *H. erectus* was
   A. dramatically larger-bodied.
   B. somewhat shorter.
   C. more or less the same body size.
   D. less skeletally robust.

9. Compared to australopithecines, *H. erectus*
   A. was smaller-brained.
   B. was larger-brained.
   C. had more or less the same brain size.
   D. was much less encephalized.

10. If the Nariokotome "boy" had survived to adulthood he would have
    A. been obese.
    B. a leader of his clan.
    C. been over 6 feet tall.
    D. had relatively long arms compared to his legs (like australopithecines).

11. What characteristic(s) distinguish(es) *H. erectus* cranial shape?
    A. Long and low skull vault
    B. Little or no forehead development with large browridges
    C. Wide cranial base with maximum breadth beneath the ear opening
    D. All of the above

12. What is a nuchal torus?
    A. a ridge of bone about the eye orbits.
    B. a ridge of bone on which the temporalis muscle attaches
    C. a projection of bone in the back of the cranium where neck muscles attach.
    D. None of the above

13. Eugene Dubois
    A. was the first scientist to understand the significance of cranial size.
    B. went out to look for evidence of the "missing link."
    C. dissected ape specimens.
    D. applied chronometric dating techniques to fossils.

14. Which of the following is **not** true of *Homo erectus* from Java?
    A. Six sites in eastern Java have yielded *H. erectus* fossils.
    B. Dating is difficult due to the island's complex geology.
    C. Most of the fossils are older than 2.0 million years.
    D. Very few artifacts have been found in association with Javan *H. erectus*

222

15. If the date range of 50,000 to 25,000 years ago for the Ngandong hominins from Java is confirmed, it would show that *H. erectus*
    A. lived contemporaneously with *H. sapiens*.
    B. had art.
    C. went extinct one million years before the appearance of modern *H. sapiens*.
    D. exhibited complex tool use.

16. The cultural remains at Zhoukoudian Cave
    A. are nonexistent.
    B. are limited to well-constructed fireplaces.
    C. consist of over 100,000 artifacts.
    D. enable archaeologists to easily reconstruct a day in the life of *H. erectus*.

17. Which of the following have been conclusively demonstrated for *H. erectus* at Zhoukoudian?
    A. They made and controlled fire.
    B. They were proficient hunters of deer and horses.
    C. They lived in the cave.
    D. None of the above (recent research has cast doubt on all three propositions).

18. An important discovery made by Louis Leakey at Olduvai Gorge in 1960
    A. is dated at 4.1 mya
    B. has a cranial capacity of 1067 cm³.
    C. has the smallest browridges of any hominin yet discovered.
    D. was found in 1980.

19. Which of the following is **not** true about WT 15000 from Nariokotome?
    A. It is the most complete *H. erectus* skeleton ever found.
    B. It dates to 1.6 mya
    C. It is the first *H. erectus* specimen from Egypt.
    D. He was about 12 years old when he died.

20. An important lesson taught to us by is the recently discovered female pelvis from Gona is
    A. that hominins were already fishing during the Lower Pleistocene.
    B. that *H. erectus* had already attained modern human height by 1.5 million years ago.
    C. that *H. erectus* had already attained a fully human language.
    D. that *H. erectus* newborns may have had brains as large as modern *H. sapiens* newborns.

21. Recent interpretations of fauna and paleoenvironment at _____ indicate H. erectus may have had limited hunting capabilities?
    A. Hexian
    B. Yunxian
    C. Zoukoudian
    D. Lantian

22. European hominin finds that date to approximately 700,000 years old have been discovered in
    A. England.
    B. France.
    C. Spain.
    D. All of the above

23. The Acheulian tool kit, the standard industry for later *H. erectus* for over a million years,
    A. served to cut, pound, scrape and dig.
    B. is only found in southern Africa.
    C. was hafted on spear shafts as an effective throwing weapon.
    D. is first found in the archaeological record of China.

24. Which Acheulian tool is considered the basic toolkit of *H. erectus*?
    A. hand axe
    B. burin
    C. scraper
    D. point

25. *H. erectus* sites around the Old World display extensive evidence of
    A. butchering.
    B. cave art.
    C. projectile hunting technology (e.g. spear throwers and bows and arrows).
    D. primitive horticulture.

SHORT ANSWER QUESTIONS (& PAGE REFERENCES)

1. Where are the earliest *H. erectus* fossils found and how old are they? (pp. 336-337)

2. What was the significance of Eugene Dubois' discoveries in Java in the early 1890s? (pp. 341-342)

3. What are the most important *H. erectus* finds made at East Turkana, West Turkana and Olduvai Gorge? (pp. 336-338)

4. What does the "Nariokotome Boy" tell us about the body size of *H. erectus*? (pp. 336-337)

5. What are some criticisms of *H. erectus* as a hunter? (p. 350)

ESSAY QUESTIONS (& PAGE REFERENCES)

1. Describe the brain size, body size, cranial shape, and dentition of *H. erectus*. How do these features differ from earlier hominins? (pp. 334-335)

2. Why are the recent discoveries at Dmanisi significant in modeling the initial migrations of hominins out of Africa? (pp. 338-340)

3. What is the importance of Zhoukoudian in the history of discovery and interpretations of *H. erectus*? How has recent research at Zhoukoudian challenged ideas about the lifeways of *H. erectus*? (pp. 342-343)

4. What is the importance of the female pelvis discovered at Gona? What can this spectacular discovery tell us about the biology and lifeways of *H. erectus*? (pp. 337-338)

5. How do the recent discoveries in Spain and Italy add to what we know about *H. erectus*? (pp. 348-349)

ANSWERS, *CORRECTED STATEMENT* IF FALSE & REFERENCES TO TRUE/FALSE QUESTIONS

1. FALSE, p. 336, Current interpretations view the first hominin migrations out of Africa taking place close to 2.0 mya

2. TRUE, pp. 348-349

3. TRUE, p. 334

4. TRUE, p. 341

5. FALSE, pp. 342-343, Zhoukoudian, a very important *H. erectus* site, is a cave located outside of *Beijing, China.*

6. TRUE, p. 336

7. FALSE, pp. 338-339, The site of Dmanisi, in the Republic of Georgia, is important because the hominin fossils found there are *among the oldest* of all *H. erectus* finds, dating to *1.7-1.8 m.y.a.*

8. TRUE, pp. 350-351

9. TRUE, pp. 350-351

10. TRUE, p. 352

ANSWERS AND REFERENCES TO MULTIPLE CHOICE QUESTIONS

1. **A**, p. 338
2. **A**, p. 331
3. **D**, p. 338-339
4. **A**, pp. 348-349
5. **A**, p. 331
6. **D**, p. 334
7. **C**, p. 342
8. **A**, p. 334
9. **B**, p. 334
10. **C**, p. 337
11. **D**, pp. 334-336
12. **C**, p. 335
13. **B**, p. 341
14. **C**, pp. 341-342
15. **A**, p. 342
16. **C**, pp. 343-346
17. **D**, pp. 343-346
18. **B**, p. 337
19. **C**, p. 337
20. **B**, pp. 337-338
21. **B**, p. 346
22. **C**, p. 348
23. **A**, p. 350
24. **A**, p. 350
25. **A**, p. 351

CONCEPT APPLICATION SOLUTION

1) In figure 12-6 (p. 339) shows a recently discovered cranium and lower jaw from Dmanisi, Georgia. This individual had only one tooth left in his mouth when he died. His jawbone showed a considerable amount of resorption indicating that this individual survived for perhaps years with few teeth. It is hypothesized that this individual lived in a group which helped him to survive and took care of him in his old age. These bones indicate a certain amount of cooperation and care in a very early small-brained hominin.

2) On page 344 we see that artifacts found at Zhoukoudian show that hominins used several kinds of tools that became more refined through time. These early hominins were thinking ahead and modifying their environment to gain resources. They also used a number of different sources of food like ostrich shells, berries, and herbs.

3) "A Closer Look" on pages 344-345 provides two alternate explanations for the material remaining in the Dragon Bone Hill site. The best evidence today shows that the hominins that frequented this cave probably shared time and space with other predators such as hyenas. There is clear evidence of tools at the site and cut marks on bones that suggests possible scavenging of meat killed by large carnivores.

CHAPTER 13
PREMODERN HUMANS

LEARNING OBJECTIVES

After reading this chapter you should be able to:
- discuss the significance of Pleistocene climatic fluctuations in regard to human evolution (pp. 356-357)
- understand the morphological changes that occurred in the transition from *Homo erectus* to premodern humans (pp. 358-364)
- discuss key *H. heidelbergensis* discoveries from Africa, Europe, and Asia (p. 359-364)
- compare the tool technology of premodern humans to that of *H. erectus* and early modern *H. sapiens* (pp. 365-367)
- discuss the physical characteristics of classic Neandertals (pp. 367-370)
- identify specific sites where Neandertal fossils have been discovered, and discuss what they reveal about morphology and burials (pp. 371-375)
- describe Neandertal technology, behavior, subsistence and burials (pp. 375-379)
- understand the genetic evidence that bears on the relationships and fate of the Neandertals (p. 379-381)
- understand the debates regarding classification of non-modern *Homo* fossil material (pp. 382-386)

CHAPTER OUTLINE

Introduction

    In the previous chapter we examined *Homo erectus*, believed by most to be the ancestor of modern *Homo sapiens*. In this chapter we take a look at the succeeding premodern humans from Europe, Africa, China and Java who display both *H. erectus* and *H. sapiens* characteristics. We then take a look at Neandertals including their physical characteristics, culture, technology, settlements, subsistence patterns and burials. We conclude with discussions on the debates surrounding Neandertal origins as well as their disappearance.

I   **WHEN, WHERE AND WHAT**
  A. The Pleistocene
     1. Middle Pleistocene: 780,000 - 125,000 ya
     2. Late Pleistocene: 125,000 - 10,000 ya.
     3. The Pleistocene is also known as the "Ice Age" as it was marked by periodic advances and retreats of continental glaciations.
       a. The Pleistocene is characterized by approximately 15 major cold periods and 50 minor glacial advances.
  B. In Africa during glacial periods, the Sahara desert expanded, blocking migration routes out of the southern portions of the continent.
  C. Glacial advances would have greatly affected migration routes in Eurasia.
     1. During glacial peaks much of western Europe would have been cut off.

227

D. Dispersal of Middle Pleistocene Hominins
1. Premodern humans were widely distributed throughout the Old World.
    a. These fossils are found in Africa, Asia and Europe.
2. Premodern humans did not extend the geographical range of *Homo erectus*; they largely replaced the earlier hominins previously exploited habitats.
3. Europe for the first time becomes more permanently and densely occupied.
E. Middle Pleistocene hominins: Terminology
1. Premodern humans generally succeeded *H. erectus*.
    a. In southeast Asia, there were 300,000+ years of coexistence.
2. Morphologically they display *H. erectus* characteristics.
    a. Including a large face with projecting brows, a low forehead and relatively thick bone of the cranial vault.
    b. Advanced *Homo sapiens*-like features include increased brain size, a more rounded vault, a more vertical nose, and less angulation in the occipital region.
    c. 500 kya of evolution during the Middle Pleistocene so it is not unusual to see increased variability across period.
3. Beginning as early as 850 kya and extending to about 200 kya the fossils from Africa and Europe are classified as *H. heidelbergensis*.
    a. This early group used to be called "*archaic Homo sapiens*"; but this designation does not take account of the real differences between these fossils.
    b. This text recognizes *H. heidelbergensis* as a transitional species between *Homo erectus* and *Homo sapiens*.

II   PREMODERN HUMANS OF THE MIDDLE PLEISTOCENE
A. Africa
1. The best known premodern human fossil is from Kabwe (Broken Hill) in Zambia.
    a. The Broken Hill cranium has a very heavy browridge, low vault, and prominent occipital torus reminiscent of *H. erectus*.
    b. But like later humans, the occipital region is less angular, the cranial bones are thinner, and the cranial base is essentially modern.
    c. Sites date from 600 kya to 125 kya
2. The cranium from Bodo, is one of the oldest specimens of *H. heidelbergensis* from Africa (estimated to be from 600,000 ya)
    a. The Bodo cranium has cut-marks similar to butchered animals, and thus provides the earliest evidence of deliberate bone processing of hominins by hominins.
3. Other crania from southern and eastern Africa show a combination of retained ancestral with more derived characteristics.
    a. The most important sites are from Florisbad, Elandsfontein, and Laetoli.
4. In Africa, the premodern humans fossils are all morphologically similar and are similar to European types.
B. Europe
1. More *H. heidelbergensis* fossils are known from Europe than any other region.
2. Europe was more widely and consistently occupied during the Middle Pleistocene than had been earlier.
3. The European fossils have a time range that extends through the Middle Pleistocene and beyond.

a. Spanish fossils from Gran Dolina dating to ~850,000 ya. may be the earliest occurrence of *H. heidelbergensis*.
4. Other *H. heidelbergensis* remains come from Steinheim, Petralona, Swanscombe, Arago, and Atapuerca.
   a. European premoderns have retained certain *H. erectus* traits, by they are mixed with more derived ones such as:
      i.   increased cranial capacity
      ii. less angled occipital
      iii. parietal expansion
      iv. reduced tooth size
5. Atapuerca Site of Sima de los Huesos
   a. Dates from 600 kya to 530 kya.
   b. This site contains more than 80% of all Middle Pleistocene hominin remains in the world.
   c. The remains of at least 28 individuals (represented by over 4,000 fragments) have been recovered.
   d. Morphology shows Neandertal-like traits that include arching browridges and a projecting midface.
C. Asia
   1. China
      a. Chinese paleoanthropologists suggest that certain (ancestral) *H. erectus* features can be found in modern Chinese such as a sagittal ridge and flattened nasal bones.
      b. To some Chinese scholars, this is indicative of substantial genetic continuity and suggests modern Chinese evolved from a separate *H. erectus* lineage in China.
      c. Dali, the most complete Chinese premodern skull displays *H. erectus* and *H. sapiens* traits.
         i. It has a relatively small cranial capacity of 1120 cm^3 while the Jinniushan skull (dated to 200,000 ya.) has a surprisingly large cranial capacity of 1260 cm^3.
      d. Recently, it has been concluded that these hominins are regional variants of *Homo heidelbergensis*.

III   A REVIEW OF MIDDLE PLEISTOCENE EVOLUTION
A. The premodern fossils from Europe and Africa resemble each other more than they do the premoderns from Asia.
   1. The European and African forms are often referred to as *H. heidelbergensis*.
   2. The Asian forms (especially Jinniushan) seem more modern than African or European contemporary fossils.
      a. Jinniushan fossils may be early *H. sapiens* or may represent a regional branch of *H. heidelbergensis*.
B. Pleistocene world forced many populations into geographic isolation from other hominin populations.
   1. Some went extinct, others evolved into later hominins.
      a. African *H. heidelbergensis* is hypothesized to have evolved into modern *H. sapiens*
      b. European *H. heidelbergensis* were ancestral to Neandertals.
      c. Chinese forms may have gone extinct.
      d. Currently, there is no consensus on the status or fate of Asian hominins.

IV   MIDDLE PLEISTOCENE CULTURE
A. Acheulian technology of *H. erectus* carried over into the Middle Pleistocene with little change until the end of the period when it became slightly more sophisticated.
1. Bone was not widely used.
2. Stone flakes tools persisted, and may have had greater variety.
B. African and European premoderns invented the Levallois technique for controlling flake size and shape.
1. This highly complex technique indicates an increased cognitive ability.
2. Where hand axes proliferate – the tool industry is referred to as Acheulian.
C. Acheulian assemblages have been found at many African and European sites.
D. There is considerable intraregional diversity in stone tool industries.
1. It appears that different stone tool industries coexisted in some areas for long periods.
a. It has been suggested that different groups of hominins made different stone industries.
b. Others suggest that the same group produced them but for different activities at different sites.
c. The type of tool manufactured was also dependent on the availability of workable stone in an area.
d. See "A Closer Look" p.352.
E. Premodern humans continued to live in caves and open-air sites.
F. There is some evidence that these early humans did control fire, although not all authorities share that view.
G. Middle Pleistocene hominins built temporary structures.
H. They exploited many different food sources – fruits, vegetables, fish, seeds, nuts, bird eggs and also exploited marine life.
I. The most detailed reconstruction of Middle Pleistocene life in Europe comes from Terra Amata in southern France.
1. The site provides evidence of short-term, seasonal visits by hominins that built flimsy shelters, gathered plants, and ate food from the ocean.
J. There is little evidence supporting widely practiced advanced hunting capabilities for premodern humans.
1. In Schöningen, Germany, well preserved wooden throwing spears were found in 1995.
2. These implements are provisionally dated to 400,000 ya.
3. Most likely used as throwing spears to hunt large animals.

V   NEANDERTALS: PREMODERN HUMANS OF THE LATE PLEISTOCENE
A. Neandertals fit into the general scheme of human evolution; however their classification is difficult.
1. Some anthropologists classify them with *H. sapiens* but as a distinctive subspecies – *Homo sapiens neanderthalensis*.
2. The wider consensus that *Homo heidelbergensis* was to the ancestor to both Neandertals and modern *Homo sapiens* has led to the placement of Neandertals into a separate species - *Homo neanderthalensis*.
B. Neandertals fossil remains have been found at dates approaching 130,000 ya.
1. "Classic" Neandertals date from around 75,000 ya. to 35,000 ya. (last major glaciation) and are primarily from western Europe.
2. Neandertals lived in Europe and western Asia for about 100,000 years.

230

C. While modern *H. sapiens* brain size averages between 1300-1400 cm^3, Neandertal brain size averaged 1520 cm^3.
   1. Large brain size in Neandertals may be associated with greater metabolic efficiency in cold weather.
   2. It may also be associated with the need for large brains to run relatively large bodies that are adapted to cold climates.
D. The Neandertal cranium is large, long, low, and bulges at the sides.
   1. The occipital bone is bun shaped but lacks the occipital angle of *H. erectus*.
   2. The forehead rises more vertically than in earlier *H. erectus*.
   3. Over the orbits are arched browridges instead of a bar-like supraorbital torus.
   4. The Neandertal face projects as if it were pulled forward.
E. Postcranially, Neandertals are very robust (heavily muscled) with shorter limbs than *H. sapiens*.
F. Western Europe
   1. In 1908 at La Chapelle-aux-Saints, in southwestern France, a nearly complete Neandertal burial was found in a flexed position with several fragments of nonhuman long bones placed over the head.
   2. Also found in associated were flint tools.
   3. The skeleton was sent to Marcellin Boule, a well-known French paleontologist, for analysis.
      a. He interpreted this find as a brutish, bent-kneed, not-fully-erect biped.
      b. This resulted in a general misunderstanding that Neandertals were very primitive.
      c. In fact, the skeleton was of an older male suffering from spinal osteoarthritis.
      d. The pathologies were misinterpreted by Boule as representing normal anatomy for Neandertals.
      e. The male skull was possibly 40 years old was large typical of classic Neandertals.
   4. At the Moula-Guercy Cave site in southern France, recent work has uncovered the best evidence of Neandertal cannibalism.
      a. Neandertal bones found here were broken and cut just like the animal bones at the site, suggesting to the researchers that the Neandertals were processed for food.
   5. Some of the most recent surviving Neandertals come from St. Césaire in southwestern France and date to ~35,000 ya.
      a. The bones were recovered from a bed including discarded chipped blades, hand axes, and other stone tools of an Upper Paleolithic tool industry.
   6. Modern *H. sapiens* were living in central and western Europe by about 35,000 ya.
      a. Neandertals and moderns were living close to each other for several thousand years.
      b. Neandertals may have borrowed technological methods and tools from anatomically modern populations creating the Chatelperronian industry.
G. Central Europe
   1. Krapina, Croatia
      a. Remains of up to 70 Neandertal individuals were recovered from this site dating to the last interglacial (130,000-110,000 ya.).
      b. Over 1,000 stone tools and flakes were found.

231

     c. Fossils from this site may be the earliest showing full classic Neandertal morphology.

     d. Krapina has one of the oldest intentional burials on record.

  2. Vindija, Croatia

     a. About 30 miles from Krapina, this site is an excellent source of material culture stratified in sequence that documents much later Neandertal occupation.

     b. Dating from 42,000-28,000 ya., 35 Neandertal specimens have been recovered.

     c. The later forms are less robust than "Classic" Neandertals leading some researchers to conclude that the Vindija hominins document some continuity between Neandertals and modern humans in the region.

H. Western Asia

  1. Israel

     a. Tabun (Mugaret-et-Tabun)

       i. This site yielded a female skeleton dated to about 120,000-110,000 ya.

       ii. If the dating is accurate, it indicates that Neandertals and modern humans lived contemporaneously in the Middle East.

     b. Kebara Site (60,000 ya.)

       i. Although the skeleton is incomplete (it is missing the skull), it boasts the most complete Neandertal pelvis yet found.

       ii. The skeleton also yielded the first ever fossil hominin hyoid bone, which is very important in reconstructing speech capabilities.

  2. Iraq

     a. The most remarkable site is Shanidar Cave in northeastern Iraq.

     b. Shanidar yielded the partial remains of nine individuals, four of whom were deliberately buried.

     c. "Shanidar 1" was a 35 to 40 year old male whose stature is estimated at 5'7".

     d. He survived extreme injuries (e.g. a crushing blow to his head, loss of the use of his right arm) suggesting to researchers that his survival would have only been possible if he had been helped by others in his group.

I. Central Asia

  1. Uzbekistan

     a. The remains of a child buried with Mousterian tools recovered at Teshik-Tash cave is the easternmost Neandertal discovery.

     b. DNA analysis indicates that the Teshik-Tash skeleton are clearly Neandertal.

     c. The skeleton was 9 years old at death and deliberately buried.

     d. Researchers have identified that Neandertals and modern humans differ in both their mitochondrial DNA and nuclear DNA.

VI CULTURE OF NEANDERTALS

A. Neandertals are generally associated with the Mousterian tool industry.

  1. These cultural remains are found in Europe, North Africa, the former Soviet Union, Israel, Iran, Uzbekistan and perhaps even into China.

  2. The Middle Stone Age industry of sub-Saharan Africa is contemporary with and similar to the Mousterian.

B. Technology

1. Neandertals improved on the previous prepared-core (e.g. Levallois) techniques by inventing a new variation.
   a. They formed a disk-shaped core, and would produce more flakes per core than their predecessors.
   b. Flakes were reworked into various forms including scrapers, points, and knives.
2. Neandertals elaborated and diversified traditional methods and may have developed specialized tools.

C. Subsistence
1. Neandertals were successful hunters, although they were not as efficient as Upper Paleolithic hunters who used spearthrowers, or atlatls.
2. Neandertals had to get close to prey to kill them, and were therefore more prone to injury.
   a. The pattern of trauma found among Neandertals is similar to modern day rodeo riders, demonstrating the danger inherent in the Neandertal lifestyle.
3. We know the most about European Middle Paleolithic culture because it has been studied longer and by more scholars than any earlier period.
4. Technology and cultural adaptations in Africa paralleled those in Europe and southwest Asia.

D. Speech and symbolic behavior
1. The prevailing scientific consensus is that Neandertals were capable of speech, and possibly capable of producing the same range of sounds as modern humans.
2. Recent genetic evidence is providing indications of when human language emerged.
   a. In humans, mutations are known to produce serious language impairments in a particular locus.
   b. There is greater variability seen in the alleles at this locus in modern humans as compared to other primates.
3. If Neandertals could speak, it does not mean that their abilities were at the level of modern *H. sapiens*.
4. Behavioral differences may explain the sudden geographical and populational expansion of *modern H. sapiens*.
5. Researchers believe that Upper Paleolithic *H. sapiens* had significant behavioral advantages over Neandertals.
   a. Neandertal brains were probably not significantly different from moderns.
   b. Most reservations about Neandertal cognitive abilities are based on archaeological data.
   c. Anthropologists are unable to verify if the extinction of Neandertals was the result of cultural differences alone or if it was also influenced by biological variation.
6. See "A Closer Look: The Evolution of Language" pp. 380-381).

E. Burials
1. Some form of deliberate and consistent disposal of the dead dates back at least to the Sima de los Huesos site, Atapuerca, Spain (500,000 ya.).
2. Burial is seen in Western Europe long before it appears in either Africa.
3. Although the burial treatments of modern *H. sapien* remains are more complex, deliberate burial was practiced by Neandertals.
   a. Many Neandertal bodies were deliberately placed in a flexed position when buried.

      b. Grave goods (e.g. stone tools, animal bones, flowers) were intentionally interred with the deceased.

    4. Unfortunately, due to poorly documented excavation, burial evidence is in question.

    5. In the 33 Neandertals burials with adequate data, only 14 show definite association with stone tools and/or animal bones.

VII GENETIC EVIDENCE

A. It is becoming fairly common to extract, amplify, and sequence ancient DNA from contexts spanning the last 10,000 years.

B. DNA analyzed from more than12 different Neandertal fossils date between 50,000 and 35,000 ya.

C. Mitochondrial DNA is extracted, amplified and sequenced.

    1. Neandertals are 3 times as different from modern populations as modern populations are different from each other.

    2. An hypothesis is that the Neandertal lineage split off between 690,000-550,000 ya.

D. Nuclear DNA analysis confirms Neandertals originated between 800,000-500,000 ya.

    1. Nuclear DNA patterns are as distinct from those of modern humans as are the differences seen in mitochondrial DNA.

E. Based on the genetic evidence, it appears reasonable for Neandertals to be considered a separate species.

VIII TRENDS IN HUMAN EVOLUTION: UNDERSTANDING PREMODERN HUMANS

A. Middle Pleistocene humans are transitional between *H. erectus* and *H. sapiens*.

B. Even though they share a common evolutionary foundation, paleoanthropologists arise at different conclusions about the best way to classify Middle/Late Pleistocene hominins.

    1. Lumpers recognize only one species of premodern fossils and classify them as *Homo sapiens* and earlier forms as *H. heidelbergensis*.

    2. Splitters identify 2 or more species distinct from *H. sapiens* (*H. heidelbergensis*, *H. helmei*, *H. neanderthalensis*).

    3. There is agreement that not all of these species left descendants.

    4. Naming these early fossil species aids our understanding of their relation to moderns.

    5. These early species are better defined as paleospecies or paleo-demes.

C. Neandertals are very closely related to modern humans, although they were physically and behaviorally distinct.

    1. Despite these differences, Neandertals never fully speciated and remained capable of interbreeding with more modern people with whom they came into contact.

    2. We can consider Neandertals incipient species.

KEY TERMS

Chatelperronian: an Upper Paleolithic Neandertal tool industry found in France and Spain, containing blade tools.

flexed: the position of the body in a bent orientation with arms and legs are drawn up to the chest This position has been observed in several Neandertal burials.

glaciations: cold climatic intervals when continental ice sheets cover much of the northern continents.

interglacials: warmer climatic intervals during which continental ice sheets retreat and melt.

Late Pleistocene: The portion of the Pleistocene epoch beginning125,000 and ending approximately 10,000 ya.

Levallois: a technique for the manufacture of tools by striking flakes from a flat flint nodule.

Middle Pleistocene: The portion of the Pleistocene epoch beginning 780,000 and ending 125,000 ya.

Mousterian: the stone tool technology mostly associated with Neandertals and some modern *H. sapien* groups; also called Middle Paleolithic. This industry is characterized by a larger proportion of flack tools than found in Acheulian tool kits.

Upper Paleolithic: a culture period usually associated with early modern humans in Europe that is characterized by technological innovation in various stone tool industries.

MEDIA EXERCISES

1) The Atapuerca sites, in northern Spain, have yielded the largest collection of premodern human fossils from anywhere in the world. This collection of localities has recently been designated a "World Heritage Site" by UNESCO.
http://atapuerca.evoluciona.org/documents/00/en/gral_foto/content/inici/01_yacimiento.html

2) Two very well-done Neandertal websites deserve a visit.
http://karmak.org/archive/2003/01/westasia.htm contains a wonderful digest of western Asian Neandertal research by Scott J. Brown.
The second is hosted by the "Neanderthal Museum," which was opened in 1996 in the Neander Valley of Germany, commemorating the recovery of the first Neandertal specimen 140 years earlier. Take a virtual tour at http://www.neanderthal.de/en/home/index.html.

CONCEPT APPLICATION

Mystery Fossils
From the hints given below, try to determine which premodern human or Neandertal fossil is being described. Give yourself 5 points if you can figure it out with only the first clue ("a"), 3 points if you need both clue "a" and "b," and 1 point if you need all three clues ("a, b & c").

1. Mystery fossil #1
   a. Dates to 35,000 ya. in southwestern France.
   b. Found in association with Chatelperronian tools.
   c. "Classic" Neandertal facial and cranial morphology.

235

2. Mystery fossil #2
   a. Found in cave deposits near Kabwe, Zambia.
   b. Has a massive browridge, a low vault and a prominent occipital torus.
   c. It dates to about 130,000 ya.

3. Mystery fossil #3
   a. *Homo heidelbergensis fossil found in* China.
   b. It is the most complete skull of a premodern human from China.
   c. It has a relatively small cranial capacity of 1120 cm^3.

4. Mystery fossil #4
   a. A male Neandertal burial discovered in Israel in 1983.
   b. It has the most complete Neandertal pelvis yet found.
   c. It has the only Neandertal hyoid bone ever discovered.

5. Mystery site #5
   a. At least 32 individuals were recovered from this premodern human site.
   b. It is a cave in the northern hills of Spain.
   c. It dates to 600,000-530,000 y.a.

6. Mystery fossil #6
   a. A 30-45 year old Neandertal male recovered from a cave site in Iraq.
   b. He survived extreme trauma including a crushing blow to the side of his skull.
   c. He was 5'7" tall and had a cranial capacity of 1600 cm^3.

7. Mystery site #7
   a. At least 70 individuals were recovered from this Neandertal site.
   b. It is located in Croatia, in central Europe.
   c. It is relatively ancient for Neandertals, dating to 130,000-110,000 ya.

8. Mystery fossil #8
   a. Marcellin Boule's description of this fossil is partially responsible for today's caricature of Neandertals as a brutish biped
   b. Discovered in a cave in southwestern France in 1908.
   c. He was an old individual afflicted with arthritis and other pathologies.

Now answer the True/False, Multiple Choice and Short Answer sample test questions. Following completion of the tests, correct them with the answers and textbook page references at the end of this Study Guide chapter. Note the areas in which you are strong and weak to guide you in your studying. Finally, answer the sample Essay Questions.

TRUE/FALSE QUESTIONS

If false, consider what modification would make the statement true.

1. Temporally, premodern humans are placed in between *H. erectus* and modern *H. sapiens*.
   TRUE   FALSE

2. Premodern humans are known from all seven continents.
   TRUE   FALSE

3. Premodern humans in Africa and Europe invented the Levallois technique for controlling stone tool flake size and shape.
   TRUE   FALSE

4. The earliest evidence of bows and arrows were discovered at the German site of Schöningen, dating to 400,000-380,000 ya.
   TRUE   FALSE

5. Neandertal brain size averaged 1100 cm^3, much less than the modern human average of 1350 cm^3.
   TRUE   FALSE

6. The first Neandertal fossils were discovered in Africa during the 1960s.
   TRUE   FALSE

7. Neandertal facial anatomy and their stocky bodies have been interpreted as adaptations to the challenges of living in glacial climates.
   TRUE   FALSE

8. Some of the latest-surviving Neandertals are from St. Césaire, in southwestern France.
   TRUE   FALSE

9. Neandertals improved and elaborated upon the tool-making techniques of their predecessors.
   TRUE   FALSE

10. Modern humans were the first people to bury their dead with grave goods (such as stone tools, animal bones and flowers).
    TRUE   FALSE

MULTIPLE CHOICE QUESTIONS

1. Which of the following is **not** a premodern human specimen?
   A. Nariokotome
   B. Broken Hill
   C. Dali
   D. Petralona

2. Which of the following is **not** a derived morphological change found in premodern humans?
   A. brain expansion
   B. increase in molar size
   C. more globular cranial vault
   D. less angled occipital

3. The premodern human finds from South and East Africa
   A. are very similar to one another, suggesting a fairly close genetic relationship.
   B. evolved from different gracile australopithecines ancestors.
   C. indicate that Neandertals evolved in southern Africa.
   D. suggest that these hominins went extinct by 25,000 ya.

4. Neandertals are found in
   A. Kenya.
   B. Cambodia.
   C. Australia.
   D. None of the above

5. Modern Chinese populations retain certain premodern human traits including
   A. extreme post orbital constriction and sagittal crests.
   B. projecting canines and diastemata.
   C. sagittal ridges and flattened nasal bones.
   D. All of the above

6. Earlier European premodern human fossils
   A. retain some *H. erectus* features such as thick cranial bones and heavy browridges.
   B. display some derived features including larger cranial capacity and reduced tooth size.
   C. are recognized as a transitional species, indicating an evolutionary relationship between earlier (*H. erectus*)and later European hominins.
   D. All of the above

7. Bodo is an premodern human site from
   A. China.
   B. Tanzania.
   C. Ethiopia.
   D. Croatia.

8. The site of Sima de los Huesos is important because it
   A. yielded the largest sample of premodern humans from anywhere in the world.
   B. documents the appearance of premodern humans in Mexico.
   C. is where Neandertal toolmakers first discovered the Levallois technique.
   D. All of the above

9. The Levallois technique for tool manufacturing
   A. arose both in Africa and in Europe.
   B. enabled the toolmaker to control flake size and shape.
   C. required coordinated steps.
   D. All of the above

10. The stone tool tradition referred to as Acheulian
    A. exhibits considerable intra-regional diversity.
    B. is restricted to eastern Asia.
    C. is uniform throughout Europe and Africa.
    D. is associated with modern humans.

11. Dali is a Middle Pleistocene site from?
    A. China
    B. Indonesia
    C. Ethiopia
    D. Kenya

12. One of the most important Neandertal discoveries was made in 1908 in what town in southwestern France.
    A. Nice
    B. La Chapelle-aux-Saints
    C. Liege
    D. Spy

13. Neandertals buried their dead in what position?
    A. northern facing.
    B. face down.
    C. flexed.
    D. Neandertals didn't bury their dead.

14. Average brain size among Neandertals
    A. is larger than among modern humans.
    B. may be related to metabolic efficiency in cold climates.
    C. is close to that of modern Inuit (Eskimo) brain size.
    D. All of the above

239

15. Which of the following is **not** typical of Neandertal crania?
    A. The skull is long and low.
    B. The browridges are arched over the orbits and do not form a bar-like supraorbital torus.
    C. The occipital bone is sharply angled.
    D. The forehead begins to appear and rises more vertically.

16. The La Chapelle-aux-Saints Neandertal was buried with
    A. flint tools.
    B. broken animal bones.
    C. a bison leg.
    D. All of the above

17. The Neandertal skeleton from La Chapelle-aux-Saints
    A. was a gracile, adult female.
    B. was an arthritic, older male.
    C. was a typical Neandertal in every way.
    D. died in his early teen-age years from a massive head injury.

18. Moula-Guercy, is significant because it
    A. is the best documented evidence of Neandertal cannibalism.
    B. provides the first evidence of fire use among premodern humans.
    C. provides the best evidence of interbreeding between Neandertals and early modern humans.
    D. documents the final extermination of Neandertals by premodern humans.

19. St. Césaire, in southwestern France, has produced a Neandertal in association with tools of what industry?
    A. Oldowan
    B. Acheulian
    C. Mousterian
    D. Chatelperronian

20. The Krapina, Croatia, Neandertal finds
    A. include fragments representing up to 70 individuals.
    B. date to around 30,000 ya.
    C. have very few stone tools associated with them.
    D. All of the above

21. The Tabun and Kebara Neandertal discoveries are from which country?
    A. Iceland
    B. Israel
    C. Iran
    D. Indonesia

240

22. The Kebara skeleton is the first Neandertal fossil to preserve which bone?
    A. patella
    B. calcaneus
    C. hyoid
    D. vomer

23. The Shanidar 1 male
    A. lived to be approximately 30-45 years old.
    B. was 5'7" tall.
    C. survived extreme trauma.
    D. All of the above

24. The tool industry that is generally associated with Neandertals is the
    A. Upper Paleolithic.
    B. Developed Oldowan.
    C. Acheulean.
    D. Mousterian.

25. Neandertal hunting
    A. utilized bows and arrows.
    B. probably required close contact with their prey.
    C. was probably rare and generally unsuccessful.
    D. was learned by copying from early modern human hunters.

26. Deliberate burial of the dead
    A. was characteristic of the Neandertals.
    B. is first observed in the archaeological record among *H. habilis*.
    C. is only a modern human behavior.
    D. was infrequent among European Neandertals.

27. What new technological breakthrough adds support to the separation of modern humans and Neandertals?
    A. The ability to use a new kind of carbon-14 dating to obtain an absolute age from ancient hominin bone that is over 100,000 years old.
    B. The use of a new kind of ground-penetrating radar to search for ancient, buried hominin skeletons.
    C. The extraction and sequencing of mtDNA from the original 40,000-year-old Neandertal fossil.
    D. The completion of the human genome project that conclusively demonstrated that Neandertals could not possibly be our ancestors.

SHORT ANSWER QUESTIONS (& PAGE REFERENCES)

1. How did climate changes affect premodern human migration? (pp. 356-357)

2. What was the importance of the Levallois technique? (p. 365)

3. What is the significance of the Chatelperronian stone tool culture? (p. 372)

4. How does Shanidar 1 represent an example of Neandertal compassion for the disabled? (p. 374)

5. Why is the extraction and sequencing of mtDNA from Neandertal fossils so exciting and significant? (pp. 379-381)

ESSAY QUESTIONS (& PAGE REFERENCES)

1. Describe the Middle Pleistocene culture of premodern humans. What archaeological evidence has been recovered that informs us about their tool use, shelter and subsistence? (pp. 365-367)

2. What is distinctive about the Neandertals? Discuss their brain size, skull shape, dentition, body size, robusticity and proportions in this context. (pp. 367-370)

3. What is the evidence for symbolic behavior and intentional burial among the Neandertals? (pp. 371, 378-379)

4. Discuss the taxonomic philosophies of "splitting" and "lumping" in the context of premodern humans and Neandertals. (pp. 382-384)

CONCEPT APPLICATION SOLUTION

Mystery Fossils (and page number references)
1. St. Césaire (p. 337)
2. Broken Hill ("At a Glance" p. 326)
3. Dali (p. 330)
4. Kebara (p. 338)
5. Sima de los Huesos, Atapuerca ("At a Glance" p. 327)
6. Shanidar 1 (p. 339)
7. Krapina (p. 337)
8. La Chapelle-aux-Saints (p. 335)

ANSWERS, *CORRECTED STATEMENT* IF FALSE & REFERENCES TO TRUE/FALSE QUESTIONS

1. **TRUE**, p. 359

2. **FALSE**, pp. 358-359, Premodern humans are known from *Africa, Asia and Europe*.

3. **TRUE**, p. 365

4. **FALSE**, p. 367, The earliest evidence of *throwing spears* were discovered at the German site of Schöningen, dating to 380,000-400,000 y.a.

5. **FALSE**, p. 367, Neandertal brain size averaged *1520* cm^3, *more* than the modern human average of 1350 cm^3.

6. **FALSE**, p. 367, 371, The first Neandertal fossils were discovered in *western Europe more than a century ago*.

7. **TRUE**, p. 370

8. **TRUE**, pp. 371-372

9. **TRUE**, p. 375

10. **FALSE**, pp. 378-379, *Neandertals* were the first people to bury their dead with grave goods (such as stone tools, animal bones and flowers).

ANSWERS AND REFERENCES TO MULTIPLE CHOICE QUESTIONS

1. **A,** pp. 359-364	10. **A**, p. 366	19. **D**, p. 372
2. **B**, p. 358	11. **A**, p. 361	20. **A**, p. 372
3. **A**, pp. 359-360	12. **B**, p. 371	21. **B**, pp. 373-374
4. **D**, pp. 367-375	13. **C**, p. 371, 379	22. **C**, p. 374
5. **C**, p. 361	14. **D**, pp. 367-368	23. **D**, p. 374
6. **D**, pp. 358-359	15. **C**, p. 368	24. **D**, p. 375
7. **C**, pp. 359-360	16. **D**, p. 371	25. **B**, p. 376
8. **A**, p. 361	17. **B**, p. 371	26. **A**, pp. 378-379
9. **D**, p. 365	18. **A**, p. 371	27. **C**, p. 379

CHAPTER 14
THE ORIGIN AND DISPERSAL OF MODERN HUMANS

LEARNING OBJECTIVES

After reading this chapter you should be able to:
- compare the three basic hypotheses for the origin and dispersal of anatomically modern humans (pp. 393-397).
- discuss the earliest evidence of modern humans including geographic distribution (pp. 397-410).
- discuss the significance of *Homo floresiensis* (pp. 410-412)
- discuss the earliest evidence of modern human technology and art (pp. 412-418).

CHAPTER OUTLINE

Introduction

In the previous chapter we looked at premodern humans including Neandertals. In this chapter we investigate the origins of anatomically modern humans. We discuss the problems in trying to determine when, where and how modern *H. sapiens* first appeared and look at the competing hypotheses that attempt to answer these questions. We then examine early modern *H. sapiens* fossils, technological artifacts and art in a wide range of geographic locations.

I   APPROACHES TO UNDERSTANDING MODERN HUMAN ORIGINS
   A. Paleoanthropologists have developed two major opposing theories
      1. Complete replacement model
      2. Regional continuity model
      3. A third model, the partial replacement model, combines aspects of first two models.
   B. The Complete Replacement Model (Recent African Evolution)
      1. This hypothesis was developed by Stringer and Andrews in 1988.
      2. According to this theory, modern humans originated in Africa within the last 200,000 years.
      3. Modern humans then migrated out of Africa and into Europe and Asia, where they replaced existing populations of archaic hominins.
      4. This theory does not accept a transition of premodern to modern *H. sapiens* anywhere except Africa.
      5. A critical deduction is that anatomically modern humans appeared as the result of a biological speciation event.
         a. This implies that migrating African modern *H. sapiens* could not have interbred with local non-African populations.
         b. The African modern humans would be a biologically different species.
         c. Taxonomically, all premodern populations outside of Africa would be classified as belonging to a different species of *Homo*.
      6. Evidence used to support this theory comes from genetic data.
         a. This approach assumes that at least some of the genetic patterning seen today can be used to view the past.

    b. Genetic patterns observed today between geographically widely dispersed humans are thought to partly reflect migrations occurring in the late Pleistocene.
    c. Researchers have studied both nuclear and mitochondrial DNA.
    d. Consistent relationships are emerging showing that indigenous African populations have greater diversity than populations from elsewhere.
    e. The consistency is highly significant because is supports a replacement model.
    f. mtDNA from 9 ancient modern skeletons from Italy, France, the Czech Republic and Russia have been sequenced.
        i. Results show mtDNA patterns very similar to living humans which is direct evidence of a genetic discontinuity between Neandertals and moderns.
        ii. The mtDNA sequences are so similar that contamination has been suspected.

C. The Partial Replacement Model
1. Modern *H. sapiens* populations first evolved in Africa and then migrated out of Africa into the Old World.
2. This model claims that some interbreeding occurred between emigrating Africans and resident premoderns.
3. Assumes that no speciation event occurred and these hominins should be considered members of *H. sapiens*.
4. Most researchers still believe that very little interbreeding occurred.

D. The Regional Continuity Model (Multiregional Evolution)
1. This model was proposed by Milford Wolpoff and colleagues (1994, 2001).
2. This theory contends that local hominin populations in Europe, Asia and Africa continued their indigenous evolutionary development from premodern forms to anatomically modern humans.
    a. They contributed, at least in part, to the evolution of their modern successors.
3. This model needs to explain how so many different populations evolved separately but became the same species.
4. This models answers this by
    a. Denying that the earliest modern humans originated exclusively in Africa.
    b. Asserting that significant levels of gene flow between premodern populations was extremely likely.
5. Through gene flow and natural selection, local populations would not have evolved independently of one another.
6. Speciation would have been prevented between regional lineages.
7. This model suggests there is no taxonomic distinction between modern and premodern hominins.
8. Proponents of this model recognize the strong influence of African migrants and that only minimal gene continuity existed in several regions.

E. Seeing the big picture
1. Most evidence suggests that a strong multiregional model is unlikely.
2. One or more major migrations from Africa fueled the worldwide dispersal of modern humans.
3. There might have been some interbreeding with local populations.

II   THE EARLIEST DISCOVERIES OF MODERN HUMANS

A. Africa
1. The earliest anatomically modern specimen comes from Omo Kibish
   a. Dated to 195,000 ya, *Omo 1* is the earliest modern human found in Africa.
   b. Two skulls found at this site show a great amount of variation.
   c. *Omo 1* is essentially modern and *Omo 2* is more robust and less modern.
2. Klasies River Mouth and Border Cave have been dated to 120,000-80,000 ya.
3. Modern humans had appeared in East Africa after 200,000 ya and migrated south by about 100,000 ya.
4. Herto (Ethiopia)
   a. The discovery of the well-preserved and well-dated discovery was announced in June 2003.
   b. The discovery is very significant because it securely dated (using argon-argon methods) near-modern human morphology from Africa to between 160,000-154,000 ya.
      i. This date is clearly older than any other modern *H. sapiens* discovery.
   c. The most complete adult cranium has a cranial capacity of 1450 cm^3, well within the modern human range and a modern, non-projecting face.
   d. It does retain primitive features such as a robust long skull, arching browridges and an occipital protuberance.
   e. Researchers have designated these skulls as *Homo sapiens idaltu* meaning that they were near modern.
   f. Further analysis shows that the morphological patterning of the crania does not specifically match that of any contemporary modern human group.
   g. The finds strongly support the African origin models.

B. The Near East
1. In Israel at least 10 individuals have been found in the Skhūl Cave at Mt. Carmel.
   a. Skhūl has been dated to between 130,000 – 100,000.
2. The Qafzeh Cave in Israel has yielded the remains of at least 20 individuals.
   a. It has been dated at around 92,000-120,000 ya.
3. There is an overlap of modern and premodern humans in Israel that runs counter to the multiregional model.
   a. Neandertals may slightly precede modern forms in the Near East, but there is still considerable overlap in the timing of occupation.

C. Asia
1. There are seven early modern human sites in China.
2. The fossils from these sites are all fully modern dating less than 40,000 ya.
3. The Upper Cave at Zhoukoudian find has been dated to 27,000 ya and consists of three skulls found with cultural remains in a site that humans regularly inhabited.
4. Liujang site revealed a nearly complete human skull and partial skeleton, but contextual dating has been compromised.
5. The skeleton from Jinniushan, dating ~ 200,000 ya. has been suggested to display some modern features.
   a. If this date is accurate, it would cast doubt on the complete replacement model.
   b. Chinese paleoanthropologists maintain a continuous evolution in their region from *H. erectus*, through archaic *H. sapiens*, to anatomically modern humans.

246

6. Tianyuan Cave is the source of another important discovery made in 2003.
    a. A fragmentary skull, a few teeth, and several postcranial bones were found.
    b. The fossil is accurately radiocarbon dated to ~40,000.
    c. The individual shows mostly modern features, with a few retained premodern traits.
    d. Researches suggest the remains indicate an African origin of modern humans, and the possibility of interbreeding with resident Archaic populations.
7. A skull with modern morphology was recovered from Niah Cave on the north coast of Borneo has been dated to 45,000 – 40,000
    a. It has been hypothesized that some earlier or contemporaneous population may have been the first group to colonize Australia.
D. Australia
    1. Sahul refers to the area including New Guinea and Australia.
        a. 50,000 ya modern gracile humans inhabited Sahul.
        b. Bamboo rafts may have been the means of crossing the sea between islands
    2. Human occupation of Australia may have been quite early since some archaeological sites there may date to 55,000 ya.
    3. Dating of the human fossils has been problematic.
        a. The earliest finds so far discovered have come from Lake Mungo in southeastern Australia
        b. Using different methods, these remains have been dated by some to 60,000 ya, and by others to 30,000-25,000 ya.
    4. The Kow Swamp people date between 14,000-9,000 ya and exhibit certain archaic traits such as heavy browridges and thick bones, suggesting to some researchers regional continuity between modern Australians.
    5. Recent genetic evidence indicates that all native Australians are descendants of a single migration dating to ~ 50,000 ya.
E. Central Europe
    1. Finds include the earliest anatomically modern *H. sapiens* yet discovered anywhere in Europe.
    2. Dated to 35,000 ya, remains at Oase Cave in Romania include crania from 3 individuals.
        a. Although robust, they are similar in form to modern humans.
    3. From Mladeč, in the Czech Republic, human fossils have been found that date to 31,000 ya.
        a. While modern, the sample exhibits a great deal of variation, including prominent browridges.
    4. It is clear that by 28,000 ya, modern humans are widely dispersed in central Europe and into western Europe.
F. Western Europe
    1. Western Europe has received the most attention by human evolution researchers.
    2. Early on theories of human evolution were based exclusively on western Europe.
    3. The best known western European modern human fossils are from the Cro-Magnon rock shelter, discovered in 1868 outside of the village of Les Eyzies in southern France.

a.　The Upper Paleolithic tool industry associated with the Cro-Magnon fossils is called the Aurignacian.

　　　b.　Cro-Magnon dates to 28,000 ya making it the earliest modern human fossil site in France.

　　4.　Most genetic evidence from Africa argues against continuous local evolution.

　　5.　The degree of admixture that occurred between Africa populations and resident premodern groups is currently being debated.

　　6.　A very important find that provides evidence of interbreeding between Neandertals and anatomically modern *H. sapiens* was found in Lagar Velho, Portugal and announced in 1998.

　　　a.　Dating to 24,500 ya., the child's skeleton recovered from this burial has been interpreted as representing millennia of admixture between modern human and Neandertal populations.

　　　b.　The burial was associated with Upper Paleolithic industry.

　　　c.　Not all researchers, however, are convinced of modern human-Neandertal hybridization by the evidence from this single specimen.

　　　d.　See "A Closer Look" p. 409.

G.　Something new and different: The "Little People"

　　1.　In Indonesia, remnant premodern populations branched off and found their way to small islands to the east.

　　2.　Under extreme isolation pressures, these groups evolved into small sized hominins.

　　3.　An incomplete skeleton of a female small-sized small-brained hominin, and fragments from 9 other individuals were discovered in 2004 in Liang Bua Cave on Flores..
　　　a.　The female skeleton is only 3 feet tall, with a brain size of 417 cm^3.

　　4.　These hominins were still living on Flores as of 13,000 ya.

　　5.　Probably evolved from H. erectus on Java.

　　6.　Insular dwarfing as an adaptation to reduced resources selected for small body size in these hominins.

　　7.　Species is called *Homo floresiensis*.
　　　a.　They most resemble *H. erectus* in cranial shape and thickness, and in dentition.
　　　b.　They also have derived features that set them apart from all other hominins.

　　8.　Some researchers have argued that the fossils are actually microcephalic *H. sapiens*.
　　　a.　The severity and rareness of this pathology make this conclusion unlikely.
　　　b.　It must be recognized that long-term, extreme isolation lead to a new species showing dramatic dwarfing in body size and reduction in brain size.

III　**TECHNOLOGY AND ART IN THE UPPER PALEOLITHIC**

A.　Europe

　　1.　The cultural period Upper Paleolithic began ~ 40,000 ya. in western Europe.
　　　a.　Upper Paleolithic cultures are usually divided into five periods based on stone tool technologies.
　　　　i.　Chatelperronian
　　　　ii.　Aurignacian
　　　　iii.　Gravettian
　　　　iv.　Solutrean
　　　　v.　Magdalenian

248

2. A warming trend lasting several thousand years began around 30,000 ya.
   a. This resulted in much of Eurasia being covered by tundra and steppe.
   b. Animals thrived on the new vegetation and predatory animals exploited the browsers and grazers which bolstered hunting opportunities.
   c. In addition, humans also began to regularly eat fish and fowl at this time.
3. It was a time of relative abundance and Upper Paleolithic people spread out over Europe.
   a. At Sungir near Moscow at 24 kya an elaborate burial was found with grave goods of red ochre, ivory beads, long spears, engravings, and jewelry.
4. Climatic pulses were common during the last glacial.
   a. Around 20,000 ya. the weather became noticeably colder in Europe and Asia.
5. Humans had an advantage in changing conditions due to their technology and culture.
   a. Humans began inventing new and specialized tools and increased the use of new materials that included bone, ivory, and antler.
6. The Solutrean industry is a good example of Upper Paleolithic skull and aesthetic appreciation.
   a. Stoneknapping developed to the finest degree ever known.
   b. Lance heads were among the finest, most expertly-knapped stone tools ever produced and may not have served a utilitarian purpose.
7. The Magdalenian was the last stage of the Upper Paleolithic and is characterized by still more advances in technology.
   a. Spear-throwers (atlatls), the barbed harpoon and perhaps the bow and arrow all make their first appearances during this culture period.
   b. Burins, chisel-like stone tools used to engrave and punch holes, were common.
8. These technological advances may have influenced human biological evolution as well.
   a. At this time there are reductions in anterior tooth size probably owing to more efficient food processing.
   b. This led to the lower face of moderns becoming less prognathic compared to premodern peoples.
9. "Symbolic representation" in the form of art is widespread during the Upper Paleolithic.
   a. For 25,000 years this kind of art was present in Europe, Siberia, northern and southern Africa and Australia.
   b. The carving and engraving of bone and ivory was improved with the use of specialized tools.
   c. "Venus figurines," female effigies, have been found in France and Italy.
   d. Small animal figures produced from fired clay at two sites in the Czech Republic date to 27,000 ya., documenting the earliest use of ceramic technology in the archaeological record.
10. The most spectacular Upper Paleolithic art is found on cave walls in Western Europe dating to the Magdalenian period.
    a. Cave art is known from more than 150 sites with the majority of cave art found in southwestern France and northern Spain.
       i. Two of the most famous sites are Lascaux and Chauvet Caves in southern France and Spain's Altamira Cave.

      b. Lascaux cave
         i. Immense wild bulls dominate the Great Hall of Bulls.
         ii. Horses and deer are drawn with remarkable skill
      c. At Altamira the walls and ceiling of an immense cave are filled with bison in red and black.
      d. In the Chauvet Cave the art is possibly 30,000 ya.
         i. Images include dots, handprints, and hundreds of animals.
         ii. Chauvet is older than Lascaux or Altamira.
      e. In other areas images were not rendered in deep caves but on rock faces.
  B. Africa
    1. Early accomplishments in rock art are seen in southern Africa (Nambia) at the Apollo 11 rock shelter site
      a. Painted slabs have been dated to 28,000-26,000 ya.
      b. Incised ostrich shell fragments found at the site may be older.
    2. More than 40 tick shell beads, incised ochre fragments, and bone tools dating to 77,000 ya were recovered from Blombos Cave
    3. Microliths and blades characterize Late African technologies.
    4. Evidence of the systematic exploitation of shellfish and the use of microliths, and ocher (possibly for personal adornment) have been found at Pinnacle Point in South Africa
      a. This site is dated to ~ 165,000 ya, providing the earliest evidence of cultural behaviors characteristic of modern humans.
    5. In central Africa bone and antler were used to make tools.
    6. The Katanda excavations have revealed well crafted bone tools that may date to 80,000 ya.

IV SUMMARY OF UPPER PALEOLITHIC CULTURE

  A. The Upper Paleolithic is a culmination of 2 million years of cultural development.
  B. For most of the Pleistocene cultural change was very slow.
  C. In the late Pleistocene of Europe and central Africa, however, cultural innovations were attained in a dramatically shorter time span.
    1. These included big game hunting with new weapons, body ornamentation, "tailored" clothing and burials with elaborate grave goods.
    2. However, this big-game hunting and gathering way of life was radically altered by the retreat of the continental glaciers.
  D. With the major environmental change, prey species became much less abundant and the stage was set for the development of plant domestication, a more sedentary lifestyle and much more complex social organizations.

KEY TERMS

atlatl: spear-thrower developed during the later Upper Paleolithic.
Aurignacian: an Upper Paleolithic stone tool assemblage dating to around 40,000 ya. and associated with early modern Europeans.
burin: small, chisel-like stone tool thought to engrave bone, antler, ivory and/or wood.

Cro-Magnon: A term commonly used when referring to early modern humans from Europe. The term derives from the rock shelter in southern France that dates to around 30,000 ya. where eight skeletons were found in 1868. The skeletons included three adult males, one adult female and four young children.

Gravettian: An Upper Paleolithic culture period dating to around 27,000 ya.

Magdalenian: The final stage of the Upper Paleolithic stone tool industry dating to around 17,000 y.a.

Solutrean: An Upper Paleolithic stone culture period dating to around 21,000 ya. Considered to be the most highly developed stone tool industry.

Upper Paleolithic: refers to a cultural period of early modern humans distinguished by innovative stone tool technologies. Dates from around 40,000 to 10,000 ya. It is further divided into five different cultural periods associated with stone tool technology. These five cultural periods (from the oldest to the most recent) are Chatelperronian, Aurignacian, Gravettian, Solutrean and Magdalenian.

MEDIA EXERCISES

1) Visit "Peter Brown's Australian and Asian Paleoanthropology" site to view images and learn about the Australian early modern human fossil evidence. Each important fossil is pictured and thoroughly discussed by Dr. Brown, Associate Professor of Archaeology and Paleoanthropology at the University of New England, Australia.
Brown's site: http://www-personal.une.edu.au/~pbrown3/palaeo.html

2) A useful site that brings together "under one roof" various resources, images and links concerning the appearance of our species is C. David Kreger's "A Look at Modern Human Origins." Kreger's purpose for the site is to help "students of paleoanthropology in the process of research, and to provide a source of information for any layperson who may or may not have access to the requisite background or general information needed to come to a fuller understanding of human evolution." (http://www.modernhumanorigins.net/)

CONCEPT APPLICATION

Mystery sites

From the hints below, try to determine what modern paleoanthropological and/or archaeological site is being described. Give yourself 5 points if you figure it out with only the first clue ("a"), 3 points if you need both clue "a" and "b," and 1 point if you need all three clues ("a, b & c").

1. Mystery site #1
   a. Dated to 14,000-9000 ya in Australia.
   b. Crania preserve certain archaic traits, such as heavy browridges.
   c. Skeletons are robust, with thick bones.

2. Mystery site #2
   a. May date between 80,000 ya in the Dem. Rep. of Congo.
   b. Has the remains of remarkably developed bone craftwork.

3. Mystery site #3
   a. Dates to 30,000 y.a. in the Dordogne region of southern France.
   b. Eight individuals were discovered in a rock shelter there in 1868.
   c. The fossils are associated with an Aurignacian tool assemblage.

4. Mystery site #4
   a. Dates to about 110,000 ya in Israel.
   b. Remains of at least 20 individuals found there.
   c. Some specimens show certain premodern, Neandertal-like features.

5. Mystery site #5
   a. The first example of advanced cave art recorded in Europe.
   b. Discovered in Spain in 1879.
   c. Filled with spectacular bison painted in red and black.

6. Mystery site #6
   a. Dates to about 33,000 in the Czech Republic.
   b. The crania display a great deal of variation, perhaps due, in part, to sexual dimorphism.
   c. Each of the crania (save one) are marked by a prominent supraorbital torus.

7. Mystery site #7
   a. A spectacular French cave art site.
   b. Dates relatively early – perhaps more than 30,000 ya.

8. Mystery site #8
   a. *H. erectus* and early modern humans found in this cave complex.
   b. Dates to 27 kya in China.
   c. The modern human fossil crania are reported to have a number of regional (i.e. Chinese) features.

9. Mystery site #9
    a. May date from anywhere between 25,000 to 60,000 ya.
    b. Site is in southeastern Australia.
    c. Reports have been published claiming that mtDNA has been isolated and sequenced from one of these fossils.

10. Mystery site #10
    a. Dates to 24,500 ya. from Portugal.
    b. A four-year-old child's burial.
    c. Skeleton displays both modern human and Neandertal features.

Now answer the True/False, Multiple Choice and Short Answer sample test questions. Following completion of the tests, correct them with the answers and textbook page references at the end of this Study Guide chapter. Note the areas in which you are strong and weak to guide you in your studying. Finally, answer the sample Essay Questions.

TRUE/FALSE QUESTIONS

If false, consider what modification would make the statement true.

1. The complete replacement model requires a biological speciation event for the origin of modern humans.
    TRUE   FALSE

2. The multiregional evolution model requires gene flow to prevent speciation between regional populations of prehumans.
    TRUE   FALSE

3. Border Cave, Klasies River Mouth and Omo Kibish are three early modern human sites in southeast Asia.
    TRUE   FALSE

4. Cro-Magnon is the earliest modern human site from western Europe.
    TRUE   FALSE

5. Lake Mungo and Kow Swamp are early modern human sites from Australia.
    TRUE   FALSE

6. The Magdalenian is earlier in time than the Aurignacian.
    TRUE   FALSE

7. The atlatl, barbed harpoon and bow and arrow are cultural innovations of the later Mousterian.
    TRUE   FALSE

8. "Venus figurines" were depictions of planetary motions.
   TRUE   FALSE

9. Grotte Chauvet Cave is significant because it is a very early Upper Paleolithic cave art site.
   TRUE   FALSE

10. Rock art in Africa may be as old as that from Europe.
    TRUE   FALSE

MULTIPLE CHOICE QUESTIONS

1. In June 2003, near-modern human fossils dating between 160-154,000 ya. were announced from
   A. Herto, Ethiopia.
   B. Lake Mungo, Australia.
   C. Border Cave, South Africa.
   D. Kebara, Israel.

2. Regarding the origin of anatomically modern humans, scientists
   A. agree that it involved a speciation event in Africa.
   B. agree that it first occurred in China.
   C. do not agree concerning the timing and geography of our origins.
   D. do not agree that there is only one modern human species on the planet today.

3. Which of the following is **not** a model of modern human origins?
   A. The Partial Replacement Model
   B. The Multiregional Evolution Model
   C. The Regional Replacement Model
   D. The Complete Replacement Model

4. The model also known as "Recent African Evolution" is based on the origin of modern humans
   A. in Africa and their interbreeding with local African populations.
   B. in Africa and their replacement of local populations in Europe and Asia.
   C. in China and their relatively recent evolution in Africa.
   D. simultaneously in Africa and China.

5. According to the partial replacement model
   A. modern humans evolved in Africa and Europe at the same time.
   B. premodern humans first evolved into modern *H. sapiens* in southern Africa.
   C. the dispersal of modern humans was relatively rapid.
   D. moderns never interbred with archaics in Eurasia.

6. According to the multiregional evolution model
   A. anatomically modern *H. sapiens* originated exclusively in Africa.
   B. modern *H. sapiens* are a separate species from Neandertals.
   C. some local populations of archaic *H. sapiens* in Europe, Asia and Africa contributed to the evolution of modern *H. sapiens* in those regions.
   D. All of the above

7. Current evidence indicates that modern *H. sapiens*
   A. evolved simultaneously in Africa, Europe and Asia.
   B. arose exclusively from Neandertals.
   C. originated in southeast Asia.
   D. fossils may appear earliest in Africa.

8. Recently, mtDNA isolated and sequenced from nine ancient modern humans revealed
   A. a similar pattern to living modern humans.
   B. a similar pattern to *H. erectus*.
   C. a similar pattern to *H. neanderthalensis*.
   D. a similar pattern to *H. heidelbergensis*.

9. The Skhūl Cave at Mt. Carmel, Israel has yielded
   A. more than 30 individuals.
   B. a single Neandertal mandible.
   C. a sample of individuals who are modern in every respect.
   D. a sample whose overall configuration is modern, but some individuals retain archaic (i.e. Neandertal-like) features.

10. The Mladeč site in the Czech Republic
    A. dates to about 31,000 ya.
    B. displays a great deal of cranial variation.
    C. suggests some continuity with Neandertals.
    D. All of the above

11. The area of the world that has produced the most evidence of early modern *H. sapiens* is
    A. Australia.
    B. southeast Asia.
    C. China.
    D. western Europe.

12. Cro-Magnon is
    A. typical of the European races of early modern *H. sapiens*.
    B. a site from southern Germany.
    C. an early human site that yielded eight individuals and is dated to 28,000 ya.
    D. a mythical bird figure that is a recurrent theme in Upper Paleolithic cave art.

13. Aurignacian refers to
    A. a tool assemblage associated with France's earliest anatomically modern humans.
    B. a site in western Spain that yielded 10 skeletons.
    C. an archaeologist who uncovered a rich site in northern Belgium.
    D. a tool tradition associated with premodern humans in western Asia.

14. A four-year-old child, dating to 24,500 ya., that displays both modern human and Neandertal characteristics was recently discovered at
    A. Vindija, Croatia.
    B. Lagar Velho, Portugal.
    C. Cro-Magnon, France.
    D. Qafzeh, Israel.

15. The Upper Cave at Zhoukoudian
    A. dates to 27,000 ya.
    B. has yielded fossils that exhibit both modern and Neandertal characteristics.
    C. may be the oldest anatomically modern find.
    D. All of the above

16. The oldest specimen with modern-like appearance in Asia is from
    A. Niah Cave, Borneo.
    B. Zhoukoudian, China.
    C. Jinniushan, China.
    D. Batadomba, Sri Lanka.

17. In Australia, the oldest archaeological sites date to
    A. 55,000 ya.
    B. 25,000 ya.
    C. 200,000 ya.
    D. 125,000 ya.

18. The earliest human site in Australia is
    A. Kow Swamp.
    B. Lake Mungo.
    C. Cooperville.
    D. Adcockton.

19. The Kow Swamp people
    A. date to 14,000 to 9,000 y.a.
    B. are robust, displaying thick bones.
    C. exhibit archaic cranial traits such as heavy supraorbital tori.
    D. All of the above

256

20. Which of the following is **not** a cultural period of the European Upper Paleolithic?
    A. Magdalenian
    B. Solutrean
    C. Mousterian
    D. Aurignacian

21. Magdalenian refers to
    A. the first evidence of religion.
    B. a geographic region in western Asia.
    C. the final phase of the stone tool tradition in the Upper Paleolithic in Europe.
    D. a type of facial structure found among early moderns.

22. In which of the following regions has Paleolithic art **not** been found?
    A. Australia
    B. Siberia
    C. North America
    D. South Africa

23. Dolni Vestonice and Predmosti from the Czech Republic yielded the first documented use of
    A. ceramics.
    B. metals.
    C. controlled fire.
    D. sewn on buttons.

24. Solutrean tools
    A. are excellent examples of Upper Paleolithic skill and aesthetics.
    B. are among the finest examples of Paleolithic flintknapping known.
    C. include beautiful parallel-flaked lance heads that can be considered works of art.
    D. All of the above

25. Which African rock art site dates to between 26-28 kya?
    A. Oase
    B. Katanda
    C. Klasies River Mouth
    D. Apollo 11

26. In Africa, we find very early evidence (40,000 ya.) of
    A. hunting weapons such as the bow and arrow.
    B. portable personal adornment in the form of beads made from ostrich eggshells.
    C. the use of fire.
    D. cave paintings.

27. Early sculptures made figures of women called
   A. Aphrodites.
   B. Venuses.
   C. Nefertitis.
   D. Chloes.

28. During the Magdalenian
   A. European prehistoric art reached its climax.
   B. humans first started cooking their meat.
   C. the European climate was warm and temperate.
   D. All of the above

29. Which of the following is **not** an Upper Paleolithic cave art site?
   A. Cro-Magnon, France
   B. Chauvet, France
   C. Lascaux, France
   D. Altamira, Spain

30. The Sungir site, not far from Moscow, is significant because
   A. it documents the efficiency of Upper Paleolithic reindeer hunters.
   B. there, for the first time, is evidence that humans buried their dead.
   C. it preserves evidence of sewn clothing dating to 22,000 ya.
   D. the first Paleolithic solar visors derive from that site.

SHORT ANSWER QUESTIONS (& PAGE REFERENCES)

1. How do the Complete and Partial Replacement models differ? (pp. 393-396)

2. Why was the Upper Paleolithic a time of relative affluence? (pp. 412-414)

3. What were burins used for by Upper Paleolithic people? (p. 413)

4. Describe the punch blade technique. (p. 415, Fig. 14-19)

5. How does the cave art at Grotte Chauvet differ from other famous cave art sites? (p.416)

ESSAY QUESTIONS (& PAGE REFERENCES)

1. Compare and contrast the Complete Replacement to the Multiregional Evolution models of modern human origins. How do these models differ in their interpretations of Neandertal taxonomy and fate? (pp. 393-397)

2. Summarize the technological advancements of the Upper Paleolithic. (pp. 412-418)

3. What interpretations have been offered to explain Upper Paleolithic art? (pp. 414-416)

ANSWERS, *CORRECTED STATEMENT* IF FALSE & REFERENCES TO TRUE/FALSE QUESTIONS

1. **TRUE**, p. 393

2. **TRUE**, p. 396

3. **FALSE**, pp. 397-399, Border Cave, Klasies River Mouth and Omo Kibish are three early modern human sites in *Africa*.

4. **TRUE**, p. 406

5. **TRUE**, pp. 404-405

6. **FALSE**, p. 413, The *Aurignacian* is earlier in time than the *Magdalenian*.

7. **FALSE**, pp. 412-413, The atlatl, barbed harpoon and bow and arrow are cultural innovations of the later *Upper Paleolithic*.

8. **FALSE**, p. 415, "Venus figurines" were depictions of *human females*.

9. **TRUE**, p. 416

10. **TRUE**, pp. 416-419

ANSWERS AND REFERENCES TO MULTIPLE CHOICE QUESTIONS

1. **A**, pp. 399-400	7. **D**, p. 397	13. **A**, p. 406	19. **D**, p. 405	25. **D**, p. 416
2. **C**, p. 394	8. **A**, p. 395	14. **B**, pp. 408-410	20. **C**, p. 412	26. **B**, p. 416
3. **C**, pp. 393-397	9. **D**, p. 400	15. **A**, p. 401	21. **C**, p. 413	27. **B**, p. 415
4. **B**, pp. 393-396	10. **D**, pp. 405-406	16. **C**, p. 402	22. **C**, p. 415	28. **A**, p. 413
5. **B**, p. 396	11. **D**, p. 406	17. **A**, p. 404	23. **A**, p. 415	29. **A**, p. 416
6. **C**, p. 396	12. **C**, p. 406	18. **B**, p. 404	24. **D**, p. 413	30. **C**, pp. 412, 414

CONCEPT APPLICATION SOLUTION

Mystery sites (and page number references)

1. Kow Swamp (p. 405)
2. Katanda (pp. 416-418)
3. Cro-Magnon (p.406)
4. Qafzeh (p. 400)
5. Altamira (p. 416)
6. Mladeč (pp. 405-406)
7. Grotte Chauvet (p. 416)
8. Upper Cave, Zhoukoudian (p. 401)
9. Lake Mungo (p. 404)
10. Lagar Velho (pp. 408-410)

CHAPTER 15
MODERN HUMAN BIOLOGY: PATTERNS OF VARIATION

LEARNING OBJECTIVES

After reading this chapter you should be able to:
- understand the history of how human racial categories were established (pp. 422-424)
- differentiate between the typological and clinal approaches to studying human variation (pp. 427-431)
- describe the current approach to understanding human variation (p. 430)
- understand racism and its influence (p. 428)
- discuss the concept of human polymorphisms with respect to human variation studies (pp. 430-432)
- list the assumptions of the Hardy-Weinberg theory of genetic equilibrium (p. 437)
- discuss the role of human cultural activities in biological evolution (p. 443)
- cite at least two instances of human biocultural evolution (pp. 444-445)

CHAPTER OUTLINE

Introduction

In preceding chapters we looked at human macroevolution. However, our species continues to evolve and in this chapter we look at the minute changes that occur within our species. This is called microevolution and, unlike macroevolution, does not result in the evolution of new species. In this chapter, we focus on polygenic traits, or traits that express *continuous* variation. We will see how these traits have been used as a basis for traditional racial classification and look at some of the issues that currently surround the topic of race in physical anthropology. We will investigate how genetic principles lie at the very foundation of the evolutionary process and how these processes interact to produce evolutionary change in living human populations. We will conclude by examining biocultural influences on humans because cultural activities have greatly influenced our evolution.

I   HISTORICAL VIEWS OF HUMAN VARIATION.
   A. The discovery of the New World led to an increasing awareness of diversity in people, plants, animals and cultures.
      1. When different groups first came into contact they tried to account for physical differences.
      2. This practice even predates European explorers.
         a. Ancient Egyptians established classifications based on skin color.
   B. Throughout the eighteenth and nineteenth centuries European and American scientists focused on description and classification as a means of managing this diversity.
      1. Linnaeus' classification of life also included humans.
         a. Linnaeus recognized four separate categories.
            i.   His groupings were based on physical traits.
            ii.   He assigned behavioral and intellectual qualities to each group.

261

b. Linnaeus ranked humans with the least complimentary traits being assigned to sub-Saharan (black) Africans.

c. Europeans were ranked highest and reflected the Eurocentric view that they were superior.

2. Johann F. Blumenbach (1752-1840)

a. Blumenbach classified humans into five races.

b. Blumenbach emphasized that racial divisions based on skin color were arbitrary.

c. Blumenbach recognized that many traits, including skin color, were not discrete phenomena.

   i. Individuals within a group that expressed traits that were intermediate would be difficult to classify.

   ii. Furthermore, many traits showed overlapping expression between groups.

3. By the mid nineteenth century racial classification resulted in ranked human groups, with (northern) Europeans being at the top of the racial hierarchy.

C. Biological determinism

1. The idea that there is a cause and effect association between physical characteristics and behavioral characteristics is called biological determinism; i.e., cultural variations are inherited.

a. It follows from this logic that there are inherent behavioral and cognitive differences between groups.

b. When biological determinism is accepted as a reasonable explanation, it is easy to justify the persecution and enslavement of other peoples.

2. Eugenics was a scientific discipline grounded in biological determinism.

a. Eugenics promoted the idea of "race improvement" and suggested that the government should be involved in this endeavor.

b. This movement was particularly important in Nazi Germany.

D. By the end of WWII, many scientists were turning away from racial typologies in favor of an evolutionary approach to appreciating human variation.

II   THE CONCEPT OF RACE

A. All contemporary humans belong to the same polytypic species, *Homo sapiens*.

1. A polytypic species consists of local populations that differ from one another in the expression of one or more traits.

a. Even within local populations, there is a great deal of genotypic and phenotypic variation between individuals.

b. Most species are polytypic.

c. Therefore there is no form that typifies the particular species.

B. The traditional concept of race

1. In the past people have been grouped by various combinations of attributes and placed into categories associated with particular geographical areas.

2. The term race is often misused and has developed various definitions.

a. Race has been used synonymously with species; the human race.

b. Since the 1600s race has been used to refer to various culturally defined groups.

c. The perception that there is an association between physical traits and many cultural attributes is still widespread.

d. While phenotypic expressions contribute to social identity: sex and age are also critically important.

3. In the 1950s the use of the term "race" was challenged and it was proposed that it should be replaced by the term "ethnicity."
C. The biological use of the word "race"
1. "Race" refers to geographical phenotypic variation within a species.
2. Even within modern biology there are no established criteria by which races of plants and animals are assessed.
    a. Classifications of non-human organisms into races are subjective biological decisions.
3. Prior to WWII, most studies of human variation focused on phenotypic variation between large geographically defined populations.
D. Modern studies of human variation incorporate evolutionary principles.
1. Specifically we want to know the adaptive significance of phenotypic and genotypic variation.
2. Application of evolutionary principles to human variation has replaced the older view that was based solely on observed phenotypes.
3. Races are no longer viewed as fixed biological entities.
4. While human variability is recognized between geographic areas, the following questions must be asked regarding this phenotypic difference.
    a. Is there an adaptive significance attached to the observed phenotypic variation?
    b. Is genetic drift a factor?
    c. What is the degree of underlying genetic variation that influences the observed variation?
E. Controversies and debates about human variation
1. The word race is an emotionally charged one with a long history.
2. Although physical anthropology is rooted in attempts to explain human diversity no modern scholar subscribes to the pre-modern view of races as fixed biological units.
3. Race is not a valid concept because the amount of genetic variation between groups is exceeded by the variation within groups.
4. Race is a creation of the human mind that tries to categorize a complex issue.
5. Forensic anthropologists find the phenotypic criteria associated with race to have practical applications.
    a. These anthropologists assist in identification of human skeletal remains.
    b. Analysis of the skeleton yields evidence of ancestry or the ethnic background of skeletal remains up to about 80% accuracy.
F. Objections to racial taxonomies
1. Such classificatory schemes are typological.
    a. The categories, or "types" are discrete and based on stereotypes that comprise a specific set of traits.
    b. Such typologies do not account for individuals who do not conform to the particular type for the group.
2. Many of the characteristics used to define races are polygenic.
    a. Recall that polygenic traits are based on the interaction of many genes
        i. Polygenic traits exhibit a continuous range of variation.
        ii. Skin color is a polygenic trait as it is influenced by many genes and populations exhibit a range in color.
    b. Using polygenic traits to define a group makes it difficult, if not impossible, to draw discrete boundaries between populations.

III RACISM

A. Racism is an unfortunate reality of human populations.
   1. It is an outcome of biological determinism.
B. Racism is based on the false belief that intellect and various cultural factors are inherited along with physical characteristics.
   1. Such beliefs commonly rest on the assumption that one's own group is superior to other groups.
   2. This perspective assumes all members of a population share the same attributes.
C. Racism is a cultural, not a biological, phenomenon, and it is found worldwide.

IV INTELLIGENCE

A. There is no scientific evidence to show that personality of any other behavioral trait differs genetically between human populations.
B. Whether or not there is an association between population affinity and intelligence has been widely debated in scientific, social, and political circles.
C. Both genetic and environmental factors contribute to intelligence.
   1. It is not possible to measure the percentage each factor contributes to intelligence.
   2. IQ scores are often confused with intelligence; IQ scores and intelligence are not the same thing.
      a. IQ scores can change within an individual's lifetime.
   3. Complex cognitive abilities, no matter how they are measured, are influenced by multiple loci and are polygenic.
D. Innate differences in abilities reflect individual variation within populations, not inherent differences between groups.
E. There is no convincing evidence that populations vary with regard to cognitive abilities.

V CONTEMPORARY INTERPRETATIONS OF HUMAN VARIATION

A. Since most physical traits used to define race are polygenic (e.g. skin color, hair form, etc.) it is nearly impossible to precisely determine the degree of genetic influence on their expression.
B. Beginning in the 1950s, the focus turned to assessing biochemical components such as blood markers and other chemical components.
   1. May of these components are not polygenic.
   2. The phenotype is very representative of the genotype.
C. More recent approaches to understanding human variation examine the underlying genetics directly through DNA sequencing.
   1. This allows genotypes to be ascertained directly.
   2. Studying differences in DNA with and between human populations will dramatically increase our knowledge of human variation.
D. Human polymorphisms
   1. Polymorphisms are traits that are governed by a locus with more than one allele.
   2. Polymorphic traits are useful in studying evolutionary differences between populations.
      a. By comparing the allele frequencies of polymorphic traits between populations we can consider the evolutionary events that link populations.
   3. By the 1960s individual polymorphic traits were being used, instead of the traditional approach, to study human variation.

264

a. Clinal distributions of human polymorphisms were used.
a. A cline is a gradual change in a value dispersed over space.
    i. Using polymorphisms, clines illustrate changes in the frequency of a trait through geographical space.
    ii. See Figure 15-4 p. 431 for an illustration of the distribution of the B allele of the ABO system across space.
b. Clinal distributions are believed to reflect microevolutionary influences of natural selection and/or gene flow.

4. Allele frequencies are then interpreted in terms of the evolutionary forces that may account for the observed patterns.
    a. Natural selection
    b. Gene flow
    c. Genetic drift
    d. Mutation

5. The ABO system is a polymorphic trait with three different alleles, A, B, and O.
    b. The frequencies of the three alleles vary tremendously, with most human groups being polymorphic for all three alleles.
    c. One exception is blood type O among South American Indians, where the allele frequency for O is 100%. This is referred to as being fixed in the population.
    d. The high frequency of the O allele is probably due to genetic drift.

6. The HLA (human leukocyte antigen) system is an antigen system found on white blood cells.
    a. HLA is the most polymorphic genetic system known in humans.
    b. This system is governed by at least six loci possessing hundreds of alleles.
    c. Because HLA alleles are so numerous, this system is very useful in investigating human population diversity.

7. Phenylthiocarbamide (PTC) is another well studied polymorphism
    a. Some find PTC to be a bitter chemical while other individuals do not taste it.
    b. The PTC genotype is inherited by simple Mendelian transmission.
    c. The distribution pattern of PTC varies between populations and is not clearly understood.
    d. The ability to taste PTC by humans may have resulted from selection to taste bitter (and toxic) plants.

D. Patterns of polymorphic variation
1. While examining single polymorphisms is informative, it is limited as a means for sorting out population relationships.
    a. The simultaneous study of several polymorphic traits is more useful.
2. Harvard geneticist, Richard D. Lewontin analyzed human diversity using 17 polymorphic traits.
    a. He assessed several populations from 7 geographical areas.
    b. Lewontin published his work in 1972.
    c. He found that only 6.3% of genetic variation could be explained by differences between these seven major continental groupings of people.
        i. Thus 94% of variation occurs within these groups.
    d. Most human genetic diversity appears to be explained in terms of differences from one village to another, one family to another, and even between one individual to another (even within the same family!).

265

e. The traits used to form races may produce a highly biased sample and not give an accurate picture of the actual pattern of genetic variation.

f. Lewontin's final conclusion is that human racial classification, shown to have no genetic or taxonomic significance, should be discontinued.

E. Polymorphisms at the DNA level

1. The Human Genome Project has permitted the study of polymorphisms directly at the DNA level.

   a. In addition, these technologies have revealed a great deal of previously unknown variability in our DNA.

2. Microsatellites are repeated DNA segments

   a. These microsatellites are extremely variable from person to person.

   b. Therefore they are very useful in providing "DNA fingerprints."

3. SNPs (single nucleotide polymorphisms) reflect patterns of variation at single nucleotide sites.

   a. Like microsatellites, SNPs are very variable from individual to individual.

   b. Already, about three million SNPs have been mapped throughout the human genome.

   c. SNPs hold the potential to inform us of the genetic history of our species.

4. Population geneticists have begun to incorporate DNA polymorphisms into human variation studies.

   a. Such can provide more accurate measures of within and between group variation that previously thought.

   b. Geneticists can use these techniques to study recent events in human population history.

   c. Worldwide patterns of variation have been examined in large portion studies referred to as "whole-genome" analyses.

   d. This new information indicates that African populations exhibit a higher degree of genetic variation than any other geographical group.

      i. All human populations outside of Africa have much less genetic variation

      ii. Implies a fairly recent origin of all modern humans in Africa.

      iii. Potentially genetic drift (founder effect) played a role in human evolution.

   e. These data may provide insight into population patterns of susceptibility to some diseases.

   f. How we address diversity, individually, and collectively, must balance the potential scientific benefits against a history of social costs.

VI POPULATION GENETICS

A. A population is a group of interbreeding individuals.

1. Populations contain a degree of relatedness and, thus, share a gene pool.

   a. The gene pool is the total complement of genes maintained by a population.

2. All members of a species are potentially capable of interbreeding, but are incapable of fertile interbreeding with members of other species.

   a. A species such as ours is a genetically closed system.

3. Mate choice is influenced by factors including geographical, ecological, and social influences.

   a. Geography, by isolating populations through barriers such as bodies of water or mountains, causes the formation of breeding isolates.

  b. However, cultural rules can also play a role by prescribing who is most appropriate among those potentially available.

  c. Human populations tend to mate within their own group; this is called endogamy.

  d. However, human populations are not completely closed and individuals may choose mates from outside of their group; this is called exogamy.

B. Once populations are identified, the next step is to determine what, if any, evolutionary forces are in operation on that population.

 1. The Hardy-Weinberg theory of genetic equilibrium is a mathematical model that helps researchers to determine if evolution is occurring at any particular genetic locus.

C. The Hardy Weinberg equilibrium postulates a set of conditions in an idealized, hypothetical population where no evolution is occurring.

 1. The Hardy Weinberg equilibrium makes the following assumptions:

  a. The population is infinitely large. This eliminates genetic drift as a factor.

  b. There is no mutation; therefore, no new variation is added at the molecular level.

  c. There is no gene flow, i.e., there are no new alleles coming into the population from another population.

  d. Natural selection is not operating. Specific alleles confer no advantage over others that might influence reproductive success.

  e. Mating is random. Each adult member of one sex has an equal chance of mating with any adult member of the opposite sex.

 2. If the above conditions are met, allele frequencies will not change from one generation to the next, i.e., no evolution will take place.

 3. By establishing the conditions that would exist if evolution were not occurring, the Hardy-Weinberg equilibrium can be used to as a comparative source to determine if evolution is occurring.

  a. Expected (predicted) genetic frequencies can be compared to observed genetic frequencies.

  b. This makes the Hardy-Weinberg equilibrium testable.

  c. The null hypothesis is that no evolution is occurring.

  d. If observable frequencies differ significantly from expected frequencies the null hypothesis is rejected.

  e. This would mean that evolution has occurred at the locus in question.

 4. The Hardy-Weinberg equation is: $p^2 + 2pq + q^2 = 1$

  a. See pp. 438-440, and Appendix D pp. 522-526.

  b. p = the frequency of the dominant allele, and

  c. q = the frequency of the recessive allele.

  d. Frequencies are simply defined as percentages of a whole, so p and q must always sum to one.

   i. $p + q = 1$

 5. Given the allele frequencies of p and q, the second Hardy-Weinberg equation is used to predict the expected genotype frequencies in that population: $p^2 + 2pq + q^2 = 1$

  a. p^2 = the expected frequency of the first homozygote,

  b. $2pq$ = the expected frequency of the heterozygote, and

  c. q^2 = the expected frequency of the second homozygote.

  d. Again, the frequencies sum to one.

D. Calculating allele frequencies
   1. The simplest example is to analyze a trait coded for by two codominant alleles at one locus.
      a. In this situation, the two alleles would produce three genotypes that directly correspond to three recognizable phenotypes.
         i. Recall that in a codominant system it is possible to identify the heterozygote based on phenotype as it exhibits a unique phenotype.
   2. In a two-allele, codominant system, you can count the individuals displaying each phenotype.
   3. From these data, you can calculate the numbers of each allele in the population and determine their frequencies, which become p and q.
      a. Recall the two allele frequencies must sum to one.
   4. Once allele frequencies are calculated, the next step is to plug those numbers into the Hardy-Weinberg equation to determine the expected genotype frequencies.
      a. Again, check your work to make sure that $p^2 + 2pq + q^2 = 1$.
   5. Finally, compare your expected and observed genotype frequencies.
   6. If the expected frequencies significantly differ from the observed frequencies (that is determined statistically), then
      a. conclude that the population is not in equilibrium, and
      b. that at least one of the above assumptions of HWE has been violated.
      c. In short, you may conclude that evolution (at that locus) has occurred.
   7. Refer to the example in your text (pp. 437-441), A Closer Look: Calculating Allele Frequencies : PTC Tasting in a Hypothetical Population (p. 442), and the Concept Application in this chapter of the Study Guide.

VII EVOLUTION IN ACTION: MODERN HUMAN POPULATIONS
   A. A number of factors initiate changes in allele frequencies. Including those that
      1. produce new variation (mutation), or
      2. redistribute variation through gene flow or genetic drift, or
      3. select "advantageous" allele combinations that promote reproductive success (natural selection).
   B. Nonrandom mating
      1. Any consistent bias in mating patterns can alter the genotypic proportions.
         a. Mate choice will not alter allele frequencies.
      2. There are types of nonrandom mating
         a. Positive assortative mating occurs between individuals who are phenotypically alike.
         b. Negative assortative mating when phenotypically different individuals mate with each other more often than expected.
         c. Neither positive nor negative assortative mating appear to have much influence in the vast majority of human populations.
      3. Inbreeding occurs when relatives mates among themselves more often than expected.
         a. This results in an increase in homozygosity and a decrease in variability.
         b. All societies have taboos against incest (matings between parent and child, and brother and sister).
         c. However, most human groups work hard at maintaining exogamy.
         d. In primates, one sex generally leaves the natal group to avoid endogamy

VIII HUMAN BIOCULTURAL EVOLUTION

A. Culture is the human strategy of adaptation.

B. Humans modify their cultural environments and this has wide reaching impacts.

C. Culture, evolution, and malaria
1. Prior to the advent of agriculture humans rarely lived near mosquito breeding areas.
2. About 2,000 years ago slash-and-burn agriculturists cleared forested areas in Africa.
3. A result of deforestation was the creation of stagnant pools of water that served as prime breeding areas for mosquitoes, the vectors for malaria.
4. The origin of the sickle cell mutation in Senegal appears to have occurred between 1,250 and 2,100 years ago.

D. Malaria has served as a powerful selective force.
1. Sickle-cell trait is a biological adaptation to malaria.
2. There is an advantage for carriers of sickle-cell, but only in malarial environments.
   a. Carriers have higher resistance to malaria and higher reproductive success.
3. After WWII extensive spraying of DDT eliminated large numbers of mosquito breeding grounds.
4. During the intervening years, mosquitoes, also subject to natural selection, have developed DDT-resistant strains with the result that malaria is again on the rise.

E. Sickle-cell trait, in which the heterozygote has an advantage in a specific environment, is an example of natural selection in humans.
1. The evolutionary mechanism in sickle-cell is called a balanced polymorphism.
   a. As defined earlier, a polymorphism is a trait with more than one allele in appreciable frequencies.
   b. When a harmful allele has a higher frequency than would be expected by mutation, a more detailed explanation must be sought.
   c. "Balanced" refers to the interaction of selective pressures to maintain both alleles in appreciable frequencies.
   d. This is due to the selective advantage of the heterozygotes who pass on both alleles.

F. Lactose intolerance is another example of human biocultural evolution.
1. Lactose is a sugar found in milk which is broken down by the enzyme lactase.
2. In most mammals the gene coding for lactase is "switched off" at the end of childhood.
3. In most adult mammals (including humans and cats) lactose in milk that is ingested is not broken down and ferments in the large intestine.
   a. This results in gastrointestinal distress.
4. Many African and Asia populations, most of the world's population, are intolerant of milk as adults.
5. This inability to digest milk is called lactose intolerance.
6. Why is there variation in lactose tolerance among human populations?
   a. Throughout most of hominin evolution, milk was unavailable after weaning.
   b. Continued action of an unnecessary enzyme might inhibit digestion of other foods.
   c. There may be a selective advantage for the gene coding for lactase production to switch off.
7. Why can some adults tolerate milk?

269

a. Peoples whose ancestors were pastoralists (such as modern Europeans and African peoples like the Tutsi and Fulani) probably drank large quantities of milk.

b. In a cultural environment where milk was consumed, strong selection pressures would act to shift allele frequencies in the direction of more lactose tolerance.

c. Some populations rely on dairying, but consume milk products as fermented dairy products such as cheese and yogurt.

    i. These populations have not developed a tolerance for lactose.

8. The patterns of lactose tolerance and intolerance illustrate how cultural factors have influenced our evolution.

KEY TERMS

balanced polymorphism: the maintenance of two or more alleles in a population due to the selective advantage of the heterozygote.

biological determinism: the concept that phenomena, including various aspects of behavior, are governed by genetic factors.

breeding isolates: a population that is distinctly isolated geographically and/or socially from other breeding groups.

cline: a gradient of genotypes (usually measured as allele frequencies) over geographical space, often maintained by natural selection.

endogamy: mating with individuals from the same group.

ethnocentrism: viewing other cultures from one's own cultural perspective. This often leads to thinking of other cultures as odd and inferior.

eugenics: a former scientific discipline, now largely discredited, that promoted the improvement of the human species through controlled breeding and sterilizations of "undesirables."

exogamy: mating with individuals from other groups.

gene pool: the total complement of alleles shared by the reproductive members of a population.

Hardy-Weinberg theory of genetic equilibrium: the mathematical relationship expressing, under ideal conditions, the predicted distribution of genes in populations; the central theorem of population genetics.

inbreeding: a type of nonrandom mating in which relatives mate more often than predicted under random mating conditions.

intelligence: mental capacity: the ability to learn, reason, or comprehend and interpret information, facts, relationships, meanings, etc.

lactose intolerance: the inability to digest fresh milk products; caused by the discontinued production of lactase, the enzyme that breaks down lactose or milk sugar.

non-random mating: patterns of mating in a population in which individuals choose mates preferentially.

polymorphism: genetic trait governed by a locus with more than one allele.

polytypic: referring to species composed of populations that differ with regard to the expression of one or more traits.

population genetics: the study of the frequency of alleles, genotypes, and phenotypes in populations from a microevolutionary perspectives.

slash-and-burn agriculture: a traditional land-clearing practice whereby trees and vegetation are cut and burned. In many areas, fields are abandoned after a few years and clearing occurs elsewhere.

MEDIA EXERCISES

1) Take a look at Syracuse University's "All of Us Are Related, Each of Us is Unique" cyber-exhibition "exploring the concept of race." (http://allrelated.syr.edu/) After reading the descriptive blurb on the first page, click on the "View the Exhibition" button towards the bottom right. That will take you to a page that displays thumbnails of all 18 panels of the exhibition. Before cycling through them, open up another browser window and click on "Full Text Panels 1-18". This will allow you to view the panels in one window while switching back-and-forth with the other so you can read the full text associated with each panel. How do the perspectives in this exhibition agree with those of your text?

2) Browse through the "Evolution and Population Genetics" section of the "Biology Web Site References for Students and Teachers." (http://www.hoflink.com/~house/) Click on "Population Genetics, Microevolution" in the Table of Contents to be taken to a series of links on numerous relevant topics including, for example: 3 sites on gene frequencies, 2 sites on gene pools, 6 sites on Hardy-Weinberg and 2 sites on heterozygote advantage. Use these sites to better understand the concepts and processes discussed in your text.

3) Log on to the following website and consider your perspectives on variation and race. http://www.understandingrace.org/humvar/

4) Consider exploring www.pbs.org for background information on their powerful film series entitled Race: Power of an illusion.

INFOTRAC

1) In *InfoTrac*, do a keyword search on "scientific racism Blakey" to read an article by Howard University physical anthropologist Michael L. Blakey titled "Scientific Racism and the Biological Concept of Race" published in the journal *Literature and Psychology* in 1999. This very thorough treatment of the subject takes you from attempts to define race, through its historical development to manifestations of scientific racism today.

2) In *InfoTrac* do a keyword search on "sickle cell malaria" and read a few of the abstracts and articles that are retrieved. What are some of the advances in knowledge that are being reported concerning the relationship of the sickle cell trait and malaria?

CONCEPT APPLICATIONS

Shaded-Box Exercise

Arrange the 16 figures (labeled A-P below) into two groups of 8. Record the criteria that guided your decisions to group the figures the way that you did. Compare your groupings to those of a classmate. Do they differ? If so, why? If they don't, is there an equally logical way to group them again so that your groupings differ from your classmate's? What does this exercise have to say about attempts to classify humans into races?

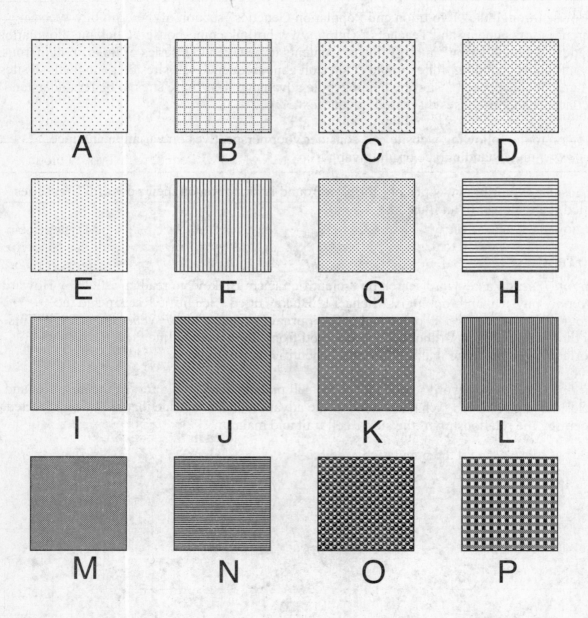

Hardy-Weinberg Walk-Through Fill-Ins

Solve the following Hardy-Weinberg problems by filling in the blanks using terms found below. Each item may be used more than once. Numerical values are not found below.

codominant	allele	population	homozygote	alleles
frequencies	blood	equilibrium	observed	M
p	genotype	two	antisera	N
phenotypes	q	heterozygotes	insignificant	locus
blood types	not	evolved	dissimilar	homozygotes
genotypes	Hardy-Weinberg	one	small	expected

Problem #1. You are a geneticist working on a breeding population of 100 individuals on an island. Your research question is to find out whether or not this population is at _____ at the MN locus. First, you draw the 100 individuals' _____ and determine their MN blood types by observing reactions with specially prepared _____. You then record the populational distribution of MN blood types:

People with Type M blood	People with Type MN blood	People with Type N blood
24	52	24

You know that because the MN system is _____, each of the three MN blood types (their _____) correspond to a specific MN _____. "Type M blood" individuals are genotype MM, "Type MN blood" individuals are _____ (genotype MN) and the "Type N blood" individuals are the other _____, genotype NN. Your next step is to determine allele _____ for M and N in this population. You know that each individual has ___ alleles at the MN locus, so that there are ___ total M and N alleles in this population (2 times the number of people in the breeding population). You also know that each person with Type M blood has two M alleles because their genotype is MM. Similarly, each Type N individual carries ___ N alleles since their genotype is NN. Finally, each Type MN person is a heterozygote and carries ___ of each allele, an __ and an __. So now you can calculate the frequencies of the M and N alleles using the following formulae:

f(M) = # of M alleles in the population / total # of M & N alleles in the population
f(N) = # of N _____ in the population / total # of M & N alleles in the _____

The table below summarizes the numbers so far:

MN blood type:	Type M blood	Type MN blood	Type N blood
# of individuals:	24	52	24
genotype:	MM	___	NN
# of M alleles:	24 X 2 = 48	52	0
# of N alleles:	___	___	___

273

so f(M) = (48 + 52) / (2 X 100) = 100/200 = .50, and since we know that the allele frequencies have to add up to ___, the f(N) also has to equal .50, but you'll check to make sure anyway:
f(N) = (52 + 48) / (2 X 100) = 100/200 = .50

Now, you start to plug those _____ frequencies into the Hardy-Weinberg formulae to determine if the population is in equilibrium. First you set the frequency of the M allele equal to __ and the frequency of the N allele to __, so f(M) = .50 = p and f(N) = .50 = q therefore p + q = 1

Next you calculate the expected genotype frequencies by plugging the values of p and q into the second _____ formula: $p^2 + 2pq + q^2 = 1$, so
the expected frequency of MM genotypes is $f(MM_{exp}) = p^2 = (.\_\_)^2 = .\_\_$, and
the expected frequency of MM genotypes is $f(MN_{exp}) = 2pq = 2(.\_\_)(.\_\_) = 2(.\_\_) = .\_\_$, and
the expected frequency of NN genotypes is $f(NN_{exp}) = q^2 = (.\_\_)^2 = .\_\_$

Next you check your math: does $p^2 + 2pq + q^2 = $ __? Since .__ + .__ + .__ = __, you move on to the next step: do the expected genotype frequencies that you just calculated match the observed _____ frequencies in the population? The observed _____ frequencies are simply calculated by counting the number of people with each MN blood type (remembering that there is a one-to-one match with blood types and _____ in this codominant system) and dividing that number by the total number of people in the population (in this case ___).
The observed frequency of MM genotypes is $f(MM_{obs}) = $ 24 Type M people / 100 people = .24
The observed frequency of MM genotypes is $f(MN_{obs}) = $ __ Type MN people / ___ people = .__
The observed frequency of MM genotypes is $f(NN_{obs}) = $ __ Type N people / ___ people = .__

Finally, you compare the observed to the expected frequencies:

MN blood type:	Type M blood	Type MN blood	Type N blood
# of individuals:	24	52	24
Observed frequencies	24/100 = .24	__/__ = .__	__/__ = .__
Expected frequencies	$p^2 = (.5)^2 = .25$	$2pq = 2(.\_)(.\_) = .\_\_$	$q^2 = (.\_\_)^2 = .\_\_$

From these comparisons, you conclude that this population is likely at _____ for the MN locus because the _____ and _____ frequencies are very _____. You attribute the _____ differences between the observed and expected values to the _____ size of the population. Therefore, this population is ___ evolving at this _____.

Now complete Problem 2. Use the same term list from the previous page to complete the following section

Problem #2. You, the geneticist, return to the same island 25 years later and discover that the next generation's breeding population has doubled to 200 individuals. You intend to investigate whether or not this population is still at _____ at the MN _____. You again draw the populations' blood and determine their MN _____ by observing reactions with specially prepared antisera. You record the following populational distribution of MN blood types:

People with Type M blood	People with Type MN blood	People with Type N blood
40	40	120

You know that because the MN system is codominant, each of the _____ MN blood types (their phenotypes) correspond to a specific MN genotype. "Type M blood" individuals are genotype __, "Type MN blood" individuals are heterozygotes (genotype __) and the "Type N blood" individuals are the other homozygote, genotype __. Your next step is to determine allele frequencies for M and N in this population. You know that each individual has two alleles at the __ locus, so that there are ____ total M and N alleles in this population (2 times the number of people in the breeding population). You also know that each person with Type M blood has two M alleles because their genotype is MM. Similarly, each Type N individual carries two N alleles since their genotype is NN. Finally, each Type MN person is a _____ and carries one of each allele, an M and an N. So now you can calculate the frequencies of the M and N alleles using the following formulae:

f(M) = # of M alleles in the _____ / total # of M & N alleles in the population
f(N) = # of N alleles in the population / total # of M & N _____ in the population

The table below summarizes the numbers so far:

MN blood type:	Type M blood	Type MN blood	Type N blood
# of individuals:	40	40	120
genotype:	__	MN	__
# of M alleles:	_____	__	__
# of N alleles:	0	40	120 X 2 = 240

so f(M) = (__ + __) / (2 X ____) = ___/___ = ___/___ = ___/___ = .__, and since we know that the allele frequencies have to add up to 1.0, then f(N) has to equal .__, but you'll check to make sure anyway:
f(N) = (40 + 240) / (2 X 200) = 280/400 = 28/40 = 7/10 = .__

275

Now, you start to plug those allele frequencies into the Hardy-Weinberg formulae to determine if the population is in equilibrium. First you set the frequency of the M allele equal to p and the frequency of the N allele to q, so f(M) = .__ = p and f(N) = .__ = q therefore p + q = 1

Next you calculate the expected genotype frequencies by plugging the values of p and q into the second Hardy-Weinberg formula: $p^2 + 2pq + q^2 = 1$, so

the expected frequency of MM genotypes is $f(MM_{exp}) = p^2 = (.\_)^2 = .\_\_$, and

the expected frequency of MM genotypes is $f(MN_{exp}) = 2pq = 2(.\_)(.\_) = 2(.\_\_) = .\_\_$, and

the expected frequency of NN genotypes is $f(NN_{exp}) = q^2 = (.\_)^2 = .\_\_$

Next you check your math: does $p^2 + 2pq + q^2 = 1$? Since .__ + .__ + .__ = 1, you move on to the next step: do the expected genotype frequencies that you just calculated match the _____ genotype frequencies in the population? The _____ genotype frequencies are simply calculated by counting the number of people with each MN blood type (remembering that there is a one-to-one match with _____ and genotypes in this codominant system) and dividing that number by the total number of people in the population (in this case ____).

The observed frequency of MM genotypes is $f(MM_{obs})$ = __ Type M people / ___ people = .__

The observed frequency of MM genotypes is $f(MN_{obs})$ = __ Type MN people / ___ people = .__

The observed frequency of MM genotypes is $f(NN_{obs})$ = 120 Type N people / 200 people = .60

Finally, you compare the observed to the expected frequencies:

MN blood type:	Type M blood	Type MN blood	Type N blood
# of individuals:	__	__	60
Observed frequencies	__/__ = ___	__/__ = ___	120/200 = .60
Expected frequencies	$p^2 = (.\_)^2 = .\_\_$	$2pq = 2(.\_)(.\_) = .\_\_$	$q^2 = (.7)^2 = .49$

From these comparisons, you conclude that this population is likely ___ at equilibrium for the MN locus because the observed and expected _____ are very _____. You note that there are less than half of the _____ that are expected and that both _____ are more frequent that you would expect given the observed _____ frequencies of M and N in this population. Therefore, you conclude that this population has _____ at this locus.

Now answer the True/False, Multiple Choice and Short Answer sample test questions. Following completion of the tests, correct them with the answers and textbook page references at the end of this Study Guide chapter. Note the areas in which you are strong and weak to guide you in your studying. Finally, answer the sample Essay Questions.

TRUE/FALSE QUESTIONS

If false, consider what modification would make the statement true.

1. All contemporary humans are members of the same polytypic species, *Homo sapiens*.
    TRUE   FALSE

2. Today, most physical anthropologists view race as the central explanatory concept to apply to human variation.
    TRUE   FALSE

3. Lewontin's 1972 study showed that only 6.3% of genetic variation could be explained by differences between major continental groupings of people (i.e. "races").
    TRUE   FALSE

4. Racism is a cultural, not a biological, phenomenon and it is found worldwide.
    TRUE   FALSE

5. Comparing populations on the basis of IQ scores is a valid use of testing procedures and provides convincing evidence that populations vary with respect to cognitive ability.
    TRUE   FALSE

6. A mating pattern whereby individuals obtain mates from groups other than their own is called endogamy.
    TRUE   FALSE

7. The Hardy-Weinberg theory of genetic equilibrium is a minor theorem of population genetics.
    TRUE   FALSE

8. According to the Hardy-Weinberg theory of genetic equilibrium, the two equations $p + q$ and $p^2 + 2pq + q^2$ must each sum to 1.
    TRUE   FALSE

9. Inbreeding will increase the amount of homozygosity, since relatives share more alleles than strangers.
    TRUE   FALSE

10. The maintenance of a single allele in a population due to the selective advantage of the recessive homozygote results in a balanced polymorphism.

    TRUE   FALSE

MULTIPLE CHOICE QUESTIONS

1. The German anatomist responsible for classifying humans into five races was
    A. Carolus Linnaeus.
    B. Charles Lyell.
    C. Thomas Malthus.
    D. Johann Blumenbach.

2. A local sheriff believes that the people in his district, who have high arrest and conviction rates, are born thieves because of their genetic constitution. Which of the following exemplifies the sheriff's attitude?
    A. relativism.
    B. homophobia.
    C. biological determinism.
    D. post-modernism.

3. The philosophy that provided "scientific justification" for purging Nazi Germany of its "unfit" was
    A. anthropometry.
    B. eugenics.
    C. genetics.
    D. monogenism.

4. Within *Ammodramus maritimus , the* seaside sparrow, there are four distinct populations that differ from one another in at least one trait. This sparrow is an example of a
    A. monotypic species.
    B. polytypic species.
    C. chronospecies.
    D. syngamic species.

5. The consensus criterion for identifying a biological race is
    A. At least 50% of the members of one population of a species must be physically distinguishable from those from another population.
    B. Two populations of the same species are located in two different geographical areas.
    C. Two populations have different vocalizations or, in humans, languages.
    D. There are no established criteria for identifying races of plants and animals (including humans) today.

6. An objection to the use of racial taxonomies is that they are
   A. typological in nature.
   B. based on polygenic traits.
   C. based on continuous traits.
   D. evolutionary in nature.

7. A gradual change in allele frequencies in populations dispersed over geographic space is called a
   A. race.
   B. phenotypic grade.
   C. cline.
   D. Hardy-Weinberg equilibrium.

8. In Lewontin's 1972 study of race, he concluded that
   A. there is more genetic variation between races than is found within any one specific race.
   B. the seven "geographic" races cluster independently, indicating that they are true races.
   C. there is more genetic variation within any one race than there is between races.
   D. the idea of race is valid.

9. What is a microsatellite?
   A. Individually unique repeated sequences of DNA
   B. differences between large geographically separated populations.
   C. Sections of mtDNA
   D. A polygenic trait such as skin color.

10. Which of the following statements is true?
    A. Many anthropologists consider groups such as the Japanese to be a race.
    B. Forensic anthropologists can identify the ethnicity of a skeleton 100% accurately.
    C. Many physical anthropologists see human race as a meaningless concept.
    D. The five races of Blumenbach are still the standard in modern physical anthropology.

11. Which of the following statements is true?
    A. Individual abilities are due only to an individual's genetic inheritance.
    B. IQ can change within an individual's lifetime.
    C. IQ scores are essentially the same thing as innate intelligence.
    D. IQ scores reflect innate cognitive differences between populations.

12. The total complement of genes shared by reproductive members of a population is that population's
    A. gene flow.
    B. gene drift.
    C. gene pool.
    D. bottleneck effect.

13. Which of the following is **not** an assumption of the Hardy-Weinberg theory of genetic equilibrium?
    A. the population is infinitely large
    B. mating is non-random
    C. no mutation is occurring
    D. there is no natural selection occurring

14. Random mating means
    A. every adult individual of one sex has an equal opportunity to mate with any other mature individual of the opposite sex.
    B. every individual of one sex can mate with any individual of the opposite sex, except close family members.
    C. that people may have as many spouses of the opposite sex as they please.
    D. that adults may mate only with those individuals from the same social standing as they are.

15. You have taken blood samples from 100 individuals. You want to know what the allele frequencies for the MN blood group is in this population. You find that 70 individuals have type M blood, 20 have type MN blood, and 10 have type N blood. What are the allele frequencies for blood types M and N?
    A. M = .7, N = .3
    B. M = .7, N = .2
    C. M = .8, N = .2
    D. M = .9, N = .1

16. You find in a population, while taking blood samples and looking at the MN blood group, that the M allele is present at a frequency of 0.7. Using the Hardy-Weinberg theorem predict the genotypic frequencies for the next generation.
    A. .64(MM) + .32(NN) + .04(NN)
    B. .36(MM) + .48(MN) + .16(NN)
    C. .49(MM) + .42(NN) + .09(NN)
    D. .25(MM) + .5 (MN) + .25(NN)

17. If significant deviations are shown from Hardy-Weinberg expectations, this may suggest
    A. equilibrium.
    B. evolution.
    C. the locus in this population is not evolving.
    D. a balanced polymorphism.

18. Patterns of mating in a population in which individuals choose mates preferentially is known as
    A. nonrandom mating.
    B. a balanced polymorphism.
    C. the null hypothesis.
    D. a cline.

19. The common result of positive assortative mating and inbreeding is to
    A. increase homozygosity.
    B. decrease homozygosity.
    C. increase heterozygosity.
    D. increase gene flow.

20. Mating with relatives more often than would be expected by chance is called
    A. nonrandom mating.
    B. negative assortative mating.
    C. inbreeding.
    D. incest avoidance.

21. Most human populations are polymorphic for the ABO system, but one notable exception is the fixed O allele among
    A. Australian Aborigines.
    B. the peoples of central Asia.
    C. South American Indians.
    D. Blackfeet Indians.

22. The most genetically complex polymorphism yet discovered in humans is the
    A. ABO blood group.
    B. HLA system.
    C. MN blood system.
    D. Rh system.

23. Which of the following is a molecular component of the human genome that is very valuable in obtaining "genetic fingerprints"?
    A. Rh factors.
    B. microsatellites.
    C. PTC tasting strips.
    D. ABO antigens.

24. SNPs are
    A. Semi-Networked Polygenes.
    B. Solid Nodal Pods.
    C. Stringy Nano-Polypeptides.
    D. Single Nucleotide Polymorphisms.

25. Many individuals have difficulty digesting milk because
    A. they have an Rh antigen producing an immune response to milk.
    B. they do not have enough lactose in their cardiovascular system.
    C. they cannot process the lipoproteins in the milk.
    D. as adults, they have ceased the production of the lactase enzyme.

SHORT ANSWER QUESTIONS (& PAGE REFERENCES)

1. What was the importance of Lewontin's 1972 genetic study? (p. 433)

2. What are breeding isolates? (p. 437)

3. Why are polymorphisms of greatest use in contemporary studies of human genetic variation? (pp. 430-431)

4. What is the importance of the HLA system? (p. 432)

5. Why is inbreeding harmful? (p. 441-442)

ESSAY QUESTIONS (& PAGE REFERENCES)

1. Review the development of the race concept in Western thought from its origins in the 16th century through its catastrophic effects during the 20th century. (pp. 422-423)

2. How do physical anthropologists regard the concept of race today? Discuss the variety of viewpoints present in the field on this topic. (pp. 425-427)

3. How do biological determinism and racism enter into the debate over IQ, intelligence and claimed cognitive differences between populations? (p. 429)

4. What is the Hardy-Weinberg theory of genetic equilibrium? What assumptions have to be met if a population is concluded to be in genetic equilibrium for a particular locus? (p. 437)

5. How does the relationship of sickle-cell trait to malaria illustrate the concepts of biocultural evolution and balanced polymorphism? (p. 443)

ANSWERS, *CORRECTED STATEMENT* IF FALSE & REFERENCES TO TRUE/FALSE QUESTIONS

1. TRUE, p. 425

2. FALSE, pp. 425-426, Today, most physical anthropologists view race as *meaningless in explaining* human variation.

3. TRUE, p. 433

4. TRUE, pp. 428-429

5. FALSE, p. 429, Comparing populations on the basis of IQ scores is a *misuse* of testing procedures and provides *no* evidence *whatsoever* that populations vary with respect to cognitive ability.

6. FALSE, p. 437, A mating pattern whereby individuals obtain mates from groups other than their own is called *exogamy*.

7. FALSE, p. 437, The Hardy-Weinberg theory of genetic equilibrium is *the central* theorem of population genetics.

8. TRUE, pp. 437-438

9. TRUE, p. 441

10. FALSE, p. 443-444, The maintenance of *two or more* allele*s* in a population due to the selective advantage of the *heterozygote* results in a balanced polymorphism.

ANSWERS AND REFERENCES TO MULTIPLE CHOICE QUESTIONS

1. **D**, p. 423
2. **C**, p. 423
3. **B**, p. 424
4. **B**, p. 425
5. **D**, p. 426
6. **A**, p. 427
7. **C**, p. 431
8. **C**, pp. 433-434
9. **A**, p. 434
10. **C**, pp. 426-427
11. **B**, p. 429
12. **C**, p. 436

13. **B**, p. 437
14. **A**, p. 437
15. **C**, pp. 439-441
16. **C**, pp. 439-441
17. **B**, pp. 437-438
18. **A**, p. 441
19. **A**, p. 440
20. **C**, p. 441
21. **C**, pp. 431-432
22. **B**, p. 432
23. **B**, p. 434
24. **D**, p. 434
25. **D**, pp. 444-445

CONCEPT APPLICATION SOLUTIONS

Shaded-box exercise

There is no "right answer" for the shaded-box exercise. One possible division of these figures would be the first two ("lighter") rows (Figs. A-H) versus the 3rd and 4th ("darker") rows (Figs. I-P). Alternatively, a division of "dots" (Figs. A,C,E,G,I,K,M,O) versus "lines" (Figs. B,D,F,H,J,L,N,P) is equally defensible. This concept application is meant to illustrate the arbitrariness of human racial typologies (See A Closer Look: Racial Purity: A false and Dangerous Ideology pp. 424-425).

Hardy-Weinberg Walk-Through Fill-Ins
Blanks are filled-in with **bolded italics**.

Problem #1. You are a geneticist working on a breeding population of 100 individuals on an island. Your research question is to find out whether or not this population is at **equilibrium** at the MN locus. First, you draw the 100 individuals' **blood** and determine their MN blood types by observing reactions with specially prepared **antisera**. You then record the populational distribution of MN blood types:

People with Type M blood	People with Type MN blood	People with Type N blood
24	52	24

You know that because the MN system is **codominant**, each of the three MN blood types (their **phenotypes**) correspond to a specific MN **genotype**. "Type M blood" individuals are genotype MM, "Type MN blood" individuals are **heterozygotes** (genotype MN) and the "Type N blood" individuals are the other **homozygote**, genotype NN. Your next step is to determine allele **frequencies** for M and N in this population. You know that each individual has **two** alleles at the MN locus, so that there are **200** total M and N alleles in this population (2 times the number of people in the breeding population). You also know that each person with Type M blood has two M alleles because their genotype is MM. Similarly, each Type N individual carries **two** N alleles since their genotype is NN. Finally, each Type MN person is a heterozygote and carries **one** of each allele, an **M** and an **N**. So now you can calculate the frequencies of the M and N alleles using the following formulae:

$f(M)$ = # of M alleles in the population / total # of M & N alleles in the population
$f(N)$ = # of N **alleles** in the population / total # of M & N alleles in the **population**

The table below summarizes the numbers so far:

MN blood type:	Type M blood	Type MN blood	Type N blood
# of individuals:	24	52	24
genotype:	MM	MN	NN
# of M alleles:	24 X 2 = 48	*52*	0
# of N alleles:	*0*	52	*24 X 2 = 48*

so $f(M)$ = (48 + 52) / (2 X 100) = 100/200 = .50, and since we know that the allele frequencies have to add up to **1.0**, the $f(N)$ also has to equal .50, but you'll check to make sure anyway:
$f(N)$ = (52 + 48) / (2 X 100) = 100/200 = .50

Now, you start to plug those **allele** frequencies into the Hardy-Weinberg formulae to determine if the population is in equilibrium. First you set the frequency of the M allele equal to **p** and the frequency of the N allele to **q**, so $f(M)$ = .50 = p and $f(N)$ = .50 = q therefore p + q = 1

284

Next you calculate the expected genotype frequencies by plugging the values of p and q into the second **Hardy-Weinberg** formula: $p^2 + 2pq + q^2 = 1$, so
the expected frequency of MM genotypes is $f(MM_{exp}) = p^2 = (.5)^2 = .25$, and
the expected frequency of MM genotypes is $f(MN_{exp}) = 2pq = 2(.5)(.5) = 2(.25) = .50$, and
the expected frequency of NN genotypes is $f(NN_{exp}) = q^2 = (.5)^2 = .25$

Next you check your math: does $p^2 + 2pq + q^2 = 1$? Since $.25 + .50 + .25 = 1$, you move on to the next step: do the expected genotype frequencies that you just calculated match the observed **genotype** frequencies in the population? The observed **genotype** frequencies are simply calculated by counting the number of people with each MN blood type (remembering that there is a one-to-one match with blood types and **genotypes** in this codominant system) and dividing that number by the total number of people in the population (in this case **100**).
The observed frequency of MM genotypes is $f(MM_{obs}) = 24$ Type M people / 100 people = .24
The observed frequency of MM genotypes is $f(MN_{obs}) = $ **52** Type MN people / **100** people = **.52**
The observed frequency of MM genotypes is $f(NN_{obs}) = $ **24** Type N people / **100** people = **.24**

Finally, you compare the observed to the expected frequencies:

MN blood type:	Type M blood	Type MN blood	Type N blood
# of individuals:	24	52	24
Observed frequencies	24/100 = .24	**52/100 = .52**	**24/100 = .24**
Expected frequencies	$p^2 = (.5)^2 = .25$	$2pq = 2(.5)(.5) = .50$	$q^2 = (.5)^2 = .25$

From these comparisons, you conclude that this population is likely at **equilibrium** for the MN locus because the **observed** and **expected** frequencies are very **similar**. You attribute the **insignificant** differences between the observed and expected values to the **small** size of the population. Therefore, this population is **not** evolving at this **locus**.

Problem #2. You, the geneticist, return to the same island 25 years later and discover that the next generation's breeding population has doubled to 200 individuals. You intend to investigate whether or not this population is still at **equilibrium** at the MN **locus**. You again draw the populations' blood and determine their MN **blood types** by observing reactions with specially prepared antisera. You record the following populational distribution of MN blood types:

People with Type M blood	People with Type MN blood	People with Type N blood
40	40	120

You know that because the MN system is codominant, each of the **three** MN blood types (their phenotypes) correspond to a specific MN genotype. "Type M blood" individuals are genotype **MM**, "Type MN blood" individuals are heterozygotes (genotype **MN**) and the "Type N blood" individuals are the other homozygote, genotype **NN**. Your next step is to determine allele frequencies for M and N in this population. You know that each individual has two alleles at the **MN** locus, so that there are **400** total M and N alleles in this population (2 times the number of people in the breeding population). You also know that each person with Type M blood has two

M alleles because their genotype is MM. Similarly, each Type N individual carries two N alleles since their genotype is NN. Finally, each Type MN person is a **heterozygote** and carries one of each allele, an M and an N. So now you can calculate the frequencies of the M and N alleles using the following formulae:

f(M) = # of M alleles in the **population** / total # of M & N alleles in the population
f(N) = # of N alleles in the population / total # of M & N **alleles** in the population

The table below summarizes the numbers so far:

MN blood type:	Type M blood	Type MN blood	Type N blood
# of individuals:	40	40	120
genotype:	*MM*	MN	*NN*
# of M alleles:	*40 X 2 = 80*	*40*	*0*
# of N alleles:	0	40	120 X 2 = 240

so f(M) = (*80 + 40*) / (2 X *200*) = *120/400 = 12/40 = 3/10* = *.30*, and since we know that the allele frequencies have to add up to 1.0, then f(N) has to equal *.70*, but you'll check to make sure anyway:
f(N) = (40 + 240) / (2 X 200) = 280/400 = 28/40 = 7/10 = *.70*

Now, you start to plug those allele frequencies into the Hardy-Weinberg formulae to determine if the population is in equilibrium. First you set the frequency of the M allele equal to p and the frequency of the N allele to q, so f(M) = *.30* = p and f(N) = *.70* = q therefore p + q = 1

Next you calculate the expected genotype frequencies by plugging the values of p and q into the second Hardy-Weinberg formula: $p^2 + 2pq + q^2 = 1$, so
the expected frequency of MM genotypes is $f(MM_{exp}) = p^2 = (.3)^2 = .09$, and
the expected frequency of MM genotypes is $f(MN_{exp}) = 2pq = 2(.3)(.7) = 2(.21) = .42$, and
the expected frequency of NN genotypes is $f(NN_{exp}) = q^2 = (.7)^2 = .49$

Next you check your math: does $p^2 + 2pq + q^2 = 1$? Since *.09* + *.42* + *.49* = 1, you move on to the next step: do the expected genotype frequencies that you just calculated match the **observed** genotype frequencies in the population? The **observed** genotype frequencies are simply calculated by counting the number of people with each MN blood type (remembering that there is a one-to-one match with **blood types** and genotypes in this codominant system) and dividing that number by the total number of people in the population (in this case *200*).
The observed frequency of MM genotypes is $f(MM_{obs})$ = 40 Type M people / 200 people = .20
The observed frequency of MM genotypes is $f(MN_{obs})$ = 40 Type MN people / 200 people = .20
The observed frequency of MM genotypes is $f(NN_{obs})$ = 120 Type N people / 200 people = .60

286

Finally, you compare the observed to the expected frequencies:

MN blood type:	Type M blood	Type MN blood	Type N blood
# of individuals:	*40*	*40*	60
Observed frequencies	*40/100 = .20*	*40/200 = .20*	120/200 = .60
Expected frequencies	$p^2 = (.3)^2 = .09$	$2pq = 2(.3)(.7) = .42$	$q^2 = (.7)^2 = .49$

From these comparisons, you conclude that this population is likely ***not*** at equilibrium for the MN locus because the observed and expected ***frequencies*** are very ***dissimilar***. You note that there are less than half of the ***heterozygotes*** that are expected and that both ***homozygotes*** are more frequent that you would expect given the observed ***allele*** frequencies of M and N in this population. Therefore, you conclude that this population has ***evolved*** at this locus.

CHAPTER 16
MODERN HUMAN BIOLOGY: PATTERNS OF ADAPTATION

LEARNING OBJECTIVES

After reading this chapter you should be able to:
- describe the adaptive significance of human variation (pp. 451-452)
- understand the relationship between skin color and solar radiation (pp. 451-454)
- discuss the human response to thermal stresses (pp. 457-460)
- describe the physiological response to high altitude environment (pp. 461-463)
- understand how infectious disease has affected human evolution (pp. 465-467)
- discuss current culturally mediated factors that may contribute to the spread of infectious disease (pp. 463-466)
- describe the patterns of infectious disease throughout human history (pp. 466-469)

CHAPTER OUTLINE

Introduction

    In the previous chapter we saw how polygenic traits have been used as a basis for traditional racial classification and how physical anthropologists view the concept of race. We learned how genetic polymorphisms have been used to study evolutionary patterns in human populations. In this chapter, we will focus on the adaptive value of polygenic traits for human populations living in specific environments. We will also examine how populations and individuals differ in their responses to environmental stress. Finally, we will consider the role of infectious disease in human evolution and adaptation.

I   **THE ADAPTIVE SIGNIFICANCE OF HUMAN VARIATION**
    A. Physical anthropologists view human variation as the result of evolutionary factors and adaptations to environmental conditions, both past and present.
        1. Environmental conditions can stress on humans.
            a. Stress acts to disrupt the balanced physiological system of the human body.
            b. The balanced system is an internal constancy of system operations called Homeostasis.
            c. Humans can adapt to environmental conditions.
    B. Physiological response to environmental change is influenced by genetic factors.
        1. Long-term (i.e. genetic) evolutionary changes characterize all individuals within a population or species.
        2. Acclimatization is form of physiological response to environmental conditions.
            a. Acclimatization can be short-term, long-term or even permanent.
            b. In the short term, acclimitization can be a temporary and rapid adjustment to environmental change
               i. Tanning by exposure to direct sunlight is an example of short-term acclimatization since the tan eventually fades.
            c. Developmental acclimatization is a response to an environmental stress that occurs during pre-adulthood.

i. If you were to move to a high altitude environment as a child, you would respond differently than were you to move there as an adult.

C. Solar radiation and skin color
  1. Skin color in indigenous populations followed a regular geographical distribution, particularly in the Old World.
     a. See Figure 16-1 p. 452.
     b. Populations with the greatest amount of pigmentation were found in the equatorial regions.
     c. Populations with lighter skin color were associated with more northern latitudes.
  2. Skin color is influenced by three substances: hemoglobin, carotene and most importantly, melanin.
  3. Melanin
     a. Melanin has the ability to absorb ultraviolet (UV) radiation, preventing damage to DNA.
        i. UV radiation can produce mutations in skin cell DNA and ultimately cause skin cancer.
     b. Melanin is produced by specialized cells in the epidermis called melanocytes.
     c. All humans appear to have about the same number of melanocytes.
     d. Exposure to sunlight triggers a protective mechanism which temporarily increases melanin production (i.e., a tan).
  4. Natural selection has favored dark skin in areas nearest the equator where the most intense UV radiation is found.
     a. In considering skin color from an evolutionary perspective, three points should be kept in mind:
        i. Early hominins lived mostly in the tropics.
        ii. Early hominins spent the majority of time outdoors.
        iii. Early hominins did not wear clothing that would have provided some protection against UV radiation.
     b. UV radiation was a powerful agent selecting for optimum levels of melanin production in early humans.
        i. Evidence suggests that less-pigmented skin in intense UV environments could reduce reproductive fitness.
     c. Melanin also prevents the destruction of folate, an important B vitamin.
        i. Folate is a B vitamin that can be degraded by UV radiation.
        ii. Folate is critical for normal neural development in fetuses.
        iii. Loss of folate can lead to spina bifida and other neural tube defects.
        iv. Healthy folate levels are important for reproductive fitness.
     d. Studies suggest early hominins may have had fair skin with body hair. With the loss of body hair, dark skin evolved to lessen the impacts of UV radiation.
  5. While we have solid explanations for dark pigmentation, why did light pigmentation evolve?
     a. As hominins migrated to the northern latitudes, selective pressures changed.
        i. Sunlight patterns are dramatically different in northern latitudes.
        ii. Europe had cloudy skies, a winter with fewer hours of daylight, and the location of the sun to the south, solar radiation was indirect.
        iii. The use of clothing for warmth further prevented exposure of the skin to sunlight.

289

    b. Selection favoring dark skin was relaxed, but there also had to be a selective
       pressure favoring lighter skin.
D. The vitamin D hypothesis
    1. Exposure to sunlight is critical for the production of vitamin D.
        a. Reduced exposure to sunlight would have been detrimental to darker-skinned
            individuals in northern latitudes as higher melanin content would filter out UV
            rays.
    2. Vitamin D synthesis in northern latitudes was as important to natural selection as the
        need for protection from UV radiation in the tropics.
    3. Vitamin D plays a vital role in mineralization and normal bone growth during infancy
        and childhood.
        a. While vitamin D is available in some foods, the body's primary source comes
            from its own ability to synthesize vitamin D through the interaction of UV light
            and a cholesterol-like substance found in the subcutaneous layer of the skin.
    4. The potential for vitamin D synthesis differs based on the pigmentation of the skin.
    5. Insufficient amounts of vitamin D during childhood results in rickets, which leads to
        bone deformities.
        a. Deformities of the bones of the pelvis are of particular concern for women
            because it can compromise the birth canal.
    6. Vitamin D is important in the body's responses many of which influence reproductive
        success.
        a. The SCL gene involved in melanin production has two alleles.
        b. A mutated allele is found in 100% of Europeans and European Americans.
            i.   93%+ of Africans, Native Americans and East Asians have the unmutated
                 form of the allele.
    7.   Evidence supports strong and rapid selection for depigmented skin in northern
        latitudes.
E.   From an evolutionary perspective, skin color provides an excellent example of how the
    forces of natural selection have produced geographically patterned variation as the result
    of two conflicting selection forces :
    1. The need for protection from overexposure to UV radiation,
    2. The need for adequate UV exposure for vitamin D synthesis
F. The thermal environment
    1. Mammals and birds have evolved physiological mechanisms which enable an
        organism to maintain a constant body temperature.
    2. Humans inhabit a wide variety of thermal environments, ranging from 120° F to -60°
        F that necessitate more than cultural innovations.
G. Response to heat
    1. Most of early human evolution took place in warm climates.
    2. Humans and many other mammalian species have sweat glands widely distributed
        throughout the skin.
        a. Sweat on the body surface removes heat through evaporative cooling.
    3. The capacity to dissipate heat by sweating is a feature found in all human populations
        almost equally.
        a.   People not generally exposed to hot conditions need a period of acclimatization
            to warmer temperatures.
        b. Loss of body hair also facilitates cooling.

c. A negative side-effect to heat reduction through sweating is that critical amounts of water and minerals can be lost.

4. Another mechanism for radiating body heat is vasodilation.
    a. Vasodilation refers to a widening (dilation) of the capillaries.
        i. Capillaries are small (in diameter) vessels that carry blood.
    b. Vasodilation of the capillaries near the skin's surface permit "hot" blood from the body's core to radiate to the outer layers and dissipate heat to the surrounding air.

5. Body size also plays a role in temperature regulation.
    a. Among mammals and birds, there is a general relationship between climate and body size (although, as always in biology, there are exceptions).
    b. Two biological rules apply to body size, body proportions, and temperature.
        i. Bergmann's rule
        ii. Allen's rule
    c. Bergmann's rule states that body size tends to be greater in populations that live in cold environments.
        i. This is because as mass increases, the relative amount of surface area decreases.
        ii. Because heat is lost from the surface, increased mass allows for greater heat retention and reduced heat loss.
    d. Allen's rule focuses upon the appendages and states that in colder climates, populations should have shorter appendages (arms, legs, and sometimes noses) to increase mass-to-surface ratios and prevent heat loss.
        i. In warmer climates, populations should have longer appendages with increased surface area relative to mass which promotes heat loss.
    e. According to both Bergmann's and Allen's rules:
        i. In warmer environments body shape should be linear with long arms and legs, such as that found today among East African pastoralists.
        ii. In cold environments people should have stocky bodies with shorter arms and legs as is found among the Inuit.
    f. There is much human variability regarding body proportions and not all populations conform to Bergmann's and Allen's rules.

H. Response to cold
1. Humans can respond to cold by increasing heat production or by enhancing heat retention.
    a. Heat retention is more efficient because it requires less energy.
2. Short-term human responses to cold include:
    a. Increased metabolic rate.
        i. Increases in metabolic rate release energy in the form of heat.
        ii. People exposed to chronic cold maintain higher metabolic rates than do those in warmer climates.
        iii. Inuit people in the Arctic maintain metabolic rates between 13 and 45 % higher than non-Inuit controls.
        iv. Inuit have a high protein and fat diet.
    b. Shivering
        i. Shivering generates muscle heat as does exercise.
    c. Vasoconstriction
        i. Narrowing of blood vessel diameters—reduces blood flow to the skin.
        ii. Vasoconstriction restricts heat loss and keeps warmth at core.

291

3. Long-term responses to cold vary among human groups.
4. Cultural and behavioral modifications meet many environmental stressors.

I. High altitude
1. Worldwide, twenty-five million people live above 10,000 feet.
2. Multiple factors produce stress on the human body at higher altitudes, including:
   a. intense solar radiation,
   b. cold,
   c. low humidity,
   d. wind (which amplifies cold stress),
   e. rough terrain and
   f. hypoxia (this is the most influential).
   g. Many of these in combination lead to a reduced nutritional base.
3. Hominins did not evolve at high altitudes.
4. Hypoxia is caused by reduced barometric pressure.
   a. The oxygen is less concentrated.
   b. To increase the body's ability to transport and use oxygen at high altitudes, certain physiological alterations must occur.
5. Reproduction is affected through increased rates of infant mortality, miscarriage, and premature births.
   a. High elevation compromises the vascular supply (oxygen transport) to the fetus.
6. Adult acclimatization to high altitude occurs when people, born at lower elevations, travel to and acclimatize to the higher elevation. These short-term modifications include:
   a. an increase in respiration rate,
   b. an increase in heart rate and
   c. an increase in the rate of production of red blood cells.
7. Developmental acclimatization to high altitude occurs in those who grow up in high altitude. They acquire the following adaptations during their growth and development:
   a. greater lung capacity,
   b. larger hearts, and
   c. more efficient diffusion of oxygen from blood vessels to body tissues.
   d. Developmental acclimatization provides a good example of physiological flexibility by illustrating how, within the limits of genetic factors, development can be influenced by environment.
8. There is evidence that populations can adapt to high attitudes.
   a. Indigenous Tibetan populations appear to have evolved accommodations to hypoxia (over the last 25,000 years) and do not have reproductive problems.
   b. This may be the result of alterations in maternal blood flow to the uterus during pregnancy.
   c. Both highland Tibetans and highland Quechua (from the Peruvian Andes) appear to utilize glucose in a way that permits more efficient use of oxygen.
   d. This implies the presence of genetic mutations in their mtDNA.
   e. This also implies that natural selection has acted to conserve advantageous mutations affecting glucose metabolism in these groups.

II   INFECTIOUS DISEASE

A. Infectious diseases are those caused by pathogens such as bacteria, viruses, or fungi.
   1. Throughout the course of human evolution, infectious disease has exerted enormous selective pressure on human populations.
   2. Infectious disease influences the frequency of certain alleles that affect the immune response.
B. The effects of human infectious disease are due to cultural and biological factors.
   1. Infectious disease was not problematic for humans until approximately 10 kya.
   2. Prior to that time humans lived in small nomadic hunting and gathering groups.
C. Approximately 10 kya, with the advent of domestication of plants and animals, populations became sedentary and had more contact with disease vectors.
   1. For a disease to become endemic in a population, sufficient numbers of people must be present.
   2. Close contact with domesticated animal in sedentary and larger groups led to the spread of zoonotic diseases.
D. Malaria has one of the highest rates of death of any other disease.
   1. Between 300-500 million people worldwide suffering from malaria.
   2. Recently some of the malarial parasites have become drug resistant.
E. AIDS (acquired immune deficiency syndrome) is a viral infection that was first reported in 1981.
   1. The virus that causes AIDS is HIV (human immunodeficiency virus).
   2. Between 30 and 36 million people were living with HIV/AIDS by January 2008.
      a. 95% of these people live in developing countries.
   3. HIV is transmitted from person to person through the exchange of bodily fluids.
   4. HIV is a slow virus and people can be asymptomatic for years.
   5. HIV can attack a variety of cell types, but its predilection is for T4 helper cells, one of the cell types that initiates an immune response.
      a. When a person's T cell count drops below minimum levels, "opportunistic" infections, pathogens present but not HIV, are able to mount an attack on the body.
      b. A receptor site is on the plasma membrane of some immune cells, including T4 cells.
      c. Pathogens, including HIV, attach to these receptors and invade the cells.
   6. Some individuals test positive for HIV, but show few if any symptoms, even after 10-15 years.
      a. This suggests that some individuals may possess natural immunity or resistance to HIV.
   7. Some individuals possess a mutant allele that results in a malfunctioning receptor site to which HIV is unable to bind.
      a. Homozygotes for this allele may be completely resistant to HIV.
      b. In heterozygotes, infection may still occur, but the progress of the disease is much slower.
         i. The mutant allele occurs mainly in people of European descent where the allele frequency is around 10%.
         ii. The allele is not present in Japanese and West Africa samples; however, it does occur at a frequency of around 2% in African Americans, perhaps due to gene flow from Euro-Americans.

293

c. The allele may have resulted from selection for an earlier disease that occurred in Europe.
d. This selection was not against HIV, but another pathogen that required the same receptor site.
e. In 1999 a group of researchers reported that a virus related to the one that causes smallpox can use the same receptor site as HIV and suggested that this may be the mysterious agent of selection.

F. Smallpox may be an example of how exposure to infectious agents can produce polymorphisms in host populations.
1. During the 18th century this disease was estimated to have been responsible for 10-15% of all deaths in parts of Europe.
2. By 1977, modern medical technology totally eradicated this killer disease.
3. Individuals who were blood type A or AB were more susceptible to smallpox than blood type O.
4. This was explained by similarities between the A antigen and one on the smallpox virus.
5. Therefore, the immune systems of blood type A and AB individuals did not recognize the smallpox virus as foreign and did not mount adequate defenses.

III THE CONTINUING IMPACT OF INFECTIOUS DISEASE
1. Humans and pathogens exert selective pressures on each other.
   a. Disease exerts selective pressures on host populations to adapt to that particular organism.
   b. Microbes also evolve (very quickly) and adapt to the various pressures exerted upon them by their hosts.
   c. From an evolutionary perspective, it is to the advantage of any pathogen to keep its host alive until it can reproduce and infect other hosts.
      i. Selection frequently acts to produce resistance in host populations (a benefit to the host) and to reduce the virulence of the disease (also a benefit to the host, but this also benefits the disease organisms because it enables them to reproduce more efficiently).
   d. Populations exposed to new disease usually die in large numbers.
2. Of the known disease-causing organisms, HIV provides the best example of how pathogens evolve and adapt.
   a. Since the 1980s researchers have compared the DNA of HIV and SIV (Simian immunodeficiency virus) which indicate HIV evolved from SIV.
   b. These primates are in contact with humans.
      i. HIV/AIDS is a zoonotic disease.
   c. human actions have impacted the the patterns of infectious disease.
   d. The interaction of cultural and biological factors has influenced microevolutionary change in humans.
3. Before the 20th century, infectious disease was the number one cause of death in human populations.
   a. In industrialized nations, during the first part of the twentieth century, improved sanitation, antibiotics, pesticides infectious diseases gave way to non infectious diseases of "old age", like cancer.

294

i. As much as half of all mortality is due to infectious disease in developing countries.
b. Recently (1980-1992) infectious disease rates have risen.
c. The increase in the prevalence of infectious disease may be due to overuse of antibiotics.
i. Antibiotics have exerted selective pressures on bacteria and some species have developed drug-resistant strains.
d. Another factor associated with today's rapid spread of disease is the widespread mixing of populations everyday; this includes the crossing of borders and penetration into remote areas.
4. Some diseases are reemerging.
a. Tuberculosis is now the world's leading killer of adults and this disease, once controlled by antibiotics, has developed drug-resistant strains.
5. Fundamental to the spread of disease is human population growth.
a. Population growth causes environmental disturbance and adds to global warming.
b. Overcrowding leads to unsanitary conditions and the spread of communicable disease.

KEY TERMS

acclimatization: physiological response to environmental change that occurs during the lifetime of an individual.

AIDS: acquired immune deficiency syndrome. A condition caused by suppression of the immune system due to the human immunodeficiency virus (HIV).

antibodies: proteins that are major components of the immune system.

coevolution: evolution of two or more species in which they are exerting reciprocal selective pressures on one another.

endemic: (referring to disease) continuously present in a population.

evaporative cooling: a physiological mechanism that helps prevent this body from overheating.

homeostasis: a state of equilibrium in which the body's internal environment remains within a stable range.

homeothermy: characteristic of mammals and birds. These animals are able to regulate their body temperatures independent of outside (ambient) temperature fluctuations.

hypoxia: a lack of oxygen, either in the body's tissues or in the atmosphere (at higher altitudes).

neural tube: the embryonic structure that forms the brain and spinal cord.

pandemic: an extensive outbreak of disease affecting large numbers of people over a wide area; potentially, a world-wide phenomenon.

pathogen: any organism or substance that causes disease.

spina bifida: the condition in which vertebrae fail to develop properly and do not form a protective barrier around the spinal cord.

stress: in a physiological context, any factor that acts to disrupt homeostasis.

vasoconstriction: narrowing of blood vessels, reducing blood flow to the skin.

vasodilation: expansion of blood vessels, permitting increased blood flow to the skin.

vector: an agent that serves to transmit disease from one carrier to another.

zoonotic: disease that is transmitted to humans through contact with animals.

MEDIA EXERCISES

1) Thinking of doing some high-country hiking or visiting the mountains for a vacation? Before you go, take a look at the "Outdoor Action Guide to High Altitude: Acclimatization and Illnesses" (http://www.princeton.edu/~oa/safety/altitude.html). This will give you some helpful tips on how us lowlanders can acclimate to high altitude, and how to avoid such nasty things as Acute Mountain Sickness and Pulmonary Edema.

CONCEPT APPLICATION

Your school has decided to make itself known to the world by having the best long-distance track team on the planet. You have been asked by the athletic department to go out, find, and recruit these world-class runners. Your budget only allows you to go to one foreign country and visit one region. Where would you go? Before you answer, think about what environmental factors would have selective pressure on running ability in human populations. What kinds of diets would these groups have? Where would they live, by the sea for the fresh air or in the mountains for the cool temperatures? Are there cultural factors that could influence a group's ability to run long distance? Is there such a thing as a "runners body?"

List your ideas and then take a look at the following web site http://www.pbs.org/frontlineworld/stories/kenya/thestory.html. Read the story and also click on FACTS & STATS to get more information that can help you answer the questions above.

Now answer the True/False, Multiple Choice and Short Answer sample test questions. Following completion of the tests, correct them with the answers and textbook page references at the end of this Study Guide chapter. Note the areas in which you are strong and weak to guide you in your studying. Finally, answer the sample Essay Questions.

TRUE/FALSE QUESTIONS

If false, consider what modification would make the statement true.

1. Acclimatization can be short-term, long-term or even permanent.
   TRUE   FALSE

2. Folate, a B vitamin that is critical for normal fetal neurological development, can be degraded by infrared radiation.
   TRUE   FALSE

3. Skin lightened as populations inhabited the higher latitudes because of the need to synthesize Vitamin A which is essential for the normal formation and growth of bone.
   TRUE   FALSE

4. Panting is the most important mechanism of heat dissipation in humans.
   TRUE   FALSE

5. In general, populations adapted to chronic cold maintain higher metabolic rates than people living in more equable climatic conditions.
    TRUE   FALSE

6. According to the World Health Organization, currently Tb is the worlds' largest killer of adults.
    TRUE   FALSE

7. Dark-skinned human populations in the tropics are protected by their melanin from the adverse affects of intense ultra-violet radiation.
    TRUE   FALSE

8. Allen's rule states that body size tends to be greater in populations that live in colder climates.
    TRUE   FALSE

9. One important stress at high altitude is hypoxia.
    TRUE   FALSE

10. HIV can be transmitted from person-to-person by casual contact.
    TRUE   FALSE

MULTIPLE CHOICE QUESTIONS

1. If an Illinoian leaves the 300 foot elevation of Urbana-Champaign and flies to Quito, Ecuador, elevation 8,000 feet, this person's body will begin to produce more red blood cells to compensate for lower oxygen levels. This type of short-term physiological change is called
    A. habituation.
    B. homeothermy.
    C. acclimatization.
    D. remodeling.

2. The pigment that absorbs ultraviolet radiation, thereby protecting the skin against its harmful effects, is
    A. carotene.
    B. melanin.
    C. lactose.
    D. hemoglobin.

3. When insufficient ultraviolet radiation is absorbed during childhood the condition resulting from a Vitamin D deficiency is
    A. rickets.
    B. gastroenteritis.
    C. cancer.
    D. trisomy 21.

4. Which of the following is **not** associated with human adaptation to heat?
   A. Vitamin D synthesis
   B. sweating
   C. vasodilation
   D. the evolutionary loss of our "fur coat"

5. Alaskan Inuits are relatively heavy for their height, while many east Africans are relatively light for their height. This is explained by
   A. Bergmann's rule.
   B. Thompson's rule.
   C. Gloger's rule.
   D. Kleiber's rule.

6. The long arms and legs of the East African Masai, and the short arms and legs of the Inuit conform to
   A. Bergmann's rule
   B. Allen's rule
   C. Gloger's rule
   D. Cope's rule

7. Which of the following processes is most associated with human acclimatization to cold?
   A. sweating.
   B. vasodilation.
   C. vasoconstriction.
   D. evaporative cooling.

8. Which of the following is **not** a short-term response to cold?
   A. increased metabolic rate.
   B. shivering.
   C. increased food consumption.
   D. vasodilation.

9. The people with the highest metabolic rates in the world are the
   A. inland Inuit of the Arctic.
   B. Ainu of Japan.
   C. Australian Aboriginals.
   D. Choctaw of Oklahoma.

10. A problem associated with high altitude stress is
    A. kidney failure.
    B. low birth weights.
    C. high red blood cell counts.
    D. high white blood cell counts.

11. There is some evidence that highland Tibetans
    A. do not need to breathe oxygen.
    B. have made genetic adaptations to hypoxia.
    C. have evolved more efficient kidneys.
    D. need to go down to lower elevations in order to reproduce.

12. A zoonotic disease currently believed to have originated in African apes and monkeys is
    A. rickets.
    B. AIDS.
    C. bubonic plague.
    D. Ebola virus.

13. Serious concern(s) of medical workers is/are that
    A. disease causing microbes are evolving resistance against antibiotics.
    B. insect vectors have developed resistance against pesticides.
    C. infectious diseases are on the rise again.
    D. All of the above.

14. Which of the following statements is true?
    A. HIV can be transmitted through casual contact.
    B. HIV can be carried by an insect vector.
    C. HIV is transmitted through exchange of body fluids.
    D. HIV is the immediate cause of death for a victim.

15. Any factor that acts to disrupt homeostasis is
    A. homeostasis.
    B. stress.
    C. adaptation.
    D. culture.

16. Balance or stability within a biological system is
    A. homeostasis.
    B. stress.
    C. adaptation.
    D. culture.

17. Which of the following has **no** influence on human skin color?
    A. melanin
    B. carotene
    C. hemoglobin
    D. insulin

18. Dark skin does **not** protect indigenous, tropical human populations from which of the following?
    A. skin cancer
    B. degradation of folate
    C. severe sunburn
    D. rickets

19. The fact that modern humans cope better with dry heat rather than cold is an indication that
    A. humans are ectothermic.
    B. we lost our "fur coat" very recently in human evolution, around 10,000 y.a.
    C. our ancestors primarily evolved in the warm-to-hot woodlands of eastern Africa.
    D. our sweating ability is poorly-developed compared to apes.

20. Desert-dwelling native Australians dealt with moderate night-time cold stress by
    A. sleeping in elaborate hide-covered huts.
    B. constructing skin and fur sleeping bags.
    C. vasodilating and shivering all night long to maintain high skin temperatures.
    D. vasoconstricting and reducing skin temperatures all night long to prevent energy loss.

21. Which of the following are lowlander responses to high altitude?
    A. increased heart rate
    B. decreased respiration
    C. fewer number of red blood cells produced
    D. All of the above

22. Highlanders, such as Tibetans and the Quechua of Peru, metabolize _____ relatively more efficiently than lowlanders, allowing more efficient use of oxygen.
    A. water
    B. glucose
    C. melanin
    D. hemoglobin

23. An agent that **transmits** disease from one carrier to another is a(n)
    A. pandemic.
    B. vector.
    C. antibody.
    D. pathogen.

24. A substance or microorganism that **causes** disease is a(n)
    A. pandemic.
    B. vector.
    C. antibody.
    D. pathogen.

25. A mutant allele that confers some protection against HIV infection is most prevalent in populations from
    A. Europe.
    B. Asia.
    C. East Africa.
    D. Australia.

SHORT ANSWER QUESTIONS (& PAGE REFERENCES)

1. What effect does ultra-violet radiation have on human skin? (pp. 452-453)

2. Why do you vasodilate when you're hot and vasoconstrict when you're cold? (pp. 457-460)

3. How do high-altitude natives acclimatize during their growth and development? (p. 463)

4. Why does smallpox have a higher incidence in people with Type A or Type AB blood compared to people who are Type O? (p. 466)

5. How has the overuse of antibiotics increased the prevalence of infectious disease? (p. 469)

ESSAY QUESTIONS (& PAGE REFERENCES)

1. What is acclimatization and illustrate your answer with one example of developmental acclimatization? (p. 451)

2. What are the selective forces that influence the maintenance of dark skin color in the tropics and lighter skin in the higher latitudes? (pp. 451-456)

3. How do HIV and AIDS illustrate the dynamic nature of the relationships between host, pathogen and human culture? (pp. 464-466)

CONCEPT APPLICATION SOLUTION

Your school has decided to make itself known to the world by having the best long-distance track team on the planet. You have been asked by the athletic department to go out, find, and recruit these world-class runners. Your budget only allows you to go to one foreign country and visit one region.

Where would you go? *I would probably go to Kenya. A Google search for New York City marathon winners shows that the Kenyans seem to have won a number in the past ten years. In fact, they have won more than any other single country in the past ten years.*

Before you answer, think about what environmental factors would have selective pressure on running ability in human populations. *Running takes strength, endurance, cardiovascular fitness, and good thermoregulation. People who grow up in environments that allow these traits to develop would be best adapted to distance running. Well-nourished people who grow up in environments that are well above sea level stand a good chance of having the necessary adaptations to carry oxygen in their blood even in hypoxic environments. Someone who grew up in the mountains might be a good choice.*

What kinds of diets would these groups have? *A group that is well nourished on a diet of carbohydrates might also be a good place to look.*

Are there cultural factors that could influence a group's ability to run long distance? *Some groups, like the Tarahumara in Mexico, are known for their long distance running. Running plays a role in their cultural practices, as part of games, and social interactions. are groups all over that world that may have traditions of long distance running.*

Is there such a thing as a "runners body?" *All humans have the ability to run but some may be more efficient at burning energy, at pumping blood, and transporting oxygen. Of course, genetics, development, and the environment all have their influences. Short, lean bodies may be the best for running long distance though.*

From the FACTS & STATS page of the story listed above.

"Kenyan women hold world records in the 20,000m, 25,000m and 30,000m track races.

Most of Kenya's success in running has come from members of a single tribe, the Kalenjin, who number 3 million. The Kalenjin live in high altitudes, between 5,000 and 10,000 feet (1,524 m to 3,048 m), giving them strong lungs and high endurance. And the temperature at that altitude is cool and ideal for running.
The Kalenjin won nearly 40 percent of the biggest international men's awards from 1987 to 1996.
In 1990, Kenya's top high school squad, from St. Patrick's Academy in Iten, outraced members of the Swedish national track team in several events organized by Swedish
http://www.pbs.org/frontlineworld/stories/kenya/facts.html "

ANSWERS, *CORRECTED STATEMENT* IF FALSE & REFERENCES TO TRUE/FALSE QUESTIONS

1. TRUE, p. 451

2. FALSE, p. 453, Folate, a B vitamin that is critical for normal fetal neurological development, can be degraded by *ultraviolet* radiation.

3. FALSE, pp. 454-455, Skin lightened as populations inhabited the higher latitudes because of the need to synthesize *Vitamin D* which is essential for the normal formation and growth of bone.

4. FALSE, p. 457, *Sweating* is the most important mechanism of heat dissipation in humans

5. TRUE, p. 461

6. TRUE, p. 469

7. TRUE, pp. 452-454

8. FALSE, p. 460, *Bergmann's* rule states that body size tends to be greater in populations that live in colder climates.

9. TRUE, p. 462

10. FALSE, pp. 464-465, HIV can be transmitted from person-to-person *only through the exchange of bodily fluids*.

ANSWERS AND REFERENCES TO MULTIPLE CHOICE QUESTIONS

1. **C**, p. 462	8. **C**, p. 461	14. **C**, p. 464	20. **D**, p. 461
2. **B**, p. 451	9. **A**, p. 461	15. **B**, p. 450	21. **A**, p. 462
3. **A**, p. 454	10. **B**, pp. 462-463	16. **A**, p. 450	22. **B**, p. 463
4. **A**, p. 455	11. **B**, p. 463	17. **D**, p. 451	23. **B**, p. 464
5. **A**, p. 460	12. **B**, p. 467	18. **D**, p. 454	24. **D**, p. 465
6. **B**, pp. 460	13. **D**, p. 469	19. **C**, p. 457	25. **A**, p. 466
7. **C**, p. 461			

CHAPTER 17
LEGACIES OF HUMAN EVOLUTIONARY HISTORY

LEARNING OBJECTIVES

After reading this chapter you should be able to:
- explain the benefits of examining human behavior from a behavioral ecological framework (pp. 473-475)
- discuss how evolution has influenced human reproductive behavior and how reproduction is embedded in culture (pp. 475-476)
- understand how humans differ from other primates in regard to birth, infancy and childhood (pp. 477-480)
- understand the onset and end of human reproductive function (pp. 484-488)
- understand how and why we age (pp. 488-490)
- discuss how an evolutionary view of medicine can contribute to understanding current health issues (pp. 490-491)
- place humans within the context of other life on the planet (pp. 491-492)
- understand the exponential increase of the human population and the effects of our species' overpopulation on us and the planet's biodiversity (pp. 492-495)
- explain how we hasten the evolution of other species and how that is not necessarily beneficial (pp.495-496)
- list and discuss the 8 Millenium development goals of helping to reduce human misery worldwide (pp. 497-498)
- answer the question: "Are we still evolving?" (pp. 498-499)

CHAPTER OUTLINE

Introduction
     As we have noted throughout the text, modern humans are the result of evolution in which there was a strong interaction between biology and culture. In this final chapter we explore the impact that human biocultural evolution has left on three levels of organization: the individual, society and our planet.

I   HUMAN BEHAVIORAL ECOLOGY AND EVOLUTIONARY PSYCHOLOGY
    A. Behavioral ecology is the examination of human behavior within an evolutionary framework.
        1. Behavioral ecologists suggest that humans, like all other animals, behave in ways that increase their reproductive success (fitness).
    B. Evolutionary psychology employs the tenets of behavioral ecology to try to explain topics such as human sexuality, aggression, and violence.
        1. Many people are uncomfortable with the idea that there may be evolutionary constraints on our behavior that are difficult, or impossible, to overcome.
        2. For example males and females have different reproductive strategies that allow them to increase reproductive fitness.
        3. Usually a compromise in strategies is the most effective.

C. Human behavior is a complex phenomenon and its expression depends upon environmental context, genes, and individual experience.
D. Behavioral ecology can generate predictions about human behavior
   1. For example, hunters are expected to use an optimal foraging strategy.
   2. There are many reasons why a hunter would choose less "optimal" game or plants.
   3. These same caveats can be said for optimal reproductive strategies.

II **BIOCULTURAL EVOLUTION AND THE LIFE CYCLE**
A. Examining human behavior as a product of evolution helps us explain and understand some aspects of our lives.
B. To appreciate biocultural evolution, growth and development must be considered.
C. There is a lot of variation in how certain characters will be manifested in individuals.
   1. Some genetic traits will be expressed in a particular fashion regardless of the cultural environment.
   2. Other features reflect a greater interaction between environment and genes.
   3. Cultural values influence growth and development.
D.   Life history theory is utilized by many physical anthropologists and primatologists.
   1. These scientists study primate and human growth from an evolutionary perspective, focusing on how natural selection has affected the life cycle, from conception to death.
   2. Life history theory is based upon the foundation that there is a finite amount of energy available to organisms for growth, maintenance of life and reproduction.
      a. The life cycle is thus viewed as a series of trade-offs among life history traits because energy invested in one process is not available for another.
   3. Humans are distinctive because our "life stages" (e.g. infancy, childhood, adult...) are relatively extended compared to other mammals.
      a. Humans have a post-reproductive phase called menopause.
      b. Most of these life cycle stages are well-marked by biological transitions.
      c.   See Figure 17-4 for a comparison of life cycle stages for various animal species.
   4. However, in humans these transitions are complicated by culture.
      a. Collective societal attitudes toward these transitions (e.g. puberty, menopause) affect individual growth and development.
E. Birth, Infancy, and Childhood
   1. Human infants are born with only 25% of their adult brain-weight, compared to 50% for most other mammals, including non-human primates.
      a.   Much of human brain growth occurs in a stimulating environment.
      b. This pattern of delayed maturation was likely established in hominin evolution by 1.5 mya.
   2. Birth is a life cycle event that takes place in the context of culture.
      a. Human mothers seek assistance because of the nature of the anatomical nature of the pelvis.
         i.   A survey of world cultures reveals that it is unusual to give birth alone.
   3. On average, Nursing typically lasts for three to four years in humans.
      a.   In Western societies nursing rarely lasts more than a year.
   4. Humans have unusually long childhoods during which a great deal of learning takes place.

305

F. Nutritional effects on growth and development
   1. Nutrition has an impact on human growth and development at every stage of the life cycle.
   2. There are necessary nutrients for growth and development:
      a. proteins,
      b. carbohydrates,
      c. lipids (fats),
      d. vitamins and
      e. minerals.
   3. However, today's Western diets are often not compatible with the nutritional requirements that our species evolved over the last 5 million years.
      a. The ancestral diet was high in protein, but low in fat.
      b. The diet was high in complex carbohydrates, including fiber.
      c. The diet was low in salt and high in calcium.
      d. Evidence indicates that many of today's diseases in industrialized countries are related to the lack of fit between our diet today and the one with which we evolved.
   4. Many of the biological and behavioral characteristics that contributed to our success as a species, may be maladaptive in our modern industrialized societies.
      a. An example of this is our ability to store fat.
         i. This was an advantage in the past when food tended to alternate between being abundant or scarce.
         ii. Today there is a relative overabundance of foods in western nations so the formerly positive ability to store extra fat has now turned into a liability that leads to degenerative diseases.
   5. Perhaps the best example of a disorder that reflects how our former hunting and gathering lifestyle is in conflict with our modern diets is the incidence of adult on-set diabetes (Type 2 diabetes or non-insulin dependent diabetes mellitus).
      a. In 1900, this disease ranked 27th among the leading causes of death in the U.S., today it the 7th leading killer.
      b. It is projected to increase significantly around the world over the next ten years as well.
      c. Rates for obesity and diabetes in the US and throughout the world have grown over the last decade, and some fear the increase is accelerating.
   6. Overpopulation in today's world also leads to malnutrition, undernutrition and starvation in many developing nations.
   7. Food inequality is a larger problem than food scarcity.
      a. While the earth may be able to produce sufficient food, economic and political forces keep the food from reaching those in need.
G. Onset of reproductive functioning in humans
   1. A number of biological events mark the transition to adolescence for both males and females.
   2. Menarche, the first menstruation in girls, is affected by several factors such as genetic patterns, nutrition, stress and disease.
      a. Sexual maturity is hormonally driven but the timing appears related to skeletal growth.
      b. Proposed that menarche begins when the pelvis reaches adult size.

306

3. Life history theory predicts that if early maturity results in higher numbers of surviving offspring, then natural selection would favor those members of a population who mature earlier.
   a. This pattern is suggested because throughout most of our evolutionary history, life expectancy was low and infant mortality was high.
   b. High rates of adolescent pregnancy reflect this ancient biological heritage.
   c. Today, delaying birth may give more advantages because of the physical and cultural benefits.
   d. Women who delay their reproduction until they are also emotionally, socially and economically mature are likely to have more surviving offspring in contemporary society.
      i. However, if young mothers have help from extended families, social and/or government agencies, their reproductive fitness may not be compromised.
   e. The path to reproductive success is clearly more complex than behavioral ecology models can predict, but hypotheses must be somewhat simplistic in order to remain testable.
4. Life history theory also informs us regarding the number and quality of care of offspring.
   a. Single births are most common among primates (monkeys, apes, and humans).
   b. Twins are rare and the survival rates for these multiple births are much lower than for singletons.
   c. The quality of parental care is compromised when there are too many dependent offspring.
   d. Although primate infanticide has been explained by behavioral ecologists, how can these researchers explain a human mother killing her own child?
      i. Behavioral ecologists have provided an evolutionary explanation for mothers that abandon their newborns.
      ii. If the mother does not have adequate resources to care for the child so that its very survival is in doubt, it pays (from an evolutionary not a moral perspective) to not invest in a doomed child but to delay further reproduction until the situation improves.
   e. This illustrates that for most indications of reproductive fitness, the quality of offspring is more important than the number of children.
5. The post-reproductive period
   a. Uniquely, human females live a significant portion of their lives after the reproductive years.
   b. Worldwide menopause has onset at approximately 50 years of age.
   c. During hominin evolution most females (males too) did not live past 50 years of age, and thus would not have lived for any length of time post reproductively.
   d. Various theories have been proposed to account for this additional phase in female human lives.
   e. One theory suggests the role of parenting is important.
      i. Since humans generally need 12-15 years to raise a child to self-sufficiency, this extra time was necessary to make sure that the last child survived to adulthood.

      ii. This suggests that the maximum human life span (before agriculture) was around 65 years, a number that accords well with current estimates of hunter gatherers.

   f. One explanation states that menopause is not selected for at all, but is simply an artifact of the relatively longer human life span.

      i. All female eggs (ova) are present at birth and have a life expectancy of approximately 50 years.

   g. Finally a third theory has been called the "grandmother hypothesis."

      i. This suggests that an older woman could increase her lifetime fitness by aiding her daughter in raising her grandchildren (who share one quarter of her genes).

H. Human longevity

  1. Compared with most mammals, humans have a relatively long life span.

   a. Human life expectancy at birth (the average length of life) has increased significantly in the last 100 years.

   b. One of the major reasons that people are living longer today is because they are dying much less frequently from childhood infectious diseases.

  2. Aging is synonymous with senescence, the physiological decline that occurs in all body systems.

   a. Recall that natural selection favors traits that increase reproductive success.

      i. Most causes of death that have their effects after reproduction are not subjected to selection.

   b. Many genes that enhance reproductive success in younger years may be detrimental in later years and lead to debilitating diseases such as hypertension and cancers.

      i. These are pleiotropic genes

        a) have multiple effects at different times in the life span or under different conditions.

   c. Free radicals are also believed to contribute to senescence.

      i. Free radicals are byproducts of cellular metabolism that can damage cells.

      ii. Vitamins and some enzymes (antioxidants) provide some protection against free radicals.

   d. There is also evidence that programmed cell death is also a part of normal senescence.

   e. The "telomere hypothesis" suggests that the DNA sequence at the end of each chromosome (the telomere) shortens each time a cell divides.

      i. During a lifetime of cell divisions, the telomeres eventually get so short that the cells no longer divide and thus the cells undergo degenerative changes.

  3. Lifestyle choices, such as smoking, diet and physical exercise are far more important than genes in influencing how we age.

  4. Life expectancy varies from country to country, between socioeconomic classes, and from sex to sex.

   a. For example, a girl born in Japan in 2006 can expect to live 86 years (a boy to age 79), and a girl born in the same year in the U.S. would have a life expectancy of 80 years (a boy to age 75).

   b. However, a girl in Mali born in 2006 has a life expectancy of only 47 years (a boy to age 44).

   c. In Zimbabwe the life expectancy was 65(prior to the AIDS epidemic), today the life expectancy is less than 37 years.

III EVOLUTIONARY MEDICINE

A. Darwinian medicine also known as evolutionary medicine applies evolutionary principles to the understanding of health challenges.

B. An inevitable outcome of fighting pathogens is that stronger pathogens that are therapy resistant will evolve.

C. The antibiotic-pathogen arms race
  1. The most deadly pathogens have short life spans and evolve quickly.

D. One suggestion aims to turn around the evolutionary process to make the pathogens less virulent.
  1. The primary argument is that medical interventions capable of responding to the processes of disease emergence and evolution are much more likely to be successful in the long run than those that target specific disease variants and their manifestations.

E. Genetic studies of human and chimps illustrate some simple differences that may impact the differential susceptibility to particular diseases.
  1. Sialic acid diffs in chimps and humans by a single oxygen molecule and likely explains the differences in disease susceptibility.

F. Understanding the conditions in which humans evolved can help in understanding disease and disease prevention in modern populations.
  1. Many point to a mismatch between the paleolithic body and modern conditions.

G. Evolutionary medicine also helps to distinguish traits that may have evolved because they enhanced survival and reproductive success in the past.

IV HUMAN IMPACT ON THE PLANET AND OTHER LIFE-FORMS

A. By most standards humans are a successful species.

B. Most humans have a pretty high opinion of our species: we often arrogantly think of humanity as the most successful and dominant species on the planet.

C. Humans do not hold this position.
  1. *H. erectus* lasted for 1.5 million years and some sharks and turtles have remained virtually unchanged for 400 million years!

D. Humans have had an excessive impact on the earth and we face challenges of our own creation.

E. Overpopulation
  1. Estimates of population size 10,000 years ago center around 5 million people.
  2. By the year 1650, the world population had grown to about 500 million.
    a. During 9650 years, human population size doubled seven and a half times.
  3. In the next 150 years however, from 1650-1800, the population doubled again to 1 billion.
    a. It only took 37 years (between 1950 and 1987) for the most recent doubling, from 2 to 4 billion.
  4. Human population growth adds another billion people every 11 years.
  5. The United Nations report on world populations notes that 95% of population growth is occurring in the developing world.
    a. Resources aren't distributed equally among all nations.
    b. Efforts to slow the rates of world population growth have focused on improving women's education, health, and rights throughout the world.

    c. This effort has been successful with declines of 4.5 children per woman in 1970-1975 to 2.65 today.
       i. Most success has been in developed world.
F. Global Warming
  1. The increased production of carbon dioxide and other greenhouse gases is of great concern to many in the scientific community.
  2. These scientists anticipate dramatic climate change in the form of global warming primarily due to human activities
    a. Deforestation reduces the number of trees available to absorb carbon dioxide.
    b. The burning of trees to clear land adds to this problem.
  3. Scientists are concerned that human produced greenhouse gases could tip the balance toward catastrophic global climate change.
    a. Hurricanes and typhoons, melting polar ice, droughts and fires are occurring with greater frequency.
  4. Global warming is the result of the interaction of many factors and the consequences of these interactions aren't possible to predict.
  5. Reversing these trends will be expensive and will require individual sacrifice and huge changes in business and industrial practices.
G. Impact on biodiversity
  1. Humans may be unique among species on Earth with respect to our ability to so greatly influence other species' survival and extinction.
    a. There have been 2 major extinction events in the last 250 million years.
    b. A third major extinction event is occurring now beginning in the late Pleistocene or early Holocene.
    c. Humans are the direct cause of this mass extinction.
    d. At the end of the Pleistocene, many large mammal species went extinct in North America, Australia and elsewhere.
    e. Human hunting has been implicated in the extinction of several large mammalian species particularly near the end of the Pleistocene 10,000 years ago.
  2. Today species are disappearing at an unprecedented rate; hunting continues to be a major factor.
    a. In North America at least 57 mammalian species became extinct mainly due to human overhunting.
    b. Human colonization killed off the moa in New Zealand in a few short decades.
    c. On Madagascar 14 species of lemurs have been exterminated over the past 1000 years.
    d. Competition with introduced nonnative species also adds to the problem.
    e. Habitat reduction is the single most important cause of extinctions.
    f. By the year 2022, half the world's remaining rain forests will be gone if destruction continues at its current rate.
  3. Should we care about the loss of diversity?
  4. Selfishly the answer should be yes because we continue to benefit from the forest for the production of drugs like taxol.
  5. Morally the answer should be yes, as how is it our right to eradicate so many species?

H. Acceleration of evolutionary processes
　1. Humans are also in the unique position to accelerate evolution in other organisms.
　　a. For example, human use of antibiotics has hastened the evolutionary development of resistance in the pathogens at which these drugs are directed.
　　b. Eventually these bacteria no longer respond to our antibiotics, so in effect, we have "created" more virulent germs.
　2. Similarly, the misuse and overuse of pesticides and insecticides on crops have had adverse affects over the years.
　　a. Plant pests, like bacteria, evolve resistance to the chemicals.
　　　i. Bt toxin, a naturally produced pesticide, has shown that insects are evolving resistance to it.
　　　ii. DDT, was extremely effective at killing mosquitoes when it was first employed.
　　　iii. However, these insects developed resistance and the chemical residues of the DDT proved deadly for many birds, including our national symbol, the bald eagle.
　3. Therefore, it is critical that we all understand the processes of evolution because we are (oftentimes inadvertently) directing its path in unforeseen (and potentially deadly) pathways.

V　**IS THERE ANY GOOD NEWS?**
A. Yes! In 2000, 150 countries agreed to support the Millennium Development Goals statement to reduce global human misery. These were the eight goals:
　1. Eradicate extreme poverty and hunger.
　2. Achieve universal primary education.
　3. Promote gender equity and empower women.
　4. Reduce child mortality.
　5. Improve maternal health.
　6. Combat HIV/AIDS, malaria and other diseases.
　7. Build environmental sustainability.
　8. Build a global partnership for development.
B. Although world population continues to grow, it appears that the rate of growth has slowed.
　1. Improved education for girls and women seems to have the ancillary benefit of reducing family size, thereby slowing population growth.
C. Environmental conservation and habitat preservation improvements have recently been reported.
　1. Costa Rica has been a model for making environmental concerns integral to social and economic development.
　　a. Ecotourism has become a primary industry.
　　b. Costa Rica's poverty levels are the lowest in Central America.
　2. The United Nations Great Apes Survival Project (GRASP) was formed to bring together great ape research and conservation efforts.
D. In 2005, developing and Western nations agreed to work together to reduce global poverty.
　1. The developed countries renewed commitments to double aid for Africa by 2010.

2. Progress has already been reported in Latin America and the Caribbean.
3. Sub-Saharan Africa have fallen further behind than when earlier agreements were made.

VI ARE WE STILL EVOLVING?

A. Culture has allowed us to transcend many of the limitations imposed upon us by biology.
   1. Our primary means of dealing with environmental stresses is via cultural menas.
   2. Socioeconomic and political concerns have powerful effects on our species today.
      a. Factors unrelated to biology such as socioeconomic status, power and control over one's life, and where you live, can have dramatic impacts.
         i. They also affect whether you will be killed at war, have adequate access to medical care or if they can get enough to eat.
      b. However, your biology still has much to do with whether you die from disease or fail to reproduce.
      c. The 4.3 million children who die annually from respiratory infections in the developing world are primarily due to cultural factors.
      d. However, untold other millions survive these conditions and their ability to do so must be in part the responsibility of their genes.
      e. Therefore, allele frequencies relevant to genetic resistance to infection are indeed changing generation by generation (in other words microevolution is continually occurring).
B. Will we speciate, evolve bigger brains, lose our little toes, go extinct?
   1. These are questions for futurists and science fiction writers, not physical anthropologists.
   2. Culture has enabled us to transcend many limits imposed by our biology.
   3. Today many who never would have been able to do so in the past are surviving and having children.
      a. This implies we are evolving

KEY TERMS

behavioral ecology: the study of the evolution of behavior, emphasizing the role of ecological factors as agents of natural selection

Body mass index (BMI) – weight in kg/height in m^2

Darwinian medicine: (see "evolutionary medicine")

evolutionary medicine – the application of an evolutionary viewpoint to medical issues in order to more fully understand contemporary health challenges.

evolutionary psychology: the study of how natural selection has influenced how humans and other primates think.

Holocene: the most recent epoch of the Cenozoic, beginning around 10,000 y.a. and continuing to the present.

life history theory: viewing growth and development from an evolutionary perspective, with an interest in how natural selection has operated on the life cycle, from conception to death.

menarche: the onset of the first menstruation in girls.

menopause: the end of menstruation in human women.

pleiotropic genes: genes that have multiple effects and can have different effects at different times during the life cycle.

senescence: the process of physiological decline in body function that occurs with aging.

telomere: the DNA sequence at the end of each chromosome that shortens after each cell division.

Type II diabetes: a disorder increasingly frequent in today's Westernized societies of sugar and fat-laden diets; adult-onset, non-insulin dependent form of the disease.

MEDIA EXERCISES

1) In your text, you read that efforts to reduce the rate of population growth in developing countries have focused on women. The United Nations Population Fund publishes comprehensive reports and population information every year. Go to http://www.unfpa.org/gender/index.htm to read about the last news on how gender equality is the cornerstone of development.

2) To discover more about evolutionary psychology, check out the University of California at Santa Barbara's "Center for Evolutionary Psychology" hosted and maintained by two of the leading figures in the field: Dr. Leda Cosmides (Department of Psychology) and Dr. John Tooby (Department of Anthropology) http://www.psych.ucsb.edu/research/cep/. Click on their "Evolutionary Psychology Primer" to learn more about the field. Navigate through their home page to read about recent research findings, ongoing projects and critiques of their discipline.

CONCEPT APPLICATION

Go to the PBS "Evolution" documentary website at:
http://www.pbs.org/wgbh/evolution/library/10/4/l_104_01.html.

Watch the short video featuring Dr. Paul Ewald.

How can communities use evolutionary thinking to "domesticate" pathogens? Use cholera as an example to explain what this means.

Now answer the True/False, Multiple Choice and Short Answer sample test questions. Following completion of the tests, correct them with the answers and textbook page references at the end of this Study Guide chapter. Note the areas in which you are strong and weak to guide you in your studying. Finally, answer the sample Essay Questions.

TRUE/FALSE QUESTIONS

If false, consider what modification would make the statement true.

1. Life history theorists view growth and development from an evolutionary perspective.
    TRUE   FALSE

2. Like all other primates, human infants are born with 75% of their adult brain weight.
    TRUE   FALSE

313

3. The incidence of Type II diabetes has been on the decline since 1900, dropping from the 5th leading cause of death then to the 25th leading cause of death today.
   TRUE   FALSE

4. The process of physiological decline in all systems of the body that occurs towards the end of the life course is known as senescence.
   TRUE   FALSE

5. Evolutionary psychologists study how natural selection has influenced how humans and other primates think.
   TRUE   FALSE

6. In our evolutionary past, it would have benefited hominid females to delay reproduction because life spans were long and infant mortality was low.
   TRUE   FALSE

7. Like apes and monkeys, human females have a significant, post-reproductive stage of life called menopause.
   TRUE   FALSE

8. Humans are the most numerous organisms on the planet.
   TRUE   FALSE

9. The greatest single challenge facing humanity is our population growth.
   TRUE   FALSE

10. By the year 2022 half of the world's remaining rainforests will be gone if destruction continues at its current rate.
    TRUE   FALSE

MULTIPLE CHOICE QUESTIONS

1. An example of a cultural factor that has a strong influence on growth is
   A. an individual's skill as an artisan.
   B. marriage status.
   C. socioeconomic status.
   D. religious beliefs that require an individual to eat a particular species of animal.

2. Examining human social behavior in an evolutionary framework is known as?
   A. Paleoanthropology.
   B. Behavior endocrinology.
   C. Anthropological economics.
   D. Behavioral ecology.

3. Humans, compared to other animals, have _____ life cycle stages.
   A. more
   B. fewer
   C. the same number of
   D. fewer than some, more than others

4. At birth the human brain is only ____ percent of its adult size.
   A. 25
   B. 50
   C. 90
   D. 95

5. Delayed brain growth may be particularly important for a species that is reliant upon
   A. carnivory.
   B. language.
   C. instinct.
   D. All of the above

6. Great apes and women from foraging societies typically nurse their children for
   A. 4-5 years.
   B. 1 year.
   C. 6-8 months.
   D. 7-8 years.

7. Which of the following are nutrients needed for growth, development and body maintenance?
   A. carbohydrates
   B. proteins
   C. vitamins
   D. All of the above

8. Nutritional deficits in mothers can be transgenerational. What does transgenerational mean?
   A. The effects skip a generation.
   B. The effects happen in only one generation.
   C. The effects can influence the child and child's children.
   D. The effects occur in only the mother's generation.

9. Which of the following does **not** characterize the preagricultural human diet?
   A. It was high in protein.
   B. It was high in complex carbohydrates.
   C. It was high in saturated fats.
   D. It was high in fiber.

10. The life cycle phase that ends with birth is
    A. prenatal.
    B. infancy.
    C. weaning.
    D. childhood.

315

11. The language centers of the brain
    A. are difficult to find on the human brain.
    B. are well developed at birth.
    C. develop in the first three years of life.
    D. do not develop until puberty.

12. The ability to store fat in our evolutionary past was
    A. maladaptive because fat is always unhealthy.
    B. adaptive because the fat could be used as a backup source of energy during lean times.
    C. irrelevant to the early hominid lifestyle.
    D. variable, with tropical populations storing much more fat than Arctic peoples.

13. Which of the following has **not** been offered as an explanation for senescence?
    A. the effects of pleiotropic genes
    B. the effects of antioxidants
    C. the effects of free radicals
    D. lifestyle factors

14. Which of the following has increased significantly over the last 100 years?
    A. maximum human life span
    B. average human brain size
    C. length of the teen-age years
    D. average life expectancy at birth

15. Behavioral ecologists suggest that humans, like other animals, behave in ways that increase their
    A. fitness.
    B. fat intake.
    C. IQ.
    D. biodiversity.

16. Human behavior is extremely complex and its expression depends on
    A. genes.
    B. environment.
    C. individual experience.
    D. All of the above

17. A clear sign of puberty in girls is
    A. menarche.
    B. pregnancy.
    C. menopause.
    D. senescence.

18. For menarche to occur normally and for ovulation to be maintained,
    A. females must have high levels of circulating calcium.
    B. high levels of vitamin D must be stored in the liver.
    C. there must be a certain amount of body fat.
    D. there must be high protein stores available.

19. Which of the following has **not** been proposed to account for menopause?
    A. Women needed to live 12-15 years after their last birth so that they could raise the last child to self-sufficiency.
    B. Natural selection caused women to live longer so that they can help men on big-game hunts after they stopped having children.
    C. Menopause is not the result of natural selection but is simply an artifact of the increase in human life span.
    D. Post-menopausal grandmothers increased their fitness by helping to feed and provide care for their grandchildren.

20. If we define biological "success" as the species that has produced the most individuals on the planet, the "winners" are
    A. bacteria.
    B. humans.
    C. fish.
    D. rats.

21. Telomeres are
    A. Skin lesions caused by melanoma
    B. Bacteria that cause cholera
    C. Drugs that prevent atherosclerosis
    D. Repeated sequences of DNA at the ends of chromosomes

22. Which of the following has/have contributed to the current crisis of overpopulation that humanity now faces?
    A. Our ability to produce food surpluses.
    B. Medical advances that have allowed many to survive formally fatal diseases.
    C. Reduced infant mortality and longer average life spans.
    D. All of the above.

23. Which of the following is **not** true?
    A. Around 10,000 years ago only about 5 million people inhabited the earth.
    B. One billion people are added to the world's population every 11 years.
    C. In 1650, the global human population was already 2 billion.
    D. In the 37 years between 1950 and 1987, human population size doubled.

24. If current human population growth rates remain unchecked, the global population will swell to 9 billion by the year
    A. 2009.
    B. 2050.
    C. 2100.
    D. 2125.

25. The current mass extinction event has been caused by
    A. continental drift.
    B. climate change.
    C. an extra-terrestrial impact.
    D. humans.

26. In what habitat do more than half of the world's plant and animal species live?
    A. deserts
    B. mountains
    C. rain forests
    D. grasslands

27. What does "domesticating pathogens" mean?
    A. Breeding pathogens specifically for life with humans.
    B. Using evolutionary processes to direct pathogens toward less virulence.
    C. These are pathogens that protect humans from disease.
    D. Breeding pathogens for greater virulence.

28. Which of the following is **not** a Millennium Development Goal published in 2000?
    A. Eradicate extreme poverty and hunger.
    B. Raise child wages.
    C. Reduce child mortality.
    D. Ensure environmental sustainability.

29. Worldwide population growth may be slowing due to
    A. improvements in education for women and girls.
    B. teenage disinterest in sex.
    C. global availability of free oral contraceptives provided by the United Nations.
    D. All of the above.

30. Which of the following is **not** true?
    A. Human cultural activities have very little influence on human biological evolution.
    B. The appearance of new pathogens will have an effect on human evolution.
    C. There is a disconnect between our biology and our 21st century cultural environment.
    D. The human species continues to evolve.

SHORT ANSWER QUESTIONS (& PAGE REFERENCES)

1. Through which life cycle stages do humans progress? (p. 477)

2. How did the ancestral diet differ from those in today's Western cultures? (p. 481)

3. What is the "telomere hypothesis" of senescence? (p. 489)

4. Why did many large mammals go extinct at the end of the Pleistocene? (pp. 495-496)

5. How are humans accelerating the evolution of bacterial virulence? (pp. 495-496)

Essay Questions (& Page References)

1. How and why does human brain growth differ from other primates? (pp. 477-479)

2. Compare and contrast the evolutionary explanations for menopause. (pp. 487-488)

3. Why is human overpopulation the single greatest challenge facing humanity? (pp. 491-493)

4. Are there reasons for us to be optimistic about humanity's future and are we still evolving? (pp. 497-498)

Answers, *Corrected Statement* if False & References To True/False Questions

1. **TRUE**, p. 476

2. **FALSE**, p. 478, *Unlike* all other primates, human infants are born with *only 25%* of their adult brain weight.

3. **FALSE**, pp. 482-483, The incidence of Type II diabetes has been on the *increase* since 1900, *rising* from the 27th leading cause of death then to the 7th leading cause of death today.

4. **TRUE**, p. 488

5. **TRUE**, p. 473

6. **FALSE**, pp. 485-486, In our evolutionary past, it would have benefited hominid females to *hasten* reproduction because life spans were *short* and infant mortality was *high*.

7. **FALSE**, p. 477, *Unlike* apes and monkeys, human females have a significant, post-reproductive stage of life called menopause.

8. **FALSE**, p. 491, *Bacteria* are the most numerous organisms on the planet.

9. **TRUE**, p. 492

10. **TRUE**, p. 495

Answers and References to Multiple Choice Questions

1. **C**, p. 476	11. **C**, p. 478	21. **D**, p. 489
2. **D**, p. 473	12. **B**, p. 482	22. **D**, pp. 491-492
3. **A**, p. 477	13. **B**, p. 489	23. **C**, p. 492
4. **A**, p. 478	14. **D**, p. 488	24. **B**, p. 493
5. **B**, p. 478	15. **A**, p. 473	25. **D**, p. 494
6. **A**, p. 479	16. **D**, p. 474	26. **C**, p. 495
7. **D**, p. 481	17. **A**, p. 477	27. **B**, p. 490
8. **C**, p. 480	18. **C**, p. 482	28. **B**, p. 497
9. **C**, p. 481	19. **B**, pp. 487-488	29. **A**, p. 497
10. **A**, p. 477	20. **A**, p. 491	30. **A**, pp. 498-499

Concept Application Solution

How can communities use evolutionary thinking to "domesticate" pathogens? Use cholera as an example to explain what this means.

Classic cholera is a particularly nasty water-borne disease. As with any pathogen, the easier it is for the bacterium to travel from one host to the next the more deadly or virulent it becomes. From the short film, we saw incredibly unsanitary water supplies in Peru that led to a devastating outbreak of cholera. Dr. Ewald suggests that by simply making the transmission of the pathogen more difficult the evolution will select pathogens that are less harmful which can survive for longer periods inside the host. Simply by cleaning up the water supply, cholera becomes less deadly.